D1259753

THE RESCUE OF EMIN PASHA

THE RESCUE OF EMIN PASHA

The story of Henry M. Stanley and the Emin Pasha Relief Expedition, 1887-1889

by ROGER JONES

'Αλλά πρῶτα θὰ δεῖς τὴν ἐρημιά
καὶ θὰ τῆς δώσεις τὸ δικό σου νόημα.
'Ελύτης.

ALLISON & BUSBY, LONDON

First published in Great Britain by
Allison & Busby Limited,
6a Noel Street, London W1V 3RB

SBN 85031 066 0

Acknowledgement is due to the Hakluyt Society and to Cambridge University Press for permission to use extracts from Dorothy Middleton's edition of The Diary of A. J. Mounteney Jephson on the Emin Pasha Relief Expedition.

THIS BOOK HAS BEEN SET IN MONOTYPE JOANNA, PRINTED BY THE ANCHOR PRESS LTD, AND BOUND BY WM. BRENDON & SON LTD, BOTH OF TIPTREE, ESSEX.

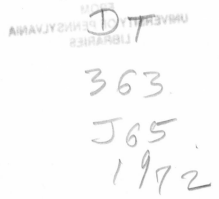

CONTENTS

Please note: The short titles used in the notes at the end of each chapter are in most cases simply an author's name printed in capitals. The exceptions are: D.A., which refers to Stanley's *In Darkest Africa*; E.P.C.A., which refers to *Emin Pasha in Central Africa*, edited by Schweinfurth and others; JEPHSON, which refers to Jephson's diary; JEPHSON—E.P., which refers to Jephson's *Emin Pasha and the Rebellion at the Equator*. Full details of all these works can be found in the Bibliography on page 455.

NOTE ON NAMES

Spellings of foreign words, especially proper names, used in this book are frankly eclectic. Where possible I have used spellings that were current at the time of the Expedition (thus *Osman Digna* rather than the modern *Uthman Diqna*; *Welle* rather than *Uele*; *Shuli* rather than *Achole*; and so on). Similarly, I have followed the practice of the Victorian explorers in applying Swahili class-prefixes even where local forms differ from the Swahili, thus: *Ganda* (stem), *Uganda* (Ganda-land), *Mganda* (a Ganda man), *Waganda* (Ganda men), *Kiganda* (Ganda language). Where contemporary sources have failed to establish a common spelling, as, for example, in the case of *Tippu-Tib* (*Tippoo Tib*, *Tippu Tip*, etc.), I have made an arbitrary selection from the alternatives and used it consistently in the narrative, while leaving the variant spellings intact in quotations. Finally, it should be noted that, since villages are frequently referred to by the name of their headman or chief, names such as *Kavalli* or *Ugarrowa* can denote either persons or places, while a place may also be known by the possessive form—*Kavalli's, Ugarrowa's*.

LIST OF ILLUSTRATIONS

LIST OF MAPS AND FIGURES

———————————

This book is dedicated to
MY PARENTS
with love

HISTORICAL INTRODUCTION

According to their first impressions of the white man, so will the natives form their estimate of our character and methods. A great responsibility thus rests on the first pioneers. The respect they claim as their due, the deference accorded to them, the trust in their courage and their justice, are heirlooms to their successors. But if they should fail to establish the character of the white man on a basis superior to any the savage has yet known, it will take long to eradicate the impression. . . .

LUGARD: *The Rise of our East African Empire* 1893

The conquest of the earth, which mostly means the taking it away from those who have a different complexion or slightly flatter noses than ourselves, is not a pretty thing when you look into it too much. What redeems it is the idea only. An idea at the back of it; not a sentimental pretence but an idea; and an unselfish belief in the idea. . . .

CONRAD: *Heart of Darkness* 1899

CENTRAL AFRICA AND THE SUDAN

About the year 1880 Central Africa stood on the threshold of the colonial era. The great days of African exploration were drawing to a close; the territorial scramble had hardly begun. It was a time when the last blanks on the map of the interior were being filled, the dotted lines of supposition giving way to the concrete realities of latitude and longitude; and a time when the polychrome shadings which symbolised the European overseas empires were hardly more than a twinkle in the eyes of patriotic cartographers.

The Emin Pasha Relief Expedition, which took place between the years 1887 and 1889, occupies a place at the watershed between the exploring and the colonising periods. It was the last of the great exploring expeditions, and it was the last expedition to be led by the greatest of the African explorers, Henry Morton Stanley. It was also the first step—or stumble—in the creation of what was to become the British East African Empire.

To isolate a historical incident from the historical process of which it is part, to pick out a single thread from a continuously-woven fabric is an arbitrary and risky business. This book, nevertheless, attempts to do just that. And first, a point must be selected at which the story may be said (loosely) to begin. For present purposes, such a point may be found in the year 1820, the year in which Egypt, under its Governor Mehmet Ali, undertook the conquest of the Sudan.

At that time Egypt was still, as it had been since 1517, a tributary province of the Ottoman Empire, ruled by governors whose authority derived from the Sublime Porte. It is, therefore, not too fanciful to regard the invasion of the Sudan as the last reflexive spasm of the Ottoman urge to conquest which had set Europe by the ears ever since the emergence of the Turkish hordes from the Asian steppes in the Middle Ages. Certainly the occupation of the Sudan was a straight-forward piece of military and economic adventurism, the object being, by extending Egyptian authority over the Upper Nile, to harness the Sudan to the Egyptian economy. The principal attractions of the region were the ivory trade and the slave trade which here, as elsewhere in Africa, went hand in hand. The military aspect of the enterprise presented, at first, no serious obtacles. The scattered sheikdoms and sultanates of the Sudan were unable, because disunited, to make an effective opposition to an Egyptian army superior in equipment and backed by the traditions of Turkish military organis-ation. The second part of the exercise—to get the Sudan to pay its way—posed problems which were never really solved. For individual entrepreneurs, particularly if they were not too scrupulous, the Sudan was from the first a bonanza ; but as far as the Egyptian government was concerned, it is doubtful whether the income levied by taxation was at any time sufficient to offset the military expenditure which the occupation entailed.

Meanwhile, behind the economic impetus to Egyptian expansion, another force was at work—nationalism. In the year 1866 the Governor Ismail extracted from the Sultan what was, de facto, a recognition of Egyptian independence when, after his successful rebellion, he persuaded the Porte to confer on him the title of Khedive (that is, "sovereign", a word of Persian origin replacing the previous Arabic title Wali, or Vali, meaning "governor"). Ismail also secured recognition of the principle of hereditary rule in his family—a concession whose significance will be obvious. But as Turkish influence in Egypt declined, so European, and especially English, influence was drawn in to fill the vacuum. Inevitably, by calling on European finance and European technical expertise to develop his newly-independent domain, Ismail was laying a mine to the foundations of that independence. The most obvious symbol of Egypt's subjection to European capital and European industrial skills is the Suez Canal, opened in 1869.

A further step towards dependent status was taken when Ismail, whose reach, financially speaking, exceeded his grasp in the grandest possible manner, endeavoured to stave off bankruptcy by the sale of his Canal shares in 1875. Though he realised four millions of sterling on the deal, he also involved his country irretrievably in England's foreign policy, and still failed to avert financial collapse. By 1878 his debts had reached £80 million and he could no longer meet the interest on his loans. England and France brought pressure to bear on the Sultan, and Ismail was deposed. Following a pattern which has since become familiar to the point of caricature, Ismail collected the liquid assets that his Treasury still contained, boarded his yacht, and sailed off to a comfortable retirement on the shores of the Bosphorus.[1]

Only the slenderest pretence was made of concealing the puppet status of his successor, his son Tewfik. To ensure Tewfik's compliance, a council of commissioners was set up representing the "powers"— France and England being paramount.

Two further links were wanting in the chain of events which was to place the responsibility not only for Egypt, but also for her Sudanese dependencies, squarely in England's lap.

The first of these events was the emergence of a powerful nationalist party under Arabi Bey. With the covert support of the Sultan, the enthusiastic backing of the army, and a highly popular anti-European platform,[2] Arabi soon found himself raised to the office of War Minister, the rank of Pasha and the powers of a dictator.

It was not long before England, fearing for the safety of the Canal, her life-line to India, was dragged into the mess caused by the Arabist risorgimento. In April 1882 a fleet of eight iron-clads and five gunboats was despatched to Alexandria, it being represented to H.M.G. that the lives and property of British subjects were at hazard. This forecast proved correct. On June 11 there were vigorous popular demonstrations in which upwards of two thousand Europeans were deprived of life or property or both. The English Consul, a Mr. Cookson, escaped (narrowly). The commander of the fleet at Alexandria sent an

B

3

ultimatum to the Arabists to desist from fortifying the harbour. The injunction was ignored and a noisy bombardment followed. The state of naval gunnery at this era was lamentable. The fleet, under perfect conditions and against negligible opposition, fired three thousand rounds at the forts. Of these only ten rounds managed to damage anything that might be considered a target.[3] As a spectacle the British Fleet at practice must have been impressive: as warfare it was laughable. However, it did have the effect of inducing the Egyptian regulars to pull out of the town. The citizenry, relieved of all restraint, improved the shining hour with a further bout of riot, mayhem and massacre. It was not until two days later that enough sailors and marines were landed to restore order in the city.

Later in the same year (1882) a full-dress Expeditionary Force under Sir Garnet Wolseley was put ashore. Arabi Pasha's army was roundly defeated at Tel-el-Kebir near Ismailia on September 13. Arabi was exiled to Ceylon (having first been condemned to death by way of a warning), Tewfik was re-installed in his palace and England found herself with what was effectively a new colony on her books.

The second link in the chain—that which added the Sudan to England's responsibilities—had its origin in 1869, the year of the Canal Opening. In this year the Khedive Ismail commissioned an English traveller and sportsman, Sir Samuel Baker, to bring the head-waters of the Nile under Egyptian rule and to extirpate the slave trade in those regions.

By the conquest of the Sudan two-thirds of the Nile had become an Egyptian waterway. Now, with Baker's help, Ismail might become the first ruler in Egypt's long history to control the river from its mouth to its source. At the same time he had other, more concrete ends in view. He would vastly increase, in fact double, the catchment area for the flow of taxes into his ever-empty coffers. His concern to put down slavery would win him confidence in Europe—an indispensable concomitant of credit. Finally, by crushing the power of the slave-traders, who had already penetrated the region in force, he would scotch what was becoming a dangerous rival to his own authority.

Here something must be said about the geography of the Sudan. For this purpose it is convenient to consider the country in relation to the river, and to consider the river as consisting of three roughly equal sections:

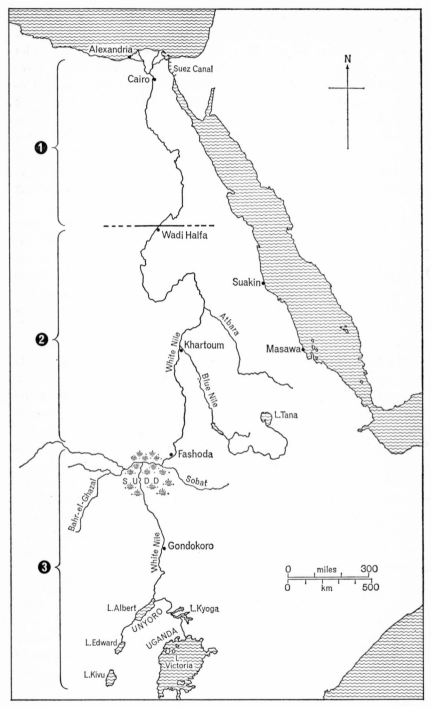

❶
❷
❸

N

Alexandria
Suez Canal
Cairo

Wadi Halfa

Suakin

Atbara

White Nile
Khartoum

Blue Nile

Masawa

L.Tana

Fashoda

S U D D
Sobat

Bahr-el-Ghazal

White Nile
Gondokoro

| 0 | miles | 300 |
| 0 | km | 500 |

L.Albert
L.Kyoga
UNYORO
L.Edward
UGANDA
L.Kivu
L.Victoria

I   The Nile System

1. The Lower (Egyptian) Nile—from the Delta to Wadi-Halfa on the Egyptian–Sudanese border.
2. The Middle (Sudanese) Nile—from Wadi-Halfa to Fashoda near the junction of the White Nile with the Sobat and Bahr-el-Ghazal. In the middle of this section stands Khartoum at the confluence of the White Nile and the Blue Nile.
3. The Upper (Equatorial) Nile—from Fashoda to the source, i.e. to the outlet on the northern shore of Lake Victoria.

It was the last of these areas towards which Baker was directed to turn his attention, and which is of particular concern to this story. This was the region that was to become Equatoria—"Hat-el-Estiva"—the southernmost province of the Sudan.

There was neither geographical nor political cohesion between Equatoria and the rest of the Sudan. South of Fashoda the culture and the peoples are Negroid, and all Arabic influence here is of external origin. North of Fashoda the Sudan belongs to the Islamic world and the people are a mixture of Hamito-Semitic and Negroid stocks. The tribes of the Upper Nile belong to the so-called "Nilotic" group of peoples, the principal tribes, from south to north, being the Madi, Bari, Dinka, Nuer and Shilluk. The distinction between these and the more or less Arabised tribes around Khartoum, while it is here over-simplified, derived a strong reinforcement from the existence of a physical barrier between the Upper and Middle Nile. This was the Sudd—the name given to the dense, shifting masses of floating vegetation which turn two hundred miles of the river south of Fashoda into a labyrinthine swamp, always difficult to navigate, often impossible. The Sudd formed a definite break in the only natural feature making for unity between the two regions—the river. And as the river was the only practicable means of north–south communication, upon which the very existence of Equatoria depended, it is clear that events there might be conditioned by the navigability of the Sudd at a given time.

The extent to which the history of Equatoria was a function of its geography will become more fully apparent in what follows. It is, in a sense, the theme of this book.

*   *   *

BAKER IN EQUATORIA

In 1870, when Baker's expedition set out from Khartoum, he was making not his first but his second visit to the southern Sudan. In 1863 he had been at Gondokoro, a pestilential collection of mud huts which at that time constituted the principal settlement south of Fashoda. Here he had met the English explorers Speke and Grant at the end of their historic journey from Zanzibar to Lake Victoria, during which they had discovered the principal source of the Nile at Ripon Falls on the northern shore of the Lake. From Speke, Baker learnt of the probable existence of another large lake to the west of Lake Victoria. Together with his beautiful Hungarian-born wife, Baker set out to find it. He succeeded (March 14, 1864), naming his trouvaille Lake Albert.

On this journey Baker had made the acquaintance of Kamrasi, King of Unyoro, through whose territory Speke and Grant had passed, the first Europeans to do so. Unyoro lay on the eastern shore of Lake Albert. South and east of Unyoro lay a second Bantu state, the Kingdom of Uganda, which together with Unyoro occupied the territory between the two lakes. Uganda and Unyoro are of considerable importance in the story of Equatoria. Both kingdoms were powerful, warlike, and had a degree of political organisation and internal coherence which made them far more formidable entities than the loose confederations of village chieftaincies which were the rule among the neighbouring tribes. Both were suspicious and fearful—with good reason—of foreign interference. The two kingdoms were frequently—indeed, almost continuously—at war with one another and with their weaker neighbours, a state of affairs which could make this area a serious obstacle to travellers or merchants in transit. Thus the existence of the two kingdoms not only set a limit to Egyptian expansion southwards; it also blocked, from time to time, communications between the Upper Nile and the East African Coast.

The strength of the two kingdoms had not yet been tested against a serious threat from the outside. In spite of what had been gleaned during the visits of Baker, Speke and Grant in the sixties, Uganda and Unyoro were still, politically, unknown quantities at the time of Baker's second expedition.

Still accompanied by the indomitable Lady Baker, Baker left Khartoum on February 8, 1870, bound for Gondokoro. His force was a strong one and well, not to say luxuriously, equipped. There were over

7

a thousand men armed with Snider rifles, half of them Sudanese recruits, half Egyptian gaolbirds. From these Baker selected a personal bodyguard which he dressed in special uniforms and christened his "Forty Thieves". There were forty-eight of them, perhaps in anticipation of casualties. His stores included artillery, a rocket battery, and a flotilla of steamboats that could be dismantled for carriage on man- or camel-back to wherever they were needed.

Baker's fleet failed to penetrate the Sudd on its first attempt. He pulled back and camped to the north of it in open water, intending to wait until the river should rise. In December he tried again. Progress was frighteningly slow and there was steady attrition of both boats and men. It was not until March 1871, and only after he had resorted to the expedient of damming the river downstream from the fleet, that Baker brought his boats out into open water again.

On May 26 he ran up the Sultan's flag at Gondokoro and solemnly annexed the surrounding country, christening it Equatoria.[4] A proclamation was issued in the following terms:

> No person shall trade in ivory, neither shall any person accept ivory as a present or in exchange; neither shall any person shoot, or cause to be shot, elephants: all ivory being the property and monopoly of the Government of His Highness the Khedive of Egypt.
> No person shall either purchase or receive slaves as presents or in exchange.
> Any person transgressing by disobedience of the above laws will be punished as the will of Baker Pasha may direct.

The rest of the year Baker spent in bloodily asserting his authority over the local tribes and over the slavers, both separately and in combination. His position was difficult. The slavers had established, by force, authority over the tribes. The only way Baker could destroy this authority was by the use of greater force. Moreover, slave-raiding, in which the slavers operated by setting tribes and villages at one another's throats, had wrecked the delicate balance of inter-tribal relationships. In addition, some of the slavers who had established zeribas (fortified encampments) in the area claimed to be representatives of the Khartoum Government. In some cases this assertion had a kind of twisted truth in so far as many of the Egyptian officials in the Sudan were actively participating in the slave-trade. So indeed was every enterprising soul in the province with two piastres to rub together.

It is doubtful if Baker appreciated how equivocal his situation was. He was employed to put down slaving; but the revenues of the government which employed him were in a great measure dependent on that trade, and ninety per cent of the government's officials were directly or indirectly involved in it or benefiting from it. This paradox was one of the rocks on which Equatoria was eventually to founder. In all probability Baker never even saw it. He had little political sense, especially of politics as they are understood in the East. Finesse had no part in his dealings with the people he administered. Despite the gusto with which he entered into the parts he played (big-game hunter, explorer, soldier, administrator), he was basically out of sympathy with the natives of Africa. He tended to regard their ways as, at best, prankish, at worst, deliberately perverse. Thus whatever problems could not be settled by a timely application of force could not be settled—or had escaped his notice altogether.

Towards the end of January 1872 Baker headed south from Gondokoro with a colonising gleam in his eye. His appetite for annexation had been whetted, not slaked. His goal was Unyoro. On April 25 he arrived at Masindi where Kabba Rega, the successor of Kamrasi, had his seat.[5] Wasting no time, Baker proceeded, in his off-handedly businesslike way, to the construction of a generously proportioned "government house", to which was added an entrenched and palisaded fort. On May 14, 1872, the annexation of Unyoro was formally announced.

It took more than a building programme and a stirring proclamation to impress Kabba Rega with the justice of the Khedive's vicarious claims. Though young and inexperienced, he was the descendant of a long line of powerful kings and had no intention of giving up his birthright at the bidding of this hairy intruder.[6] At the beginning of June he struck back. His opening move was a present of poisoned banana beer to Baker's camp. The next day, while many of Baker's men were incapacitated by the effects of the King's Greek gift, the Wanyoro mounted a massive surprise attack. They were beaten off and Baker was able to go over to the offensive. An hour later Masindi was in flames. But Baker, for all the power of his rifles, was hugely out-numbered and the enemy tenacious. Continual harassing attacks left him no alternative but retreat (June 14).

Ten days later the remains of Baker's column reached Foweira, the nearest station across the border of Unyoro, after a nightmare retreat which had cost him heavily both in men and supplies.

From here Baker moved north to Fatiko where he set up a new head-quarters and from where, when he felt strong enough, he attacked and defeated Kabba Rega's forces—not decisively enough to permit the reoccupation of Unyoro, but sufficiently to salve his pride. He then turned his attention to "pacifying" the tribes of southern Equatoria.

In 1873 Baker's four-year contract with the Khedive expired. In August he was back in Cairo en route for England. He left behind, as he thought, a province in which slavery was stamped out and the seeds of "civilisation" sown. Certainly Baker had, on paper, nearly doubled the extent of the Khedive's Sudanese possessions. But the problems of Equatoria were more resilient than he supposed.

One of his successors in Equatoria recorded this judgement on Baker's efforts:

> Whoever read the reports of Sir Samuel Baker to the President of the Royal Geographical Society, afterwards published in The Times, would have thought that slavery was completely suppressed, and that a great part of the African territory had been annexed to Egypt. But this expedition, which cost more than half a million sterling, had no important result . . . All the owners of seribe (zeribas) conspired against him, and offered a vigorous resistance. Finally, worn-out, and beaten by the enemy who burned all his provisions in the various depots, he found himself compelled to retreat. The supposed conquests and suppression of slavery were proved a chimera; the trade flourished more than ever, and the country again had to endure the horror of its oppressors.[7]

This rather harsh judgement overlooks the fact that, though the results of Baker's campaigns were not as lasting as he would have liked to believe, his rule had nevertheless laid down the broad lines which the occupation of Equatoria was to follow during the remainder of its brief history. The occupying troops, under Baker as under his successors, maintained the authority of the Khedive by force rather than by policy.

"Pacification" was both patchy and impermanent. Revolts were frequent. Often these were stimulated either by the machinations of Kabba Rega or the King of Uganda, or by the Arabs; but more often the cause was the mere presence of the troops. The soldiers lived parasitically off the natives, making "razzias" or raids upon the villages whenever they felt the need for fresh supplies of corn, cattle or concubines. These raids often provoked bloody retaliation, which in turn provoked repression—and so on. Such a system naturally gave the tribesmen a somewhat lopsided view of the benefits of civilised government. At best they had exchanged the haphazard predations of the Arabs for the more calculable piracies of a legally-constituted authority—a difference which might well have appeared to them not necessarily advantageous.

*   *   *

GORDON IN EQUATORIA

Gordon was recruited to the Egyptian service in Istanbul in 1872 after a meeting with Nubar Pasha, the Khedive's Prime Minister. Gordon, at that time serving on the International Danube Commission, was asked by Nubar if he could suggest a successor to Baker. Gordon suggested himself. Perhaps the idea of governing Equatoria seemed to offer the kind of challenge that appealed to the broad streak of knight-errantry in Gordon's character. Permission was obtained from H.M.G. for Colonel Gordon once more to enter the service of a foreign power[8] and in February 1874 Gordon arrived in Cairo. Asked to name his own salary, he demonstrated his disinterestedness by refusing to accept more than two thousand pounds a year, a startling contrast with Baker's ten thousand. (Without undue cynicism one may doubt whether this gesture made a favourable impression on the Khedive and his ministers; they are more likely to have concluded that they were dealing with a lunatic.)

By April 16, 1874, almost exactly a year after Baker's departure, Gordon had reached Gondokoro to take up his new duties.

His inheritance consisted of three stations—Gondokoro, Foweira and Fatiko—the remnants of Baker's troops including the Forty Thieves (who by now had earned their title a thousand times over) and all Baker's unsolved problems. Gordon, unlike Baker, realised that among these problems was the ambiguity of his relationship to a government whose agents, at all levels in the hierarchy, were personally involved in slave-taking, slave-dealing, slave-owning, or all three. Gordon did his best to mitigate the evils of the system, but at the end recognised that he had failed; it was too deeply engrained.

As long as the Khedive and the Pashas keep eunuchs and slaves, so long must one doubt their sincerity, whatever they may say . . . Have the Khedive and the Pashas ever moved a little finger against the slave-trade except under coercion from without? Is it not true that the moment this coercion ceases the slave-trade recommences? It is engrained in the bones of the people. Sir Samuel Baker's appointment, my appointment, and the appointment of every European in the Soudan respecting the slave-trade have been the result of either government or public (European) opinion forced on Khedives or Pashas.[9]

Just how deeply engrained the system was is eloquently suggested by a casual aside from one of Gordon's letters:

My German (*servant*) is away with my boat, and I have no interpreter. I have only two little scraps of Shillook boys whom I bought for some dhoora (*millet*) at Saubat . . .[10]

In the face of a predatory administration, a slave-based economy, and an almost total lack of support from his superiors, Gordon struggled hard and well to alleviate the lot of the black peoples of Equatoria. His dedication was total and his energy almost unbelievable.[11] If he failed it was because he had taken on a task in which no one could have succeeded.

But the slave problem was not his only preoccupation during his governorship, and in other areas he accomplished a great deal in his three-year tenure. His activities may be summarised under three headings:

1. Establishment of internal communications.
2. Exploration of the Nile system.
3. Expansion of the administration.

(1) *Communications*
Between Gondokoro and Duffile, a hundred miles higher up the river, the Nile is broken by a series of rapids which make steamer navigation impossible. Having moved his headquarters from Gondokoro to a less malarious site at Lado, a few miles away, Gordon set about opening up the river between Duffile and Lake Albert. To this end he began the laborious transfer

from Lado to Duffile of Baker's two steamers—the *Khedive* (108 tons) and *Nyanza* (38 tons)—plus two smaller collapsible steel boats. This was done partly by winching the boats up the rapids, partly by dismantling them for difficult and exhausting portages. It was to be nearly three years before both steamers were afloat at Duffile, but meanwhile Gordon had brought up the steel boats with comparatively little trouble. In these he sent one of his European assistants, the Italian Romolo Gessi, to make the first exploration of the Nile between Duffile and Lake Albert and the first circumnavigation of the Lake (March to April 1876).

The opening of the Nile between Duffile and the Lake had, as Gordon was aware, a significant effect—that of shifting the centre of gravity of the province considerably further south, and, in so doing, of weakening the already tenuous contacts between Equatoria and Khartoum. Lado was no longer the centre of Equatoria. Although it remained the nearest point directly in touch with Khartoum and Cairo, it was not as well placed as Duffile for contact with the rest of the province. While remaining officially the capital, it eventually became in effect a border town.

Gordon had in mind a plan which, if carried out, would have taken this southward shift a great deal further. It involved three distinct operations:

—Exploration of the Nile between Lake Albert and Lake Victoria, with an eye to using it for steamer communication.
—Occupation of the plateau between the two lakes—i.e. Unyoro and Uganda. (Gordon had a high opinion of the potential value of this area by comparison with Equatoria proper.) [12]
—Abandoning the Nile route as the principal line of communications with Egypt and opening instead an overland route to Mombasa or some other point on the East African Coast. [13]

Each part of the plan broke down.

Surveys upstream from Magungo, where the Nile flows into Lake Albert, showed that steamer navigation between the two lakes was clearly impossible, thanks mainly to the falls which blocked the river's course at two points.

As regards Unyoro and Uganda—Gordon had neither the

means nor the inclination to repeat Baker's mistake of attempting a straightforward military occupation. He therefore sent negotiation missions to Kabba Rega, and to Mutesa the King of Uganda. Ultimately he failed to reach a concrete agreement with either potentate.[14] It could hardly have been otherwise, as the interests of the two parties nowhere coincided. The only agreement which would have suited Gordon's plans would have involved a renunciation by Kabba Rega and Mutesa of their sovereignty, and neither king had any intention of allowing this to happen. The sole result of the negotiations was to increase the kings' suspicions respecting Egyptian intentions. They adopted and maintained an attitude of defensive hostility which was to be a fertile source of future trouble to the administration of Equatoria.

The attempt to open the East Coast route produced Gordon's most spectacular failure. In January 1875 he wrote to the Khedive to suggest sending an expeditionary force to seize a beach-head on the East Coast.

> I have proposed to the Khedive to send 150 men in a steamer to Mombaz Bay, 250 miles north of Zanzibar, and there to establish a station, and thence to push towards Mutesa . . .[15]

And again:

> I propose . . . concentrating myself in the south, near Kaba Rega, and trying to do the only thing which will open Africa, viz., coming down on the coast at Mobaz Bay, north of Zanzibar. The navigation between this (i.e. Lado) and Khartoum is a terrible affair . . . Any way it is better to open a route to the sea. Zanzibar, a large place, is near Mombaz, and I hope the Khedive will let me do it. It is the only mode of helping these countries. All the northern part of my province is marsh and desert, and useless for any one. The rich parts are the lake districts.[16]

Essentially this was not a scheme for improving the communications of the Equatorial Province, but a scheme for extending Egyptian domination over most, if not all, of East Central Africa. The Khedive, who should have known better, received the idea with enthusiasm. He was perfectly aware, as was Gordon, that the section of coast he proposed to occupy formed part of the domain of the Sultan of Zanzibar and that the Sultan was quite capable of resenting (if not of resisting) such an intrusion. Ignoring this detail, the Khedive blithely despatched three warships and six hundred soldiers to put Gordon's plan into effect. The raiders, commanded by a British naval captain named McKillop on loan to the Khedive, landed troops at three points on the coast north of Mombasa. The Sultan's garrisons surrendered without a fight, the Sultan's flag came down and up went that of the Khedive. So far everything had gone splendidly. But having gone so far, no one knew where to go next. Gordon, at the end of a 6,000-mile-long line of communications, could exercise no control over the development of his plan. Indeed, the first intimation he had of the Khedive's reaction to his proposal was the news that McKillop's force had set out, and that he (Gordon) was to make immediately for the coast to effect a junction. Gordon, however, had neither the leisure nor the men for an overland march.[17] McKillop, for his part, had orders to sit tight and wait for Gordon. There was an embarrassed pause, partly filled by the loud and energetic protestations of the Sultan of Zanzibar vis-à-vis the British Government. English opinion, in particular the noisy anti-slavery lobby, tended to side with the Sultan. The Khedive was quietly persuaded to withdraw. McKillop re-embarked his troops and sailed back to Suez.

Gordon regarded the failure of his scheme as due to the Khedive's bungling, and the Khedive's withdrawal as a lack of will. "I see," he commented bitterly, "that 'the Khedive withdrew his troops from Juba by command of the British Government'. He is a Hindoo Prince, as the French say he will be." One is allowed to gather that Hindoo Princes stood fairly low in Gordon's estimation.

(2) Exploration

When Gordon came to the Sudan the mystery of the Nile sources was still only partly unravelled. The existence of the two great lakes was known, but neither had been mapped. That a considerable river ran from East to West between the two was also known, but the identity of this river with the Nile proper was a matter of inference rather than demonstration. The river which ran north through Gondokoro might or might not be the same as the river which ran west from Lake Victoria and might or might not pass through Lake Albert on its way. The size of Lake Albert—Baker had declared it to be virtually limitless—was another unsolved question, and a matter of political as well as geographical importance. If it ran as far south as Baker maintained, and if it discharged into the Nile, then Egypt would have in her hands a waterway into the heart of Africa and the possibility of easy communication as far south as Lake Nyasa. There was even a remote but exciting possibility that Lake Albert belonged not to the Nile but to the Congo system and would provide a water link with the West Coast.[18]

Gessi's circumnavigation established the relatively modest limits of the Albert and the fact of its discharging into the Nile.

Meanwhile another of Gordon's assistants, a compatriot of Gessi's named Piaggia, had made his way upstream in an attempt to trace the course of the river as far as Lake Victoria. He penetrated to Lake Kyoga, whose southern end is about sixty miles from Ripon Falls. Here, weakened by fever and confused by the irregular conformation of the swampy shoreline, Piaggia had to turn back. However, the remaining portion had already been traversed by Speke and Grant, so with the work of Gessi and Piaggia, plus Stanley's circumnavigation of Lake Victoria (1875), the riddle of the Nile sources, the "coy fountains", was largely solved. There remained details to be cleared up, but the principal facts of the Nile watershed system were now well and truly on the map.

(3) *Administration*

In the administrative field Gordon's principal innovation was a considerable increase in the number of government stations. Baker's three posts became a chain running south from Lado to Lake Albert and then south-east along the northern bank of the river as far as Mruli. Between Lado and the Lake he established stations at Rejaf, Bedden, Kirri, Muggi, Duffile and Magungo. The posts along the Unyoro border were eventually given up after the demise of Gordon's hopes for extending his influence over Unyoro and Uganda; they served no useful purpose once this scheme had been abandoned and were too difficult to maintain in the face of opposition from Kabba Rega and Mutesa.

The multiplication of administrative centres strengthened Gordon's hold over the tribes. At the same time, by ensuring that as far as possible no two stations were more than a day's march or steamer journey apart, he simplified and speeded up internal communications. While the hazards of overnight camps had had to be reckoned with, it had been impossible to send parties of less than a hundred men from place to place. The new posts made it possible to relax this cumbersome precaution.

As part of Gordon's pacification scheme the posts were to be as nearly self-supporting as possible. If the soldiers could be induced to grow their own food they would have less incentive to plunder the natives under their care, and the natives, by the same token, would have less cause for armed opposition to the soldiers' presence. If the system never operated properly, it was not Gordon's fault. In a country where nothing operated properly—least of all any project which depended on the co-operation of large numbers of people—it is wonderful that Gordon's policies achieved even a measure of success. By comparison with the rest of the Sudan at the time, Gordon's achievement was astonishing. It was said that by the end of his governorship it was possible for a traveller to move about alone armed only with a walking stick.[19]

In October 1876, exhausted by his efforts and weighed down by the enormity of the problems which still beset the Sudan, Gordon turned his back on Equatoria. On December 24 he was back in London. But the respite was brief and the call of duty still strong. In February 1877 he returned to Egypt as Governor-General of the whole of the Sudan.

The last act of the drama, which would see the death of Gordon at the hands of his Sudanese subjects and an English army on the Nile, was still some years in the future.

*   *   *

EXPLORATION AND COLONISATION IN CENTRAL AFRICA

In the fifteenth century the Portuguese navigators had begun to trace the outline of the African continent. Once their daring but hesitant probes to the south had established that ships did not burn up at the Equator,[20] it was not long before the external configuration of the whole land mass was known. But for three hundred years following these early discoveries the interior remained "dark" and for most purposes Africa meant little more than an awkward interposition between Europe and the great overseas empires—Portuguese, Dutch and British—which sprang into being to tap the fantastically rich resources of India, China, Japan, and the Spice Islands. Until the middle of the nineteenth century, only thirty years before the events with which this story deals, the map of the African interior remained a virtual blank. But in those three decades the initiative, courage and endurance of a handful of travellers—Livingstone, Burton, Speke, Schweinfurth, Nachtigal, Baker, Stanley, Cameron—had illuminated the ignorance of centuries. From Khartoum to the Zambesi and from Zanzibar to the mouth of the Congo, the main features of that tremendous tract of land had been subjected to the curious scrutiny of European eyes. The Great Lakes—Nyasa, Tanganyika, Victoria, and Albert—had been discovered, circumnavigated and mapped. The legendary snow-capped mountains of the Equator—Kenya and Kilimanjaro—had been established as facts. The fabled pygmies of the Great Rain Forest, unvisited by Europeans since the sixth dynasty of Pharaonic Egypt, had been located and studied. The courses of the Nile, Niger, Congo and Zambesi had been followed from source to mouth.

It is beyond question that the greatest single contribution to this extraordinary burst of activity was that of Henry M. Stanley. It is also ironic that of all the explorers Stanley alone seems to have been motivated by none of the usual incentives to this kind of work: he did not travel because he loved travelling; he did not travel in Africa because he loved Africa; he had neither sympathy with nor interest in the inhabitants; missionaries and scientists he regarded with equal contempt. Ambition drove him. For Stanley, Africa was an enemy, a dangerous opponent to be struggled with and overcome, his journeys a series of contests in which the stakes were—quite literally—death or glory.

He was born in Denbigh in 1841. His father, a farmer's son, and his mother, a butcher's daughter, were not married. Their child was given his father's name, John Rowlands. At the age of five, his mother being unable (or unwilling) to support him, he became a charge on the parish and lived in the workhouse at St. Asaph where he remained, in circumstances of Dickensian horror, until, at the age of fifteen, he ran away to sea. At Liverpool he signed on as cabinboy on a merchantman bound for America. Arriving in 1859 in New Orleans, he jumped ship.

He found a job in the counting-house of a wealthy cotton broker named Stanley. This man adopted the young Welshman, who in turn took his benefactor's name. When the elder Stanley died, however, the young man suffered a new rejection: his adoptive family refused to recognise his claims on the estate or their consideration, and turned him loose to fend for himself. Two years later the American Civil War got under way. Stanley decided to participate. He entered the war as a private in the Confederate States Army and emerged from it as an ensign in the United States Navy. After the war he resigned his commission and took his first journalistic assignment, covering General Hancock's expedition against the Cheyenne and Kiowa (1867). In 1869 he reported the British invasion of Abyssinia for the *New York Herald* and then moved to Spain for one of the innumerable Carlist insurrections then in progress there. From Madrid in the same year he was called to Paris where his employer, James Gorden Bennett, proprietor of the *Herald*, presented him with the following brief:

> I wish you to go to the inauguration of the Suez Canal first and then proceed up the Nile. I hear Baker is about starting for Upper Egypt. Find out what you can about his expedition, and, as you go, describe as well as possible whatever is interesting for tourists; and then write up a guide—a practical one—for Lower Egypt: tell us about whatever is worth seeing and how to see it. Then you might as well go to Jerusalem; I hear Captain Warren is making some interesting discoveries there. Then visit Constantinople, and find out about that trouble between the Khedive and the Sultan. Then— let me see—you might as well visit the Crimea and those old battlegrounds. Then go across the Caucasus to the Caspian Sea; I hear there is a Russian expedition bound for Khiva. From thence you may get through Persia to India; you could write an interesting letter from Persepolis. Bagdad will be close on your way to India: suppose you go there and write up something about the Euphrates Valley Railway. Then, when you have come to India, you can go after Livingstone . . . and, if you find he is dead, bring all possible proofs of his being dead. That is all.

Stanley embarked on the programme set him without turning a hair:

> I went up the Nile, and saw Mr. Higginbotham, chief engineer in Baker's Expedition, at Philae, and was the means of preventing a

duel between him and a mad Frenchman, who wanted to fight Mr. Higginbotham with pistols, because that gentleman resented the idea of being taken for an Egyptian, through wearing a fez cap.[21] I had a talk with Captain Warren at Jerusalem, and descended one of the pits with a sergeant of engineers to see the marks of the Tyrian workmen on the foundation stones of the Temple of Solomon. I visited the mosques of Stamboul with the Minister Resident of the United States and the American Consul-General. I travelled over the Crimean battlegrounds with Kinglake's glorious books for reference in my hand. I dined with the widow of General Liprandi at Odessa. I saw the Arabian traveller Palgrave at Trebizond, and Baron Nicolay, the Civil Governor of the Caucasus, at Tiflis. I lived with the Russian Ambassador while at Teheran, and wherever I went through Persia I received the most hospitable welcome from the gentlemen of the Indo-European Telegraph Company; and following the examples of many illustrious men, I wrote my name upon one of the Persepolitan monuments.[22]

This little tour occupied nine months of Stanley's valuable time. In August 1870 he reached India and in October of the same year he sailed from Bombay for Zanzibar on the start of his first African expedition. It was to be a turning point in his life. He undertook the search for Livingstone as a journalist, not as an explorer. But suddenly, as a result of his journey, his life moved into another plane: he was no longer a faceless recorder of other men's deeds but the leading actor in his own drama. When he returned to England with Livingstone's journals and a heavily dramatised account of his meeting with the Doctor at Ujiji on the shores of Lake Tanganyika, a hero's welcome awaited him.

Nothing could exceed the warmth with which the general public gave expression to their admiration of the pluck and daring with which Mr. Stanley had carried out his splendid achievements. At banquets, luncheons, and public meetings, he was received with the utmost enthusiasm. The freedom of the principal cities of the empire was conferred upon him at the unanimous wish of their corporations, and he had a personal interview with the Queen.[23]

The lesson was not lost on Stanley: between the travelling correspondent and the heroic explorer there was a great gulf fixed, and

Stanley had no hesitation about deciding on which side of the gulf to station himself.

In the next two years he consolidated his reputation by his book on the Livingstone expedition and by lecture tours in England and America. He also reverted briefly to his role as war-correspondent, covering Wolseley's Ashanti Campaign, still for the *New York Herald*.

In 1874, with the combined backing of the *Daily Telegraph* and the *New York Herald*, he set out on his second expedition. Starting again from Zanzibar, he marched to Lake Victoria, sailed round it, calling on Mutesa in Uganda,[24] marched to Lake Tanganyika, sailed round it, and then, still spoiling for something to achieve, turned his attention to the Lualaba River. The Lualaba lay to the west of Lake Tanganyika and from there ran north to no one knew where. The direction of its flow had tempted some, including Livingstone, to believe that it might be the Nile. Others thought it might be the Congo, still unexplored except for a short stretch running inland from the west coast. Stanley solved the problem by the simple though desperately hazardous proceeding of sailing down the river to the sea in his collapsible boat the *Lady Alice*. It was the Congo. A thousand days after leaving Zanzibar the starving remnants of the expedition[25] emerged at the mouth of the river having crossed the continent from east to west and added more to the sum of geographical knowledge about Africa than any previous expedition.[26] At the same time Stanley's achievement had considerable practical significance: he had revealed the existence of a third water-highway into the heart of Africa to add to the two already known, the Zambesi and the Nile.

It was not long before someone was found willing to exploit this discovery. In 1876 King Leopold of the Belgians had called an international geographical conference in Brussels to discuss ways and means of opening up the African oyster. The conference gave birth to the "Association Internationale Africaine", a body whose avowed purpose was to exert the civilising influence of European commerce on the benighted savages of the interior. Under the auspices of the Association several expeditions were sent inland from Zanzibar without much furthering what was, from Leopold's point of view, the real object of the exercise—namely, to ensure that little Belgium was not entirely left behind in the African "scramble". Stanley's opening of the Congo in 1877 dealt Leopold a card which he lost no time in playing. In January 1878, only weeks after his return to England, Stanley was interviewed by Leopold's commissioners. This was followed by meetings in Brussels of various interested parties and the birth of a new organisation solemnly entitled the "Comité d'Études du Haut-Congo". This body, too, had pretensions to "international" status but Leopold's rather obvious leanings towards commercial rather than scientific endeavour had already caused the withdrawal of foreign scientific organisations such as the British Royal Geographical Society; and a general lack of interest among the "powers" (including Belgium) in other than purely national schemes for colonial exploitation had left Belgium with a virtual monopoly of the project. In 1879 the "Comité d'Études" became the "Association Internationale du Congo" and Leopold, its head, returned all foreign subscriptions. From this point the internationalism of Leopold's projects was no more than a polite fiction.

Meanwhile, in 1879, Stanley had been despatched to Africa to begin operations in the field, or, as he put it in a letter to the Committee: "We go to spread what blessings arise from amiable and just intercourse with people who hitherto have been strangers to them."

In five years of almost continuous exertion Stanley set up a chain of stations along the Congo from Boma at its mouth to Stanley Falls on the Upper Congo some one thousand four hundred miles distant. The forts were garrisoned with European officers and native troops,[27] "treaties" were made with the chiefs of the riverine tribes, and steamers were brought in to handle internal communications.[28]

In those five years Stanley had built, single-handed, a brand-new state of about the same dimensions as Saudi Arabia. The effect on the map of Central Africa was drastic. Where five years before had been a great tract not only unclaimed but unknown, was now the "Congo Free State". A substantial piece of the African continent had, almost overnight, been eliminated from the stockpile of unclaimed territory. The field for colonial enterprise in Central Africa had suddenly been reduced by half.

That left East Africa. In this area the principal contenders for the honour of spreading "what blessings arise from amiable and just intercourse" were three: England, Germany, and the Sultan of Zanzibar.

In the centuries which followed the first great surge of Islamic expansion, the East African Coast from Kilwa to Mogadishu had become an integral part of the Arab-dominated trading system of the Indian Ocean. Even after the Arabs had lost their near-monopoly of the carrying-trade to the successive irruptions of the European maritime empires, the East Coast remained largely under Arab domination. A substantial, though reduced, flow of seaborne trade continued between its ports and those of the Red Sea, the Persian Gulf and the Malabar Coast. In the nineteenth century an important focus of this trade network was the Island of Zanzibar. It had already been an Arab possession for two hundred and fifty years when, in 1832, the Sultan of Muscat transferred his capital there and established a hegemony over the whole of the coast from the Portuguese colony of Mozambique in the south to Somali-land in the north. The Sultan and his successors exercised little more than a nominal control over the coast, but it was sufficient for their purposes to control the ports and harbours which were the outlets for the caravan trade between the coast and the interior. The rulers of Zanzibar also claimed suzerainty over the tribes and countries of the hinterland, though they neither exercised, nor attempted to exercise, actual control. The Sultan's flag was carried by the caravans moving about the interior, but this was no more than a symbolic gesture.

Despite its lack of administrative strength, however, the Sultanate of Zanzibar was of considerable importance at this time. As the chief port of the central East African Coast and because of its position at the interface of the Negro and Arab cultural zones, it was a natural base for the European exploring expeditions of the 1850s and following decades. It was also, by virtue of its bi-cultural status, the unofficial capital of the so-called Swahili people or Wangwana. Of these, some were the descendants of the original inhabitants of the coast; some had been drawn there by the prospect of finding employment as caravan-porters—the traditional speciality of the Wangwana; others, probably the majority, had been brought to the coast from widely-scattered points in the interior by Arab slave-caravans to meet the demand for domestic slaves in the Arab world, and for labourers on the clove plantations of Zanzibar and Pemba. As a people they fancied themselves superior to the unregenerate natives of the interior whom they referred to pejoratively as Washenzi (savages). Nominally they were Muslims and they had their own language, Swahili, which became the lingua franca of East Africa.[29]

Zanzibar, furthermore, was an obvious choice as a base for the naval squadron which Britain maintained in these waters from about 1850 onwards. The function of this force was, by blockading the coast, to put a stop to the slave-trade out of the coastal ports. In this it was ineffective[30] but in the long run it had a more important effect:

23

English interest in the suppression of the slave trade was given a powerful impetus by the revelations of Livingstone and other travellers concerning the activities of the Arabs in Central Africa, and the presence of the fleet actualised England's moral involvement in the area. Thus it happened that, as with Egypt and the Sudan, popular emotional involvement proved stronger in the end than the government's disinclination to embark on fresh colonial ventures. It was in spite of, not because of, government policy that England became responsible for Egypt and the Sudan; the same is largely true of East Africa.

Germany, on the other hand, was[31] overtly and specifically interested in East Africa as a sphere for empire-building.

> On April 3, 1884, the Society for German Colonization had been founded at Berlin, and at the end of the same year Dr. Peters had, under its orders, started on his famous flag-hoisting journey, which ended in the peaceful subjugation of the territories of Useguha, Nguru, Usegara, and Ukami. On February 27, 1885, the Emperor, William I, sanctioned the acquisition of the new districts by the issue of a charter. On April 25 the Sultan Burghash was officially informed of the fact, and at once raised a protest at Berlin by telegraph. He insisted that the chiefs had had no right to alienate the districts acquired by Germany, for these—so ended the very sharply worded protest—belonged to him "since the days of his father". The claims of the Sultan were, naturally, not acknowledged by the German Foreign Office. . . .[32]

The British Government, at first, regarded these events with equanimity. Let Germany embroil herself in Africa; England knew better than to indulge in harebrained schemes of colonial expansion. Eventually, however, driven partly by popular emotional involvement in the suppression of the slave trade, and partly by pressure from mercantile interests[33]—but most of all by a vague feeling that the Germans might after all be on to something, and whatever that something was, Britain should have a share of it—the Government took a hand in the game, if only on the diplomatic level. In October 1886 a territorial agreement was signed with Germany. German and British "spheres of influence" in East Africa were delimited by means of a line drawn from the eastern shore of Lake Victoria to a point on the Coast a little way north of Zanzibar (corresponding to the present boundary between Kenya and Tanzania). South of this line, as far as the Rovuma River (the northern boundary of Portuguese East Africa), was Germany's sphere; north of it, as far as the Tana River, England's. The Sultanate of Witu, lying just north of the Tana River, was also recognised as a German enclave. (Later, when it was realised that this German beach-head on the northern boundary of the British zone could, if properly handled, be extended in such a way as to reduce the British claim to a mere corridor, Germany's Protectorate over Witu became a main source of German-English friction.) No arrangement was made in the Agreement for any territory lying further west than the eastern shore of Lake Victoria. This omission was shortly to become a matter of crucial significance.[34]

In all this, the advice and opinion of the Sultan of Zanzibar—whose property the High Contracting Parties were so casually disposing of— were not asked. His existence was, however, recognised in so far as his dominions were arbitrarily defined as consisting not (as the poor man supposed) of a vast empire stretching inland to the Great Lakes and beyond, but of Zanzibar and some other offshore islands plus a coastal strip ten miles wide from Witu to the Rovuma River. Even this modest territory was not long to remain his in anything but name. He soon found himself "leasing" the coastal strip to England and Germany, while England, after disputing the honour with Germany for some years, in 1890 assumed a Protectorate over the island of Zanzibar itself.

Against this diplomatic background, the period between 1887 and 1888 saw the creation of a British counterpart to Germany's East Africa Company. The founder of what emerged in September 1888 as the Imperial British East Africa Company, the man who had long been the leading proponent of a British commercial effort in Central Africa, was a Scot named William Mackinnon. He was a man who comes so close to the conventional notion of *homo victorianus* as to seem almost a caricature, a man of whom Samuel Smiles would have approved mightily—self-made, devout, hard-working, and possessed to a high degree of the Victorians' happy facility for the simultaneous worship of God and Mammon.[35] From an insignificant clerkship in a Glasgow trading house he had risen by energy, vision and ability to the command of a vast commercial empire. His enterprises were based on shipping. His chief creation was the British India Steam Navigation Company—a network of cargo-, mail- and troop-transports which stretched from England to Australia through East Africa, Aden, the

Persian Gulf, India, Burma and the East Indies. By the year 1893 Mackinnon had built up a fleet of no fewer than one hundred and ten vessels. In the 1870s he had turned his attention, or a part of it, to Central Africa. In 1875 he had begun sending his ships to Zanzibar and in 1878 he had negotiated a commercial agreement with the Sultan of Zanzibar which would have brought him substantial concessions in the interior if his plans had not foundered on the covert opposition of his own government. He had then shifted his ground to West Africa and taken an active part in the proceedings of King Leopold's various associations and committees. But here again he had been frustrated, this time by Leopold's bias towards an exclusively Belgian programme. It was not until 1887, the year of the Emin Pasha Expedition, that Mackinnon saw his dream of British commercial enterprise established on the African mainland on the way to becoming a reality.

*   *   *

THE ARABS IN CENTRAL AFRICA

It has been estimated that in 1876 only ten per cent of Africa was under European occupation and this occupation was almost entirely confined to the coastal belt.[36] A number of countries, notably France, Britain, Portugal and Germany, were laying wild claims to tremendous pieces of the interior without, in many cases, so much as the formality of a visit, but these were still only paper empires, what one traveller called "chartographical flourishes".[37] However, while the nations of Europe were jockeying for position on the starting lines, another power had already established itself among the lakes, rivers and forests of Central Africa—the Arabs.

They had two principal spheres of operation:

(1) A broad belt stretching right across the continent from east to west between the lower edge of the Sahara and the northern edge of the Rain Forest. The trade in this area was channelled through the slave markets of the Sudan and the Red Sea ports—Massawa, Suakim, Zeila and Berbera.

(2) A second belt, further to the south and running inland from the Zanzibar and Mozambique coasts to Lakes Nyasa and Tanganyika and embracing huge areas of the forest regions

beyond the lakes. The principal base for this area was Zanzibar and there were important staging posts at Ujiji on Lake Tanganyika and Tabora some two hundred miles further east.

As the search for ivory and slaves had brought the Arabs to the southern Sudan, so it had brought about their penetration of the Lakes Region and the Upper Congo. In both areas the trade in these two commodities went hand in hand. The demand for slaves in the Muslim world (where slavery had a recognised status in Koranic law) was apparently insatiable.

Two reasons for this have been suggested: (i) that the working life of the slave was short—on average only eleven years—and, (ii) that the rate of reproduction among the slave population was extremely low.[38] Another point to be borne in mind is that between the East Coast and the interior, human porters were the only means of transport; not only were there no roads and hence no wheeled traffic, but no pack animal except of the species *homo sapiens* had been found which could survive in the conditions which existed there. Camels, oxen, elephants, mules, donkeys and even zebras were all tried at various times. None was very successful. The greatest obstacle was the prevalence of the tsetse fly, which causes "nagana" disease, a form of trypanosomiasis, in cattle and horses and renders, to this day, thirty-seven per cent of the African land mass untenable to cattle. And if human pack animals also tended to succumb in large numbers, at least they were easy to replace. If *hired* porters were used, costs could be alarmingly high. The European companies found that it could cost them (in 1890) anything from £150 to £300 a ton to get their goods from the Coast to, say, Lake Victoria. It was natural therefore that the Arabs should concentrate on ivory; it was the one product which was reasonably plentiful and at the same time sufficiently valuable to repay the cost and trouble of transport.[39] Under these conditions the use of slaves to transport the ivory was a stroke of genius. The economic elegance of using one commodity to transport another and then selling both is too obvious to need elaboration.[40]

At grass-roots level—that is, in the slave-hunting grounds as opposed to the ports and slave-markets—the majority of those engaged in the trade were not, in fact, Arabs. The leader of a raiding caravan would probably be an Arab, though he might be of mixed blood or a muslimised Negro representing an Arab merchant. His

men, however, would be either muslimised Negroes from the coast—
slaves or freed slaves—or mercenaries recruited in the interior as part of
the Arab policy of setting tribe against tribe. Of the latter sort were the
Wahenga of Lake Nyasa, and the dreaded Manyuema, a cannibal
tribe whose home was to the west of Lake Tanganyika but who,
through their alliance with the slavers, were making their presence
felt over thousands of square miles on the Upper Congo and Aruwimi
rivers.

The annual loss of life by enslavement and massacre in East-Central
Africa has been estimated by Coupland at between eighty and one
hundred thousand. Livingstone, not a man given to wild talk, put the
figure five times higher.[41] Large areas were totally depopulated. The
damage done to the balance of inter-tribal relationships was incalcul-
able and irreversible. And the system was as wasteful as it was destructive. Coupland calculates that "four or five lives were lost for every
slave delivered safe to Zanzibar" and gives this account of the slavers'
methods:

> The composition of a caravan was always much the same—two or
> three Arab merchants in charge with their half-caste hangers-on, a
> body of armed slaves, and the long string of porters, slave or free,
> with the scarlet flag of the Sultan at their head—but its numbers
> varied from a hundred or so to a thousand or even more . . . At all
> points on the way inland and back again the traders were anxious
> to pick up slaves if only in twos and threes . . . But the main
> sources of supply were the organised slave-raids in the chosen
> areas, which shifted steadily inland as tract after tract became
> "worked out". The Arabs might conduct a raid themselves, but
> more usually they incited a chief to attack another tribe, lending him
> their own armed slaves and guns to ensure his victory. The result, of
> course, was an increase in inter-tribal warfare till "the whole
> country was in a flame".[42]

For this description a hundred parallels can be drawn from contemporary accounts.[43] The activities of the slavers and ivory-hunters
are well documented. Nearly all the Europeans who travelled in the
region during the great age of African exploration—from roughly
1850 to 1890, a period which corresponded with the peak of Arab
expansion—have recorded their comments on the subject. The following will serve as a sample:

Sometimes these Arab traders will actually settle for a year or two in the heart of some quiet community in the remote interior. They pretend perfect friendship; they molest no one; they barter honestly. They plant the seeds of their favourite vegetables and fruits—the Arab always carries seeds with him—as if they meant to stay for ever. Meantime they buy ivory, tusk after tusk, until great piles of it are buried beneath their huts and all their barter goods are gone. Then one day, suddenly, the inevitable quarrel is picked. And then follows a wholesale massacre. Enough only are spared from the slaughter to carry the ivory to the coast; the grass-huts of the village are set on fire; the Arabs strike camp; and the slave-march, worse than death, begins.

This last act in the drama, the slave-march, is the aspect of slavery which, in the past, has chiefly aroused the passions and the sympathy of the outside world, but the greater evil is the demoralisation and disintegration of communities by which it is necessarily preceded. It is essential to the traffic that the region drained by the slaver should be kept in perpetual political ferment; that, in order to prevent combination, chief should be pitted against chief; and that the moment any tribe threatened to assume a dominating strength it should either be broken up by instigation of rebellion among its dependencies, or made a tool at their expense . . .

. . . It was but yesterday that an explorer, crossing from Lake Nyasa to Lake Tanganyika, saw the whole southern end of Tanganyika peopled with large and prosperous villages. The next to follow him found not a solitary human being—nothing but burned houses and bleaching skeletons. It was but yesterday—the close of 1887—that the Arabs at the north end of Lake Nyasa, after destroying fourteen villages with many of their inhabitants, pursued the population of one village into a patch of tall dry grass, set it on fire, surrounded it, and slew with the bullet and the spear those who crawled out from the more merciful flames. The Wa-Nkonde tribe, to which these people belonged, were, until this event, one of the most prosperous tribes in East Central Africa . . . (But) years ago an almost unnoticed rill from that great Arab stream, which with noiseless current and ever-changing bed had never ceased to flow through Africa, trickled into the country. At first the Arab was there on sufferance; he paid his way. Land was bought from the Wa-Nkonde chiefs, and their sovereignty acknowledged. The Arab force grew. In time it developed into a powerful incursion, and the

Arabs began openly to assert themselves. One of their own number was elevated to the rulership with the title of "Sultan of Nkonde". The tension became great, and finally too severe to last. After innumerable petty fights the final catastrophe was hurried on, and after an atrocious carnage the remnant of the Wa-Nkonde were driven from their fatherland.[44]

Even when allowance is made for Victorian sententiousness and over-writing, this is not a pleasant picture. To some extent, of course, the accounts of European travellers must be distorted by their prejudices and the limitations of a purely Western outlook. But in a sense this is immaterial; the important fact, historically, is that rightly or wrongly the Europeans saw Arab influence in Africa as an evil, and one that could only be expunged by European intervention.[45] The naval blockade on the East Coast was the first step in this direction; the partition of Africa took the process to its conclusion. Inevitably this brought the colonisers—British, German and Belgian—into armed conflict with the Arabs. The British fought the Arabs on Lake Nyasa; the Germans fought them in Tanganyika between 1888 and 1892. And in 1886 an incident occurred, involving the Arabs and the forces of the Congo Free State, which has a particular bearing on the story of the Emin Pasha Expedition.

For the background to this incident we must turn for a moment to consider the career of Hamed bin Mohammed, otherwise known as Tippu-Tib.[46] The life of this extraordinary man, who carved out for himself what amounted to a private empire in Central Africa stretching from Lake Nyasa to the Aruwimi River, coincided with the sudden expansion of Arab power inland (beginning about 1840) and with the heyday of the semi-independent "sultanates" established by the Zanzibar merchant-raiders.

Tippu-Tib was born in Zanzibar about 1842 to a family of prosperous Muscat Arabs.[47] His father, a trader, had established himself at Unyamyembe and at the age of eighteen Tippu-Tib joined him there. From Unyamyembe he made his first independent foray into the interior. The venture was successful and, thus encouraged, Tippu-Tib was able to find financial backing for more ambitious schemes.[48] He took a leading part in the penetration of the forest region beyond Lake Tanganyika. When Livingstone met and was helped by him near Lake Mweru in 1867,[49] Tippu-Tib was already on the way to fame and fortune. By a judicious mixture of force and cunning he established himself as the paramount chief of one of the most turbulent and aggressive tribes of the region, the Manyuema. Later, in 1874, Tippu-Tib met and helped another explorer, Cameron, who was then engaged on his crossing of the continent. Then, in 1876, his path crossed that of a third European traveller in a meeting that was to be fertile of consequences. Stanley, about to embark on his trip down the Congo, met Tippu-Tib near Nyangwe on the Lualaba River. The meeting is recounted in the following extract from Tippu-Tib's autobiography—an extract which, incidentally, shows the simple excellence of Tippu-Tib's prose style and reveals something of the qualities which made him so brilliantly successful in the hard world of business:

A month passed there until one afternoon Stanley appeared. We greeted him, welcomed him and gave him a house. The following morning we went to see him and he showed us a gun, telling us, "From this gun fifteen bullets come out!" Now we knew of no such gun firing fifteen rounds, neither knew of one nor had seen such. I asked him, "From a single barrel?" He said they came from a single barrel. So I asked him to fire it so that we could see. But he said we should produce a fee of twenty or thirty dollars for firing it once. In my heart I thought he was lying. A single-barrelled gun: the second I thought was a cleaning-rod! How could the bullets come out of one barrel one after another? I said to him, "Over in Rumami there's a bow which takes twenty arrows. When you fire, all twenty fly together. And each arrow kills a man." At that he went outside and fired twelve rounds. Then he took a pistol and fired six rounds. He came back and sat down on the verandah. We were amazed. I asked him how he loaded the bullets and he showed me.

Stanley now persuaded the Arab to accompany him with a large party some distance downriver. Tippu-Tib agreed, though stipulating that Stanley would have to pay for this service. A bargain was concluded and the combined parties set out on what proved to be an excessively arduous and uncomfortable march through country that not even the Arabs had visited. After some distance the Arabs announced their intention of turning back. A dispute arose as to whether they had covered a sufficient distance to comply with the terms of the agreement. It will never be known with whom the right lay in this dispute. Stanley, on his return to England, noisily denounced Tippu-Tib's perfidy. Tippu-Tib's own version of both the agreement and disagreement differed substantially from Stanley's. He maintained that Stanley had broken faith with him over the matter of payment and had promised him presents (on reaching England) which had never materialised. He also maintained that he (Tippu-Tib) had saved the expedition since Stanley's men had mutinied when the Arabs turned back, and only Tippu-Tib's threatening to shoot any of Stanley's men who returned to Nyangwe had prevented them deserting in a body. One can only take one's choice as to whom to believe. It must be said that Stanley's testimony is generally unimpeachable in all that concerns places, dates and distances, but—as the account of the Emin Pasha Expedition will show—he is totally unreliable in whatever concerns the behaviour, character and motives of other people, particularly people whose actions impinge in any way upon himself. Tippu-Tib, on the other hand, had already helped both Livingstone and Cameron, and this help was given voluntarily, gratis, and in the face of opposition from his colleagues and followers. He had nothing to gain by attempting to cheat Stanley since Stanley was in a position to withhold payment if not satisfied, and such a thing ill accords with Tippu-Tib's character as established by Stanley's predecessors and Tippu-Tib's later behaviour.

Whatever the truth of the matter, the encounter between Stanley and Tippu-Tib had two important results. In the first place it left an atmosphere of distrust between the two which was to colour their future dealings. In the second place it turned Tippu-Tib's attention towards the hitherto unexploited regions of the Lualaba-Congo between Nyangwe and the confluence with the Aruwimi. Thus it happened that, a year or so later, while Stanley was working his way back up the Congo from the west, establishing the forty or so stations that were the material embodiment of the Congo State, the Arabs were simultaneously working downstream from Nyangwe.[50] The two forces met at Stanley Falls where Stanley established the last of his posts and claimed the district for the Belgians, and Tippu-Tib arrived with a numerous band of Manyuema to annex the district to the nebulous domains of the Sultan of Zanzibar. The Arabs set up a base in the neighbourhood of the Falls (1884) and sent out parties in all directions to examine the commercial possibilities of the area. Friction was inevitable. The Arabs established all over the interior were beginning to feel themselves driven into a corner by the combined pressures of the English in the south, and the Germans in the east, and now the Belgians in the west. Some, of whom Tippu-Tib was one, saw the approaching end of the Arab hegemony in Central Africa and were prepared, fatalistically, to bow to the inevitable and make the best terms they could with the interlopers. Others decided to fight. The Arabs had recognised too late that not all Europeans were defenceless, penniless, and presumably witless explorers, that these lunatic seekers after unknown rivers and mountains were the outriders of a society whose commercial and military strength came as an unpleasant surprise. By the time surprise had turned to defiance the moment for effective resistance had already passed. But it was in this spirit of defiance that in 1886 the Arabs attacked the Belgian fort at Stanley Falls. Tippu-Tib himself was absent at the time; the Arabs were led by his cousin and partner, Bwana Nzige, and Nzige's son Rashid. The fort was defended by two Europeans, Deane and Dubois, with two Krupp screw-guns and a handful of Hausas. After a spirited defence the Fort fell to the greatly superior forces of the Arabs. Most of the garrison, including Deane himself, escaped, though Dubois was drowned in the flight across the river.[51] The station remained in the hands of the Arabs and there the situation rested until the events which will be dealt with in a later chapter.

NOTES AND REFERENCES

HISTORICAL INTRODUCTION

1   An early example of this behavioural pattern occurs in the *Phyllada tou Megal-exandrou*, a mediaeval Greek version of the life of Alexander the Great. There it is recorded of a (mythical) Egyptian potentate called Nektenavos that, "when he saw that his kingdom was lost and that he would be conquered . . . he shaved off his beard, disguised himself, laid hold of all the money he could, and left Egypt secretly". He chose Macedonia for his retirement, and there fathered the future world-conqueror.

2   The appeal of Arabi's xenophobic programme is easy to understand when it is borne in mind that Egypt had been continuously under foreign domination since the time of Alexander the Great. The same consideration is relevant to an understanding of the loyalty of present-day Egyptians to the regime of Colonel Nasser, a man who embodied the first successful alternative to foreign rule in over two thousand years of Egypt's history.

3   See Admiral Sir Percy Scott: *Fifty years in the Royal Navy*.

4   Gondokoro he christened Ismailia, but the name seems not to have stuck.

5   In later years Kabba Rega kept his capital further south, for obvious reasons.

6   The Wanyoro called Baker M'bdizu ("Beardy").

7   GESSI pp. 3–4.

8   In 1863–4 Gordon had made his name, literally, in China by organising and leading a mercenary army to defend European interests during the Taiping rebellion; this won him the sobriquet "Chinese" Gordon.

9   Note by Gordon appended to "An address from the British and Foreign Anti-slavery Society to the Right Hon. W. E. Gladstone", December 1880.

10 Letter of September 25, 1874. Confirmed by Gessi (p. 64) who mentions four pounds of millet as the amount involved in the transaction.

11 Thus, in three years (1877–9) while Gordon was Governor-General of the Sudan (the post to which he was promoted on leaving Equatoria) he travelled 8,490 miles on mule- and camel-back.

12 "The only valuable part of this country is that formed by the tablelands of the Kingdom of Uganda, whilst the country south of Lado and Khartoum is but a miserable marsh." Gordon qu. CASATI II p. 218.

13 Cairo is as near to Moscow as it is to Lake Albert. And Lake Albert is nearer to Mombasa than to Khartoum. (Straight-line distances.)

34

14 See BIRKBECK HILL p. 183 and p. 192.

15 BIRKBECK HILL p. 65.

16 BIRKBECK HILL p. 68.

17 Letter of January 18, 1876: "He sent off McKillop and Long to Juba and told them to wait for me. They will wait a long time I expect. I am not going to try this with the undisciplined wretched troops I have here. . . ."

18 GESSI pp. 99–100.

19 Possible perhaps, but not wise. Only a few weeks before he left Equatoria, Gordon's party was ambushed on the march and his butter-tin destroyed by a stray assegai. (See BIRKBECK HILL p. 190 and compare Moorehead *The White Nile* pp. 175–176).

20 Even before the Portuguese started serious exploration of the West Coast of Africa, the men of Dieppe in Normandy had been trading with the Guinea Coast. When, after nearly forty years, internal conditions in France forced them to suspend operations, they attempted to protect their market for future possible use by spreading the most amazing and hair-raising stories about the dangers of sailing beyond Cape Noun. This ruse was successful to the extent that in 1417 King Jao I of Portugal had the greatest trouble in finding sailors to man a fleet destined for those regions. (See Toussaint: *A history of the Indian Ocean.*)

21 An indignity that could never have overtaken Stanley once he had adopted the unique hat which was to become a sort of moving landmark all over Africa.

22 *How I found Livingstone* (Introduction). Illustrious people must have been in short supply in Jerusalem if Stanley was reduced to visiting the "pits" with a Sergeant of Engineers.

23 *Stanley and Africa* p. 431.

24 In one of his despatches Stanley announced that Mutesa was ripe and eager for conversion to Christianity. A party of missionaries sent out by the Church Missionary Society in response to this advertisement set up shop at Mutesa's in 1877. Shortly after, a rival commando of French Catholic missionaries under Père Lourdel arrived on the scene. Islam had already been known in Uganda for some years, thanks to the presence of Arab traders from Zanzibar, the first foreigners to penetrate the country. The simultaneous presence of the proponents of three conflicting orthodoxies led to an unedifying tripartite tug-of-war for the spiritual allegiance of the Waganda. This quickly developed political overtones and ultimately ripened into a seven-year civil war (1885–92).

25 Stanley's omelettes were remarkable for the number of broken eggs that went into them. He left Zanzibar with 356 porters and three white assistants. All three white men perished—two of disease, one by drowning. Of the porters, 242 were lost by desertion, sickness, fighting, starvation, or other accidents.

D

26 There had been two previous crossings of the continent, both using routes further to the south than Stanley's: in 1853–6 Livingstone had crossed from Loanda to Kilimane, and in 1873–5 Cameron had crossed from Zanzibar to Loanda. Other crossings, soon after Stanley's, were those of the Portuguese Serpa Pinto (1877–9) and the German von Wissmann (1880–2).

27 Hausa levies were imported for this purpose.

28 The Congo is unnavigable for two hundred miles above the mouth while it descends from the Central African plateau in a "staircase" of rapids. This section of the route had to be covered by relays of porters until, decades later, a railway was built to connect the Congo mouth with the Upper River.

29 The name derives from the Arabic *sahil* meaning "coast". The basic syntax and morphology of the language are Bantu but the vocabulary contains a high proportion of loan words from Arabic, Hindustani, and other languages.

30 In the opinion of at least one contemporary observer who studied the situation closely at first-hand. See LUGARD I pp. 199–200 and *passim*.

31 Or, more accurately, seemed. See below, Chapter 10.

32 BRODE p. 169.

33 In British attitudes, both official and private, to the acquisition of territory in East Africa, can be clearly seen that curious ambivalence in the way the British regarded their Empire. The apparent inability to decide whether they were acting for their own benefit or for that of their subject peoples is easy to label hypocrisy. But to do so is to ignore the complexity of a phenomenon which is more than interesting, which is, perhaps, the central problem in the history of British imperialism. It may be salutary to note that Lugard, writing in 1893, found it necessary to remind his readers: "It is well . . . to realise that it is for our *advantage*—and not alone at the dictates of duty—that we have undertaken responsibilities in East Africa." He then goes on to adduce several pages of argument and quotation in support of his thesis.

34 The settlement of Anglo-German territorial disputes arising over the partition of East Africa is dealt with below in Chapter 10.

35 It is not immediately apparent why 20th century Man, having abandoned the worship of God the better to devote himself to that of Mammon, should feel himself morally superior to his Victorian forbears.

36 Townsend: *European colonial expansion since 1871*.

37 DRUMMOND p. 217.

38 See LUGARD p. 170 and authorities quoted by him.

39 Regarding the value placed on ivory, it has been suggested that the principal stimulus to the trade came from a sudden increase, from about 1850 onwards, in the demand for billiard balls. (For example: D.A. I p. 230 or Emil Ludwig

The Nile I v.) If true, it might seem rather a poor joke that the heart of Africa should have been laid waste to satisfy a fad for a stupid parlour game.

40 Alas! Since the above was written, the author's attention has been called to recent research which indicates that the idea—widely held at the time—that captured slaves were used to carry ivory, may be a "myth". (See Alison Smith in Oliver & Mathew (eds.) *History of East Africa*, Vol. I pp. 268–269.) However, there appears to be be room for doubt on the point; the passage has therefore been allowed to stand—on sentimental grounds. As Anatole France once wrote, "Old errors are easier to live with than new ones, and since we must make mistakes, it is best to stick to illusions which have moss on them."

41 Coupland: *Exploitation of East Africa* p. 234. See also LUGARD I pp. 199–200.

42 Coupland: *Exploitation of East Africa* pp. 136–138.

43 For example, the massacre at Nyangwe witnessed by Livingstone in 1871.

44 DRUMMOND pp. 70–74. Corroboration, and a more detailed account of events in Nkonde, will be found in LUGARD I Chapters III–VI. The Nyasa Arabs subsequently came into conflict with the Europeans in the area and a small war ensued. Led by Lugard, the Europeans fielded a scratch army of merchants, missionaries, big-game hunters and unemployed gold-miners. They checked but failed to extirpate the pestiferous slavers. In the course of the fighting Lugard was wounded by a bullet which left six holes in him.

45 See for example: CASATI I p. 280, D.A. I pp. 229–230, or DRUMMOND pp. 74–75. European protection was not, of course, in every case an unmixed blessing. In South West Africa, for instance, from 1904 to 1911, the protecting power (in this case Germany) waged a war of extermination against the Herero and Hottentot populations which reduced their numbers from 130,000 to 37,000. (Cd. 9146). Without wanting to push an invidious comparison too far, it may be noted, in fairness to the Arabs, that the Herero War lacked even the justification of a coherent economic motive since it left the settlers without a labour force.

46 "Tippu-Tib" was the name conferred on him by the natives of the interior. It probably referred to a personal peculiarity of his—a nervous twitching of the eyes—though he himself maintained, perhaps from vanity, that it referred to the noise made by the bullets from his guns among the jungle foliage. (BRODE.) The Manyuema knew him as Mtipoora, meaning "footsteps". (JAMESON p. 242.)

47 For this and most of what follows, see BRODE. The extract from Tippu-Tib's autobiography (below) is taken from Whiteley's translation p. 111.

48 The money behind most Arab enterprises in the interior came ultimately from Indian merchant-financiers (known as "banyans") established in Zanzibar.

49 On his last journey (1867–73) Livingstone received help from a number of Arab traders—help which, on one occasion, at least, saved his life. (See Coupland: *Livingstone's Last Journey*.) The Arab penetration of Manyuema-land

roughly coincided in time with Livingstone's presence there, i.e. about 1869–71.

50   The Belgians later blamed Stanley bitterly for having, as they saw it, brought the Arabs down on their necks.

51   Deane was killed by an elephant in 1888.

EMIN IN EQUATORIA
(1876-1886)

> I don't know who he is or what he is,
> except that he is a poor abandoned fellow,
> hemmed in all round, and with no clothes,
> and that Gordon stuck him there. . . .
>
> HERBERT WARD

When Gordon left Equatoria in 1876 and took up his new post as Governor-General, the governorship of the southern province passed successively to two Americans, Mason Bey and Prout Bey. Their tenures were brief; both left when their health broke down. There followed a series of native governors "under whose abominable rule the province rapidly deteriorated to a pitiable condition. Oppression, injustice, brutality and downright robbery grew like the Upas tree. . . ."[1] When the last of these gentlemen, one Ibrahim Fauzi, was relieved of his functions and condemned to death,[2] the question of a successor was mooted. The celebrated Russian-German traveller Dr. Junker, who knew the region well, was consulted:

> Asked by Gordon what I thought or whom I could suggest, I proposed Dr. Emin Effendi. Gordon at first objected, but at last assented, and appointed Dr. Emin Governor of the Equatorial Provinces, with the title of Bey.[3]

Emin was not the Doctor's real name; it was Eduard Karl Oskar Theodor Schnitzer. He had been born on March 28, 1840, at Oppeln (Prussian Silesia), the son of Ludwig Schnitzer, merchant. In 1858 Emin (it is convenient to use the name by which he was later known) embarked on the study of medicine at the University of Breslau, the provincial capital. Later he transferred to Berlin where he graduated M.D. in 1864, but without passing the state examination which would have entitled him to practise in Germany. When he tried to enter his name for the examination he was told that his application was too late.

By the end of his student years the dominant traits of Emin's character were already apparent. Already he was a solitary, but one who badly needed the approbation and acceptance of men he admired, especially intellectuals and savants. He showed an unusual sensitivity to criticism, which would later develop into the touchy and irascible vanity that lost him many friends. In his work he was scrupulous, methodical, painstaking, and a keen observer of facts. Even before leaving the university he had developed the habit of contributing to learned journals, a practice that was to be a mainstay of his lonely existence in Africa. Above all, he was mercurial, alternating inexplicably between boundless optimism and morbid pessimism. His biographer says:

> In considering Schnitzer's student life, one cannot deny that he possessed certain fantastical leanings—a tendency to fluctuate between extremes. . . . We cannot help feeling that external trifles too frequently had a determining influence on him, and that he often lacked the necessary determination to suppress his feelings. What one day he looked upon as highly promising, he would reject the next day as completely hopeless. In all things he inclined to exaggeration.[4]

Under these conditions, and in the light of his later career, it seems possible that his rejection by the Examining Board had a traumatic effect on him. Certainly Emin was not the man to take rejection, or what he interpreted as such, in his stride; and what happened next—his precipitate departure from the fatherland to seek his fortune abroad—has more the appearance of a sudden flight than a necessary or reasonable next step.

In rapid succession he applied to the British for a post in Africa, to the Turks for a post in the Imperial service, and to the Austrians for a post with Maximilian's expeditionary force just leaving for Mexico. All three turned him down.

The Turkish consulate in Vienna, however, had told him that he might apply in person at Constantinople. This seemed his best hope. Accordingly he made his way to Trieste, intending to take ship for the Sultan's dominions as soon as might be. By now he was practically destitute, but he managed to scrape together enough money to pay his passage across the Adriatic, intending to complete the journey on foot. On December 21, 1864, he disembarked at Antivari "carried ashore on the back of a dirty-looking Turk".[5]

Instead of proceeding to Constantinople, Emin remained in Antivari. From an unpromising start as a penniless and unconnected immigrant he succeeded, by a combination of hard work, adaptability and good luck, in establishing himself as medical officer for the district and port quarantine officer. At the same time he mastered three new languages,[6] adopted the fez, learned to smoke chibouk and narghile, and carved out a solid niche for himself among Antivari's cosmopolitan set.[7]

In 1871 he joined the staff of a highly-placed Turkish official named Ismail Hakki Pasha with whom he travelled in Albania, Epirus, Anatolia, Armenia, Persia and Syria. During this period Emin not only acquired a thorough knowledge of the Turkish Middle East, but also perfected his own muslimised persona. "I am now completely naturalised," he wrote in 1872, "and have even adopted the disguise of a Turkish name." His name (Emin was now calling himself "M. le docteur Hairoullah Effendi") was, he wrote, merely a convenience to shield him from the embarrassments to which the lone "Frank" might otherwise be subject. To both his sister and his mother he wrote that he had not turned Mohammedan. However, the point is not proved by these assertions since later, in Equatoria, he persistently asserted the contrary—that he was a Muslim.[8] Both his biographers (Felkin and Schweitzer) insist that Emin's Mohammedanism was a necessary fiction, but they offer no evidence beyond Felkin's statement that Emin was a keen supporter of Christian missionary endeavour.[9] The matter remains an enigma.

Another enigma appears in Emin's life at about this time—that of his relationship with his employer's wife. In January 1872 he wrote to his sister:

> More than a year has elapsed since I received your last letter, and it is just as long since I wrote to you. Do not ask me why. I have passed through a great many trials, and so I was perhaps entitled to one year's contented and happy life, although I should never have dreamt of finding my life's ideal in a Turkish harem!

There is nothing here to identify Emin's "ideal" with Madame Ismail, but the missing year in Emin's correspondence coincides with the first year of his engagement with Ismail Pasha. And a month later Emin was writing to his sister:

> For nearly four months past, since our arrival here (Trebizond), I have had ample time for reflection, having nothing to employ me beyond a daily visit to the harem. Madame Ismail is a native of Transylvania, who speaks German, French and Italian, and is very kind and amiable. We are thus on very good terms. She is probably between twenty-nine and thirty. . . .[10]

In 1873 Ismail Pasha died. Emin occupied himself with settling the estate. Then, in August 1875, he suddenly materialised at his family's home in Neisse with an entourage consisting of Madame Ismail, her four children and her retinue of Circassian slave-girls. Emin's reunion with the Schnitzer lares and penates must have been a rather strained affair. His family had all along viewed his "naturalisation" with an alarm which can hardly have been diminished by their son's arrival with a complete harem in tow. To complete their discomfiture Emin gave out that Madame Ismail was now his wife. This she almost certainly was not, but whether Emin was here practising another of his seemingly pointless deceptions, or merely offering a clumsy sop to German small-town conventions, it is impossible to be sure. It appears that Madame Ismail did, in fact, want to marry Emin, but he—

> . . . seems to have found the support of eleven persons far more than he could manage, and on the 18th of September he left Neisse for Breslau to visit some old University friends, and then suddenly disappeared.[11]

It is clear that this sudden departure represented a conscious and deliberate break with his family. He left no address, and it was fifteen years before he wrote to any of them again.

Madame Ismail and the children, deserted by their protector, stayed some weeks more with Emin's parents before they too left and returned to Turkey—in what state of mind can only be guessed at.

Having disposed of his responsibilities in this rather summary fashion, Emin made his way to Cairo and thence to Khartoum, where he arrived on December 3, 1875, in the company of some Syrian traders. Giegeler Pasha, an Austrian in the Egyptian service, gives this account of Emin's arrival in the Sudan:

> He remained with these merchants for the first few days of his stay, in a public warehouse, and was still living there when he introduced himself to me, and to Friedrich Rosset, then German Vice-Consul, as a Turk who had been brought up and educated in Germany. He persisted in keeping up this fiction all through, notwithstanding the fact that he soon presented his passport to Rosset in which he was described as "Dr. Schnitzer, a German". . . . As he was entirely without means, Rosset and I took upon ourselves to provide for his wants. He used to take his dinner with Rosset and his supper with me, and I remember with much pleasure the delightful and enjoyable evenings he used to spend at my house, when we passed the time conversing about our far-off native land, and playing chess—Emin was a very good chess-player. Sometimes we would go to my neighbour the Austrian Consul Hansal, who had a piano. There Emin, who was a splendid pianist, would play Mendelssohn and Chopin to us. . . . At the same time he was industriously collecting plants and animals which he sent to Europe.[12]

In the meantime Giegeler had written to Gordon about Emin and received a reply inviting Emin to join Gordon at Lado. Emin left Khartoum by steamer on April 17, 1876.

He maintained to Gordon the story that he was a Muslim by birth. In a letter of September 1876 Gordon refers to ". . . the Doctor, who, by the way, is a German, and who, now professing the Mussulman religion, pretends to me that he is an Arab by birth and religion. Emin Effendi is his name in Arabic. . . ."[13]

It is not clear at what precise point Hairoullah Effendi became Emin Effendi (or Mohammed Emin Effendi in the full version).[14] Even less is it clear what purpose Emin hoped to serve by thus clinging to a transparently fictitious identity. In Turkey it might have been a convenience, but in the Sudan, where European administrators were a normal feature of the scene, this no longer obtained. The most likely explanation is that in this way Emin was consciously or unconsciously trying to raise a barrier between himself and the society that had, as he thought, rejected him.

Whatever Gordon thought of his new acquisition, he soon found work for him. A detachment of Sudanese troops under an officer named Nur Aga had rather incautiously advanced into Uganda and now found themselves virtual prisoners in Mutesa's capital. "We are in the same state as Baker was at Masindi," remarked Gordon in a letter to his sister. "Mutesa has annexed my soldiers, he has not been annexed himself." Emin was sent to Mutesa's to negotiate for their withdrawal. Gordon, disillusioned by the failure of his "forward policy", meant to wash his hands of both Uganda and Unyoro. The impossibility of dealing with Mutesa was brought home to Gordon by the letters which Mutesa kept sending him, the work of one Mufta Dallington, an escapee from a slave-dhow, educated by missionaries in Zanzibar, and who had apparently been wished on Mutesa by Stanley. These letters irritated Gordon intensely. The following is a specimen:

To SIR CANNELL GORLDON. February 6th, 1876.
My dear friend Gorden hear this my word be not angry with Kaverega sultan of unyoro I been heard that you been brought two manwar ships but I pray you fight not with those Wanyoro for they know not what is good and what is bad. I am, Mtesa king of Uganda for if you fight with governour you fight with the king. I will ask you one thing but let it may please you all ye Europeion for I say if I want to go to Bommbey if the governour and if the governour of Bommbey refuse me to past will I not find the orther road therefor I pray you my friends hear this my letter stop for a moment if you want to fight put ships in the river nile take west and north and I will take east and south and let us put wanyoro in to the middle and fight against them but first send me answer from this letter. Because I want to be a friend of the English. I am Mtesa son of Suna king of Uganda let God be with your Majesty even you all Amen.
Mtesa king of Uganda.[15]

Emin found that Mutesa had a curious preoccupation, almost amounting to a mania, with religious questions. (In a way this is partial confirmation of what Stanley had earlier said about him.) The King was thrown into confusion by the discovery that Emin, though white, was a Muslim. The visit, however, passed off amicably. The negotiations were successful and by September 9, 1876, both Emin and the troops under Nur Aga were back at Mruli.

Gordon was now preparing to leave Equatoria. The question of

Emin's future employment was raised. It was agreed that Gordon, instead of leaving the question to his successor (Prout), would present the next Governor with a *fait accompli* by appointing Emin Inspector of Stores for the Equatorial Province.

After Gordon's departure Emin made two visits to Khartoum, on the second of which (May 1877) he had an interview with Gordon, who offered him a job as interpreter and personal assistant. Emin asked instead to be confirmed in the post of Chief Medical Officer for Equatoria. Gordon assented and Emin returned to the south. They never met again.

In September 1877 Emin paid a visit to Kabba Rega in Unyoro, and conceived a great liking for him. From Unyoro he went again to Uganda to visit Mutesa bearing presents and protestations of friendship from the Egyptian Government. These were purely diplomatic visits; nothing occurred beyond the exchange of mutual expressions of goodwill.[16] Needless to say, both Mutesa and Kabba Rega continued to entertain well-founded suspicions of Egyptian intentions. Sporadic outbreaks of fighting continued, in the years which followed, along the Somerset Nile where the tribes were torn between the claims to suzerainty of the Egyptian Government on the one hand and the kings of Unyoro and Uganda on the other. These troubles were exacerbated by the Egyptians' sponsorship of a certain Anfina, a pretender to Kabba Rega's throne. By the time the logical step had been taken (long after the abandonment of the forward policy which was their reason for being) of giving up the exposed outposts such as Mruli and Foweira, more serious problems had arisen for the Province.

On his return to Lado Emin continued his explorations of the Upper Nile. He made a number of excursions round Lado, and north towards Shambe and Fashoda. Everywhere he went, in addition to his administrative and medical duties, he was endlessly busy with his specimen collections and with observing and recording an incredible welter of information on the peoples and regions through which he passed. There was nothing that did not interest him. Ornithology was his speciality and his passion, but he found time, too, for researches into anthropology, linguistics, botany, zoology, ethnology, cartography and meteorology. All that he observed went into his journals or into his official reports, and much of it found its way back to Europe in the form of contributions to learned publications and letters to fellow-savants such as the botanist Schweinfurth and the ornithologist Hartlaub. His observations are remarkable as much for their precision as for their range. In a tribal dance, for instance, where nine travellers out of ten, unless trained musicologists, would have seen merely a spectacle, comic or barbaric according to taste, Emin saw what he saw everywhere—an assemblage of data:

Chief Tombe had placed his big drum underneath the votive tree which stood in the open space before my hut, and it soon sent forth the sound of invitation to a dance, three strokes at a time being continually repeated. Immediately the people collected together, and in a minute two long lines were formed, one of women, the other of men, each person holding two sticks made out of the excellent wood of the Diospyros mespiliformis, which, when struck, gives out an almost metallic sound. The big drum then began to beat in three quaver time, accompanied by a small drum, while the sticks were struck against each other. . . .

A few lines later, the speculative mind asserts itself:

The men dancing around the women, who encourage them by alluring pantomimic movements, may be seen also in the animal world; and the fundamental ideas underlying all Negro dances point to their common origin. . . . But how are we to account for the fact that the Negroes, although they are eminently musical, and have an exquisite perception of time, have never yet succeeded in harmonising their choruses?[17]

Junker recorded an impression of Emin at this period:

Dr. Emin is a slender, almost thin man, of little more than medium size, with a narrow face framed by a dark, full beard and deep-set eyes, looking forth with a keenly observant glance through his powerful spectacles. His pronounced short-sightedness compels him to strain and concentrate his sight upon the person before him, which imparts to his look a hard and sometimes, apparently, a frowning expression. The head, which is interesting from an artist's point of view, and in which intelligence is unmistakably manifest, does not in any way suggest a German; its undeniably Oriental stamp materially helped Dr. Emin in the rôle of a Turk, which he had assumed towards the official world and the people at large, and which, more especially during the first years of his stay in the Soudan, he unswervingly kept up. Every Friday one would see him going to the mosque, where he would recite the prescribed prayers. His bearing, as well as his movements, exhibited a studied stateliness and self-command calculated to make him appear dignified and self-conscious. This was particularly noticeable whenever he had intercourse with his subordinates in his capacity as Egyptian official. His external appearance showed an almost punctilious neatness and great care in his dress. . . .[18]

In July 1878 Emin received his appointment to the Governorship of Equatoria.[19]

The first four years in which he held this office were uneventful. Emin was able to devote himself to his private pursuits and to the welfare of his province. He enlarged the orbit of his explorations, pushing north-west towards Bahr-el-Ghazal, west into Monbuttu, and south to the far end of Lake Albert. New stations were built, existing ones submitted to regular tours of inspection. Agreements had to be made with tribal chiefs, their grievances heard and disputes settled. Meanwhile he was experimenting endlessly with new crops, new seed strains, new animals, new raw materials, in an effort to make the country pay. He was so far successful in that in 1882–3 the budget showed a surplus of £8,000. Ivory, however, remained the principal cash crop.

Emin's head was perpetually buzzing with schemes and projects—for domesticating the buffalo, for importing colonists from China,[20] for reorganising the administration of the Sudan, for a railway to the coast, for making soap and cloth, for training elephants to transport work and for starting rubber plantations. At the same time:

Despite his heavy load of care, his work went on as evenly as ever. His meteorological observations were continued, and entered in his diary each morning in the neatest of hands. For the ornithological collection he kept and paid a naturalist, Gasm Allah, an Arab. This was his huntsman. He would often come early in the morning for Emin Bey's orders as to the hunting expeditions; at other times he would scour the more remote districts for weeks together. Being extremely short-sighted, Emin had to give up hunting, and in fact everything that required long-sight; he could not recognise any one a dozen yards away. Gasm Allah used to come back in the middle of the day with the birds he had secured, strung on a little stick. Emin would then take their exact measurement and note down any pertinent observations, the Arab then taking the birds away to be skinned and bringing them back later on, prepared and strung as before. Of course, the comparing, classifying, careful labelling and packing, Emin saw to himself. The hours of attendance, morning and afternoon, at the divan were kept with scrupulous regularity. A perfect master of Arabic and Turkish, Emin conscientiously perused every document and sealed it himself. This would not take up all the office hours, and leisure often remained for private work. . . .[21]

Emin's efforts went a long way towards making the province self-supporting. In Gordon's time, for example, wheat had to be brought up to Lado from Khartoum. Emin, "by encouraging agriculture and regulating the collection of the tribute, succeeded in filling the granaries with sufficient quantities of corn to meet the requirements of the province. By distributing seeds of all kinds, which he obtained from Egypt and Europe, he promoted the cultivation of the soil. . . ."[22] Had he not done so, it is likely that Equatoria, far from flourishing, would have collapsed under what amounted to an economic blockade imposed by the vagaries of the Sudd acting in concert with the inefficiency and indifference of the authorities in Khartoum. Between Emin's taking office in 1878, and the final isolation of Equatoria in 1883, only nine steamers reached Lado from Khartoum, and only six of these brought supplies.[23]

In mitigation of Khartoum's neglect of Emin's Province it can be said that they had matters of more immediate pith and moment on their hands. In 1881, two years after Gordon's departure from the Sudan, the Mahdi had appeared on the scene.

*   *   *

The man who called himself the Mahdi—a title that carries the same kind of spiritual and emotional connotations in Islam as does the word "Messiah" in Judaeo-Christianity—was an obscure Dongolawi by the name of Mohammed Ahmed. In 1881 he was living on Abba Island in the Nile south of Khartoum in a hole he had dug for himself. Two of his brothers lived on the same island where they worked as

48

boat-builders. Mohammed Ahmed's exceptional austerities and holiness, plus a talent for power-politics, gained him fame and followers. When he felt sufficiently sure of himself, he began sending out letters to chosen correspondents announcing that the Mahdi, the "Guided One", had arrived, and those desirous of assisting at the

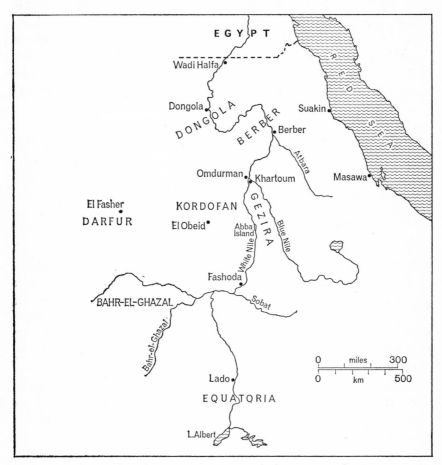

2   The Sudan, showing main towns and administrative districts

forthcoming millennium should join him without delay at his present address.

The success of the Mahdi, the readiness with which he gained supporters, is not difficult to explain in the light of the almost universal discontent among the population of the Sudan. The mass of the people were at the mercy of the Egyptian tax-gatherers who swarmed like locusts over the land, imposing, as is the way of tax-gatherers, the heaviest burdens on those least able to bear them. That the government was inefficient and corrupt was beside the point; but it was a foreign government, and the Turkish and Egyptian intruders and their infidel henchmen offered a broad target to the slings and arrows of local xenophobia. The interference with the slave trade had alienated an influential section of the population; the merchants who made their living by dealing, directly or indirectly, in ivory and slaves found the one made a government monopoly and the second forbidden altogether. Finally, the Mahdi's programme of religious reform appealed to the latent fanaticism of the tribes. The promise of an impending jihad—in which, it may be said without cynicism, the idea of loot loomed as large as did the notion of defending the Faith—added a last, lethal ingredient to the brew. To encourage those who might think that in fighting the Egyptians the Sudanese would be making war on their co-religionists, the Mahdi did not scruple to assert that the Egyptians were no longer to be counted among the faithful, as they had sold themselves heart and mind to the Christians.

Above all, the Mahdi's power fed on the failures of his opponents. The campaign, or series of campaigns, which followed as first the Sudanese, then the Egyptian and then the British governments attempted to settle the Mahdi's hash, are possibly unique in the annals of human conflict. Such persistent incompetence is rare, even in warfare. It was almost as if the generals believed that the recipe for success was to get there the lastest with the leastest, and to this policy they adhered scrupulously.

In August 1881 two companies of soldiers were sent by steamer to Abba Island to bring in the Mahdi before he should begin to make a nuisance of himself. The officer of the company that effected the capture was to be rewarded with a promotion. As a result, a spirit of healthy competition was rife and military science, in the heat of the moment, went by the board. The Mahdi, who had taken the precaution of raising the local population to his defence, had no trouble in sur-prising and slaughtering the over-excited soldiery. A handful got back to Khartoum.

The Mahdi now removed to southern Kordofan where he had greater freedom of action and where his prestige continued to grow. In December the Governor of Fashoda with fifteen hundred men and a German photographer named Berghof[24] marched out against him, again with a fine contempt for precaution. They fell into an ambush. The Governor, Berghof, and fourteen hundred soldiers died almost before they had time to fire a shot.

The jihad was now on in earnest. Those who had been hanging back, waiting to see which way the cat of victory would jump, put aside their scuples and rallied to the Mahdi's banner. The provinces of Kordofan and Sennar were overrun and Khartoum itself threatened. Panic-stricken, the authorities appealed to Cairo for reinforcements. Their request was blocked by Arabi Pasha, now at the height of his power, who scented a ruse on the part of his enemies and preferred to keep the army in Egypt where it was safely under his eye.

In the following year (1882) six thousand men under Yussef Pasha took the field against the Mahdi. Yussef was a brave and experienced soldier, but on this occasion fatally over-confident. On June 7 his camp, which he had casually neglected to fortify, or even to guard properly, was surprised at dawn. The army was annihilated. Yussef Pasha died in his nightshirt at the door of his tent.

The Mahdi-ists now moved against El Obeid, the chief city of Kordofan. The defenders held out bravely, but five months later, in January 1883, were starved into submission.

The British Government, already committed to meddling in Egyptian affairs (the battle of Tel-el-Kebir was fought in September 1882), now decided to take a hand. An officer named Hicks was seconded to the Egyptian service and posted to the Sudan with the rank of Pasha. By sending a British general they were, as they thought, saving themselves the expense of sending a British army. The principle of too-little-too-late was still being adhered to.

In March 1883 Hicks reached Khartoum. In September he marched out at the head of eleven thousand very shaky troops, five and a half thousand camels, six Nordenfeldt guns and ten Krupp mountain guns. Forming his army into a vast square he trundled off in the direction of El Obeid, bent on its recapture. On November 3 a force of two hundred thousand Mahdi-ists fell on him. In a three-day running battle, Hicks and his entire army simply disappeared from the face of the earth. His name, no doubt, will live in history with those of General Custer and the Emperor Valens for the completeness of the disaster that overtook him.[25]

Meanwhile the rising had spread to the Eastern Sudan,[26] threatening Suakin and hence communications with Khartoum. (The fastest route from Cairo to Khartoum was by boat from Suez to Suakin and then overland.) The man in charge of the Mahdi-ist operations in this area was a former slave-dealer, the redoubtable Osman Digna. The man chosen to oppose him was Valentine Baker Pasha, brother of Sir Samuel, who had begun his career in the British Army but after being cashiered had gravitated to the Egyptian service as head of the Cairo Gendarmerie. In December 1883 Baker left for Suakin to begin the pacification of the Eastern Sudan:

> While it was absolutely certain in England that Baker's force would suffer a crushing defeat, and suspected in Egypt, the General himself does not seem to be aware of any danger, or if there be, he courts it. . . . Baker possessed ability and courage in abundance; but the event proved that prudence and judgment were as absent in his case as in that of the unfortunate Hicks.[27]

In February 1884 Baker's little army, nearly four thousand strong, met the rebels at El Teb near Suakin. In the ensuing massacre Baker lost two-thirds of his men. (By now the demoralisation of the Egyptian troops was so far advanced that many of the soldiers could not even be persuaded to defend themselves and died like sheep, their throats cut.) Baker himself only preserved his life by brisk horsemanship.

The situation in the Sudan now appeared hopeless. Only military intervention on a very large scale could reverse the position, and this was something the Egyptians were no longer capable of and which the British, though they had now tacitly assumed the direction of Egyptian affairs, were unwilling to contemplate. As always, Her Majesty's Government was tragically torn between the desire to control the situation and a reluctance to become involved. The policy of the Prime Minister, Gladstone, was to establish a strong "native" government in Egypt as the prelude to an early British withdrawal. The Egyptians, meanwhile, would have to be restrained from embroiling themselves in an effort to hold on to the Sudan. At the insistence of the British, therefore, the abandonment of the Sudan was decided on. The Egyptian Prime Minister, Sharif Pasha, resigned in protest against what he considered a humiliating decision. He was replaced by a more amenable successor, Nubar Pasha, and the plans for the withdrawal, if plans they may be called, went ahead. It was desirable that someone should be found to organise the evacuation of the remaining Egyptian garrisons and the foreign community. The British cast about for someone of sufficient stature to pull even this modest chestnut out of the fire. The job was offered to Gordon. He accepted.

Since leaving Egypt in 1880, four years earlier, Gordon—

> . . . had successively occupied posts in India as secretary to the Viceroy; in China, where he had settled the dispute about Kashgar between Russia and the Celestial Empire; in Mauritius, where he had been the very lifespring of British influence; at Suez, whither he went to meet his brave and devoted friend Gessi, who died there of fever in March 1881; and at the Cape, where he had been entrusted with the settlement of the Basuto-land question.[28]

At the beginning of 1884 Gordon had just entered the Belgian service and was about to embark for the Congo to relieve Stanley in Leopold's infant colony. On being asked to return to the Sudan, Gordon, as susceptible as ever to the call of duty, asked Leopold to release him from his engagement and sailed for Egypt. By February 1884 he was back in Khartoum for the third, and last, time.

The decision to send Gordon back to the Sudan turned out as disastrously as every other decision that had so far been taken in the attempt to deal with the Sudanese rebellion. Gordon, instead of organising the evacuation, set about righting the wrongs of the Sudan.

> From the very first moment of his entry he displayed the most prodigious energy; he held public audiences; he instituted a council of notables; he visited the prisons . . .; he administered justice; he provisioned the white troops at Omdurman, on the left bank of the Nile; he entrusted the defence of Khartoum to the Soudanese regiments; he abolished tolls and remitted payment of arrears of taxes; he placed boxes in various quarters of the town for the reception of claims and complaints, and finally issued a proclamation announcing that henceforward the Soudan would be independent, and recognising as legitimate that slavery, which, according to a former decree of the Khedive, had been definitely prohibited . . . through all the districts between Assouan and the great lakes.[29]

These measures, though in themselves admirable, were lamentably mistimed. The middle of a revolution is not the moment for reform. Moreover they could have no effect on the situation in the country at large, as Gordon was now bottled up in Khartoum by the Mahdi's armies.

Meanwhile the British Government, spurred on by clamorous public anxiety regarding Gordon's fate, despatched a belated and essentially pointless army of British troops under Wolseley to Gordon's relief. Wolseley advanced up the Nile to Wadi Halfa. In January 1885 his leading column was nearing Khartoum. After hard-fought actions at Abu Klea[30] (January 17) and Metammeh (January 19) an advance guard was pushed on to Khartoum. It arrived on January 28 only to find that the city had fallen two days before and Gordon with it.

Wolseley withdrew to Wadi Halfa without more ado. The Sudan was left to its fate.[31]

*   *   *

In the southern provinces, Equatoria and Bahr-el-Ghazal, thanks to their geographical isolation from the rest of the Sudan, the effects of the Mahdi-ist revolt did not immediately make themselves felt. Emin's first intimation of the state of affairs in the north came during a visit to Khartoum in the first half of 1882. It was here that he heard of the Mahdi's early successes, and at Fashoda, on his way back to Equatoria, he learnt of the destruction of Yussef Pasha.

Emin does not at first seem to have realised that these events constituted a threat to his own province. In the letter in which he recounts his trip to Khartoum, he expresses relief at returning to the calm and security of Equatoria. "It appears", he writes, "that the most distant province of Egypt, the Equatorial province, is at this moment the only part of her dominions which is perfectly tranquil. . . ."[32]

But already ripples of the disturbances in the north had reached the other southern province, the Bahr-el-Ghazal, and in the same letter Emin writes of risings among the natives "incited by the emissaries of the Mahdi". Even so, it was not until a year later that Emin began to appreciate the seriousness of the situation in the neighbouring province and to hear the first rumblings of the storm that was soon to break over Equatoria. In June 1883, while travelling in Monbuttu, the region adjoining Equatoria on the west, Emin received letters from Bahr-el-Ghazal which told him that the Dinka had risen and cut off the rest of the province from Meshra-er-Rek, its outlet to the north. At this time the Governor of Bahr-el-Ghazal was an Englishman named

Frank Lupton. He was another of Gordon's "finds", a former merchant seaman who had worked for a time under Emin in Equatoria and been given his own province in 1881 after the recall and tragic death of Gessi.

It now became clear that the troubles in Bahr-el-Ghazal were more than an isolated piece of fractiousness and that the natives were being systematically encouraged and supported by the Mahdi-ists in Kordofan and Darfur. The capacity of the tribes to cause trouble was increased by the presence in the country of numbers of Danagla (Dongolawis). They had originally come from the north as mercenaries in the pay of the Arab slavers and had always constituted a problem to the authorities. Some had been integrated into the administration; most had not, preferring to maintain themselves in out-of-the-way zeribas or as self-appointed village chiefs. As a chronically disaffected minority, and co-religionists of the Mahdi, these people were a natural fifth-column, ready to lend themselves to all manner of mayhem.[33]

In addition to Lupton and Emin, two other Europeans were affected by the threat this outbreak posed. One was Dr. Junker; the second was another traveller, an Italian by the name of Gaetano Casati. Both these men had parts to play in the subsequent history of Equatoria.

In 1883 Junker was happily nosing about in the basin of the Welle (Uele) River which drains Monbuttu and the country of the so-called "Niam Niam" or Zande people inhabiting the Nile–Congo watershed. For years there had been speculation as to whether the Welle belonged to the Nile, the Congo, the Shari or even the Niger.[34] Junker was hot on the trail, within weeks of a final solution by his own estimate, when Lupton's letters caused him to turn back. (If he had followed the Welle far enough it would eventually have brought him to a confluence with the Congo just south of the Equator.) He found his route to the north blocked by the Dinka. He therefore made his way east into Equatoria to wait until a steamer got through from Khartoum. Failing that he would head south through Unyoro and Uganda in the hope of reaching the coast at Zanzibar.

At the beginning of 1884 Junker joined Emin at Lado.

Casati, the second traveller cut off by the rising in Bahr-el-Ghazal, was a former captain of Bersaglieri who had come to the Sudan in 1880 to help survey the southern provinces. In Bahr-el-Ghazal he had met Gessi, the Governor, and worked with him until Gessi's recall. Casati had then drifted south into Niam Niam and Monbuttu. During this period he had made the acquaintance of Dr. Junker. In early 1883 he had come to Lado to meet the steamer—the last to get through— which arrived there in March. Then, apparently careless of the ring that was closing around the southern provinces, Casati had returned to Monbuttu, he too having developed an interest in the "Welle problem".

Casati seems to have been a lonely man who found it difficult to make friends. Possibly he was one of those to whom the loneliness of the traveller is an attraction in itself. Later, when he became involved in Emin's efforts to save the province, he clearly did so only out of a sense of duty. Such involvement was distasteful to him.

In July 1884 he received a letter from Emin which revealed a drastic worsening of the situation. The long-expected invasion of Bahr-el-Ghazal had finally materialised in the form of a "dervish" army under the Emir Keremallah Kurqusawi, a lieutenant of the Mahdi. Emin quoted news he had received from Lupton:

April 12th, 1884.

Dear Emin,

The Mahdi's army is now camped six hours' march from here; two dervishes have arrived here, and want me to hand over the Mudireh (province) to them. I will fight to the last. I have put my guns in a strong fort, and if they succeed in capturing the Mudireh, I will, I hope, from my fort be able to turn them out again. They come to you at once if I lose the day, so look out. Perhaps this is my last letter to you. My position is desperate, as my own men have gone over to them in numbers. I am known now by the name of Abdullah. I win the day or die, so good-bye. Kind regards to Dr. Junker. If steamers come to you, write to my friends and let them know I die game.

Yours truly,
Frank Lupton.[35]

Even after this alarming intelligence Casati did not at once return to Lado but lingered for several months longer before making up his mind. In August 1884 he went back as far as Wandi on the eastern edge of Emin's domain and there he remained as if unwilling to take the plunge into the chaos that the affairs of Equatoria was rapidly becoming. He finally reached Lado in January 1885 "with a very considerable following, including a chimpanzee".[36] Junker had now been there for almost a year.

Equatoria was now preparing to fight for its life. Since Casati's previous visit the situation had been deteriorating steadily. In May 1883 the Dinka had overrun the stations on Emin's north-western border. Not long after, Emin had lost Shambe, on the Nile, his most northerly station. Then, in May 1884, only a few days after Lupton's letter, had come the news of his fall. For two years he had struggled bravely against the insurrection in his province. In the end he had neither won the day nor died. Deserted by his men, he had had no alternative but to surrender.[37] Equatoria was now the only remaining portion of the Sudan not in the hands of the rebels, and nothing stood between it and the Mahdi-ist onslaught.

The Emir Keremallah, from whom Emin had learnt of Lupton's fate, now sent a stream of letters urging Emin to surrender himself to the will of God. From the same source came the news of the fate of Hicks Pasha and of the encirclement of Khartoum. It was therefore useless to hope any longer for relief from the north. "The prospect", Emin wrote, "was not brilliant."[38] His soldiers were scattered over a huge area in penny-packet garrisons. They could only be concentrated by abandoning ground, since the natives would immediately rise in the rear of a departing garrison. The officers, mostly Egyptians, were of doubtful quality—Equatoria had traditionally been a sort of penal colony for the worst elements of the Egyptian army—besides which, the greater part of Emin's officer corps was subject to the Levantine mania for plotting. The soldiers were mostly Negroes levied locally, with a sprinkling of the original Egyptian and North Sudanese regulars. They had never been tested in battle and their loyalty was uncertain.[39]

The news of Lupton's surrender swung the pendulum of Emin's temperament to an extreme of pessimism. He decided to go to Keremallah and surrender his province. Almost immediately, however, the pendulum reversed its swing. Perhaps things were not so desperate after all. Emin called a meeting of his officers and sounded their opinions. The general feeling was in favour of submission. Emin decided to hedge his bets. Instead of going to make his surrender in person he sent a deputation to try to make terms. The deputation achieved nothing, merely changing sides as soon as it got within range of the enemy. The net result was to increase the atmosphere of uncertainty. Emin had neither resolved to fight nor to submit. In so far as his intentions are at all clear, he seems rather to have wanted to do neither.

His behaviour at this time is ominously significant. At the moment of crisis, instead of giving a firm lead embodied in unequivocal orders, he had sought the advice of his subordinates and then simply concurred in a majority decision. At such a moment Emin's unwillingness to make and impose his own decisions was fatal. From this time he begins increasingly to exhibit a disastrously misplaced desire to please everyone, which his officers were prompt to take advantage of. They interpreted Emin's behaviour as a signal that each one was now free to pursue his own ends, and Emin seems to have felt obliged to go along with them, even to the extent of agreeing to plans which he knew to be foolish or impractical. Thus a situation which called imperiously for firm control fostered instead a democracy that verged on—and finally collapsed into—anarchy.

The extent of the degeneration may be judged from the following extract from one of Emin's letters:

> On April 1 the civil and military officers in Lado handed me a document, wherein they petitioned that all the stations in the south should be given up . . . Suicidal as such a suggestion was . . . persuasion would have effected little, and so I had to give at least an apparent consent, and issue the necessary orders.[40]

Casati viewed Emin's vacillations with gloomy foreboding.[41]

Meanwhile, though Keremallah's expected onslaught had still not materialised, by the combined effects of encroachment and retrenchment, Equatoria continued to shrink. In May 1884 the outposts in Monbuttu were abandoned and in August the eastern and south-eastern districts were evacuated. Emin's province was now firmly based on a chain of river stations from Lado in the north to Wadelai (a station founded by Emin in November 1879) in the south. His most advanced station—that is, the one nearest to the enemy in Bahr-el-Ghazal—was Amadi, about a hundred miles north-west of Lado.[42]

In December 1884 Keremallah moved against Equatoria. His forces advanced and laid siege to Amadi. The outcome was surprising. The garrison, though ill-equipped, disunited and badly-led, resisted fiercely. Only when on the point of starvation did they abandon the town, cut their way through the besiegers and fall back towards the Nile. Keremallah had received a check, but with Amadi gone, the way to Lado was open.

Now, instead of moving at once against Emin's capital, the Mahdi-ists turned aside to attack Makraka. Here, at Rimo, a second action was fought and the Mahdi-ists, again to everyone's surprise, were repulsed with heavy losses; again, enough time was gained for the garrisons to be withdrawn.

Even so, to Emin at Lado the situation appeared desperate, the more so as Keremallah had been prompt to inform him of the fall of Khartoum and the melancholy fate of its defenders. Emin decided to abandon Lado and fall back on the line Wadelai–Duffile.

On the face of it this was a sensible decision. Emin would hold only those stations which were served by the steamers, and thenceforward would be fighting on strong interior lines—a sound strategic move. (It will be remembered that the steamers could not operate north of Duffile on account of rapids.) In addition, food was becoming scarce around Lado while further south it was plentiful. Thirdly, by holding Wadelai, Emin was in a better position to defend his line of retreat (should retreat become necessary) through Unyoro–Uganda to Zanzibar. But though his reasons were sound, the decision to abandon Lado was disastrous.

Emin secured, as he thought, the officers' approval of the move (much to the disgust of Casati who thought he had just persuaded Emin to retreat in the opposite direction—north-east to the Sobat[43]) and on April 25, 1885, Emin left Lado for the south. As soon as he had left, the officers at Lado sent a message after him politely informing him of their decision to stay put. Instead of promptly returning to Lado, Emin continued his journey southward as though nothing had happened, until in July he reached Wadelai and made his headquarters there. The result of his failure to act decisively against the disobedience of the Lado officers was that the province was now split in two. Emin controlled the stations from Duffile southward, but the northern stations of Lado, Rejaf and Bedden were in a state of more or less open mutiny, nominally acknowledging Emin's authority but in practice acting as they saw fit.

Casati washed his hands of the matter:

On the 9th of May, 1885, I departed from Lado, and on the 23rd took up my abode at Muggi, in order to abstain from any interference in the affairs of the province, regretting the rapid succession and accumulation of unpleasant entanglements; and from that day I retired to a private and solitary life.[44]

The principal reason for the soldiers' reluctance to move south was the belief that Emin intended to retreat into Unyoro. This belief was well-founded, as Emin had certainly considered the possibility of falling back through Unyoro in an attempt to reach Zanzibar. But behind the unwillingness of the troops to fall in with this plan was more than a natural reluctance to leave what was, for most of them, their homeland. Somehow the idea had got abroad that Emin meant either to abandon the soldiers in Equatoria or to sell them as slaves to Kabba Rega. The only evidence that Emin had ever entertained such a plan is a statement of Casati's (regarding a conversation at which he was not present):

> On May 27 (1884), in the midst of general discouragement, Emin, anxious to find an anchor of safety and to save his prestige from total ruin, had uttered these imprudent words: "We, white men, shall escape—I answer for it. We will give our black soldiers to my good friend Kabba Rega, the King of Unyoro, and he will permit us to cross his boundaries." These words were repeated by the loquacious Egyptians, and the chief's intentions were soon known by the black soldiers. . . . Suspicion and mistrust at first led to disobedience, and later on open rebellion was resorted to.[45]

And later:

> The unfortunate words uttered in Lado bound us like a chain. The soldiers alone could extricate us from our difficulties, but they, remembering the spectre they had seen, contemptuously declined to do so.[46]

Whether or not Casati's story is correct—and it is only barely credible—there can be no doubt of the genuineness of the soldiers' suspicions. And these suspicions had a greater influence than any other single factor on the ultimate fate of Equatoria.

Ironically, the (unilateral) decision to fall back on Duffile need never have been taken. At the end of April, when its outposts were only a few hours' march from Lado, Keremallah's army mysteriously vanished. Recalled to deal with an emergency in Darfur, Keremallah had withdrawn and marched back to Bahr-el-Ghazal. At the eleventh hour the invasion had receded—though for how long no one could tell. Possibly Keremallah had withdrawn only *pour mieux sauter*. However, for the moment at least Emin had leisure to consider his long-term prospects. They were not good. Equatoria was now completely isolated, cut off from the mother country by a thousand miles of enemy-infested territory. This left three possible courses of action open for consideration:

—to stay put, hoping to beat off any further attacks, until the Sudan should be reconquered from the north;
—to withdraw to the south, possibly as a first step in the evacuation of the entire province to Egypt via Zanzibar;
—to restore the viability of Equatoria as an administrative unit by opening either a permanent line of communications with the East Coast, or at least a route along which news and relief supplies might reach Equatoria.

There was no certainty that the Sudan would be reconquered in the near future; it might not happen for several years, if at all. In any case there was no action Emin could take to further this eventuality. As to an evacuation, the difficulties seemed insuperable. Even had the soldiers been willing, the numbers involved—and hence the administrative and logistical problems—would be enormous. Emin had perhaps fifteen hundred soldiers. In addition there were some two hundred officials and clerks, mostly Egyptians and Copts. But for each man, whether soldier or civilian, had to be counted anything from two or three to a score of dependents—wives, concubines, children and slaves. Emin estimated the total number involved at about ten thousand. Could ten thousand people, the majority women, children and slaves, be marched in a body across Africa?

The third plan was adopted for mere lack of a practicable alternative.

As a first step, in January 1886, Junker set out for Unyoro to open negotiations with Kabba Rega, whose goodwill and co-operation were indispensable to the scheme.

Junker had already made one attempt to escape to the south. He had spent almost the whole of the preceding year wandering about in the territories on the Nile border of Unyoro seeking admission to Kabba Rega's territory until "finding all his proceedings futile, he made his way back to Wadelai".[47] Behind Junker's desire to escape lay more than a readiness to serve as Emin's messenger. He had already been forced to abandon his precious collection of scientific and ethnological specimens. There remained his journals,

61

and he was deperately anxious to get these, the fruits of his labours, back to civilisation. (They subsequently formed the basis of his three-volume *Travels in Africa*.)

Accompanied by Vita Hassan, Junker duly presented himself at Kabba Rega's. From here he hoped to make contact with the Uganda missionaries (now led by the famous Alexander Mackay) who in turn were in contact with Zanzibar by the Arab trade-route. Soon after his arrival, Junker was approached secretly by an Arab trader named Mohammed Biri, a man who had once been in the employ of the Congo Free State. Biri was ready, at some risk to himself, to act as intermediary between Equatoria and Uganda. His offer produced a gleam of light. In March, however, the situation worsened. The chronic hostility between Unyoro and Uganda moved into one of its periodic phases of open warfare and Kabba Rega ordered Junker out of the country. Junker moved south, made a perilous crossing of the war-torn border and succeeded in reaching the Ugandan capital at Kampala. The situation he found there was not reassuring. Mutesa had been succeeded in 1884 by his son Mwanga, a young man of weak character and vicious habits.[48] In October 1885 Mwanga had ordered the murder of the missionary Bishop Hannington, ostensibly out of respect for a local tradition that his country would be conquered by invaders from the north-east (Hannington had attempted to enter Uganda via the north-east corner of Lake Victoria).[49] This was the prelude to a massacre of Christian converts, as a result of which the missionaries, both British and French, found themselves in an extremely dangerous position. They had every reason to believe that Mwanga shortly proposed to include them in the holocaust. Nevertheless, Junker managed to arrange for the purchase and despatch to Emin of £400-worth of cloth—a commodity which was one of Emin's most pressing needs. Mohammed Biri undertook to convey the goods to Wadelai, and faithfully executed the commission.

In July, Junker left Mwanga's and embarked in a mission boat for the southern end of the Lake.

Meanwhile in Equatoria, Casati had been recalled from his "private and solitary life" to take Junker's place at Kabba Rega's (an event which Casati referred to as "my Calvary") and Emin, through the good offices of Mackay, had received his first instalment of mail, and the first direct news from the outside world to reach him in three years. One of the letters was from Nubar Pasha. It informed Emin of the abandonment of the Sudan and left him free to attempt a withdrawal or not, as he saw fit. "A cool business despatch", commented Emin in a letter to Schweinfurth. "Not a syllable in recognition of three long years of anxiety and struggle with Danagla, Negroes, hunger and privation. . . . It seems tolerably certain that our difficulties have not been realised either in Egypt or elsewhere; people simply point out the way to Zanzibar, as if the matter were a promenade to Shubra."[50]

His only hope of a more material improvement in his lot now lay with Junker, who, like an embodied cry for help, was struggling on alone towards the coast.

NOTES AND REFERENCES

CHAPTER I   EMIN IN EQUATORIA

1   E.P.C.A. Felkin's Introduction.

2   Gordon later reprieved him.

3   Junker qu. SCHWEITZER I p. 66.

4   SCHWEITZER I p. 3.

5   Emin: letter of December 1864. Antivari is now Bar in Yugoslavia, near the Albanian border.

6   Turkish, Demotic Greek and "Illyric" (Serbo-Croat). Emin had a facility for languages which rivalled Burton's. As well as these three and his native tongue, he picked up, at one time or another, French, English, Italian, Albanian, Arabic, Persian, Swahili, and an unknown number of South-Sudanese languages and dialects.

7   Three in number excluding Emin himself: two Greeks in the Turkish medical service and a Neapolitan priest. "The circle is somewhat mixed, but select," Emin wrote home.

8   Cf below pp. 43, and 46–47.

9   E.P.C.A. Felkin's Introduction.

10 In other words, roughly Emin's age. And much younger than her husband.

11 SCHWEITZER I p. 24.

12 Qu. SCHWEITZER I pp. 26–27.

13 BIRKBECK HILL p. 187.

14 The apothecary Vita Hassan, a Sephardic Jew From Tunis who shared Emin's later exile in Equatoria, gives a reason for Emin's choice of name: in his book *The Truth about Emin Pasha* he states that Emin simply adopted the name of Gordon's previous medical officer. No confirmation of this has been found in other sources.

15 A facsimile of this letter appears in BIRKBECK HILL at p. 160.

16 At Mutesa's Emin met the C.M.S. missionary C. T. Wilson. He did not make the acquaintance of Wilson's colleague R. W. Felkin until October of the following year. (See Wilson and Felkin: *Uganda and the Egyptian Soudan.*) Emin and Felkin became firm friends and Felkin, back in Europe, was later to play an important part in promoting the relief of Equatoria.

17   E.P.C.A. pp. 303 and 304.

18   Qu. SCHWEITZER I p. 64.

19   There is some disagreement about the month. Compare: GESSI p. 191; Felkin's Introduction to SCHWEITZER p. xx; ZUCCHINETTI p. 5.

20   Gordon opposed this scheme on the grounds that the Chinese were the most immoral nation in the world. For another view, see LUGARD I p. 491.

21   Junker, qu. SCHWEITZER I p. 175.

22   CASATI I p. 257.

23   1878—one; 1879—none; 1880—two; 1881—four; 1882—one; 1883— one (the last steamer).

24   Berghof was officially employed as an anti-slavery inspector.

25   Among the dead were Mr. O'Donovan, the correspondent of the *Daily News*, and Mr. Vizetelly, a war artist employed by the *Illustrated London News*. The latter had performed the unusual feat of walking all the way from Suakin to Khartoum to have the privilege of joining Hicks and his army on their ill-starred excursion. One of the very few survivors of the battle was O'Donovan's servant, a German by the name of Klootz. Klootz cannily deserted before the massacre got under way, embraced Islam and changed his name to Mustafa.

26   This region, the Red Sea littoral of the Sudan, was (and is) inhabited by Kipling's "fuzzy-wuzzies"—the Beja tribes (Bisharin and Hadendoa), speaking a Cushitic language and ethnically akin to the Somal.

27   D.A. I p. 17.

28   WAUTERS p. 32.

29   WAUTERS pp. 34–35.

30   One of the casualties of Abu Klea was the remarkable Colonel Fred Burnaby, hero of the "Ride to Khiva" and other equestrian exploits. Metammeh cost the lives of the force commander General Stewart, and two more luckless journalists —Mr. Herbert of the *Morning Post* and Mr. Cameron of the *Standard*.

31   The Mahdi only survived his victory by a few months. He died in June 1885 and was succeeded by the Khalifa Abdullah. The Sudan remained in the hands of the Mahdi-ists until reconquered by the British under Kitchener in 1896–9. The wily Osman Digna escaped alive from the Khalifa's last battle and was not laid by the heels until January 1900.

32   E.P.C.A. p. 432.

33   E.P.C.A. pp. 408 ff.; COLLINS pp. 22–23. Emin used the name "Danagla" as a synonym for "Mahdi-ists". Other observers used the term "dervishes". Neither was very accurate. The term used by the Mahdi-ists to describe themselves was "Ansar". (See COLLINS p. 20 n.)

34 CASATI I pp. 224–227. The Welle was the old stamping-ground of the distinguished botanist Dr. Schweinfurth, the first explorer to visit it. His passion for plants earned him the name "Leaf-Eater" among the natives. Emin regarded Schweinfurth as a friend; though the two never met, they corresponded copiously from 1880 onward.

35 Emin showed the originals of Lupton's letters to Jephson, who took copies which were subsequently printed in his Emin Pasha (pp. 359–360).

36 SCHWEITZER I p. 175. Casati collected a large household of servants and retainers, to whom he was devoted.

37 Lupton sent two more letters to Emin after that of April 12, 1884, quoted above. In the second (April 20) he gave details of Keremallah's strength and equipment. In the third and last (April 26) he wrote: "It is all up with me here, everyone has joined the Mahdi . . . I am perfectly alone . . . Look out you; some 8,000 to 10,000 men are coming to you well armed. Hoping that we shall meet." Lupton died of typhus while a captive in the Mahdi's camp.

38 Letter to Schweinfurth, August 14, 1884. The Mahdi-ist generals were past-masters of this form of psychological warfare—the despondency-producing message in which you make your adversary a present of the news he most dreads to hear. The call to surrender delivered in the guise of friendly advice was another of their specialities. An important feature of the technique was the insistence that whatever befell the Mahdi's enemies was the work of God, in no way dependent on the will or actions of the Mahdi-ists themselves. This neatly suggested the utter futility of resistance: one might hope to defeat a Mahdi-ist army, but to bear arms against the Almighty is clearly a quick road to suicide. Typical is one of Osman Digna's letters to a British general, which reads in part: "Know that the gracious God has sent his Mahdi suddenly who was expected, the looked-for messenger of the religious and against infidels, so as to show the religion of God through him, and by him to kill those who hate Him, which has happened. You have seen who have gone against him from the people and the soldiers, who are countless. God killed them, so look at the multitudes." The tone seems to carry an echo of the terms in which Chingis Khan's armies summoned cities and nations to surrender: "If you do not, we do not know what will happen to you. Only God knows." (It need hardly be pointed out that in reality everybody knew what would happen—that city or that nation would disappear from the face of the earth.)

39 In the event, the loyalty of many of the black troops to the Khedive, and to the flag of a country most of them had never seen, proved unshakeable. It is one of the most surprising, and touching, facts in the sad and muddled history of Equatoria.

40 E.P.C.A. p. 480.

41 CASATI I p. 296: "Cunning, contradictory expedients, derived from error and groundless hope, inspired the leadership of the war . . ." Casati often sounds like a bad translation of Virgil.

42 By accident, Emin also held (if that is the right word) Bor on the Nile 100 miles north of Lado. Its garrison had ignored an order to evacuate. Cut off, it fell, in September 1885, to the Dinka.

43 CASATI I p. 310: "The policy of equivocation commenced that day."

44 CASATI I p. 218.

45 CASATI I p. 294.

46 CASATI I p. 334.

47 WAUTERS p. 94.

48 To wit—pederasty and bhang-smoking.

49 The prophecy was accurate. Uganda was ultimately annexed for the British by Lugard, who entered by the same route.

50 SCHWEITZER I pp. 190–191.

MODEST PROPOSALS
October 1886-January 1887

Why should a shrewd Scottish merchant be suddenly smitten with the idea of spending enormous sums in extricating an Egyptian official whom until that moment he did not even know by name?

SCHWEITZER

On December 1, 1886, almost a year after leaving Wadelai, Junker reached Zanzibar.

On the last stage of the journey—from Tabora to the Coast—he had had the good fortune to be escorted by Tippu-Tib who was making one of his infrequent visits to Zanzibar. Tippu-Tib hereby once more proved himself a friend to European travellers in need, though, as Brode says, Junker "had to pay dearly for the honour". The Arab charged him double the cost of the porters he supplied.

Leaving Zanzibar, Junker arrived at Suez on January 10, 1887, to begin agitation in Egypt for the relief of Emin. Agitation, however, was already under way in other quarters. Letters forwarded by Mackay had preceded Junker to the Coast. They contained the first news to come out of Equatoria in three years and their effect was electric.

During that long silence the world had not, in fact, been entirely indifferent to the fates of Emin, his fellow-prisoners and his province. Already two attempts had been made to get through to Equatoria. Dr. Junker's brother, a St. Petersburg banker, had financed an expedition under Dr. Fischer, an experienced traveller who at that time was acting as personal physician to the Sultan of Zanzibar. In December 1886 Fischer had reached the Kavirondo district at the north-east corner of Lake Victoria, but then had turned back. The second attempt, by an Austrian named Oskar Lenz, had been even less successful. Lenz had the notion of approaching Equatoria from the west. To this end he had himself shipped up the Congo by government steamer, intending to raise a caravan on the Upper Congo and then strike overland to Lake Albert. Lenz was defeated before he started by the fact that no porters could be found willing to traverse the dangerous and unknown country that lay between the Congo and the headwaters of the Nile.

In England very deep and widespread emotions had been raised by Gordon's mission to the Sudan, and his death had produced what almost amounted to a national trauma. But public enthusiasm can only thrive for a limited period on a total lack of news, and since 1885 interest in the Sudan had necessarily subsided. The idea of "Sarawaking the Sudan"—that is, of turning it over to individual (European) enterprise[1]—had died with Gordon.

Junker's dramatic reappearance, and the news that Equatoria still held out against the Mahdi's fanatical hordes, had an immediate and startling effect.

From Msalala, Mackay's depot at the southern end of Lake Victoria, Junker had written to his friend Schweinfurth:

It is absolutely necessary that Emin Bey should at once have relief. . . . It would be a dire disgrace if Europe makes no effort now. . . . Let Emin Bay be delivered from danger! Let the Equatorial provinces be reconquered!

From Emin's pen came similar, if rather less exclamatory, appeals:

We shall hold out until we obtain help, or until we perish.[2]

In Europe these urgings found a ready audience, and especially so in England where the ground was already prepared by the depth and extent of popular interest in events in the Sudan. Even before Junker reached the coast, the first initiative had been taken. On November 8, 1886, the Secretary of the British and Foreign Anti-Slavery Society addressed the following communication to Salisbury's Foreign Secretary, Lord Iddesleigh:

My Lord—At a meeting of the Committee of this Society, held on the 5th instant, I had the honour to lay before them a letter addressed to myself by Emin Bey, and one from him to Dr. Felkin, a former traveller in the Equatorial Provinces, and a member of this committee. Dr. Emin Bey, who was appointed by General Gordon to administer, on behalf of the Egyptian Government, the equatorial provinces on the Upper White Nile, has long been cut off from all help from the civilised world, and is now, as shown by his letter, in a very precarious position. After considering the subject-matter of the two letters (of which I have the honour to enclose a proof copy), the following resolution was passed unanimously, and I was directed to forward a copy to your lordship.—I have the honour to remain, your lordship's obedient servant, Charles H. Allen Secretary.

RESOLVED: That in view of the services rendered by Dr. Emin Bey, both in the suppression of the slave-trade and in administering for a considerable period a settled and peaceful government in the Equatorial provinces of Egypt, the committee consider that the position of Dr. Emin Bey presents a very strong claim upon her Majesty's Government. While not suggesting any measure of a military character for his relief, the committee hold that both Her Majesty's Government and that of Egypt are bound to be sparing of neither exertion nor expense in order to rescue him from the destruction which seems to await him, or by the supply of money and goods to enable him to hold a friendly position among the natives of his province.

A few days later, on November 23, again at the prompting of Emin's friend Felkin, an almost identical resolution was passed by the Edinburgh Geographical Society and forwarded to Lord Iddesleigh. The Foreign Secretary's heart may well have sunk at what must have seemed the prospect of another Sudanese débâcle. But the cry of Something-Must-Be-Done, once raised, demanded to be appeased. That not a dozen people in England had, until this moment, ever heard of Emin Bey, mattered not at all. The idea of a lone European to be rescued from imminent peril in a remote outpost of empire—even someone else's empire—battened with a fatal facility on the minds of the newspaper-reading public, and generated a clamour that might be difficult to still by anything short of action. In a contemporary view:

Both through articles and letters in the press and the conversation of the people it was manifested that something would have to be done. The public heart ached over the delays to relieve Gordon which had occurred, to the everlasting pain if not the shame of England, before the Government was aroused to send Lord Wolseley to the Soudan. And this fact caused the conviction to grow that another brave man's life ought not to be sacrificed.[3]

"Henceforth", as another writer put it, "the voice of the public did not let the matter rest. The question was no longer whether an expedition should be sent, but what route the expedition should take."[4]

However, the imagination and sympathies of Her Majesty's Government were less easily engaged. From their point of view England had already burned her fingers badly in the Sudan. The blunder of sending Gordon to Khartoum and the bungling of his "relief" had left a bitter taste. The same memories which now produced in the British public an enthusiastic and open-hearted desire to relieve Emin's plight produced an opposite reaction in the British Government.

Fortunately, the reluctance of the administration to accept responsibility for the fate of Equatoria was not put to the test of a full-dress confrontation with popular excitement. Private enterprise was already on the move. Sir William Mackinnon, who had fish of his own to fry in Africa, was already investigating the possibilities of the situation. As early as October, Mackinnon had begun discussions with Stanley on the possibility of getting an expedition through to Emin. At this stage two questions were at issue: if an expedition was sent, who would lead it? and who would pay for it? Joseph Thomson, the Scot who in 1883 had pioneered the route through Masailand to Lake Victoria, had expressed his willingness to go, in a letter to The Times (November 24, 1886). But Stanley, too, was willing, despite the fact that he was about to embark on a lecture tour of the United States. Mackinnon and Stanley were old friends through their common association with the Congo; and Stanley, being thoroughly acquainted with the political and commercial aspects of African exploration, was exactly the sort of man Mackinnon needed for the sort of expedition he had in mind.

On November 15 Mackinnon informed the Foreign Office that Stanley was prepared to lead, free of any charge for his services, any expedition that the government might care to set afoot out of a "desire to respond to the general feeling" that "some effort should be made to open up communication with Emin Bey, and that the Government should in some way or other take immediate action in the matter".[5] The answer was, of course, that the government had no intention of responding to the general feeling in any way whatever, if "responding" implied—as it did—the disbursement of public monies and the acceptance of public responsibility.

From what might have been an embarrassing impasse the Foreign

Secretary was timely relieved by a communication from Sir Evelyn Baring in Egypt reporting the progress of events there.[6] Baring stated that the Egyptian Government was prepared to give £10,000 to a relief expedition organised by Schweinfurth and Junker and which Junker would lead in person. The mention of that £10,000 was the magic key which unlocked the situation. By December 4 matters had been agreed as follows: the money offered by Egypt to Junker would be diverted to Mackinnon's expedition and a further £10,000 (Stanley had estimated the cost at £20,000) would be raised privately by an Emin Relief Committee to be formed under the chairmanship of Mackinnon. The contribution of the British Government would consist of "approval".[7]

This approval was only granted on the understanding that H.M.G. was strictly not liable to any "consequences" if the expedition ran into trouble. This assurance was given by Sir Percy Anderson, Head of the Foreign Office African Department and one of the venture's few supporters in the Administration. In a minute of December 3 Anderson wrote that even if Stanley were killed, "there would be no more obligation on the British Government to avenge him than there is to avenge Bishop Hannington".

Stanley, meanwhile, had left for the United States to begin his tour. On December 11 Mackinnon cabled him:

Your plan and offer[8] accepted. Authorities approve. Funds provided. Business urgent. Come promptly. Reply.

Stanley, with his journalist's flair for squeezing drama from the banal, contrived to receive the telegram not in his hotel room or even in his bath, but "as I was about to step on to a platform in a town in Massachusetts" to deliver a lecture. He replied and came promptly.

On December 24 he was back in England.

From that moment, impelled by the force of Stanley's tremendous energy, events moved at high speed. It took him precisely twenty-six days to complete the arrangements for the expedition. On Friday, January 21, 1887, he left England on the first stage of his journey to Equatoria.

The expedition that took shape during that hectic month differed in several important respects from Stanley's previous ventures. The basic personnel would consist, as before, of Wangwana porters—six hundred in number—recruited in Zanzibar. But an important difference lay in Stanley's enlistment of a number of assistants—gentleman volunteers, the Elizabethans would have called them—to serve under him as "officers". Initially seven were chosen from the hundreds who applied to take part in the expedition.

Four were soldiers or ex-soldiers: Major Edmund Barttelot (7th Fusiliers), Captain R. H. Nelson (Methuen's Horse), Lt. W. G. Stairs (Royal Engineers), and Mr William Bonny (late Sergeant, Army Medical Department). A fifth, John Rose Troup, had worked under Stanley for the Congo Free State. The remaining two, Mounteney Jephson and James Jameson, obtained their places principally, it would seem, by virtue of their being willing to subscribe £1,000 apiece to the Emin Relief Fund.[9] All except Jephson had previous experience of the tropics either as soldiers or travellers. Barttelot, for example, had served in the Second Afghan War and in Wolseley's Sudan campaign. Jameson, a keen amateur naturalist, had hunted and travelled in Borneo and South Africa. Nelson was, in Stanley's (rather odd) phrase, "fairly distinguished in Zulu campaigns". Troup had spent three years on the Congo.

Each man on joining signed a contract whereby he agreed to submit to Stanley's authority and—an important point—to publish no account of the expedition until six months after the official (sc. Stanley's) account had appeared.

The significance of this last clause must be briefly elucidated. Stanley's two previous exploring expeditions—the Livingstone Expedition of 1871 and the Trans-African Expedition of 1874–7— had been virtually solo exploits. In 1871 Stanley had engaged two European assistants, and in 1874 three, but all of them had died en route. Even had they survived they were not likely to have challenged Stanley's position as leader. They were the kind of men—one, for example, was a carpenter, another the Cockney third mate of a merchant ship—who could be relied on not to steal Stanley's thunder by publishing books of their own, or rise above their stations to a place in Stanley's limelight. And quite apart from the question of sharing the kudos, there was another, more sinister, side to the matter. Both Stanley's earlier expeditions had given rise to a considerable amount of controversy, some of it quite unsavoury. After his relief of Livingstone Stanley had made a misguided attempt to blacken the reputation of Livingstone's friend and helper Sir John Kirk, then English Consul at Zanzibar, by the suggestion that Kirk had been content to abandon Livingstone to his fate. Stanley's motives for this slander are not hard to discern: the contrast between his own energetic and selfless exertions in Livingstone's behalf, and the alleged callous slackness of Livingstone's supposed friend Kirk, could only be to Stanley's advantage.[10] The Expedition of 1874–7 had also, as we have seen, been the occasion of an acrimonious and undignified dispute, this time with Tippu-Tib. Here again, it was clearly to Stanley's advantage that Tippu-Tib's part in the success of the Expedition should be played down to add to the lustre of Stanley's exploit. Furthermore, both expeditions had earned Stanley an evil reputation among humanitarians by his brutality towards the native Africans. He freely (naively, in fact) admitted to using the whip to maintain the discipline and impetus of his porters; and his accounts contained, for some tastes, far too many incidents in which he had used his guns to impose his will on the natives.[11] The contrast with Livingstone's unfailing gentleness and forbearance (not to mention the obvious similarities between Stanley's methods and those of the Arab slavers) was too pointed to be lost on those of Stanley's audience, who thought the whipping and shooting of Africans no fit occupation for an Englishman and a gentleman, and who concluded, quite correctly, that Stanley was neither.

These questions have been raised here, not to discuss the ethical aspects of Stanley's preferred mode of travel, or the rights and wrongs of the disputes in which he entangled himself, but to make the point that in all these disputes Stanley himself, was for practical purposes, the sole witness of the events at issue. He therefore enjoyed an almost unrestricted freedom to adapt his account to his own needs. In the Emin Pasha Expedition, on the other hand, he no longer had this security. With the exception of Bonny, all Stanley's officers were his social equals (if not his superiors) and quite capable both of giving their own versions of whatever took place, and of commanding an audience. (In fact all the participants but Nelson, Stairs and Bonny subsequently published, or had published, their own accounts.) Hence Stanley's caution in framing the articles of enlistment. Events proved it to have been a wise, but insufficient, precaution.

Simultaneously with the enlistment of the Expedition's officers, there was the matter of supplies to be attended to. African expeditions normally carried very little in the way of food. The usual practice was to buy provisions from villages along the route. The principal item of a caravan's baggage was, therefore, the trade goods which would be exchanged for food, or used to buy the friendship and co-operation of village headmen and local chiefs. The customary media of exchange were: cheap cotton cloth, usually of Indian or American manufacture; cowrie shells; glass beads of various shapes, sizes and colours;[12] and brass, copper or iron wire, either in coils or cut into rods about eighteen inches long and called "mitako". As currency these commodities were not without disadvantages: cloth was bulky, and liable to rot in a damp climate; brass wire was heavy; and the acceptability of beads was subject to the vagaries of taste and fashion as between the different regions of Africa.

Stanley sent an order ahead to Zanzibar for:

> 27,262 yards of various kinds of cloth
> 3,600 pounds of assorted beads
> 1 ton of brass, copper and iron wire

The food which these would buy was to be supplemented, for the benefit of the officers, by a limited quantity of "European provisions" —tea, coffee, jam, meat extract and the like:

> Messrs. Fortnum and Mason, of Piccadilly, packed up forty carrier loads of choicest provisions. Every article was superb. . . .[13]

Next in importance on Stanley's shopping list came armament. Included under this heading were:

510 Remington rifles
100,000 rounds of Remington ammunition
2 tons of gunpowder
350,000 percussion caps
30,000 Gatling cartridges
35,000 special Remington cartridges
50 Winchester repeaters
50,000 rounds of Winchester ammunition
1 Maxim machine-gun (firing 330 rounds per minute)
  with portable stand and shield.[14]

Miscellaneous stores included:

100 shovels
100 hoes

100 axes
100 bill-hooks
40 pack donkeys
10 riding donkeys with saddles

Other important items were:

—tents (made by Edgington's of canvas impregnated with copper-sulphate preservative);
—medicines (Burroughs and Wellcome donated "nine beautiful chests replete with every medicament necessary to combat the endemic diseases peculiar to Africa");
—a 28-foot-long steel boat, built in twelve sections, each of which could be carried (just) by two men.

All these stores, excluding the donkeys, had to be made up into "loads" for porterage. The standard weight of a porter's load was sixty or sixty-five pounds, though in practice it was often more since the figure did not include the porter's personal gear—blanket, spear (or rifle and ammunition pouch), cooking-pot, canteen, rations, etc. The boat sections weighed approximately seventy-five pounds each— not unduly heavy, but extremely awkward over bad ground or on narrow trails.

The total cost of stores and equipment came to £7,354.3s.11d.[15]

In addition to the business of hiring men and ordering supplies, the Expedition's organisers had a third, and crucial, preoccupation—the choice of route. The normal approach to Equatoria, by the Nile, was clearly ruled out by the unfriendly posture of the Mahdi-ist armies. When some of the more whimsical suggestions, such as an approach through Abyssinia, were ruled out, there remained a choice of four basic routes to Equatoria from the East Coast:

1. Zanzibar—Msalala—Uganda—Unyoro—Wadelai.
(This might be called the "normal" route in so far as it was in constant use by Arab traders travelling to Unyoro and Uganda, and was also the one used by the early explorers and the Uganda missionaries.)
2. Zanzibar—Msalala—Karagwe—Nkole—Wadelai.
(A variation of (1) designed to avoid Uganda by a swing to the south.)
3. Zanzibar/Mombasa—Masailand—Kavirondo—Mruli—Wadelai.

(The route followed by Thomson and Fischer, though neither had pursued it further than Kavirondo.)

4. Zanzibar—Tabora—Ruanda—Lake Albert—Wadelai.

(A variation of (2) accentuating the swing to the south so as to avoid not only Uganda but its feudatory Karagwe and the Kingdom of Nkole.)

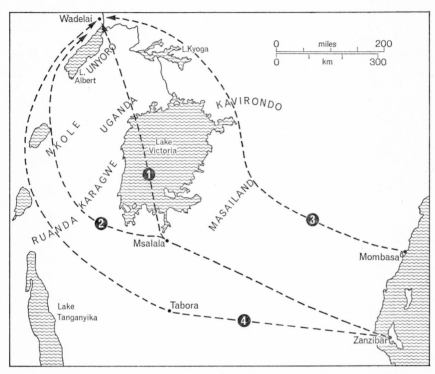

3   The choice of routes open to the Relief Expedition, showing possible approaches to Wadelai from the East Coast.

Stanley had objections to all these routes: (1) the passage through Uganda would certainly involve heavy fighting and might aggravate the already precarious situation of the French and British missionaries there. (2) The same applied since Karagwe was tributary to Uganda; and Nkole, whose people "number 200,000 spears", would be a formidable obstacle. (3) The last stage, between Kavirondo and Wadelai, though untried, was reported by Junker to be exceptionally difficult. Emin, he stated, had lost a great many men "trying to open communications" through this area. (4) An approach from the south via Ruanda also entailed an unknown quantity since Ruanda had never been penetrated by European travellers, and experiments were too risky in view of Emin's pressing need.

Finally, all four routes were objectionable because of the impossibility of preventing the Wangwana from deserting as long as they had Zanzibar at their backs or were in the vicinity of areas frequented by the Arabs.

To a startled public Stanley now announced that he proposed to follow none of these routes. Instead, though starting from Zanzibar, he would approach Wadelai by way of the Congo and Aruwimi rivers.[16]

At first blush it was a curious proposal, roughly analogous to a journey from London to Oxford by way of Madrid and Penzance. On the other hand it offered, in Stanley's view, the following advantages:

1. Certainty of reaching Emin.
2. Transport up the Congo River by State steamers to a point 320 geographical miles from Lake Albert.
3. Allaying suspicions of Germans that underlying our acts were political motives.
4. Allaying alleged fears of French Government that our Expedition would endanger the lives of French missionaries.
5. If French missionaries were endangered, then English missionaries would certainly share their fate.
6. Greater immunity from the desertion of the Zanzibaris who were fickle in the neighbourhood of Arab settlements.[17]

The arguments for and against the various routes, as set out in Stanley's book, are anything but convincing. One may be forgiven for suspecting that the muddled and patchy way in which his ideas are set out is a deliberate cover for threadbare and inconsistent reasoning.[18] The disadvantages he urged against the East Coast routes—notably: native hostility, unknown territory, and the risks of desertion—may have been real enough. But whether or not they constituted valid objections must be weighed against the drawbacks of the Congo route, which nowhere in Stanley's book are so much as hinted at:

1. The country between the Congo and Lake Albert was completely unknown. It might, therefore, present obstacles as great as or greater

than the much-vaunted perils of Karagwe, Nkole, Kavirondo or Ruanda.

2. It followed that there was no greater "certainty of reaching Emin" by this than by any other route.

3. Stanley was perfectly aware that the Congo route would take him through a major zone of Arab influence—the Stanley Falls area. His "immunity from desertion" was, therefore, wishful thinking at best.

4. The suspicions of the Germans regarding the underlying political motives of the Expedition were thoroughly justified (as will shortly be explained), and the passage of the Expedition through the Congo did nothing to allay them.[19]

5. The enormously longer distance that would have to be covered by the Congo route (even if the sea voyage from Zanzibar to the mouth of the Congo is disregarded) could only be justified by the certainty of adequate steamer transport up the river to the point where the overland march would have to begin. No such certainty existed. King Leopold had, it is true, offered the use of "the whole of his naval stock"—but in plain fact the State had only one considerable boat, the *Stanley*, in working order on the river. And Leopold's offer was conditional upon the "naval stock" not being simultaneously required for the State's own use.

In the light of these counter-objections, of all of which Stanley was well aware, it is difficult to believe that the East Coast routes were, by comparison, as chancy as he claims to have thought them. Were the perils really as formidable as he maintained? Was the road which Dr. Junker had travelled practically alone, or the route which Thomson had travelled with a handful of companions, really expected to present serious difficulties to a well-armed, well-supplied and well-led party several hundred strong?

The point of the foregoing is not to attack Stanley's competence as a leader and organiser—the soundness of his judgement may be assessed in the light of later events—but that it leads us to the question of whether or not Stanley may have had other, undisclosed, reasons for choosing the Congo route.

The key to this question lies in his relations with King Leopold. Stanley presented his decision to travel by the Congo as being taken primarily, if not solely, at Leopold's insistence. But this reason, as stated, hides as much as it reveals. It must be borne in mind that at this time Stanley was still nominally in the employ of the Congo Free State. His explanation is as follows:

> We were in full swing of preparations to meet the necessities of the overland march from Zanzibar, east to the Victoria Nyanza, when, as will be shown by the tenor of the following letter, it became necessary to reconsider our route.

The relevant portion of the letter, written on Leopold's behalf, dated Brussels, January 7, and signed "Comte de Borchgrave", reads:

> The Congo State has nothing to gain by the Expedition for the Relief of Emin Pasha passing through its terrritory. The king has suggested this road merely so as to lend your services to the Expedition, which it would be impossible for him to do if the Expedition were to proceed by the Eastern coast. According to your own estimate, the Expedition proceeding by the Eastern coast would occupy about eighteen months. His Majesty considers that he would be failing in his duty towards the State were he to deprive it of your services, especially as the latter will certainly be needed before the expiration of this lapse of time.[20]

For reinforcement, Stanley then quotes the following communication from Mackinnon:

> I had a short pleasant letter from the King showing how anxious he is the Congo route should be taken, and how unwilling to allow a break in the continuity of your connection with the Congo State, as he considers you a pillar of the State. He asks me to banish (sic) any divergent sentiments, and get all parties to agree to the Congo route. . . .[21]

In Stanley's version of the affair, he discussed, on January 9, Leopold's request with two other members of the Emin Relief Committee, Sir Francis de Winton (former Administrator-General of the Congo Free State) and Col. J. A. Grant (Speke's exploring-companion). They then wrote back to Leopold requesting definite information about the availability of river transport. On January 12, at a further meeting of the Committee, ". . . The answer as regards the Congo route being satisfactory was decided upon (sic), and this has now been decided unanimously." And on January 14:

Crossed over Channel last night towards Brussels via Ostend to see King Leopold. Saw King and gave my farewell. He was very kind. Left for London in evening at 8 p.m.[22]

It is not to be believed that no more was involved in what Stanley thus represents as a *change* of plan than Leopold's desire to retain an option on Stanley's services, or that no more was discussed at their meeting than Stanley's goodbyes. Nor is it possible to accept the implication that Stanley had undertaken to lead the expedition without first obtaining Leopold's consent. The question, then, naturally arises whether Leopold intended to avail himself of Stanley's services during the Expedition, and if so to what end? Stanley himself offers no direct information on this point, but a knowledge of later events makes it easy to divine the true nature of Leopold's involvement. Since the affray at Stanley Falls, which had left the Arabs in undisputed possession following the flight of the Governor, Deane, the State had made no effort to reassert its authority. Worse—now that the Arabs were masters of the Falls district, the whole eastern half of the Free State lay open to them, since the most easterly Belgian station was now at Bangala, some four hundred miles down-river. It was therefore urgently necessary at least to stabilise the situation before any more ground was lost. It remains uncertain whether the plan for doing this which Stanley later put into effect was decided on in detail before he left for Africa; but there can be no doubt whatever that measures to check the eastward spread of Arab power formed part of Stanley's brief.

The second service which Stanley was to perform for Leopold was nothing less than to arrange for the annexation of Equatoria to the Belgian Congo. Since Egypt had officially renounced the Sudan, Equatoria was now fair game for any power willing and able to take and hold it. Leopold, an opportunist if he was anything, was perfectly within his rights, by the standards of international behaviour then current, in moving to occupy this or any other vacant square on the African chessboard. But obviously the thing was only possible if it could be proved that a practicable line of communications existed between Equatoria and the rest of Leopold's territory. It is morally certain that the need to test this possibility was the real reason behind the choice of the Congo route. The discussion of the logistical and geographical merits and demerits of the various other routes was merely a smokescreen for a decision that was predetermined on purely political grounds.

These arrangements between Stanley and King Leopold were quite separate from Stanley's arrangements with Mackinnon.[23] Here again the nature of the "services" Stanley had undertaken to perform has to be deduced from external evidence, as Stanley makes no mention of them in his account of the planning of the Expedition.

The "relief" of Emin was presented to the public in the guise of a philanthropic gesture pure and simple. But the plaintive suspicion of the German Ambassador in London, that Mackinnon "was not alone actuated by philanthropic aims", [24] was too obviously true to be worth voicing. For evidence one need hardly look further than the subscription list of the Emin Relief Fund, which bristles with the names of Mackinnon's business associates—men like J. F. Hutton, the President of the Manchester Chamber of Commerce, who had co-operated with Mackinnon in a number of West African enterprises. And it can hardly have been due to the operations of blind chance that the three men chiefly responsible for the business organisation of the Expedition—Mackinnon, de Winton, and Mackinnon's associate G. S. Mackenzie[25]—were, within a year, to become the founding fathers of the Imperial British East Africa Company.

The background to Mackinnon's involvement in Africa has already been touched on. The Anglo-German agreement on spheres of influence was signed, as we have seen, in October 1886. In the same year Britain was offered a chance to add Equatoria to her share of East Africa. Emin, desperate in his isolation and abandoned by his own government, wrote to Mackay that he would be willing to submit his province to a British protectorate. Mackay dutifully passed the information to Zanzibar and from there it filtered back through diplomatic channels to the Prime Minister, Lord Salisbury. Salisbury hastened to decline what must have looked to him like a white elephant of an extremely embarrassing variety. As Emin was a German, he remarked, Equatoria was Germany's business. Salisbury's reason for refusing was not primarily his reluctance to upset the Germans by acquiring territory outside the area governed by the agreement. A more potent consideration was the memory of the Khartoum fiasco, combined with the knowledge that to establish what nowadays would doubtless be called a "British Presence" in Equatoria would have been a weighty undertaking. Not only would the province have to be made secure against the Mahdi-ists, it would also need reliable communications with the outside world. This in turn would require, as a minimum, the pacification (and probably occupation) of Uganda, and the building

I (ii) GENERAL CHARLES GORDON

I (i) SIR SAMUEL BAKER

2 (i) EMIN aged twenty-five

2 (ii) HENRY M. STANLEY aged fifteen

and manning of a chain of fortified posts from Lake Victoria to the sea. Such an adventure, quite apart from the blow to national and governmental prestige that would accrue from any failure, implied a large outlay in men and money for an uncertain return.

Salisbury's initially negative reaction to the possibilities of the situation has to be viewed in the light of the fact that he had not yet had the time to develop, as it were, an East African point of view. Equatoria belonged not to the as yet almost non-existent category of East African Affairs, but to the well-established category of Egyptian Affairs; and in this area the dictates of policy were unequivocal. Salisbury's administration had inherited Gladstone's policy of disengagement from Egypt at the earliest possible moment.[26] This automatically ruled out any attempt to hold on to Equatoria, as it had ruled out any attempt to hold on to the northern Sudan. On the other hand, as Baring saw, if the "relief" of Emin was to be interpreted as relieving Emin of his post, thus cutting the last link with the Sudanese incubus, it was clearly in the Egyptian (and British) interest to support any expedition with this aim. It was this considera-tion which caused Baring to throw the weight of his approval behind the plans of first Junker and then Mackinnon. It does not, however, explain the government's curious lack of interest in the Expedition's territorial motives.

But if the government declined to involve itself in territorial adventures, it did not go so far as to forbid individual citizens to try—however rashly—their luck. Mackinnon and his friends were, of course, no better placed than the government to undertake so daunting a venture; they were merely more willing. But they could not simply walk into East Africa and take it over. The country was still largely unexplored. It would have to be surveyed, pacified and administered—three separate tasks, each of enormous scope and difficulty—before commercial operations could even begin. On the other hand, the existence of Equatoria, complete with Governor, civil service, army, and vacant freehold, was too good an opportunity to let slip, particularly as, if Britain missed it, Germany could be counted on to seize it with both hands.[27]

Stanley's mission for Mackinnon, then, was—depending on the out-come of his mission for Leopold, and on the state of affairs he found on arrival in Equatoria—to recruit Emin to the East African Company Mackinnon and his partners were hoping to form. If Emin accepted, he might then continue to govern Equatoria on the Company's behalf, or, if

G

retreat from Equatoria was preferable or inevitable, he might withdraw to the south-east and establish himself in the Kavirondo district, which would then become a *point d'appui* for further operations inside the British zone.[28]

Of the outcome of Stanley's exertions in his employers' behalf more will be said in due course. For the present it is sufficient to have indicated that there was more to the Emin Relief Expedition than appeared in the face it presented to the world at large.

The public side of the Expedition was epitomised in a speech made by Stanley on January 13, 1887, a week before leaving England. On this day, after a ceremony at the Guildhall to confer on him the Freedom of the City of London, Stanley attended a luncheon in his honour at the Mansion House. (". . . a distinguished party present, and affair most satisfactory", he noted in his journal.[29]) His address in response to the Lord Mayor's toast summarised the avowed aims and proposed methods of the forthcoming expedition. He dwelt on the difficulties and dangers of the East Coast routes and then went on to relate how, with the Committee facing a crucial choice between so many conflicting hazards, King Leopold's generous offer had miraculously resolved the dilemma, opening up a safe and speedy alternative route. The baseless suspicions of the Germans that the Expedition was a cloak for mercenary or political adventures were touched on in passing, and brushed aside by the assertion that the sole objects of the Expedition were: firstly, to supply Emin with the ammunition he needed to hold his position, and secondly, to escort to the Coast such of Emin's non-combatants as wished to leave the province.[30]

This statement of the Expedition's purpose,[31] disingenuous as it was in view of all that it omitted, needs closer examination. Even if the political background is left out of consideration, the bare assertion that Stanley was going to "relieve" Emin can hardly be accepted as a rational programme. A question needs to be asked which should have been asked more often and more insistently before the Expedition set out (rather than in the form of recriminations after its return): What exactly, or even approximately, was meant in this context by the word "relieve"? Did it mean what Baring thought it meant? Did it mean what Emin hoped it would mean? And what did it mean to Stanley, if anything?

In the public mind there existed two analogies for the forthcoming enterprise: Wolseley's relief of Gordon, and Stanley's relief of Livingstone. Neither analogy was valid in the present case. Wolseley's expedition, setting aside its political futility, had been a relief expedition in the accepted military sense of the term—its aim was to raise the siege of Khartoum and permit the withdrawal of Gordon, the Egyptian garrison and the European population. The relief of Livingstone had consisted in the delivery of a caravan of supplies to a lone European stranded in the interior by his lack of medicines, trade goods and provisions. But now Stanley was setting out to rescue, not a single man, nor even a city, but a whole province. It was an undertaking greater in scope than that for which a full-scale military expedition under Wolseley had proved inadequate; yet the means Stanley proposed to employ were only marginally more substantial than those that had been required for the relief of Livingstone, a single individual.[32]

The aims of the Expedition, as publicly stated, derived, of course, from the current situation of Emin and his province, as far as these could be judged from information available at the end of the year 1886. Emin's letters during the period when he was actually under attack were more pessimistic in tone than those written after and just before Junker's departure. At first Emin had toyed with a number of variations on the theme of withdrawal; but by the beginning of 1886 the words "retreat", "escape" and the like are less frequently heard, as by this time Emin had shifted to a more heroic (or perhaps more fatalistic) posture. The latest information available to the organisers of the Relief Expedition was that Emin intended to remain at his post until the last bullet, etc.

The question of bullets was a crux.

Stanley had seized on a phrase in one of Emin's letters in which reference was made to the possibility of ammunition running short, and inflated it until it became the fundamental rationale of the whole operation. Emin must not be allowed to run out of ammunition!—that was why Stanley must go to Equatoria.

> It is the relief of Emin Pasha that is the object of the Expedition, the said relief consisting of ammunition in sufficient quantity to enable him to withdraw from his dangerous position in Central Africa in safety, or to hold his own if he decides to do so for such length of time as he may see fit.[33]

The notion that the relief was to be effected by the mere transporting of a few boxes of cartridges across the African continent was patently at variance with the realities of Emin's situation; but it served to lend the Expedition a meretricious appearance of purpose, a kind of phantom concreteness, which its organisers badly needed to prop up the public-relations side of the venture.

Since nothing could be said in public of the Expedition's commercial and political aims, Stanley was driven to adopt, and later to defend, what was at best an extremely shaky thesis: that the relief which provided the Expedition with its official reason for existence was to consist—apart from a few details such as a new dress uniform for Emin—*solely* in the one hundred thousand rounds of Remington ammunition given by the Egyptian Government. A hundred thousand cartridges may have looked impressively bulky piled on a dock in Zanzibar; but the stark fact remained that even if every single round arrived intact at Wadelai, the net result would have been seventy-five rounds per man for Emin's troops—enough at best for a day's brisk skirmishing.

The essential futility of such a proceeding—which Stanley tried desperately to conceal before, during and after the event—should have been glaringly obvious from the start. That it was not, can only be accounted for by the fog of popular emotion surrounding Emin's plight and Stanley's plans, and by the prestige of Stanley's name which, for the public at large, effectively precluded critical appraisal of his actions.

The stage was set for a fiasco.

NOTES AND REFERENCES

CHAPTER 2   MODEST PROPOSALS

1 In 1841 James Brooke, the "White Rajah", had established himself, independently of the British Government, in his own private colony in Sarawak,
   northern Borneo.

2 Emin to Mackay, November 1884.

3 *Stanley and Africa* p. 595.

4 WAUTERS p. 127.

5 C.5601 No. 4—Mackinnon to Foreign Office (15/11/86).

6 C.5601 No. 9—Baring to Foreign Office (23/11/86).

7 C.5601—Nos. 10, 12, 15, 22.

8 Stanley's generosity in giving his services gratis was a little marred by the
   loudness and frequency with which he let it be known that he had renounced an
   income of £10,000 by abandoning his lecture tour. ("My agent was in
   despair . . ." D.A. I p. 34.)

9 Jephson's contribution was paid for him by his cousin the Countess de Noailles.

10 For a detailed account of Stanley's allegations against Kirk and the repercussions
   of the dispute, see Coupland: *Livingstone's Last Journey.*

11 A notorious but by no means isolated example was Stanley's "chastisement"
   (his own term) of the islanders of Bumbire, Lake Victoria. (See Stanley's
   Through the Dark Continent, 1887.) For a sample of hostile comment on this and
   similar affairs, see FOX–BOURNE pp. 14–20.

12 There is an imposing collection of trade beads in the Ethnographical Gallery of
   the British Museum (unless it has fallen victim to the current mania for reorganisation of the Ethnographical exhibits).

13 D.A. I p. 39. To those whose very lives depended on them, these superior
   picnic baskets seemed both ill-conceived and miserably inadequate. See
   TROUP pp. 149–150.

14 The first four items were donated by the Egyptian Government. The Gatling
   cartridges for the Maxim gun were furnished (gratis) by the War Office—a fact
   which Sanderson interprets as a form of covert official support for the
   Expedition. (See SANDERSON Ch. II.) The machine-gun itself was the gift of
   its proud inventor, Mr Hiram S. Maxim, an ex-factory hand and failed boxer
   whose creative career had opened with the invention of a mouse-trap. The

world, far from beating a path to Maxim's door, had ignored his contributions to the sum of human welfare until he turned his attention to the more rewarding field of weapons research. The gift of a gun to the E.P.R.E. was a promotion stunt forming part of a no-holds-barred rivalry with the Nordenfeldt Company which was currently occupying Maxim's attention. The Nordenfeldt gun, though demonstrably inferior, was being promoted by the redoubtable Basil Zaharoff, the man in whose honour the term "merchant of death" was originally coined. The duel between the two companies ended, in 1888, in a merger.

15   D.A. II p. 460.

16   Wauters claims to have been the first to suggest the Congo route for reaching Equatoria—in an article dated December 6, 1886, in *Le Mouvement Géographique*, of which he was Editor. He is careful to point out (WAUTERS pp. 130–133) that he refers to the Congo–Aruwimi route, not the route striking north-east from the Lualaba envisaged by the luckless Lenz. In fact, the first person to suggest the Congo route was almost certainly Gordon, in January 1884. (See R. W. Felkin in the *Scottish Geographical Magazine*, Vol. II (1886) p. 713.)

17   D.A. I p. 45.

18   Stanley could be wonderfully indifferent to logic when it suited him. See for example the statements above regarding French and English missionaries. Again, he rebutted the "curious idea" of Schweinfurth and Junker "that because the Expedition was to be armed with several hundred Remingtons and a machine-gun of the latest invention, it was to be an offensive force", by asserting that the indiscipline of the Zanzibaris was so great and their shooting so wild that they were incapable of doing any damage.(!) (D.A. I pp. 52–53.)

19   The Germans were less worried about how the Expedition got to Equatoria than about what it would do when it got there. An informal agreement was in force at this time by which Germany and England agreed to abstain from annexations in the hinterlands of their respective "spheres" in East Africa; the Germans suspected, with good reason, that Stanley's Expedition covered designs calculated to violate this agreement both in the spirit and the letter. Hence their objections to Stanley's passing through their sphere. Even so, it is hard to believe that Stanley found this objection a valid reason for avoiding the East Coast routes since, on the return journey, he led the Expedition back through German territory without a qualm, at the same time signing "treaties" (the accepted precursors of annexation) left and right with the native chiefs along his road. The same general argument—the fact that Stanley returned by the East Coast route—applies to most of his other objections, and reinforces the suspicion that the dangers of the road were chimeras deliberately fabricated to justify the choice of the Congo route and discarded when they had served their purpose. Casati formed the same opinion. (See CASATI II pp. 156–157.)

20   D.A. I p. 43.

21   D.A. I p. 44.

22   D.A. I pp. 46–47.

23 If the extent to which Leopold and Mackinnon were aware of each other's plans is something of a historical puzzle, the question of how Stanley proposed to reconcile the mutually-exclusive aims of his two employers is more mysterious still. The question is discussed in ANSTEY. See also SANDERSON pp. 34–36 and refs.

24 Qu. PERHAM p. 173n.

25 Mackenzie was connected with Smith, Dawes & Co. (who acted as shipping agents for the Expedition, besides contributing £1,500 to the Relief Fund) and with Smith, Mackenzie & Co., the East African agents for Mackinnon's British India Steam Navigation Company.

26 Baring, who served in Cairo under both the Gladstone and Salisbury administrations, ensured the continuity of this policy. It was he who had insisted on the withdrawal from the northern Sudan. And it was he who dictated to Nubar the terms of the letter to Emin which, ironically, had caused Emin to turn in desperation to the British for help.

27 Preparations for the German Emin Relief Expedition did not actually begin until April 1888. (PETERS p. 3.)

28 D.A. I pp. 386–388; PERHAM p. 167. When Stanley put this proposal to Emin, he stated that he was doing so without authority. But the broad lines of the policy (at the very least) must have been agreed between Stanley and Mackinnon before the Expedition's departure, since the agreement signed with Mackinnon's East Africa Company by Felkin on Emin's behalf (and of which Stanley, in Africa at the time, could have had no knowledge) embodied precisely the same proposals. (See below, Chapter 10.)

29 D.A. I p. 46. One gets the impression that it needed "affairs" like this to make the explorer's life worth while.

30 Estimated by Junker at 600—clerks, storekeepers, etc., and their dependants (D.A. I pp. 54–55).

31 See report of Stanley's speech in The Times, January 14, 1887.

32 On the Livingstone Expedition Stanley took 189 men, excluding himself and his two assistants. To "rescue" Emin he took 711.

33 D.A. I pp. 52–53.

3

LONDON TO YAMBUYA
January to December 1887

... the most perfectly organised expedition that has hitherto entered
tropical Africa ...

CONSUL HOLMWOOD

... the ill-managed slave-gang ...

FOX-BOURNE

On January 21, 1887, fortified by a visit to Sandringham and a
farewell banquet from Mackinnon, Stanley made his way to Charing
Cross Station, where he arrived shortly before eight o'clock in the
evening. A cheer greeted him from the Distinguished Party gathered to
wish him godspeed. After a distribution of handshakes, Stanley
entered a reserved compartment on the continental mail train. The
start was signalled. The train began to move. "When will you be
back?" called a voice from the crowd. "As soon as I can," replied the
departing hero gaily.[1] The Distinguished Party raised another cheer.
Stanley bowed his acknowledgements from the carriage window and
the train bore him out of sight.

With the exception of Troup, who was to start later and sail
direct to the Congo, the Expedition's officers had already left England.
Major Barttelot had set out for Aden a week earlier to recruit a
number of Somalis to accompany the Expedition. Jameson was
making his way independently to a rendezvous with Stanley at Suez.
And the day before Stanley's own departure, Nelson, Stairs and
Jephson had left for Egypt aboard one of Mackinnon's ships, the
Navarino. ("The vessel is bad," wrote Jephson, who began his diary on
the day they sailed, "surprisingly so for one of the British India
vessels.") Bonny, who was also to have travelled on the *Navarino*,
contrived by a quite bewildering piece of mismanagement to miss the
boat:

Mr William Bonny started from my rooms with black boy Baruti[2] to Fenchurch Station at 8 A.M. Arriving there he leaves Baruti after a while and proceeds to the Tower of London! He says that returning to the station at 2 P.M. he found the boat had gone. . . . Baruti found deserted in Fenchurch Station, very hungry and cold. Colonel J. A. Grant finds him and brings him to me.[3]

Bonny and Baruti were despatched the following day to board an India-bound vessel at Plymouth. It would perhaps be an overstatement to call this episode significant; yet it has the same flavour, at once faintly ludicrous and somehow inexplicable, which invests many of the later mishaps that were to overtake the Expedition.

Stanley reached Alexandria on January 27 and made his way directly to Cairo. Here he was met by Sir Evelyn Baring, who informed him "in his clearest and most straightforward manner that there was a hitch somewhere." Nubar Pasha and the Khedive, it appeared, were manifestly dissatisfied by the turn affairs had taken. Stanley's announcement of his intention to travel by the Congo indicated a wide departure from the aims of the Expedition as originally envisaged in Egypt. Junker and Schweinfurth too, in Stanley's phrase, "had both been struck by consternation", and Nubar had raised a protest to the Foreign Office. Since Junker and Schweinfurth were the original promoters of the venture, and the Egyptian Government was its chief backer, the objections they raised could not simply be ignored but would have to be reasoned away. The first person Stanley had to win round was Baring himself, the arch-proponent of the evacuation policy. Stanley's response to Baring's exposition of the "hitch" has a patronising, even insolent, quality which characterises so much of his man-to-man conversational style:[4]

"Well, Sir Evelyn," I said, "do you not think that there are as clever men in England as Messrs. Schweinfurth and Junker? On the Relief Committee we have Colonel James Augustus Grant— companion of Speke, Colonel Sir Francis de Winton—late Administrator General of the Congo, Colonel Sir Lewis Pelly—late Political Agent at Zanzibar, the Honourable Guy Dawnay of the War Office, Sir John Kirk—late Consul-General at Zanzibar, the Rev. Horace Waller, and several other distinguished and level-headed men. Nothing has been settled without the concurrence and assent of the Foreign Office. We have considered everything, and I have come this far resolved to carry the project out as the

91

Committee and myself have agreed." And then I gave Sir Evelyn the pros and cons of the routes, which satisfied him.[5]

Whether or not Baring really was satisfied by Stanley's explanations, he had no choice but to acquiesce, having received specific instructions from Salisbury to put the weight of his influence behind Stanley in an attempt to silence the objections of Nubar and the Khedive. (Of course the real issue, coolly ignored in Stanley's account, was not the geographical and logistical arguments regarding the various routes, but the political implications of Stanley's commitment to King Leopold.)

The discussions with the various interested parties occupied Stanley for the next three days. By the end of that time their objections had been either overruled or soothed away and Baring was able to report:

> . . . I have accompanied Mr. Stanley on visits both to the Khedive and Nubar Pasha, and . . . after an explanation of his views on the subject, they have both expressed themselves thoroughly satisfied of the wisdom of Mr. Stanley's choice in adopting the Congo route in preference to that from Zanzibar.[6]

During the same period Stanley had pumped Junker for information on affairs in Equatoria, and on Emin himself, about whom Stanley, like the rest of the world, knew next to nothing; he had interviewed Mason Bey, an ex-governor of Equatoria, and received from him a map embodying the results of Mason's survey of Lake Albert; he had received permission to use the Egyptian flag as the banner of the Expedition; and he had been entrusted by the Khedive and by Nubar with messages for Emin. (The contents of these last were merely a reiteration of what had already been made plain to Emin in the despatch which had produced so depressing an effect on him the previous year: that he and his men might return to Egypt or stay where they were, but should they elect to stay, they were no longer Egypt's concern.)[7]

Finally, Stanley had added to the Expedition's strength an Anglo-Irish medical officer, two Syrian interpreters, and sixty-two Sudanese regulars of the Egyptian army. His purpose in taking on the Sudanese troops was twofold: as the Expedition would otherwise consist solely of untrained and undisciplined Zanzibari porters, the regulars would enhance its ability to defend itself; secondly, when they reached Equatoria they could be advanced as living witnesses of the genuineness of Stanley's claim to be the emissary of the Khedive.[8] The Medical Officer, whom Stanley had engaged in Cairo, was a friend of Barttelot's, Surgeon T. H. Parke of the Army Medical Department. Until that time the post of medical officer had been left vacant. It had been offered to an old Congo hand, Dr. R. Leslie, but Leslie had objected to the clause in his contract which debarred him from publishing anything about the Expedition until six months after the appearance of Stanley's account. He had wanted to insert a modifying clause, "except in the case of my reputation being attacked". This concession had been refused him, and Leslie in turn had declined the post.[9] In view of the attacks later made by Stanley on the reputations of no fewer than five of his officers, one can only admire Dr. Leslie's prescience.

His business concluded, Stanley, with the inevitable Distinguished Party present to wave goodbye, left Cairo for Suez on February 3. Here he met Jameson and sent him on to Aden to assist Barttelot. Three days later, with Parke and the Sudanese, Stanley joined Stairs, Nelson and Jephson on board the Navarino.[10] Proceeding to Aden, they picked up Barttelot, Jameson and the twelve Somalis Barttelot had hired, and transferred to another B.I.S.N. vessel, the Oriental, which was to take them to Zanzibar. ". . . a small and rather dirty ship," Barttelot noted, "full of red ants and huge cockroaches." Perhaps Mackinnon preferred to keep his ships busy rather than clean.

The voyage to Zanzibar lasted ten days. The officers spent their time getting to know one another, drilling the Sudanese, and taking their first lessons in Swahili—a necessary accomplishment if they were to be able to communicate with the Zanzibaris. Bonny travelled second class. One of the Sudanese was found to have smallpox. Parke isolated him and began a programme of vaccinations, starting with the officers. Jephson refused Parke's ministrations, professing himself an "anti-vaccinationist".

On February 22 they dropped anchor in the harbour of Zanzibar.

*   *   *

Here, as in Egypt, "There were", as Stanley put it, "a few things to be done." His first and most pressing piece of business lay with the Sultan of Zanzibar, the aged Seyyid Barghash. To him Stanley hastened with a letter of introduction from Mackinnon and when this had been duly presented, "We then entered heartily into our business."

The matter under discussion was the concession Mackinnon hoped to obtain to trading rights in that portion of the Sultan's domains which had fallen to England by the Anglo-German agreement of October 1886. In a letter to "a friend" dated March 9, 1887, Stanley described the background to the negotiations in the following terms:

> I have settled several little commissions at Zanzibar satisfactorily. One was to get the Sultan to sign the concessions which Mackinnon tried to obtain a long time ago. As the Germans have magnificent territory east of Zanzibar, it was but fair that England should have some portion for the protection she has accorded to Zanzibar since 1841. The Germans appeared to have recognized this, as you may see by the late Anglo-German Agreement. . . . This concession that we wished to obtain embraced a portion of the East African coast, of which Mombasa and Melindi were the principal towns. For eight years, to my knowledge, the matter had been placed before His Highness, but the Sultan's signature was difficult to obtain. Arriving at Zanzibar, I saw that the Sultan was aging, and that he had not long to live. Englishmen could not invest money in the reserved "sphere of influence" until some such concessions were signed.[11]

The Sultan showed himself agreeable, in principle, to a settlement:

> . . . I obtained from him the answer needed. "Please God we shall agree. When you have got the papers ready we shall read and sign without further delay and the matter will be over."[12]

A second "little commission" had to do with Tippu-Tib. Stanley had two objects in view: he wanted to secure at least the compliance, and if possible the assistance, of Tippu-Tib in the Expedition's passage through his territory (the Stanley Falls district); and he wished, on behalf of King Leopold, to resolve the uncertain situation which had persisted in that region since the expulsion of Deane by the Arabs the previous year.

Tippu-Tib was still in Zanzibar, having remained there since his arrival with Junker in December 1886, and Stanley lost no time in entering into negotiations with him. Agreement was quickly reached and two contracts were drawn up: the first—which more closely

94

resembles an excerpt from a Gilbert and Sullivan scenario than a serious piece of diplomacy—was between Tippu-Tib and Stanley as the representative of the Congo Free State; the second between Tippu-Tib and the Emin Pasha Relief Expedition. The terms of these documents may be summarised as follows:

I. Tippu-Tib consented to become Governor of the Stanley Falls district on behalf of the Congo Free State at a salary of £30 per month. In return for this honour he would:

(1)—fly the State's flag over the Falls and all other stations within the Governor's jurisdiction;[13]

(2)—accept a resident "Secretary" appointed by the State and who would act as intermediary with the State authorities;

(3)—stop, suppress, put down, prevent, and otherwise put an end to, slave-raiding in the district under his control.

So that Tippu-Tib could assume his new functions without delay, Stanley offered free passage for him and his party from Zanzibar to Stanley Falls.

II. Tippu-Tib contracted to supply the Expedition with extra carriers at £6 "per loaded head" between Stanley Falls and Wadelai. The number of carriers was not specified, but Stanley subsequently insisted that six hundred was the number agreed on. It was also stipulated, though Stanley does not mention it in his account, that the Expedition would provide powder and percussion caps for each man provided by Tippu-Tib.[14]

In theory at least these contracts would advance Stanley's plans in a number of ways. In the first place he secured himself against interference from Tippu-Tib's mercenary hordes who, since their ousting of Deane, were liable to interpret the Expedition's arrival on the Upper Congo as a revanchist move on the part of the Belgians, and to react accordingly. At the same time the dispute over the ownership of the Falls district would be settled in the most elegant fashion—recognition of Tippu-Tib's de facto jurisdiction being neatly converted into an apparent reassertion of Belgian authority.

In the second place, the extra porters were vital; without them the Expedition would be virtually helpless. Stanley's plans had already provided for the hiring of six hundred Zanzibaris, a number which, though impressively large, was in fact totally inadequate, as the number of loads to be carried far exceeded the number of Zanzibaris available to carry them. On the Congo this would not matter; Troup had undertaken to arrange for extra porters on the overland stage between the river mouth and Stanley Pool, and steamer transport would solve the problem on the second stage as far as the Aruwimi River. But on the final stage between the Aruwimi and Lake Albert, even if no allowance was made for losses among the Zanzibaris, their numbers would only be sufficient to move approximately one half of the Expedition's effects.

Apart from this consideration Stanley had in mind another use for the extra carriers which he hoped Tippu-Tib would provide. While in Egypt, he had learned from Junker that Emin's magazines contained an estimated seventy-five tons of ivory, which the blockade of Equatoria had prevented Emin from exporting. If this could be got out of Equatoria, it would bring in, at an average of eight shillings a pound, a dazzling £60,000—enough to repay the Expedition's backers three times over. With this in mind, Stanley planned to use Tippu-Tib's porters to help him carry ammunition to Emin and to bring, on the return journey, at least a part of the ivory out of the Province.[15]

It is clear then that from Stanley's point of view the arrangement with Tippu-Tib might be thought of as affording grounds for self-congratulation. Equally clearly, however, the ointment contained some fair-sized flies. For one thing, Stanley's previous dealings with Tippu-Tib had, as we have seen, given rise to acrimony, reproaches and mutual distrust, and nothing had since occurred to dissipate these feelings. Moreover, the notion of Tippu-Tib's serving under the Congo Free State was one which may (conceivably) have looked well on paper, but which had obvious affinities to the deleterious Roman practice of hiring barbarians to defend the Empire.[16] And the idea of giving the greatest slaver in Central Africa the job of suppressing slave-raiding in those regions can hardly have looked well anywhere. In its defence Stanley invoked the analogy of Gordon's dealings with Zubeir, thinking, perhaps, of Gordon's scheme for making that notorious slaver Governor of the Sudan. If so, while the analogy is exact, the argument is a poor one, since one might be forgiven for taking the view that both schemes were equally harebrained.

Finally the agreement contained two fatal weaknesses. First, Stanley stood to gain far more than did Tippu-Tib from fulfilment of its conditions. Tippu-Tib's appointment as Governor merely recognised a situation which the Belgians were for the time being powerless to alter. And the profit Tippu-Tib would realise on the hire of his men as porters was pin-money in comparison to what the same men could earn in pursuit of their more usual vocations as slave-catchers and ivory-hunters. Second, and most important of all, should any dispute arise over fulfilment of the contract, there was absolutely no way in which Stanley could enforce its terms. Once the Expedition reached the Upper Congo all the advantages in terms of power were on the side of the Arabs; there could be no recourse to arms (since the Arabs had sufficient forces in the area to make a meal of Stanley's party)[17] and no recourse to law in a region where Tippu-Tib was the law. Stanley wrote that: "On the breach of any article in the contract (with the State) being reported, the salary is to cease." Hardly a daunting sanction.

Whether or not these objections crossed Stanley's mind, it is impossible to say. The impression given by his account of the negotiations is that he felt himself to have pulled off a shrewd piece of diplomacy.

Having arranged matters to his satisfaction with Tippu-Tib and with the Sultan, Stanley was free to attend to the affairs of the Expedition proper. A letter was despatched to Emin ("for transmission . . . by couriers overland, who will travel through Uganda into Unyoro secretly") announcing the good news of Stanley's imminent arrival. At the same time arrangements were made for forming a depot of stores at the southern end of Lake Victoria for the use of the Expedition on the homeward march. Two hundred loads of goods were to be sent up to Msalala, timed to arrive around March 1888, by which time Stanley fondly hoped he would be approaching Msalala on his way back to the Coast.

Meanwhile Mackinnon's agent in Zanzibar, with the help of Holmwood the Consul, had completed the selection and hiring of the Zanzibari porters and was ready to start embarking them. Many were already known to Stanley from previous expeditions. Each man was given four months' advance on his wages. As soon as each batch of fifty had been paid, it was transferred to a waiting lighter and ferried out to the steamer waiting in the harbour. As a further precaution against advance-jumping, when the full complement of Zanzibaris was aboard, the steamer retired to another anchorage, sufficiently far from the shore to discourage even strong swimmers.

By midnight on February 24 the Zanzibaris, Sudanese, Somalis, Europeans, Arabs, and all the stores were safely aboard.

The muster roll showed:

  623 Zanzibaris (600 men, 23 boys)

    97 Arabs (Tippu-Tib and followers, of which 35 were
          the wives of Tippu-Tib)

    62 Sudanese

    12 Somalis

     9 Europeans (Stanley, Barttelot, Jameson, Nelson,
          Stairs, Jephson, Parke, Bonny, Hoffman)

     2 Interpreters

     1 Baruti

TOTAL 806[18]

The ship that was to take them from Zanzibar to the Congo was yet another of Mackinnon's argosies, the S.S. *Madura*. The Relief Committee had originally petitioned the Admiralty for the loan of a navy vessel to cover this leg of the journey. Their Lordships had turned down the request, less out of meanness than out of deference to the government's decision to withold a too obvious support for the Expedition. The Committee had, however, obtained free bunkering for the *Madura*.[19]

At daybreak on February 25, 1887, she weighed anchor and steamed away to the south. Holmwood, in a despatch dated the same day, wrote:

> The relief party which has just left Zanzibar is in every way the most perfectly organised expedition that has hitherto entered tropical Africa. . . .[20]

*   *   *

The officers, for once, had no complaints about the quality of the B.I.S.N. Company's accommodation, but the seven-hundred-odd men crowded below decks with the temperature in the nineties found it less easy to settle down in their new quarters. Two hours out from Zanzibar, fighting broke out in the forward hold between the Sudanese and the Zanzibaris.

> It rose from a struggle for room. . . . They were all professed Moslems, but no one thought of their religion as they seized upon firewood and pieces of planking to batter and bruise each

3 (i) Equatorial irregular troops

3 (ii) TIPPU-TIB

4 (i) EMIN. Photograph taken
at Khartoum in 1882

4 (ii) HENRY M. STANLEY in
1885

other. The battle had raged for some time before I heard of it. As I looked down the hatchway the sight was fearful[21]—blood freely flowed down a score of faces, and ugly pieces of firewood flew about very lively. A command could not be heard in that uproar, and some of us joined in with shillelaghs, directing our attacks upon the noisiest. It required a mixture of persuasiveness and sharp knocks to reduce the fractious factions to order, especially with the Sudanese minority, who are huge fellows. The Sudanese were marched out of their place and located aft, and the Zanzibaris had all the forward half of the ship to themselves. . . . The result of the scrimmage is ten broken arms, fifteen serious gashes with spears on the face and head, and contusions on shoulders and backs not worth remark, and several abrasions of the lower limbs. (STANLEY)[22]

Parke's version of the casualty list is notably less gory:

One Nubian had his left middle finger broken; and a Zanzibari was disabled by having both bones of his forearm badly smashed. The other injuries were less considerable.

The remainder of the voyage to the Cape was uneventful. Parke continued his programme of vaccinations. Several of Tippu-Tib's wives became seasick. Parke dosed them with "Eno's".

The Expedition was now put on a quasi-military footing. The men were divided into companies and allotted to the various officers. Barttelot was given the Sudanese. The other officers had companies of Zanzibaris.[23] These arrangements were embodied in a written "General Order" signed "H. M. STANLEY, Commanding Emin Pasha Relief Expedition". Stairs, Nelson, Jameson and Jephson were made "Captains"—a proceeding which somewhat shocked Major Barttelot by its irregularity since only one of these (Stairs) currently held the Queen's commission.[24]

On March 8 they arrived off Cape Town to begin coaling.

March 10th. Went on shore with Jephson and Nelson to buy a lot of things and to get dogs. . . . Mr. Stanley bought two fox-terriers—one for himself, and one as a present for Tippu-Tib.[25] Jephson and I secured two large bull-terriers, and tossed up for them. The large brindled one fell to me, and a horribly low white one to Jephson.

H

99

They are about the two most ruffianly-looking dogs I have ever seen. (JAMESON)

While the others bought dogs, Parke bought medicines.

At Cape Town another European joined the Expedition, an engineer named Walker. He was to accompany them only as far as the Aruwimi, his sole function being to get Leopold's "naval stock" in working order and nurse it up the river.

As soon as the coaling was completed, the Madura left her moorings and turned to steam north up the West African coast. Several incidents occurred to give the journey a lugubrious flavour. Jameson recorded:

March 13th. A donkey died: the first death on board, with the exception of a few goats. . .
March 14th. A Zanzibari died today, and was consigned to the deep. It is horrible the way the natives neglect their sick. . . .
March 15th. Jephson, disgusted with the low habits and appearance of his dog, flung him overboard in the dead of night, with a furnace-bar attached to him. . . .
March 16th. Another Zanzibari died today, of inflammation of the lungs. . . .

Eight days after leaving the Cape, they dropped anchor off Banana Point at the mouth of the Congo. The following day, March 19, disembarkation began. A flotilla of small steamers was got together, these being the property of various trading companies—British, Portuguese, Belgian and Dutch—which maintained stations on the Congo mouth.[26] The men and stores were transferred by sections from the Madura to the small steamers and conveyed upstream to the neighbourhood of Matadi, the limit of navigation. By March 21 the disembarkation was complete.

*   *   *

The overland march to Stanley Pool which now faced them was the Expedition's first real test—a test of Stanley's capacity for leadership and organisation, of the officers' ability to face up to the unpleasant realities of African travel, and of the willingness and endurance of the Sudanese and Zanzibaris. It was a test which all, to a greater or lesser extent, failed. The supply situation was chaotic from the start, as was the march discipline of the Zanzibaris and the Sudanese. Loads were lost, left behind, or thrown away. Desertions began almost from the first day. Sickness—fever, dysentery and bronchial infections —sapped the energies of the men and took a steadily mounting toll of lives; the Sudanese and Somalis, unused to the humid climate of the rain forest, were the worst sufferers. Relations between Stanley and his officers, from a bad start, got steadily worse.

All these things might have been expected. But perhaps the most depressing fact which emerges from the records of these first weeks is the almost immediate disillusion of the young Englishmen who had volunteered with such pathetic eagerness, and been so proud of being chosen, for what was to have been a glorious adventure and now revealed itself as a squalid nightmare. It was not the physical discom- forts of their situation—heat, rain, insects, sickness and fever, sore feet, wet clothes and poor rations—which produced this effect. It was rather the moral degradation of the work they were called on to do, work which all too often seemed to consist solely in cajoling, bullying and whipping groups of sullen, bewildered or disorderly Africans into a semblance of orderly movement. "The work we are doing", wrote Jameson disgustedly, "is not fit for any white man but ought to be given to slave-drivers." It was not for this that they had come to Africa, and they all had moments when their overmastering feeling was one of simple futility. Jephson, in the depression of a first bout of dysentery, wrote:

> The lonely feeling of being left alone with nothing but native noises & native smells about one makes one's thoughts turn to home" with the feeling of "shall I ever see it again". It is miserable, everything looks black & hopeless & useless—what is the good of doing anything, all is vain, all useless—why all this worry of oneself, why all this pushing forward & the everlasting "cui bono" repeats itself again & again in one's mind as one tosses backwards & forwards on one's bed trying to find an easy position & finding it nowhere.[27]

Bad relations between the officers and Stanley made things seem far worse than they might otherwise have been. For all the qualities of drive, determination and decision which he so eminently possessed, Stanley's behaviour was not always that of a man who knows how to get the best out of his subordinates. In previous enterprises he had been accustomed to dealing directly with the men under his command, and had no talent for exerting his will through the medium of subordinate officers. One result was that the officers instinctively felt, and strongly resented, that in his dealings with them Stanley was not delegating responsibility but merely distributing dirty jobs he was unwilling to do himself. The situation was complicated by the fact that Stanley alone had sufficient Swahili to convey orders directly to the men; by thus short-circuiting the chain of command, he undermined the authority of his officers to such an extent that, rightly or wrongly, they felt that he was doing so deliberately.[28] Because of the language problem, too, the men took their complaints direct to Stanley, again short-circuiting the command-process, again wounding the officers' pride and adding fuel to their outraged conviction that Stanley was all too ready to take the part of the men, to believe their word before that of the Europeans, and to react to reported disputes before he had even heard the other side of the case.[29] Stanley, in his account, is eloquent on the subject of his own "patience" and "forbearance". "I reserved for myself", he wrote, "the rôle of mediator between exasperated whites and headstrong, undisciplined blacks." Such an assertion is pure eyewash, firstly because if Stanley did indeed play such a role he played it extremely badly, simply exacerbating the friction between officers and men; and secondly because the role of "mediator" is not the business of a leader, merely the quickest way to forfeit the trust of both parties. And for all his talk of patience he was subject to outbursts of violent—and frequently misdirected—anger. He was prone to favouritism, moody, inconsistent, secretive, and in some things petty. As a matter of policy he kept aloof from social contact with his officers, living and dining alone in a tent which, as if to emphasise its owner's separation from the common herd, was so large that it required forty men to carry it. Finally, though he handed out blame in plenty, for real or fancied blunders, he gave no praise at all for work well done; and his distribution of blame was sometimes wildly unfair.

As an illustration of the kind of incident which adversely affected both Stanley's relations with his officers and theirs with their men, the following, recorded by Jameson, will serve:

This morning Mr. Stanley placed me a very false position with my men. Just as we were starting, I told him that one of my chiefs[30] was very ill indeed, and that I did not think he could go on.

He told me not to bring him any reports of the kind, that he would not listen to them, and that his orders were for all the sick to go on, and that I was to see that they did so. I only said, "Very well, sir." I behaved very cruelly in making the man get up, amidst the murmurs of all the chiefs, and then driving him on. In a few yards he fell down, and could not get up. Mr. Stanley, on passing, recognized him, and went up to see how he was. He called to Dr. Parke to come to him, and told him that, as he was a good man, we must not lose him; gave him medicine then, and left more with him, at the same time telling one of the officers of the State to look after him, get him into a hut, and do everything he could for him. Of course all the men now look on me as a brute, and Mr. Stanley as a sort of guardian-angel. . . .

Three days were spent in camp organising the column for the march. The stores were broken up into sixty-pound loads and distributed among the carriers. Arms were served out: Remingtons or spears to the Zanzibaris, Winchesters to the officers and a few picked men. Each of the officers was given a riding-donkey.[31]

On the 25th (of March) the trumpets sounded in the Sudanese camp at 5.15 A.M. By 6 o'clock tents were folded, the companies were ranged by their respective captains, and near each company's stack of goods, and by 6.15 A.M. I marched out with the vanguard, behind which streamed the Expedition, according to companies, in single file, bearing with us 466 separate "charges" or porter-loads of ammunition, cloth, beads, wire, canned provisions, rice, salt, oil for engines, brass rods and iron wire. The setting out was admirable, but after the first hour of the march the mountains were so steep and stony, the sunshine was so hot, the loads so heavy, the men so new to the work after the glorious plenty on board the "Madura", and we ourselves were in such an overfed condition, that the Expedition straggled in a most disheartening manner to those not prepared for such a sight. (STANLEY)

The column was now ascending the western escarpment of the central African plateau. ". . . one of the worst roads I have ever seen," wrote Jameson, "up and down masses of cinder-like rock and broken quartz."
On the third day out from Matadi a new recruit was enrolled, a

young Englishman named Herbert Ward. He had already spent three years on the Congo, working first under Stanley for the Belgians and later for the Sanford Expedition. Before that he had led a roving life in Borneo, New Zealand, Australia and in the merchant navy. At the beginning of 1887 he was preparing to leave the Congo when a chance meeting with the missionary Charles Ingham brought Stanley's forthcoming expedition to his knowledge.[32] Ward promptly decided to join, if possible, in an adventure which promised broader horizons and a chance to escape from the routine drudgery of organising porter-transport on the Congo. In these respects both Ward's situation and his reasons for joining the Expedition were identical with those of Troup (the two were old comrades), though Troup had left the Congo and was in England before he heard of the Expedition and decided to enlist. Ward's attitude towards the Expedition may be judged from his own words:

> ... I knew nothing of Emin Pasha, and truth compels me to confess that about him I cared not at all. Of his sufferings and trials, of his dangers and difficulties, I was in entire ignorance. Life with Stanley promised new experiences, unthought of adventures, and all those things which from my early days had appeared to my sporting mind to make life worth the living. For glory or profit I had no need; but for sport and adventure I was keen and excited.[33]

This boyish and rather naive excitement was not peculiar to Ward. Compare it for example with Parke's account of how he was recruited by Barttelot at their meeting in Alexandria:

> ... he informed me that he had been selected by Mr. Stanley to accompany him as one of the officers of the Emin Pasha Relief Expedition. ... Barttelot seemed quite radiant with the romantic idea of traversing unknown regions in search of the lost European hero, and urged me to accompany the expedition, if I could obtain release from my present duties. On enquiring who Emin was, I was told he was "some chap who wanted to get out of Africa and couldn't". The idea pleased me. ...

With the same unthinking enthusiasm, Ward—

. . . soon gathered some three hundred of the required porters together, and losing no time set out with them to meet Stanley and his company. With the much-desired supply of porters as an outward and visible argument in my favour, I felt pretty confident that my request for permission to join the Expedition as a volunteer would not be refused.

On March 28 the path of Ward's caravan met that of Stanley's advancing column. Ward's description of the meeting is given here at length as containing the only graphic description extant of the Expedition on the march:

I had broken camp early one morning, and was marching rapidly along ahead of my caravan, when in the distance coming over the brow of a hill I saw a tall Sudanese soldier bearing Gordon Bennett's yacht flag.[34] Behind him, astride of a fine henna-stained mule, whose silver-plated strappings shone in the morning sun, was Mr. Henry M. Stanley, attired in his famous African costume.[35] Following immediately in his rear were his personal servants, Somalis with their curious braided waistcoats and white robes. Then came Zanzibaris with their blankets, water-bottles, ammunition belts and guns. Stalwart Soudanese soldiers with dark-hooded coats, their rifles on their backs, and innumerable straps and leather belts around their bodies; and Zanzibari porters bearing iron-bound boxes of ammunition, to which were fastened axes and shovels as well as their little bundles of clothing, which were rolled up in coarse sandy-coloured blankets. . . . At one point a steel whale-boat was being carried in sections, suspended from poles which were each borne by four men; donkeys heavily laden with sacks of rice were next met with, and a little further on the women of Tippoo-Tib's harem, their faces partly concealed, and their bodies draped in gaudily-covered cloths; then at intervals along the line of march an English officer with whom, of course, I exchanged friendly salutations; then several large-horned African goats, driven by saucy little Zanzibari boys. A short distance further on, an abrupt turn of the narrow footpath brought into view the dignified form of the renowned Tippoo-Tib, as he strolled along majestically in his flowing Arab robes of dazzling whiteness, and carrying over left shoulder a richly-decorated sabre, which was an emblem of his office conferred on him by H.H. the Sultan of Zanzibar. Behind him at a respectful distance followed several Arab sheiks, whose bearing was quiet and dignified. In response to my salutation they bowed gracefully.

"Haijambo," said I.

"Sijambo," they replied.

"Khabari ghani?" (what news?), I inquired.

"Khabari njema" (good news), was the reply,

and in that way I passed along the line of 700 men, in whose ranks were represented various types from all parts of eastern equatorial Africa, each wearing the distinguishing garb of his own country. All the accoutrements looked bright and gay, for the Expedition had disembarked but a few days previously. As the procession filed along the narrow, rugged path, it produced an effect no less brilliant than striking. Its unbroken line extended over a distance of probably four miles.[36]

Stanley accorded Ward a brief interview, offered him a cigar from a silver cigar-case, mentioned that the cigar-case in question was a parting gift from H.R.H. the Prince of Wales, and accepted the offer of Ward's services. No firm agreement was made at this stage but Stanley gave Ward to understand that he was prepared to enlist him for the duration of the Expedition.

> He asked me many questions about the steamers at the Pool, their condition, etc., and then told me . . . that if I could manage to clear out the 1,000 loads from Matadi, and be up at the Pool by the end of April, he would "take me along".[37]

Ward now continued down to Matadi while the main column pressed on for Stanley Pool. He had seen the Expedition at its best. The officers' diaries for March and April suggest that the overland journey was less distinguished by an air of barbaric pageantry than by blood, sweat, tears and plain muddle. A few extracts will serve to show that, for them at least, this first march was on the whole a less than enjoyable experience:

March 28 (BARTTELOT): Left Palabella at 5 a.m.; a bad road, very much up and down hill, and greatly fatiguing to the men. This is my birthday; I am twenty-eight years old. At 4.30 p.m. we reached camp—about twelve miles—and I bathed with Jephson in a muddy stream. One of my Soudanese tried to kill a goat, but was stopped in time; his excuse was, the goat charged him, and was possessed with a devil.

March 29 (JAMESON): Marched to the deserted native village of Congo da Lemba, which, until burnt by the Congo Free State, was a flourishing native town. . . . On arriving in camp one has to go over all the loads to see that they are correct, then stack them and interview the men about the loads that have gone wrong; so that it is dark before one has even time to wash. I have given up all hopes of collecting, although I have seen many birds, and especially butterflies, that I should dearly like to have obtained.

April 2 (JAMESON): In the morning we had a general parade of all the men, and Mr. Stanley addressed each company in turn, and I noticed that all the lazy blackguards, who had given us the most trouble, were foremost in shouting out all sorts of fine things about going to the end of the world with him! After this came a drenching storm of rain, and then we marched six or seven miles across the valley and camped.

April 6 (JAMESON): . . . On reaching the top of a hill, I found all the baggage and tents lying on the side of the road, the men being about a quarter of a mile off in a native garden, pulling up manioc, and seizing whatever they could. No shouts on my part or from the chiefs could bring them back, so, taking up a good stick, I ran down the hill towards them, and having waded through a swamp for about 150 yards, I met the first man trying to sneak back. I applied my stick, and he made such a row that all the others decamped, and when I regained the top of the hill, I found all the tents and baggage gone on. On arrival at Mwembi, the news was brought to us that one of our chiefs had been shot dead, and one of Tippu-Tib's men shot in the hand by some of the natives of a village which they had been looting. Went to bed dead beat.

April 7 (PARKE): Today Mr. Stanley decided that it was necessary to enforce a stricter discipline, as the stragglers were continually wasting our time in trying to keep them up. . . . The number of desertions since we left Mataddi now amounted to about thirty, and the straggling and pilfering were becoming intolerable. Accordingly, Mr. Stanley decided to ride in the rear of the caravan, which made a very happy difference in our progress—after a few examples had been made by whipping in the incorrigible loiterers. . . .[38]

The happy difference was short-lived. The next day the Sudanese staged a near-mutiny, complaining bitterly of bad treatment and short rations. Stanley firmly rejected their demands, threatened to have them all shot, and afterwards blamed Barttelot for the incident in terms which all but suggested that he had been its instigator. A quarrel ensued in the course of which Stanley threatened to ruin Barttelot's army career on their return to England. The following day, April 9, at a general parade, all the worst men—loiterers and troublemakers—were weeded out and added to Barttelot's Sudanese company. Barttelot was then packed off like a naughty schoolboy with orders to make his own way to Leopoldville keeping one day's march ahead of the main column. "This", wrote Barttelot, "was Stanley's revenge."

In fact the Sudanese continued difficult and their progress was so bad that Barttelot and the defaulters were overtaken by the main column two days later.

April 11 (PARKE): . . . we settled down for the night very close to the river's bank, and I suspended my hammock between two trees. Presently the rain came down in torrents; we were soaked through and through; and, in a few hours, the stream had swollen and overflowed its banks to such an extent that the tree to which my hammock had been secured now appeared to be in the middle of the river. . . . In the evening our leader asked me to his tent to have a cigar, and we conversed on the various topics suggested by the progress of the Expedition. We discussed the question that had been raised of Major Barttelot's having threatened to shoot Uledi,[39] but decided that it was not meant for earnest; also rumours about the European provisions having been tampered with, which were false.[40]

Jephson at this stage was on detached duty. Stanley had given him charge of the collapsible boat which was being used to ferry the Expedition across the numerous small tributaries of the Congo that intersected the line of march. Possibly Jephson had earned this duty on the strength of his once having trained as an officer in the merchant service (though he had not entered the profession). Some of the Somalis were attached to the boat party.

I was up at four this morning & got the caravan started by twenty minutes to five—I was anxious to start early for I wanted to do a long march today & as some of the Zanzibaris & five out of the six Somalis were sick, it was as well to get on before the sun grew hot. One of the sick Somalis had not come into the camp the night before so I sent the only one that was well to bring him on—he has just come in with the news that the sick man died on the way. It gives one a horrid feeling to hear a man with whom one has been working is suddenly dead but one is gradually becoming used to it, for many of our men are already dead & many are sick. It was a cool day and we were able to do the march well & get into camp by twelve. . . . (JEPHSON)

By now the Expedition was beginning to shake down, at least as far as march discipline was concerned:

April 15 (JAMESON): . . . It is now quite a pleasure to see the men walk along cheerily with their loads. . . . Some of the glimpses of the river were very beautiful. I would give anything to have time to make a sketch, no matter how rough, of some of them. . . . About half an hour from here we passed a dead native tied upright to a pole, by the side of the path. Mr. Stanley says it is the body of a thief, put up thus as a warning to others, and that he was executed by the natives themselves. The body was there when Mr. Stanley camped in the same place three or four years ago. . . .[41]

But although the Expedition was marching better on the last stages of the journey to Stanley Pool, there were still unpleasant incidents. On April 18, Jameson reported a box of ammunition missing from his company's loads:

Mr. Stanley ordered the whole company to fall in, and then made each man take a load from the heap of loads brought in. He asked the chief who had received the loads in camp to recognize . . . the men who had brought in theirs. He did not remember seeing one unfortunate man, so Mr. Stanley fixed upon him as the man who had lost his box, although he is really one of my best carriers, and swore he brought in his box, and showed Mr. Stanley the tree he had cut down to keep his boxes off the ground. Mr. Stanley then called the Somalis, and gave all my chiefs, with the exception of the one who had received the loads in camp, fifty cuts each with a stick, whilst they were held down on the ground. He then gave to the man, whom he accused of having lost the box, a hundred lashes, asking him several times during the beating where the box was,—the man each time still swearing that his box was in camp. He then chained and padlocked the chiefs all together, and accused me of losing three boxes of ammunition (which I flatly denied), and told me that in '77 it would have been death, and if it happened again we must part. (JAMESON)

While on detachment Jephson had fallen in with one of the Sanford Expedition's caravans on its way up to Stanley Pool. It was led by Roger Casement, at that time twenty-three years old. Casement's character, his kindness and friendliness, seems to have impressed all the Expedition's officers.[42] (Jephson was also impressed by the style in which Casement travelled—". . . a *real* dinner at a *real* table with a table cloth & dinner napkins & plenty to eat with Burgundy to drink . . . & this in the middle of the wilds. . . .")

April 21 (JEPHSON): . . . I got the boat started & sent the people ahead to catch up Stanley, for I felt I could march but slowly that day. I travelled slowly, each step being painful, & got about half through the march when I came upon Casement who was camping for breakfast in a deserted village. I could not go further & I was fain to lie down in an old hut, whilest Casement got his bed made up & put me on it. For a couple of hours I tossed about in a half sleep dreaming that Stanley was far ahead & that I was struggling to catch him up with the boat & couldn't overtake him. Casement gave me ten grains of quinine & when it got a little cooler put me in a hammock & sent four men to carry me into camp. . . .

On the same day the Expedition reached Stanley Pool and went into camp near Leopoldville. In spite of every mishap and confusion they had covered two hundred and thirty-five miles in twenty-eight days, an average of eight and a half miles a day. To Stanley, feverish always to get on, this result may have seemed less than impressive, but the time was not far off when a daily average of eight and a half miles would seem like an impossible dream.

The cost, both in men and material, had been considerable:

April 24th—Mustered Expedition and discovered we are short of 57 men and 38 Remington rifles. . . . Of bill-hooks, axes, shovels, canteens, spears, &c., we have lost over fifty per cent—all in a twenty-eight days' march. (STANLEY)

Parke's returns for this date show a loss of fifty-three men since leaving Zanzibar—eleven deaths, sixteen desertions, and twenty-six "invalids", that is, men left behind as unfit to travel.

For the officers the cost seems to have been as much moral as physical. Of the reactions of Nelson and Stairs we know nothing. Of the others, Jephson and Parke stood up best to their first experience of working under Stanley—Jephson because he had sufficient resilience to accept what came his way, and Parke because he was evidently endowed with a quite ruthless determination to look on the bright side of whatever presented itself to his view, people as well as events. Those who came out worst from the experience were Barttelot and Jameson. Barttelot's relations with Stanley, never good, deteriorated rapidly after Matadi and were shortly to deteriorate still more dramatically. Barttelot's Sudanese were included under the umbrella of Stanley's odium (". . . he does hate them so", Barttelot wrote), but the reasons for this are not apparent. Of all the officers it is the sensitive and artistic Jameson who shows the least readiness to adapt after an initial disillusion, and the least willingness to overcome his distaste for the work he was called on to do. In a letter to his wife (he was the only married man among the officers), Jameson summed up his feelings:

The march from Matadi was one of the most disgusting pieces of work I have ever had to do. . . . A lot of slave-drivers of the old days would have done it much better, for that—slave-driving—is what it often resolved itself into. . . . It must take a great deal of glory to make up for it all.

For Stanley, the arrival at Leopoldville was no time for retrospection, even had his character inclined him to it—which it decidedly did not, at least while there was still work to be done. He was immediately confronted two serious problems: transport, and food.

The Expedition had now practically exhausted the rations—principally rice, of which they had consumed thirteen tons during the march from Matadi—which had up to now supported them in however haphazard a fashion. The moment had come to start living off the country. But on arrival at Leopoldville they found the district in the grip of near-famine.[43] As a temporary expedient Jameson was sent out to shoot hippos for the pot, while Stanley turned his attention to the problem of getting the Expedition away to regions of greater plenty as soon as might be. This brought him face to face with the question of transport for the next stage of the journey up-river to the Aruwimi.

From the moment of the disembarkation at Banana Point, Stanley had been assiduously gathering intelligence as to the condition and availability of Leopolds' vaunted river-navy. The results had been ominous, and the state of affairs that met him at the Pool confirmed his worst fears.

The State's naval stock currently comprised four vessels: *Stanley*, *En Avant*, *Royal* and *Association Internationale Africaine (A.I.A.)*. The *Stanley* was the largest, the others being "little more than steam launches" (Troup). The *Stanley*, it now appeared, was indeed at the Expedition's disposal. But the *Stanley* alone was quite inadequate to the task in hand, and of the other three, the *Royal* had just been broken up, the *En Avant* had lost her engines, and the *A.I.A.* was cruising about somewhere on the upper river.[44] At the same time there were three other vessels on, or almost on, the river: *Peace*, property of the English Baptist Mission; *Henry Reed*, property of the American Baptist Mission; and *Florida* (still on the slips and without engines), property of the Sanford Expedition. Finally there were Stanley's own whaleboat the *Advance*, and two or three other whaleboats belonging to the State or the Missions.

Stanley's problem was to get a sufficiently large fleet together to move seven hundred and fifty men and some ninety thousand pounds of stores up-river, preferably in one trip. If the Expedition had, in addition to the *Stanley*, the use of the only other engined boats, the *Peace* and the *Henry Reed*, plus as many as possible of the engineless craft towed as barges, the thing should be possible. Unfortunately the chances of Stanley's getting his hands on the Mission steamers were, at first blush, poor. The prevailing image of Stanley in missionary and humanitarian circles was something not dissimilar to the Great Beast from Revelations. He had applied before leaving England for the loan of the *Peace* and had been met with a flat refusal, plus the advice to "repent and believe the Gospel" before it was too late.[45] However, by a stroke of luck, the English missionaries on the spot, Messrs. Bentley and Whitley, were unaware that the use of their boat had already been refused by their superiors in England. Stanley was not the man to apprise them of their mistake. Very far from it. With the connivance of

the State authorities he promptly took steps to have the missionaries'
mail intercepted to prevent them receiving instructions about the
disposal of the boat.[46] Deprived of the backing of higher (human)
authority, and confronted by the full force of Stanley's personality, the
English missionaries gave in after a token resistance. The Americans,
however, were of sterner mettle. The precise means by which Stanley
got possession of their boat is clouded in a certain murk, since
Stanley's account of the proceedings agrees in almost no particular
with those of his subordinates. But a comparison of his version with
those of Troup, Jephson, Jameson, Parke, Barttelot and Ward yields the
following picture:[47] on the first approach, the Americans, Billington
and Sims, refused point blank to lend the Henry Reed. The reason given
was that the Rev. Mr. Billington, who happened also to be the engineer,
was shortly leaving for the coast to marry a lady missionary of his
acquaintance. To reinforce his argument Billington had cunningly
removed some vital parts of the Henry Reed's machinery, rendering her
engines useless. Stanley, to show that he meant business, riposted by
sending Jephson with a detachment of armed Sudanese to put the
boat under guard while Barttelot, at the head of a second detachment,
marched on the Mission House to demand the surrender of the missing
parts. Mr. Billington, unshaken, returned that he had considered the
matter "prayerfully, even unto the third watch" and the answer was
still no. At this nasty impasse, the State authorities intervened in the
person of Lt. Liebriechts, the District Commissioner for Stanley Pool.
Liebriechts announced to the embattled missionaries that the State,
exercising its prerogative of requisition, was taking the Henry Reed
for its own use. He then handed the boat over to Stanley. "This
appeared also to be a crooked proceeding," commented Ward, "and in
all probability will cause some controversy when it becomes known in
Europe."[48] A charter fee of £100 a month was fixed on. Walker would
act as engineer.

It is impossible to be sure whether Liebriechts was acting on his
own initiative or under Stanley's direction. He must, however, have
been quite as anxious as Stanley himself to speed the departure of
seven hundred and fifty omnivorous men from his famine-stricken
district.

There were now three steamers at the Expedition's disposal, plus the
Florida, the En Avant and the whaleboats. It was a considerable flotilla,
but even so it proved inadequate to move all the men and all the
loads at one go; some double journeys would be necessary. As a

first move, Barttelot, Parke and one hundred and fifty-three men were sent two days' steaming up-river on board the *Stanley* to an area where, it was hoped, supplies were more plentiful. Their orders were to disembark, send the steamer back to Leopoldville, and then continue overland to the mouth of the Kwa River (about a hundred miles above Stanley Pool) where they would wait to be picked up. This measure eased the food situation at the Pool and reduced the number of men remaining to a level where they could all be got away at once. It also had the effect (though such may not have been the intention) of separating Stanley from Barttelot and the Sudanese. Barttelot's group left in the *Stanley* on April 25.

On the last day of April, Ward and Troup, having completed the despatch of stores from Matadi, got into Leopoldville. They found Stanley in unusual good humour, perhaps occasioned by the success of his *coup de main* against the monstrous regiment of Bible-thumpers. That night he and his officers were the guests of the Dutch represent-ative M. Greshoff:

> Ours was a very enjoyable evening. Mr. Stanley was in his most entertaining mood,[49] full of anecdotes, and inclined to chaff one and all of us. No wonder the great explorer was feeling at his best. . . . His great Expedition was fairly started and all was, so far, going well. He could doubtless see in his mind's eye his ultimate triumph. (TROUP)

For Troup the pleasure of the evening was marred by the knowledge that he alone would not be going up on the steamers. He had been detached to remain behind at Leopoldville in charge of the loads—five hundred of them—for which there would be no room on the first trip. When the main body had been disembarked at the Aruwimi, the steamers would return for Troup and the stores. He swallowed his disappointment, consoling himself with the thought of the adven-tures and excitement that lay in store for him on the march to Lake Albert.

On May 1, the flotilla got under way:

> Today at about ten o'clock we started up river. Stanley & Ward in the *Peace* carrying 50 men, & having in tow a lighter belonging to the State, carrying 50 men, & the missionary boat *Plymouth* carrying 35 men. The *Henry Reed* having Tippu Tibs men numbering 50 &

towing the En Avant (a hull) with 50 men, & our boat, the Advance with 35. The Stanley with 168 men, with Stairs, Nelson, Jameson & myself on board, towing the Florida with 168 men and 9 donkeys. There were also 594 loads distributed among the steamers. (JEPHSON)[50]

Troup led the cheering from the shore.

The Peace, with Stanley aboard, was the last to cast off. She had no sooner got out into the current than her steering-gear gave way. This event may have caused a degree of unchristian but pardonable satisfaction to the English missionaries, who had advanced her dilapidated conditions as grounds for not lending her. After hasty repairs she rejoined, the following day, the other boats waiting for her at the head of the Pool.

The first part of the river journey was without incidents of moment. The numbers of sick continued to grow, especially among the Somalis and Sudanese, and there were some deaths. Attrition by disease, exhaustion, and bad and insufficient food continued at a steady trickle. It was not yet the flood that was to come, but like a dripping tap this ceaseless yet unspectacular mortality was a constant reminder of a situation that could only get worse. Jameson commented on a fact that had struck Livingstone, observing the deaths among the victims of a slave-march:

When they once get sick they neither eat, nor drink, nor move; in fact . . . they simply make up their minds to die.

One new factor that was to have an increasingly deleterious effect on the Expedition's health was their reliance—now that supplies of rice were exhausted—on manioc as a staple food.[51] The manioc tuber contains a form of cyanide which must be carefully eliminated by preparation or cooking before the manioc is safe to eat. There are several methods of extracting the poisonous principle, but all are time-consuming, especially to a very hungry man. If it is not done, the immediate effects of ingestion are giddiness, fainting, cramps and nausea; in the long term it leads to degeneration of nervous tissue, particularly the optic nerve, and ultimately blindness. "Our Zanzibaris", wrote Parke, "were instructed how to prepare the manioc for food; but with their usual recklessness and want of forethought, they were sometimes too lazy or careless to take any trouble with the

tubers, and ate them raw. They always paid dearly for this folly. . . ."[52]
Parke might have added that their recklessness was often stimulated by
long periods of near-starvation followed by sudden plenty.

All the officers went down intermittently with dysentery, or with
"go"s of fever which lasted anything from a few hours to a few days.
When not ill, and when not ashore supervising the endless drudgery of
cutting wood for the steamers, they were observing, and gingerly making contact with, their new environment. Jameson was a keen amateur
naturalist and sportsman. His plans for "collecting" had been one of
his chief motives for joining the Expedition. Now he filled his diary
and letters to his wife with observations on the birds, beetles and
butterflies which teemed around him, fretting the while at his inability
to get down to serious collecting. Ward, who had very considerable
artistic gifts, spent much of his free time sketching. Jephson made
tentative experiments in field anthropology:

> One old fat chief who was smoking a pipe with a stem five & a half
> feet long came up & made friends with us shaking hands & saying
> "Botay" a great many times, "Botay" literally means "good" but it is
> their term of greeting to friends. By & bye he brought up a large
> calabash of palm wine, "Molaffo" as the natives call it, & we all
> sat round with a lot of chiefs & drank it—in my opinion it is very
> nasty. I asked the chief to show me his beard, which I measured &
> found was four & a half feet long, he seemed highly delighted when
> I made a note of it in my note book. The beard consisted of only a
> few tangled hairs in some places & was encrusted with palm oil &
> the dirt of ages & my hands were horrible after touching it.

The gaiety, however, of a shared adventure, to which they had all
looked forward, persistently eluded them. Perhaps it was Stanley's
moody and irritable aloofness that cast a pall on the enterprise. Or
perhaps it was the strangeness of the brooding, sullen and unpredictable river up which they were passing. Jameson, the most receptive of
them to such impressions, wrote:

> I have never been on a trip where there is so little enjoyment of
> any kind; it is all so serious, and a kind of gloom hangs over it all.
> If one does say anything which raises a laugh, it is the most ghastly
> imitation of one, and dies a sudden death, not to be raised again,
> perhaps, that day.

And earlier, even the boyish Jephson had confided to his diary:

> It is peculiar what a feeling of hatred the river inspires one with. One hates it as if it were a living thing—it is so treacherous & crafty, so overpowering & relentless in its force & overwhelming strength. . . . The banks too have a dreary ghostly appearance, black jagged rocks stand out from the banks as if ready to devour anything that came near them & the very kites and cranes seem to add to the inexpressible dreariness of the scene—it is all like a bad night mare. . . . The Congo river god is an evil one, I am persuaded.

These reactions bear more than a passing similarity to those of Conrad who made the same journey and later described it in the following incomparable words:

> Going up that river was like travelling back to the earliest beginnings of the world, when vegetation rioted on the earth and the big trees were kings. An empty stream, a great silence, an impenetrable forest. The air was warm, thick, heavy, sluggish. There was no joy in the brilliance of sunshine. The long stretches of the waterway ran on, deserted, into the gloom of overshadowed distances. On silvery sandbanks hippos and alligators sunned themselves side by side. The broadening waters flowed through a mob of wooded islands; you lost your way on that river as you would in a desert, and butted all day long against shoals, trying to find the channel, till you thought yourself bewitched and cut off forever from everything you had known once—somewhere—far away—in another existence perhaps. There were moments when one's past came back to one, as it will sometimes when you have not a moment to spare to yourself; but it came in the shape of an unrestful and noisy dream, remembered with wonder amongst the overwhelming realities of this strange world of plants, and water, and silence. And this stillness of life did not in the least resemble a peace. It was the stillness of an implacable force brooding over an inscrutable intention. It looked at you with a vengeful aspect.[53]

On May 12 the three steamers arrived at the populous settlement of Bolobo, two hundred and fifty miles above Stanley Pool. The *Peace*, afflicted with something resembling terminal asthma, had to be towed in by the *Henry Reed* and again repaired. The *Stanley*, too, had come near to being a total loss when she fouled a submerged reef and was holed below the waterline. Walker the engineer was now earning his keep. With the assistance of the engineers from the other boats, and working up to his waist in water, he had managed to patch up the *Stanley*'s bottom with sheets cut from old oil drums.

At Bolobo the men disembarked and the *Stanley* was sent back down to pick up Barttelot's contingent. On May 14 she was back at Bolobo.

Stanley now had to decide who to leave behind on the next leg of the journey. He weeded out the weakest and sickest of his men so that the steamers would be carrying only those fit for the work which lay immediately ahead. An officer would have to be left in charge of the invalid contingent, and inevitably Stanley had marked Barttelot down for the post of nursemaid. It is even possible that he meant to install Ward, who had been enjoying a great deal of Stanley's company during the river journey, in Barttelot's place as second-in-command. Ward writes:

> In the course of our interviews Stanley informed me of his intention to appoint me to the position of Executive Lieutenant in charge of his No. 1 Company of Zanzibaris. Subsequently, however, in the course of the arrangements in connection with the Bolobo Camp, I learned to my disgust that this plan had been changed, and that I was to be left behind at Bolobo in command of the camp there, with Bonny and 125 men. . . . The real reason, however, for my being left behind was, that some of my fellow officers had urged upon Mr. Stanley that it would be unfair to allow me to go ahead at the expense of any one of them being left, when they had journeyed with the Expedition from England, and I had only been "picked up" by the way in Africa. There was a good deal of fairness in the argument, I admit, and it is with no idea of complaining that I refer to the matter; nevertheless it was an unlucky day for me when I was left behind at Bolobo. . . .

Stanley, as will appear in the next chapter, had another scheme in mind for separating himself from Barttelot.

The day after the *Stanley*'s return, the Expedition, minus Ward, Bonny and the hundred and twenty-five sick, resumed the voyage.

A few days later there occurred a dispute so violent and so unreasonable that it came near to breaking up the Expedition:

May 20 (JAMESON): This morning, I am sorry to say that the most disgraceful row I have ever heard of happened between Mr. Stanley and Jephson and Stairs. It appears that early this morning a number of men and chiefs went to Mr. Stanley, and complained that the officers had flung away their rations for one day. Mr. Stanley sent for Stairs. The men swore they had bought the food at the village they looted. . . .[54] Stairs told Mr. Stanley this, assuring him that only stolen stuff was taken away from them, and sent for Jephson, who gave the same testimony. It is still quite evident that Mr. Stanley takes the word of the Zanzibaris on every occasion before that of the white men, and when he saw that he had hold of rather the wrong end of this stick, he attacked them about their tyranny to the men. He attacked them in a frantic state, stamping up and down the deck of the "Peace". He called Jephson all sorts of names, a "G-d d-n son of a sea-cook," "You d-d ass, you're tired of me, of the Expedition, and of my men. Go into the bush, get. I've done with you. And you, too, Lieutenant Stairs, you and I will part today; you're tired of me, Sir, I can see. Get; away into the bush." Then he turned round to the men (about 150) sitting down, and spoke Swahili to the effect that the men were to obey us no more, and that if Lieutenant Stairs or Jephson issued any orders to them, or dared to lift a hand, they were to tie them up to trees. He had already told Stairs that he had only to lift his hand for the men to throw him into the sea. He lastly offered to fight Jephson. "If you want to fight, G-d d-n you, I'll give you a bellyful. If I were only where you are, I'd go for you. It's lucky for you I'm where I am". Mr. Stanley was on the deck of the "Peace", Jephson on shore. All this was said before the missionaries, Tippu-Tib, and everyone. As for Stairs or Jephson being tired of the Expedition, no men could work harder or have their hearts more in it. . . . He also called Jephson, "G-d d-d impudent puppy." . . . I had no idea until today what an extremely dangerous man Stanley was.

Stanley nowhere mentions this scene, but Jameson's account is corroborated by those of Barttelot and of Jephson himself, though neither attempts to follow Jameson in reproducing Stanley's picturesque language.[55] Since all accounts agree that Jephson and Stairs had merely tried to prevent looting and that the Zanzibaris' complaint was completely fabricated, Stanley's rage is difficult to understand. A clue may lie in Barttelot's account of his own efforts to square things between the disputants.

> . . . He also said to Stairs, before Jephson came up, that a mutiny was brewing, and that if he only raised a finger, the Zanzibaris would rush upon him and crush him, or club him to death. I was astonished when Stairs and Jephson returned and told me about it, especially in Stairs' case, for no kinder officer to the men, or more zealous and hard-working officer, is there in the Expedition, besides being most efficient and capable. . . . I gave him (Stanley) time to cool down, shaving in the meanwhile, and then went over to see him. We were lying 200 yards up stream. On the way I met Parke, who told me that Stanley had called him on to the "Peace", and opined that we were talking about him; that it was apparent to him that we had formed a compact against him and were tired of the Expedition, and only made a row to get sent back. Parke assured him of our loyalty, and earnest wishes to carry on the work. I then saw Stanley, and told him that I was sorry for what had happened, asking to know his wishes concerning Jephson and Stairs, whether they were really dismissed. He said they were. Harped back to his old idea of the compact. I assured him to the contrary. He said he could carry on the Expedition without any of us.
>
> I asked him whether I was to tell Jephson and Stairs that his decision was irrevocable. He hesitated, and then said, "As regards myself it is." By that alone I knew he was bluffing. I went away, and Jephson and Stairs came over, at my advice, and squared it.

Stanley's behaviour on this occasion exhibits definite symptoms of incipient paranoia—specifically, the delusion that his officers were plotting against him.[56] But any consideration of the peculiarities of his personal conduct must be made in the light of the enormous responsibility that sat on his shoulders. He alone, finally, was accountable for the success or failure of a frankly gigantic undertaking. He alone had the will-power and personality to hold the Expedition together and drive it on. It would therefore be both reasonable and charitable to interpret his moments of apparent mental unbalance as due to the overmastering strength of his desire to bring to a successful conclusion the venture on which he was embarked. He said of himself, with every appearance of sincerity, "The dearest passion of my life has been, I think, to succeed in my undertakings."[57] However, reading between the lines of Stanley's writings and Stanley's career, one becomes aware of the possibility of a somewhat different interpretation: that it was not the desire to succeed which drove him on and placed him under such terrible strain, so much as the fear of failure. Far from being a distinction without a difference, this can be plausibly seen as the key to Stanley's entire life. "No other famous man of his time", wrote Sir Reginald Coupland, "got so high from a start so low. No one can understand him who forgets that. He never forgot it himself."[58] Given his birth and background, it is not too difficult to form some idea of what "success" must have meant to Stanley. But it is perhaps less easy to remember and to appreciate (since we are considering in retrospect a figure whose place in history we know to be assured) that every step Stanley took up the ladder to fame was taken at the risk of everything he had already achieved. His standing in the world's eye was underpinned by neither family, nor fortune, nor intellectual attainments; his position was at all times precarious. One failure would cost him all that he had earned with so much pain. When he undertook to "rescue" Emin, he threw his entire career into the pot. Thus, obstacles, delays, reverses, and above all the incompetence—real or imagined—of his subordinates, were perceived as threats to his achievement, not merely of immediate goals, but of a whole life's work. That his reaction to such threats should sometimes come close to a kind of madness, while hardly laudable, is at least comprehensible.

The quarrel with Jephson and Stairs was smoothed over, but not forgotten. Meanwhile the boats pressed on. The end of May saw them at Bangala, the last Belgian station on the river. It had a garrison of sixty Hausas and two Krupp guns. The Governor, Lt. van Kerckhoven, was away at the time of the Expedition's arrival. He was an energetic and capable officer who was later to play a part of his own in the history of Equatoria.

> This station . . . is, compared to the other stations, a good one, but that is not saying much, still there are signs of cultivation and care about it which are refreshing after the neglect and decay of the other stations. (JEPHSON)[59]

At Bangala Stanley prepared to part company with Tippu-Tib. They were now approaching the Congo–Aruwimi confluence where Tippu-Tib's party would turn south up the main branch of the Congo to Stanley Falls while the remainder of the Expedition would follow the Aruwimi due east to the limit of navigation represented by the rapids at Yambuya—the nearest approach they could make by steamer to their goal at Lake Albert. Barttelot and forty Sudanese were told off to board the Henry Reed to escort the new Governor to Stanley Falls and see him safely installed in his post. The Sudanese were selected for this duty, according to Stanley, "that none of the Zanzibaris might become acquainted with the fact that Stanley Falls was but a few days' march from Yambuya". (How it was proposed to prevent the Sudanese subsequently passing the information on to the Zanzibaris is not clear.)

The Stanley and the Peace left Bangala on June 1, a day behind Barttelot in the Henry Reed.

From this point on, the disposition of the natives whose villages lined the banks was an unknown quantity. At this time the area between Bangala and Stanley Falls was a kind of no-man's land subject to the depredations of both sides—the Belgians in the west and the Arabs in the east. The inhabitants, besides a penchant for cannibalism (supposedly symbolised by their filed teeth), were likely to view with a certain reserve the approach of strangers. When it became necessary for the steamers to put into the shore for food or fuel, the initial approach had to be made with caution. The basic policy—and this was to remain true, with modifications, throughout the Expedition— was overt friendliness backed by a readiness to fight:

> . . . we made for the middle village, and upon our approach to land, all the natives rushed down to the shore with their spears, shields and guns, yelling and shouting at us to keep back. . . . As wood was very short, and we must get food for the men, we ran the steamer straight for shore, and they all stood about forty yards off, making a terrific noise. They at length listened to our spokes- man,[60] and agreed to allow us to land if one of the white men would come on shore and be made blood-brother to their chief. Stairs and the Captain of the steamer landed, and the ceremony was performed with much pomp. Stairs' arm was slightly cut until blood came, and the chief's also, then the bleeding parts were rubbed together, each man swearing to be a "true brother" to the

other. All this time a wild song was kept up by the natives, beer was drunk, and the chief sent us a present of a goat. The fierce natives of half an hour ago were in one moment transformed into the sharpest and most eager traders, ready to sell everything they possessed. (JAMESON)

This scene was to be repeated with variations across the breadth of the continent.

On June 12, the *Stanley* and the *Peace* arrived at Basoko, a large complex of villages at the Aruwimi confluence. It was a place of doubtful reputation. Its inhabitants had recently distinguished themselves by devouring two of Deane's Hausas, captured during the flight from Stanley Falls. It happened, however, to be the home of Stanley's boy Baruti, and through him contact was established.

> . . . the natives paddled back to the village & brought Baruti's brothers and sisters. They immediately asked if he had a mark on his arm where a crocodile had bitten him, upon his showing them the mark they were satisfied that he was their long lost brother & a good deal of weeping & kissing resulted. (JEPHSON)

Despite this touching incident, the inhabitants refused to sell food to the Expedition. Stanley decided not to make an issue of it but to press on.

Above Basoko the Aruwimi narrows rapidly. On June 15, at about five in the afternoon, the steamers reached Yambuya, ninety-six miles above Basoko. This was as far as the steamers could go, for at Yambuya were the first of the Aruwimi rapids.

The river journey from Stanley Pool had taken six weeks. So far progress had been good. The Expedition was on schedule. They were now nearly thirteen hundred miles from Matadi, the place they had left just under three months earlier. In that time they had come half-way across the African continent. If ever a place deserved to be called the "heart of Africa", Yambuya was that place.

The boats made fast to the north bank. None of those aboard who now turned to inspect the village that faced them from the opposite shore had any reason to suspect that for many of them this was journey's end.

NOTES AND REFERENCES

1 Ask a stupid question . . .

2 A Congolese youth given or sold by Tippu-Tib to Sir Francis de Winton and by him to Stanley. "Baruti" means "gunpowder" in Swahili—an example of the diverse origins of the Swahili vocabulary, since the word started its career as a Turkish adaptation of the Greek "πυρίτης" (cf. "pyrites").

3 D.A. I p. 48.

4 In mitigation: (i) it must be remembered that all direct speech in Stanley's writings is strictly Thucydidean; (ii) that the unfavourable impression one gains of Stanley from reading his reports of conversations he claims to have had may simply be due to his incompetence (product of journalistic over-writing) in handling written dialogue.

5 D.A. I pp. 50–51.

6 C.5601 No. 27—Baring to Salisbury (2/2/87).

7 Stanley prints the translation of the Khedive's firman of which the original was in Arabic. He does not reproduce Nubar Pasha's letter, which he refers to as a "letter of recall"—it was nothing of the kind—and adds: "Nubar's letter conveys the wishes of the Egyptian Government, which are in accordance with those of the English Government, as expressed by Sir Evelyn Baring." (D.A. I p. 58.)

8 D.A. I p. 62 and pp. 67–68.

9 TROUP p. 30; BARTTELOT pp. 51–52; PARKE pp. 1–7.

10 The errant Bonny also rejoined at Suez. It may be noted at this point that Bonny's name occurs rarely in the narratives of the other officers, and when it does, it is clear that they both disliked and looked down on him. Another name that hardly ever occurs is that of Stanley's young servant William Hoffman. Stanley's account contains only two direct references to him in a thousand-odd pages of text and even then he is not named. Hoffman, of German parents but brought up in London (Parke refers to his Cockney speech), had been with Stanley since 1884. In 1938 he published a book entitled *With Stanley in Africa*.

11 A characteristic ploy: Stanley suggests that the negotiations had been dragging on since 1878, and hence—by implication—that it took the intervention of Stanley to settle in a day what others could not settle in eight years. In fact Mackinnon had completely lost interest in East Africa after the Government

had sabotaged his hopes for a concession in 1878. Moreover, the matter cannot be said to have been "settled" by Stanley's talks with the Sultan; final agreement was not reached until the incorporation of the Imperial British East Africa Company in 1888.

12 D.A. I p. 62.

13 Stanley thoughtfully provided Tippu-Tib with a supply of flags for this purpose. (BRODE p. 100).

14 Stanley's reticence about the powder (an action he might be called to account for in Europe) is understandable. But see TROUP p. 152; BARTTELOT p. 108 and p. 113; JAMESON p. 74; BRODE p. 200.

15 D.A. I p. 64 & p. 71. After Stanley had left England, a slightly sordid wrangle broke out between the Relief Committee and the Egyptian Government over the distribution of this rich booty. (See C.5601 Nos. 31, 32, 33, 37, 41.) They were, as it turned out, disputing a phantom prize. Not a pound of Emin's ivory ever reached the coast. In the confusion which attended the evacuation of Equatoria, most of it was dumped in the Nile and the rest fell into the hands of the Mahdi-ists. (COLLINS p. 57.)

16 The idea of Tippu-Tib's taking service under the Belgians had been discussed between him and Junker during their journey to the Coast. Junker had been enthusiastic for the idea and had put it to Stanley when they met in Cairo. But, according to Junker, "Stanley objected that an arrangement of this nature could scarcely be made with such a notorious slaver as Tippu Tib." (JUNKER pp. 568–569.)

17 The majority of Tippu-Tib's followers were cannibal Manyuema. Holmwood, the British Consul at Zanzibar, estimated that Tippu-Tib had 3,000 fighting-men at or near Stanley Falls at this time. (C.5601 No. 39.)

18 Minor discrepancies between the various narratives tend to appear from time to time in estimates of the Expedition's ration-strength. Here, for example, Stanley, Parke and Jameson give the number of Somalis as 12; Barttelot, who hired them and should have known, states that there were 13. The above figures are, therefore, a consensus. This method has been followed elsewhere—faute de mieux—in dealing with other small divergences on points of fact.

19 C.5601 Nos. 19, 20, 23.

20 C.5601 No. 39—Holmwood to Salisbury.

21 ". . . as if hell itself was let loose . . ." (JEPHSON). ". . . exactly like an 'Inferno' by Gustave Doré . . ." (JAMESON). ". . . a decidedly animated scene . . ." (PARKE).

22 Where the chronology is sufficiently clear to make a page-reference superfluous, extracts from the Expedition narratives will be accompanied by a notation consisting of the author's name only. This is a cunning device to reduce footnote-load.

23   The Somalis were first allotted to Barttelot's company but Stanley subsequently formed them into a sort of palace guard under his personal command. He used them as lictors and camp police. Jephson also found them apt as boatmen.

24   Stanley seems to have had trouble remembering the ranks he had conferred on his assistants. Stairs, in Stanley's account, is sometimes Captain Stairs and sometimes Lieutenant Stairs. Jephson, too, is frequently demoted from Captain to Lieutenant and sometimes broken all the way down to Mr.

25   Considering the low status of dogs in the Arab world, and the importance attached to giving and receiving presents, it would be difficult to imagine a less tactful choice. Brode records Tippu-Tib's dismay on a previous occasion at receiving from Stanley in place of the "rich presents" he had been promised, a signed photograph of the great man. (BRODE pp. 130–131.) Tippu-Tib promptly passed his dog on to Jephson. Stanley's own dog is later made the hero of one of his humorous-dramatic "set-pieces" (D.A. I p. 213.)

26   In the early days the Belgians preserved a jealous monopoly of trade on the Upper River, the only exception being the concession granted in 1886 to the "Sanford Exploring Expedition". This company was the creation of Henry Shelton Sanford, an American entrepreneur/diplomat and close collabo-ator in Leopold's various schemes. Sanford was an important lobbyist for Leopold in the States and his concession was the reward for having got the U.S. to recognise the newly-created Congo Free State in 1885, before any other country had done so.

27   [Sic] Jephson's punctuation and orthography are idiosyncratic, even in times of good health.

28   Stanley's *Autobiography* contains a long apologia on the subject of his relations with his officers (pp. 380–381). On this particular point he says (p. 385): "It took the officers some months to learn that, when they stood at the head of their companies, and I repeated for the benefit of the natives in their own language the orders already given to them in English, I was not speaking about themselves!" This assertion must be viewed in the light of an incident, recorded below, in which Stanley allegedly told Stairs's and Jephson's men to tie their officers to trees if they "raised a hand" to them.

29   For other instances, see JAMESON, entries for April 18 and 19; BARTTELOT, March 26 and April 18; PARKE, April 9 and 10. Jameson and Barttelot were the ones who enjoyed the worst relations with Stanley. Only of Nelson can Stanley say that, with him "I do not remember to have had a single mis-understanding." (*Autobiography* p. 383.)

30   I.e. headmen of the porters, "wanyampara" in Swahili.

31   Jameson tells how he distributed ". . . spears, which from their rottenness are comparatively harmless, half of them being already without their heads". This is the first of a number of recorded comments on the shoddiness of the Expedition's stores. See also, for example, TROUP pp. 105–106; JAMESON, p. 75. None of the donkeys lived long.

32 Ingham, a Congo veteran, had been offered a place on the Expedition but had refused. (TROUP p. 31.) He had, however, agreed to help Troup with the transport arrangements between Matadi and Stanley Pool and was engaged on this work at the time of his meeting with Ward.

33 WARD p. 3.

34 It amused James Gordon Bennett, proprietor of the *New York Herald* and Stanley's former employer, to have Stanley carry this pointless emblem to and fro across Africa.

35 Particularised as follows by Troup: "He was arrayed in his usual African *war-paint*, viz. a Norfolk jacket, with continuations in the shape of knicker-bockers, which displayed most decidedly well-developed calves; his head-gear was a large flat-topped cap with a peak in front such as is worn by officers in the German army." (TROUP pp. 88–89.)

36 WARD pp. 5–7, quoting his own *Five Years with the Congo Cannibals* p. 33.

37 Ward to Joseph Hatton, May 6, 1887, qu. Ward, S.: *A Valiant Gentleman* pp. 65–66.

38 "Stanley, as rear-guard, got on A1. He flogged loafers, and they all kicked amazingly." (BARTTELOT) "How he did lay his stick about the lazy ones, and the Somalis whacked away too. It was a sight for sore eyes to see the lame, the sick, the halt, and the blind running with their loads as if they were feathers; and I was delighted to see some of my men catch it hot, after I had been told by Mr. Stanley himself not to strike them." (JAMESON)

39 Uledi was an old travelling companion of Stanley's, having made the great crossing of the Continent with him in 1874–7 as coxwain of the boat *Lady Alice*. (See Stanley: *Through the Dark Continent*). Barttelot writes: "I never threatened Uledi."

40 Stanley had apparently believed a story told him by the Zanzibaris that the officers had been stealing the European provisions. Parke had in fact opened one of the Fortnum and Mason boxes to get arrowroot for Stanley who was suffering a bout of dysentery. ". . . Parke in answer to Stanley, said 'Yes,' but the only person who had had any of the contents was himself, and that he should advise him to put a little more trust in his officers, who were, at any rate, gentle-men and not accustomed to be accused of that sort of thing." (BARTTELOT).

41 It was still there three years later to catch the eye of another traveller who passed along that road—Joseph Conrad. (See Conrad's *Congo Diary*—entry for July 29, 1890.) It made a sufficiently strong impression on him to be incorp-orated, years later, into the story *Heart of Darkness*, which he based on his experiences in the Congo. (See below, Appendix II.)

42 "An uncommon nice fellow," was Barttelot's judgement. Conrad, who met Casement in the Congo in 1890, was also favourably impressed. Indeed, of all the Europeans Conrad met in the Congo, Casement was the only one who did impress him favourably. (See below, Appendix II.)

43 (TROUP pp. 85–86; D.A. I p. 90; JEPHSON pp. 93–94.) The cause of the famine was the depopulation of the district (rather than vice versa); the cause of the depopulation was Belgian mismanagement. It was already the case, and in the next two decades was to become more obviously so, that depopulation and desolation were the distinguishing marks of those districts that had been most intensively subjected to the civilising activities of the State's administrators and commercial agents.

44 Troup (p. 67) says that it was the *A.I.A.* that was engineless at the Pool and the *En Avant* which was away up-river, but the consensus of other accounts is against him.

45 D.A. I p. 47. Stanley gives the full text of what he calls this "quaint reply". Its author was Robert Arthington, a Leeds industrialist of strong philanthropo-evangelical leanings who had been the first promoter of English missionary effort on the Congo.

46 Ward to Hatton, May 6, 1887: "At the N'Kissi River we met Baron von Reichlin, who had been sent down to intercept the mails of the A.B.M.U. and also the B.M.S. missions—as Stanley thought that probably news would come from England which might tend to the refusal of the steamers. This struck me as a crooked proceeding." This is confirmed by Barttelot (p. 87). Troup gives the name of the Baron as von Reichland. For insecurity of mails on the Congo see also JEPHSON p. 110.

47 TROUP pp. 86–87; JEPHSON pp. 94–95; JAMESON pp. 27–28; PARKE p. 44; BARTTELOT pp. 87–88; *A Valiant Gentleman* p. 67. There are two versions of Stanley's side of the story: that in D.A. I (p. 92) and that in his despatch to the Committee from Leopoldville which was printed in *The Times* for June 17, 1887.

48 Ward to Hatton, May 6, 1887. The most glaring inconsistencies between Stanley's and the other versions are: (1) In Stanley it is Jephson who wants to seize the *Henry Reed* but is dissuaded by Stanley urging patience and moderation; (2) Liebriechts' part is reduced to merely arguing with Billington; (3) the soldiers sent to arrest the boat and intimidate Billington are simply not mentioned. All accounts but Stanley's are consistent with each other and differ only in points of detail and in how much of the story they include.

49 Stanley was, by all accounts, an outstanding conversationalist, and when he was so minded his charm could be as overpowering as his rages. (See, for example, JAMESON p. 33; JEPHSON p. 70 and p. 81; BARTTELOT, p. 53.)

50 The *Stanley* and *Henry Reed* were both stern-wheelers and so, instead of towing their consorts, had them lashed alongside. Five more "invalids" were left at Leopoldville.

51 Bitter cassava, *manihot utilissima*.

52 PARKE p. 494.

53 *Heart of Darkness*, Chapter II.

54 The looting is described in JEPHSON, JAMESON and BARTTELOT.

55 Parke mentions the affair briefly, but in his usual good-natured way he plays it down as far as possible, merely referring to "some feverish language". (Both Stairs and Jephson were, according to Parke, "ailing" at the time.)

56 For another instance, see Jameson's entry for June 6, in which he relates how the *Peace* took a wrong turning among the channels of the river and became separated from the *Stanley*. Stanley, on board the *Peace*, jumped to the conclusion that the disappearance of the other steamer showed an attempt at mass desertion to be in progress.

57 D.A. I p. 183.

58 Coupland: *Livingstone's Last Journey.*

59 This is not the only place in which Jephson—who, writing in the privacy of his diary, can hardly be accused of axe-grinding—expresses less than admiration for the visible manifestations of Belgian rule. (See also JEPHSON p. 84 and pp. 93–94.) His opinion was shared by some at least of his brother officers. (JAMESON p. 29 and p. 50; PARKE p. 46.)

60 One of the Zanzibaris knew the language. So varied were their origins that there appears to have been hardly a tribe in Eastern and Central Africa linguistically beyond the reach of one or another of them.

YAMBUYA TO LAKE ALBERT
June to December 1887

The earliest date at which Mr Stanley can arrive at Wadelai is about the middle or end of July.

MACKINNON TO SALISBURY (10/2/1887)

On the morning of June 16, the Expedition crossed the river, disembarked in skirmishing order, and occupied the village of Yambuya. The inhabitants deserted their huts and fled into the surrounding jungle.

The stores were unloaded from the steamers and work was immediately put in hand for converting the native settlement into a fortified camp. The bush was cleared to a depth of fifty yards around the village and parties were told off to begin the construction of a fortified perimeter consisting of a six-foot-high stockade surrounded by a ditch.

That night Baruti deserted:

(He) came into my hut in the dead of night, armed himself with my Winchester rifle and a brace of Smith and Wesson revolvers, a supply of rifle and revolver cartridges, took possession of a silver road-watch, a silver pedometer, a handsome belt with fitted pouches, a small sum of money, and, possessing himself of a canoe disappeared down river to parts unknown, most probably to his tribe. (STANLEY)

There were probably few men in the camp that night who, if they had known what lay before them, might not have been tempted to follow Baruti's example.

The next day and the days which followed, while work on the fortifications went ahead, Stanley began to show increasing anxiety about the non-appearance of Barttelot and the *Henry Reed*. Stanley had expected him back from the Falls on June 17. On the 22nd, convinced that Barttelot had fallen victim either to a native attack, shipwreck, or Arab treachery, Stanley gave written orders to Stairs to take the Peace[1] and the Maxim gun and go in search of the missing steamer. (It is fair to say that Stanley showed more concern about the possible fate of the boat than about the fate of Barttelot and his men.) Stairs was to set out on the morning of June 23. On the evening of the 22nd, Barttelot returned.

Tippu-Tib's installation had passed off without accident. There had been some fighting between Tippu-Tib's men on the Peace and the natives of one of the villages where the steamer had put in, but the main cause of Barttelot's lateness had been the necessity of making frequent stops so that Tippu-Tib could hold "palavers" with the local headmen and his own subordinate chiefs along the river below Stanley Falls.

Barttelot was furious when he discovered that Stanley had been about to send Stairs in search of him. He seems to have interpreted Stanley's anxiety as a lack of confidence in his (Barttelot's) capacity. This may well have been the case, but Stanley, perhaps to appease Barttelot, insisted that it was Tippu-Tib he did not trust. This failed to satisfy the Major, who very reasonably objected that if such were the case, it was a curious proceeding to have put the Expedition in a position of such dependence on the Arab chief. This was an un-answerable objection, and a point which is crucial to the under-standing of future events.

Barttelot's report, on his return, included the ominous information that Tippu-Tib was already beginning to hedge in the matter of the promised porters. On parting from Stanley at Bangala, Tippu-Tib had promised to present himself at Yambuya at the head of his men nine days after his arrival at Stanley Falls. On the way up to the Falls, however, he had learnt from Barttelot that the ammunition for his men was still at Leopoldville. He then gave Barttelot to understand that he considered Stanley's failure to have the ammunition ready on demand a breach of contract. The discussion between Barttelot and Tippu-Tib then ended on a rather inconclusive note:

I effected a sort of compromise by making him half-promise to supply, at any rate, 200 men with ammunition, to be repaid.[2]

Stanley, amazingly, appeared perfectly unperturbed at this unsatis-factory and tentative agreement, merely informing Barttelot that he never expected Tippu-Tib to keep to the nine-day deadline and that, if the worst came to the worst, the Expedition would manage without the extra carriers altogether.[3]

Stanley's apparent nonchalance regarding Tippu-Tib's intentions can only be explained, if at all, by the fact that his own plans for the next stage of the Expedition were laid in such a way as to make him personally quite independent of anything Tippu-Tib might or might not do. Briefly, his plan was this: the Expedition would now be divided into two parts. Barttelot, supported by Jameson, would take charge of the entrenched camp at Yambuya and would keep with him most of the stores, most of the Sudanese and all the sick. Here he would remain until (a) the *Stanley* returned with Troup and the loads left at Leopold-ville, and with Ward, Bonny and the one hundred and twenty-five men left at Bolobo, and (b) Tippu-Tib arrived with the extra porters. Meanwhile Stanley at the head of what he was pleased to call the "Advance Guard"—three hundred picked men and a relatively small proportion of the loads—would press on at once for the lake.

The division of forces at Yambuya, since it subsequently cost the lives of some two hundred men, became the subject of violent controversy on the Expedition's return to England. It is sufficient here to comment on just two aspects of the plan:

(1) Neither at the time nor at any subsequent time did Stanley advance a single coherent reason for dividing the Expedition. Indeed, it is perfectly impossible to discern what reason he could have advanced had he been inclined to do so. To say that the pre-cariousness of Emin's situation made speed essential[4] is no reason at all: Stanley's arrival at Lake Albert without the supplies which were the Expedition's *raison d'être* could in no way lessen the putative mishaps threatening Emin and his province. What then did Stanley hope to gain? There is no answer.

(2) The "Rear Guard" was left at Yambuya without a clear under-standing having been reached regarding its future actions. The whole proceeding was conducted in such a manner as to leave the Yambuya force in a situation bristling with ambiguities and uncertainties. Stanley not only failed to take Barttelot and the other officers fully into his confidence regarding his intentions, he failed even to provide the men he was leaving behind with unambiguous orders—either written or verbal—to guide their future actions. These omissions were made doubly dangerous by the fact that once the separation had taken

place it was unlikely (and in fact proved impossible) that there could be any communication or consultation between the two halves of the Expedition.

It is not even clear at what point Stanley made the decision to divide his forces. The first direct reference from any of the officers to such a plan occurs in Barttelot's diary for April 28, three days after leaving Stanley Pool, where he wries: "Stanley intends leaving me in the rear, I think, at least he told me so at Leopoldville." (This may, however, be a reference to Stanley's unrealised plan for leaving Barttelot at Bolobo.) Stanley had certainly decided his tactics, at least in outline, before leaving Leopoldville. His despatch from there to Mackinnon, dated April 26,[5] refers to "forming an entrenched camp" and then "pushing on lightly equipped". But there is nothing to suggest that he had discussed the plan with his officers. Possibly Stanley had entertained the notion even earlier, since on March 16, while still on board the *Madura*, Barttelot had noted enigmatically: "He (*Stanley*) has got some special job for me, but he won't tell me yet what it is."

The first intimation the other officers had of the plan seems to have been on May 15 during the stop at Bolobo. The relevant passages are as follows:

(JEPHSON): He has decided on taking the Sudanese on to the entrenched camp (i.e. *instead of leaving them at Bolobo*) & to leave Barttelot & Jameson in command with 100 men under them, whilest he, Stairs, Nelson & myself push on to Wadelai.
(PARKE): It is now arranged that Barttelot is to remain at the proposed entrenched camp at Yambuya.
(BARTTELOT): Jameson is, I believe, to stay behind with me at the Falls.
(JAMESON): Alas for all my bright dreams about the march from the Falls to Wadelai. Today Mr. Stanley informed me that I was to be left with Major Barttelot in command of the entrenched camp on the Aruwimi.

It may be noted that Parke, Jephson and Jameson refer to "the" entrenched camp, which suggests that the idea had previously been discussed and that all that was decided at Bolobo was who was to command it. At the same time, Stanley must have been playing his cards extremely close to his chest since Ward, who was present at

Bolobo, was not informed *at any time* of the decision to divide the Expedition and merely arrived at Yambuya to find Stanley gone.[6] The diary entries, too, are sufficiently laconic to imply that at this stage Stanley neither explained his plans in detail nor promoted any discussion of what was involved. Barttelot had apparently not even been told where the entrenched camp is to be located. However, his next reference to the matter is more explicit. On June 23, the day after he reached Yambuya, Barttelot wrote to a friend:

> Stanley intends to leave Jameson and me here; we are to await his return, which will be about five months; but I am going to try and persuade him otherwise.

This is the only unequivocal statement from any source on a crucial question: did Stanley propose to return to Yambuya after reaching Lake Albert, or did he intend Barttelot to follow in his tracks? From the above it is clear that originally Stanley intended to return for Barttelot and the stores. (This explains why Stanley was indifferent to the possibility of Tippu-Tib's being late with the carriers— Barttelot was not expected to move anyway. It does not, however, help to understand why Stanley made his dash for the Lake in the first place.) But the phrase "I am going to try and persuade him otherwise" again throws the whole issue in doubt, since it remains very far from clear what was decided when Barttelot applied to Stanley for permission to move on as soon as he could. That permission was granted, we know from Barttelot's own evidence,[7] but even this does not resolve the vital question of whether Barttelot's leaving Yambuya before Stanley's return was decided on as a definite policy, or left open as an option which Barttelot could adopt if he chose to do so. On balance the evidence favours the latter interpretation (despite Stanley's insistence that the contrary was true).

The day after Barttelot's interview with Stanley, in which Stanley had accorded permission for the Rear Guard to march under its own steam, Stanley delivered to Barttelot his famous "Letter of Instructions". This letter is not what Stanley later claimed it to be, a written order, but a list of instructions for the management of the Yambuya camp plus suggestions on how to conduct the march *should Barttelot decide to undertake it*. If it is not understood in this light, it cannot be understood at all since, while it clearly refers to the possibility of Barttelot's deciding to sit tight and await Stanley's return, it contains no guidance as to the circumstances under which such a decision is to be made. Moreover, while it refers to the eventuality of Tippu-Tib's failing to provide the full complement of carriers, it says nothing about the possibility of his providing none at all—the inference clearly being that in such a case Barttelot would not be undertaking the march, and that consequently the letter of instructions would not apply.

After digesting the "instructions" Barttelot had a second interview with Stanley, described by Barttelot as a "row" and by Stanley as a "conversation". The two versions—Barttelot's and Stanley's—of what passed between them differ wildly.[8] The only point they have in common is that one of the topics under discussion was the reliability of Tippu-Tib. Presumably Barttelot felt, as did Jameson, that this obviously vital issue needed some elucidation,[9] but the interview rapidly degenerated into a quarrel and nothing was decided. The result was that, for all the interviews, conversations, rows and letters of instructions, when the Advance Guard marched out of Yambuya on June 28, still no firm decision had been taken as to whether Barttelot was to await Stanley's return or march on his track. Stanley, writing after the event, does everything possible to make it seem that it was generally assumed that Barttelot would march the Rear Column to the Lake independently. If this were so Jephson would not have written in his diary for June 28 (the day of departure):

> The camp looked quite deserted & melancholy as we marched out, & Barttelot & Jameson felt very disconsolate at the prospect of their six months stay there with no prospect of anything to eat but rice and manioc.

*   *   *

In setting out from Yambuya and plunging into the forest to march to Lake Albert, Stanley was once more in his life taking a leap into the completely unknown. The only facts he had to guide him were that the south end of the Lake lay due east of Yambuya, and that the straight-line distance between the two was some three hundred and eighty miles.[10] But that three hundred and eighty miles was a total blank on the map. It had never before been traversed, not even by the Arabs:

... this is absolutely unknown. Is it all a forest?—then it will be an awful work. How far does the forest reach inland? A hundred—two hundred—three hundred miles? There is no answer. (STANLEY)

Stanley's calculations for the journey were premised on the assumption that the forest they would have to pass through shared the same general characteristics as other, known parts of the Congo Rain Forest: in particular, that the patterns of habitation and cultivation along the Aruwimi would be broadly similar to those along the Congo. Without villages at reasonable intervals the forest would be impassable, firstly because the Expedition was going to depend entirely on the inhabitants for food—manioc, plantains, maize and beans, grown in jungle clearings—and secondly because without villages there would be no paths. In his orders for the march Stanley wrote:

A conception of the character of more than half of the country to be traversed may be had by glancing at our surroundings. It will be a bush and forested country with a native path more or less crooked connecting the various settlements of the tribes dwelling in it. The track now and then will be intersected by others connecting the tribes north of our route and those south of it.

On the assumption that a straight-line distance of three hundred and thirty miles might entail a march of nearly double that distance, "say five hundred and fifty miles at an average of six miles per day, we should reach Lake Albert about the last day of September". It was a reasonable calculation, but one which events were to prove terribly wrong.

On June 27 a holiday was declared to permit the men to celebrate Bairam. Everything was now ready for the march. The *Peace* and the *Henry Reed* had been sent back to the Pool; the work on the fortifications was almost complete; Barttelot—much to his disgust—had been through a brotherhood ceremony with a local chief; the men had been organised into companies, the stores divided up.

The Advance Guard was to consist of three hundred and eighty-four men and five officers—Stanley, Jephson, Nelson, Stairs and Parke—a total of three hundred and eighty-nine. Barttelot's garrision would number one hundred and twenty-nine. This included seventy-six Zanzibaris, of whom forty were too sick to travel, and the majority of the surviving Sudanese. (Stanley took twelve Sudanese with him and left the remainder on the grounds that, as they were regular soldiers, they were best fitted for garrison duty.) One hundred and sixty-seven loads were left at Yambuya. Between two hundred and fifty and three hundred, including the Maxim gun and the steel boat, went with the Advance Column.

At the last moment there was some question of leaving Stairs behind. He was seriously ill and might even be dying. At his own insistence it was decided to take him along. Ten men were told off as litter-bearers.

> It is rather a rash undertaking to carry a man in his condition, though, if death is the issue, it comes as easy in the jungle as in the camp. (STANLEY)

And so, on the morning of June 28, the Advance Guard marched out of Yambuya camp with flags, drums and trumpets, and disappeared into the forest.

Stanley had a parting word for Barttelot: "Now, Major, we are in for it. Neck or nothing! Remember your promise and we shall meet before many months."

To which Barttelot replied: "I vow to goodness I shall be after you sharp. Let me once get those fellows from Bolobo and nothing shall stop me."[11]

*   *   *

The order of march was by three divisions. First went a group of forty picked "pioneers", armed with Winchesters and carrying axes, billhooks and machetes to clear the path. Behind them came the main division consisting of the loaded porters; in addition to their loads, each of them carried a rifle, bandoleer, rations and personal kit, so that many were carrying as much as eighty pounds' weight. (A Remington rifle alone weighed nine pounds.) Last came a rearguard of thirty men, also armed, but carrying no loads. Their duty was not so much to protect the rear of the column as to prevent straggling. The command of the various divisions was rotated daily among the officers.

At the first village they came to, they found the inhabitants drawn up in arms to contest their passage. The approach had been booby-trapped with hundreds of poisoned wooden skewers artfully concealed under leaves and twigs. They were about a foot long, sharp enough to

137

pierce the sole of a boot, and notched at the end so that the point would break off in the wound. Stanley was disinclined to waste time parleying. He ordered the advance guard to clear a way with their rifles, and the column passed through the village without loss, leaving the huts on fire behind them. Jephson, at the rear of the main division, saw nothing of the fighting but its aftermath:

> At about half past four we heard the guns going ahead & knew that a fight of some sort was going on. . . . As we approached the camp we heard the angry cries of the natives who had retired to an island a little way down the river. Soon we came to a village which had been burnt & was still burning & amongst the huts was a native who had been caught in the fire & the heat had burst his skull, it was a horrible sight.

The first day they made ten miles, but in the days and weeks that followed there were few days on which progress was so good. A few days after leaving Yambuya, Stanley wrote:

> Naturally, penetrating a trackless wild for the first time the march was at a funereal pace, in some places at the rate of four hundred yards an hour, in other more open portions, that is of less under-growth, we could travel at the rate of half, three-quarters and even a mile per hour—so that from 6.30 A.M. to 11 A.M. when we halted for lunch and rest, and from 12.30 P.M. to 3 o'clock or 4 P.M. in from six to seven hours per day, we could make a march of about five miles.

The difficulties attending the normally uncomplicated act of walking were terrible. Much of the track, where a track existed at all, lay through swamps and marsh.[12] In the neighbourhood of villages the paths were invariably found to be sown with poisoned skewers, and the game trails which the Expedition was often forced to follow for lack of a man-made path presented the added attraction of concealed game pits which were impossible to detect except by falling into. There were hundreds of streams and small rivers to be crossed. The tree canopy— in many places a hundred feet and more above their heads—shut out the sun and confined them in a grey twilight not merely gloomy but permanently damp. The temperature varied wildly from the bone-chilling mists of early morning to a mid-day heat which made the air a steam bath. Storms were frequent and violent. Everyone's clothes were permanently wet. At night it was impossible to sleep without a fire and often impossible to make one. And if a malevolent combination of topography and climate were insufficient, personal discomfort was further assured by animate pests in the form of ant armies, swarms of hornets and wasps, mosquitoes, chiggers,[13] and a particularly nasty species of tick which "fixes itself to the lining membrane of the nose, and requires forcible removal with a forceps, when it sometimes carries the mucous membrane with it, and is invariably gorged with blood". (PARKE)

Under such circumstances, five miles a day from barefoot, near-naked and underfed men with 80-lb. loads on their heads seems astonishingly good going. That they could be persuaded in the first place to undertake such work, under such conditions, for so little reward, and for an end of which they knew nothing, defies explanation.

By the end of the first week, the combined effects of the foul climate, hard physical work and irregular and insufficient food were beginning to show. In order to release as many men as possible from the necessity of bearing loads, Stanley decided to assemble and launch the steel boat. This automatically freed the forty-four men needed to carry it. Into it went the loads of another fifty carriers, and ten of the most seriously sick. The latter included Stairs, who, though recovering from his fever, was still too weak to march.

Thenceforward the Expedition advanced in two columns, one on the river and one by land, moving—subject to the idiosyncrasies of local topography—parallel. This arrangement committed the Expedition to keeping to the river, even though this might entail a lengthening of the march since the Aruwimi seemed to show a tendency towards the north. Stanley was willing to accept this disadvantage, as moving the whole column by land would reduce his reserve of unloaded carriers and force him to leave behind either the sick men or some of the loads, once the number of healthy carriers fell below a certain level. He reasoned, besides, that the most thickly settled areas would be found close to the river.

From time to time they were able to "secure" a canoe, and ultimately built up a flotilla of sixteen vessels.

With rare exceptions, the natives were not friendly. This entailed a number of added unpleasantnesses, not to say dangers, to the Expedition's already painful progress. In the first place, the inhabitants normally deserted their villages on the column's approach so that it became much more difficult to obtain food; meat became a rarity, as the villagers invariably took their livestock (goats and chickens) with them into the bush; often they took with them also their stored food (maize and beans), so the Expedition was reduced to what it could steal of manioc, corn and plantains from the garden plots. In the second place, the opposition of the natives was by no means merely passive. From now on the marching men were continually harassed by the Parthian attacks of unseen bowmen. Stragglers who fell out on the march, or unwary individuals who strayed from the camp in search of food, were frequently to pay with their lives for their carelessness; and neither stern warnings, nor harsh punishments, nor the unpleasant fate which overtook the unwary, would cure the Zanzibaris of their habit of wandering off alone or in twos and threes at peril of their lives. Finally, when the natives declined face-to-face contact, the only way to secure guides was by capture.

> Stanley always gets natives when he can, to get information from them, he puts them in chains for a few days & when he has got all the information he can out of them he lets them go. (JEPHSON)

Information was not the only commodity obtained by force:

> . . . Stanley pursued a canoe with four men in it—he shot one of the men & the others jumped ashore and got off. We towed the canoe to the other side of the river with the wounded native in it, but he bled to death before we reached the bank & the men threw him overboard.[14] He had been shot in the thigh. The men then washed the canoe & we manned & put loads into her. (JEPHSON)

Incidents of this kind are reported frequently in all the narratives. It is beyond the scope (and competence) of this account to inquire into the ethical side of the European impact on Africa. The moral imbalance which permits a man to kill another man in order to take his canoe from him, and yet allows him still to believe himself the representative of a morally superior race, is an interesting topic but external to the matter in hand.

On July 20, two men disappeared. There was no way of knowing what had happened to them, whether they had lagged behind and been killed by the natives or whether they had deserted.[15] And a few days later (August 2) the Expedition had its first death since leaving Yambuya—from dysentery—after thirty-six days of what Stanley termed "a most extraordinary immunity considering the hardships and privations to which we were all subjected". On the same day one of the donkeys died. There was no grass for them in the forest.

August 4 saw the Expedition at Panga Falls. They had covered approximately one third of the distance from Yambuya to the Lake, but in order to do so they had had to make a march of two hundred and seventy-two miles, and had taken thirty-six days to do it. It was a discouraging result. After thirty-six days they should have been more than half-way to their goal; and not only had they already fallen badly behind on Stanley's original estimates, but the advance was getting slower all the time as the health of the men got worse. There could be no hope of better marching until they got clear of the forest.

They portaged round the Falls and pressed on.

On August 14 a portion of the column was attacked from the far side of the river by a strong force of bowmen firing needle-pointed arrows tipped with poison. Sustained rifle fire drove off the attackers, but not before several of the Expedition had been wounded, among them the luckless Stairs, who had but recently recovered from his previous skirmish with mortality. An arrow entered his chest and broke off leaving the point embedded in the wound only an inch from the heart. These arrows were so small and the points so fine that the wounds seemed mere pinpricks. But a week later the wounded began one by one to die in agony, racked by spasms of what appeared to be tetanus. ("Wherefore I take it," remarked Stanley sagely, "to be a vegetable poison.") Stairs alone eventually recovered, though he carried the arrow-head in his chest wall for the next fifteen months.

Other men had been disabled by stepping on the pointed skewers. One had been shot in the foot by a careless or vindictive comrade, and Parke had to amputate the mangled extremity. Many of the men were incapacitated by huge sloughing ulcers which, starting from a scratch or pinprick, in a few days ate through to the bone.[16] The glossy skins of the Zanzibaris had turned a dull and deathly grey.

A muster on August 22 showed:

Healthy	316
Sick.................	57
Dead or missing	16
TOTAL	389

"Healthy" must be understood as a relative term. It meant "able to walk".

Wounds and disease were not the only causes of deterioration in the Expedition's physical state. From now on the diaries of Jephson and Parke show an increasing, and at times almost exclusive, preoccupation with the problem of getting enough to eat. Thus Parke—

August 22— . . . We are having a hard time of it. There is now no meat to eat—only unripe plantains to live on, and the work is dreadfully fatiguing. . . .

August 23— . . . I have eaten five small unripe plantains today, and feel very empty still.

August 26— . . . We encamped in a village just opposite the Falls,[17] where we got a supply of plantains and manioc.

August 27—We remained in camp all day, and the stronger men were sent in detachments to look for food. The plantains are improving as we go on. . . . Later on in the evening some unsuspecting chickens returned from the bush to roost in our village and they furnished us with some useful exercise in trying to catch them.

August 28—This perpetual marching through an apparently never-ending, dark, unbroken forest has (very naturally, I think) a most depressing effect on the men. . . . We are all looking worn-out—man and beast declining. Of the six donkeys we brought from Yambuya on the 28th of June, but three now survive, and one of these possesses at present but a very limited expectation of life. . . .

August 30— . . . It is marvellous how our men obey us so well, stick to their loads under such extreme hardships. Our last box of biscuits is still missing, although a party was sent back to look for it, but they failed to find it or its bearer. We had been keeping this box for an emergency. The emergency has come now, but where is the box of biscuits? . . .

August 30 was the day on which Stanley announced that the half-way mark had been reached—a calculation based on comparison of their present longitude with those of Yambuya and Lake Albert. In his letter to Emin, Stanley had allowed fifty-five days for the march to the Lake. August 30 was the sixty-fourth day out from Yambuya.

*　　　*　　　*

"The morning of that evil date, August 31st, dawned as on other days", wrote Stanley, looking back on a day that was to mark a drastic change for the worse in the Expedition's affairs.

They had reached the cataract of Basopo, a few miles above the Nepoko confluence and two hundred and ninety-six miles' march from Yambuya:

> We had 163 geographical miles in an air line to make yet, which we could never accomplish within 64 days as we had performed the western half of the route. The people were in an impoverished state of body, and mentally depressed, ulcers were raging like an epidemic, anaemia had sapped their vitality. They were told the half-way camp was reached, but they replied with murmurs of unbelief. (STANLEY)

On the morning of August 31 the boat had been taken out of the water and the men were cutting a road through the bush for the portage up the cataract. The work was nearly finished when Hoffman, Stanley's servant, dashed up to his master with the news that Emin Pasha was approaching down-river in a canoe flying the Egyptian flag. Stanley dropped what he was doing and galloped off to the head of the cataract to see for himself.

The canoe contained not Emin Pasha but fifty Manyuema. The flag was not the Khedive's but that of the Sultan of Zanzibar.[18]

The Manyuema, it appeared, were the followers of a Zanzibari slaver named Uledi Balyuz ("Uledi the Consul") and known to the natives as Ugarrowa.[19] He was camped some distance up-river having reached the Upper Aruwimi a few months earlier by an overland march from a point on the Congo between Nyangwe and Stanley Falls. The Manyuema in the canoe were a scouting party sent down by Ugarrowa to discover what river they were on and to explore the possibility of a water route to the Falls. Stanley gave them the information they sought and they departed, promising to prepare a welcome for the Expedition in a village some miles higher up.

Stanley's Zanzibaris were delighted at this meeting in the heart of an unknown wilderness with men who spoke their own language. The knowledge that an Arab encampment lay ahead had a revitalising effect on their morale. But for Stanley this sudden revelation of the Arabs' presence in an area he had supposed free of them was the worst of bad news. Up to now the Zanzibaris, despite their rapidly worsening condition, had been surprisingly amenable to the discipline imposed by the Expedition's aims; now, as Stanley foresaw, the proximity of the Arabs was likely to serve as a stimulus to desertion, and under present conditions even a few desertions might be accompanied by a total breakdown of discipline and morale among the remainder. A second and even more serious corollary of the Arabs' presence was its likely effect on the availability of food. The destructiveness of the ivory-hunters was notorious. They lived like locusts off the land and people, and what they did not consume they wantonly destroyed. In any country they had passed through the likelihood of the Expedition's finding the plentiful supplies it so desperately needed was much reduced.

On the day after the meeting the Expedition reached the village where the Manyuema scouts had camped. It was deserted.

At the gate was a dead male child, literally hacked to pieces; within the palisades was a dead woman who had been speared. The Manyuema had disappeared. (STANLEY)

We found some native children lying dead about the village ... — one poor little boy was still alive though his entrails were protruding from a spear wound in his stomach. (JEPHSON)

That night two men deserted, one with a box of ammunition, the other with the Expedition's entire supply of salt. A third man "was caught trying to desert with a box of European provisions—Stanley wished to hang him as an example to the rest but the chiefs would not hear of it & he was only put in chains." (JEPHSON) The crack-up had begun.

Extracts from Parke's diary convey the tone of the next few days' march:

September 3— ... I was on rear guard, and was obliged to leave one Zanzibari behind for want of transport, as he could not march. Before leaving camp we buried several tusks of ivory, some shovels, axes, &c., as we did not have sufficient hands to carry them further.

September 4— ... so many men have deserted since we met with Ugarrowa's people that it has been causing considerable confusion, and threatens disaster. Twelve men absconded last night with their rifles, and already about a dozen boxes of ammunition have been lost or taken by desertion . . . The rifles of a good many of the men—whom Mr. Stanley saw reason to suspect—were now disabled by having the spring taken out.

September 5—We are all without food. We left camp early; I was in advance, and we arrived early in the day at some villages where we got some plantains and three goats. The feasting which followed was simply luxurious, as we have been starving for so long. It takes at least two of our men in their present condition to bring one goat to a standstill. . . . Mr. Stanley never anticipated these difficulties, as he thought we should be at Wadelai about the 15th of August. . . .[20]

September 6— . . . We were so tired that we have opened some brandy (for the first time) and added it to our tea. Three men, who were unable to march, have been carried all day.

September 8— . . . This is the seventy-third day of our march; it is slow, and tries one's patience. . . .

September 9— . . . Foraging parties were sent across the river here; the men returned (very late) with large quantities of plantains, tobacco, and *bhang*—i.e. Indian hemp—which the natives smoke, and all of which we confiscated, as it is very injurious. . . .[21]

September 10— . . . Nelson's donkey, which had been on the eve of dying of starvation, strayed away into the bush and is lost: it is too weak to give us notice of its whereabouts by braying.

September 11— . . . Nelson had an unsuccessful hunt for his donkey. I went foraging with a party of forty men, and succeeded in getting some plantains. We were obliged to leave our Somali boy behind; he was unable to travel further, being literally reduced to a living skeleton—integument and bone.

September 12— . . . three sick men left behind in camp, as they were unable to march. . . .

September 13—Saadi . . . a chief in No. 2 Company, was sent back early this morning to hunt up one of his men who had not come in with his box of ammunition. As there is no sign of the return of either, we conclude that the Washenzi[22] have caught him. . . .

Meanwhile, the country through which they were passing showed evidence of the Arabs' destructive habits:

Navabi must have been a remarkable instance of aboriginal prosperity once. It possessed groves of the elais[23] and plantain, large plots of tobacco and indian corn; the huts under the palms looked almost idyllic; at least so we judged from two which were left standing. . . . Elsewhere the whole was desolate. Some parties, which we conjectured belonged to Ugarrowa, had burnt the settlement, chopped many of the palms down, levelled the banana plantations, and strewn the ground with the bones of the defenders. Five skulls of infants were found within our new camp at Navabi. (STANLEY)

And on September 14 some scouts reported finding the bodies of fifteen natives lying in the road, killed with bullets. The inference— that where bullets were, the Arabs were not far away—was borne out two days later. On September 16, as the Expedition was preparing to go into camp, a flotilla of canoes appeared on the river; a volley of musketry and the booming of many drums heralded the arrival of Ugarrowa in person:

About fifty strong, robust fellows accompanied him, besides singers and women, every one of whom was in prime condition of body. . . . Upon asking him if there was any prospect of food being obtained in the vicinity of his station, he admitted, to our sorrow, that his followers in their heedless way had destroyed everything, that it was impossible to check them because they were furious against the "pagans" for the bloody retaliation and excesses committed against many and many of their countrymen in their search for ivory. (STANLEY)

Although the country round had been devastated,[24] food—rice, onions, beans and corn—was grown at the settlement. On September 17 the Expedition encamped just below the village and a market was opened where the Zanzibaris could trade for food.

Ugarrowa showed himself an amiable host. "A nice looking man of the regular African-Arab type", wrote Jephson, "and speaks in a well mannered way." Stanley received presents of goats, rice, and "curried fowl, a dish I am not fond of, but which inspired gratitude in my camp".[25] The chief's treasures were paraded for Stanley's admiration. These included, in addition to a large store of ivory, a captive pygmy girl, the first of that race Stanley had seen:[26]

She measured thirty-three inches in height, and was a perfectly formed young woman of about seventeen, of a glistening and smooth sleekness of body. Her figure was that of a miniature coloured lady, not wanting in a certain grace, and her face was very prepossessing. Her complexion was that of a quadroon, or of the colour of yellow ivory. Her eyes were magnificent, but absurdly large for such a small creature—almost as large as that (sic) of a young gazelle; full, protruding and extremely lustrous. Absolutely nude, the little demoiselle was quite possessed, as though she were accustomed to be admired, and quite enjoyed inspection. (STANLEY)

The halt at Ugarrowa's lasted two days. During this time Stanley concluded a deal with Ugarrowa whereby the Expedition's sick would be left with the Arabs, who undertook—for a consideration—to lodge and feed them. Payment would take the shape of three hundredweight of gunpowder from the supplies carried by the Rear Column on their arrival. Ugarrowa further agreed to send a party down-river with despatches for Barttelot.

These arrangements considerably alleviated Stanley's immediate worries. "Once more", he exulted, "the Expedition consisted of picked men. My mind was relieved of anxiety respecting the rear column, and of the fate which threatened the sick men." The company returns now showed:

Able to march.........	271
Sick.................	56
Lost by death and desertion	62
TOTAL	389

On September 19, the two hundred and seventy-one men with one hundred and eighty loads left Ugarrowa's and continued the march. As before they proceeded in two columns, one by land and one by water. That evening some of Ugarrowa's men arrived by canoe at the Expedition's camp. They had with them three of Stanley's deserters, bound. Stanley expressed his thanks for the gift and rewarded the bearers. The prisoners were tied to trees for the night.

The next morning the men were assembled and it was explained to them "in fitting words" that the deserters had by their action imperilled the lives of their more loyal comrades. For this the punishment must be death. The men, according to Stanley, concurred heartily in their leader's reasoning. They agreed—or rather, Stanley proposed and no one objected—to hang one culprit per day for the next three days:

> They drew lots. . . . Mabruki was the first to go; so a rope was placed about his neck, and he was tied to the top of a flexible tree which was pulled down for the purpose. This tree, however, cracked; and, accordingly, could not rebound, so the rope was thrown over a strong branch, and he was pulled up by his comrades who were prisoners. When a short interval had elapsed and Mr. Stanley asked the question, "Is he dead?" I answered, "Yes," and the column immediately filed out of camp, leaving Mabruki's lifeless body hanging to the tree. (PARKE)[27]

The next day it was found that one of the two surviving prisoners had got away in the night.[28] Stanley took the head chief on one side and quietly let it be known that he would be amenable to a plea for clemency on behalf of the remaining prisoner. Accordingly, when the victim of the day was standing ready with the rope about his neck, the chiefs, at a prearranged signal, threw themselves at Stanley's feet begging loudly for his life. Stanley assented gravely and the man was pardoned. Stanley then improved the occasion by a stirring oration which, according to his own version, had an immediate and dramatic effect on morale, and provoked scenes of astonishing emotional violence. The men loudly protested their unshakeable loyalty till the forest shook with cries of—

Death to him who leaves Bula Matari![29]
Show the way to the Nyanza!
Lead on now—now we will follow! etc.

The days which followed were haunted by a desperate scarcity of food. A man whose ration for one day consisted of two unripe bananas or a single ear of Indian corn thought himself well off; the next day he might well have less. Their sustaining hope was that, having left Ugarrowa's village behind them, they must be nearing the outer edge of the Arabs' raiding circle, the area ravaged and made desolate by the "heedless" practices of Ugarrowa's men. But on the last day of September, ten days and fifty-one miles from the Arab village, this hope was taken from them. A group of half a dozen Manyuema, letting off their muskets to announce their presence, stalked into the camp. They were not Ugarrowa's men but belonged, they said, to another chief named Kilonga-Longa, whose station was some five days' march further on. This station, Stanley learnt to his dismay, formed the centre of a second raiding circle sited contiguously with that of Ugarrowa. Thus the Expedition, starving, and exhausted after a harrowing march of one hundred and twenty-six miles through country stripped bare of food and people by one Arab band, found itself on the outer edge of just such another area. There was no going around it; the only way was east along the river. They must go on or go back. Stanley made the only possible decision—to push on as fast as possible to Kilonga-Longa's station. There, at least, there must be food.

For five days, then, the march continued. But at the end of that time there was still no sight of the promised settlement, though there was ample evidence that the Expedition was moving through an Arab zone—in five days they had found only one spot where food (in this case bananas) was to be had. It was now evident to all the officers that a crisis point had been reached. Since Kilonga-Longa's village had not revealed itself at the end of five days, there was no way of knowing how many more days the journey would take; it might be another five, it might be fifteen or even fifty. Many of the men had reached a point where they were not merely too weak to continue the march, they were actually dying of hunger. Among those who could no longer continue was Nelson, whose legs and feet were a mass of putrid sores. And of those who were still able to walk, many were too weak to carry loads. The nature of the country, too, had changed, posing added difficulties. The river had shrunken considerably and was so much broken by rapids that a point was approaching where river travel was no longer a tenable proposition. The landscape, while still forested, was hilly and broken by ravines full of huge boulders. It was becoming increasingly difficult for the land and river columns to remain in touch.

On October 6 Stanley called a "shauri" (council) of the officers and chiefs to decide what should be done. It was decided that Nelson and fifty-two sick men too weak to travel should remain where they were. All the loads for which no carriers could be found would also be left. The steel boat was taken out of the water and taken to pieces for carrying. The canoes were sunk with stones where they could be recovered later if needed. A party of Zanzibari chiefs consisting of four volunteers under the head chief was detailed to leave immediately and, travelling light, endeavour to make contact with the Arabs and return with a relief party. Stanley, Jephson, Stairs, Parke and the remainder of the column would press on as best they could with the boat and as many loads as they could carry.

There was a strong probability, as they were all aware, that Nelson and many, if not all, of those with him were being left to their deaths. Yet it is hard to think of how, under the circumstances, matters could have been arranged in any other way. And it is typical of Stanley that once the decision was taken, he acted upon it with what appeared—to Jephson at least—a callous disregard for the likely fate of the men he was leaving behind. It would be, in a sense, irrelevant to take exception to this trait in Stanley's character. Had he been a man easily swayed by the possible consequences to others of his actions, he would not have been Stanley, or have achieved what Stanley achieved, any more than a general could plan or carry through a battle if he saw the realisation of his plans in terms of the cost in human suffering. It is the prerogative of the detached observer to see, if he so chooses, Stanley's crossing of the continent in terms of a trail, two thousand miles long, of dead, dying and crippled men. Such a notion was a luxury Stanley could hardly have afforded, even had his character rendered him capable of entertaining it.[30]

Stanley marched off with his loads without hardly taking the trouble to say goodbye to Nelson & left us to look after the loads as best we could—he certainly never troubles himself to say a good word or a nice thing to us and gives his orders with a kind of snarl. . . . We got off by about two o'clock & said goodbye to poor old Nelson very sadly, for his position is very precarious & our chances of relieving him slight. . . . (JEPHSON)

And for Parke—

It was altogether the most heart rending goodbye I have ever experienced or witnessed. I cannot fancy a more trying position than that of abandoning in this wilderness of hunger and deso-lation our white companion and so many faithful men; every one of whom has risked his life dozens of times for the relief of our hypothetical friend, Emin Pasha.

Travelling was by now a nightmare of weakness, hunger and privation. The men were so enfeebled, and so much time was lost in foraging for food, that they averaged only three miles a day. Their diet was as meagre as it was repulsive. They subsisted principally on edible fungi and "a sort of large flat bean which drops from the trees, it has a very unpleasant taste like a horse chestnut." (JEPHSON) In addition—

Grubs were collected, also slugs from the trees, caterpillars, and white ants—these served for meat. The *mabengu* (nux vomica) furnished the dessert, with *fenessi* or a species of bastard jack-fruit. (STANLEY)

Men who collapsed on the march, or crawled off into the forest at the side of the path to die, were simply left where they lay. The rear-guard picked up the rifles and loads of the fallen. Many of the porters no longer had the strength to lift their loads onto their heads or shoulders, and one of the officers had to lift their burdens into position for them after each halt or rest. Desertions, despite the exemplary hanging, continued:

Kajeli stole a box of Winchester ammunition and absconded. Salim stole a case containing Emin Pasha's new boots and two pairs of mine and deserted. Wadi Adam vanished with Surgeon Parke's entire kit. Swadi, of No. 1 Company, left his box on the road, and departed himself to parts unknown. Bull-necked Uchungu followed suit with a box of Remington cartridges. (STANLEY)

On October 15 one of the two surviving donkeys was killed for food.[31] Stanley gave one pound of meat to each man. The Zanzibaris fought like dogs for the hide, intestines and hoofs. Some of them even lapped the spilled blood from the ground. In a few minutes there was nothing left of the wretched beast but a handful of hair and a stain on the earth.

The next day their spirits were somewhat raised when the pioneers came on a well-used track where the trees bore the unmistakable blazes of the Manyuema—"a discovery that was transmitted by every voice from the head to the rear of the column, and was received with jubilant cheers". (STANLEY) They now had reason to hope that the Arab settlement really was within reach.

We were frightfully thin, the whites not so much reduced as the coloured men. We thought of the future and abounded with hope, though deep depression followed any inspection of the people. . . . Hunger followed by despair killed many. . . . They had fared badly and suffered greatly. It is hard to walk at all when weakness sets in through emptiness; it is still worse to do so when burdened with sixty pounds weight. Over 50 were yet in fair condition; 150 were skeletons covered with ashy grey skins, jaded and worn out, with every sign of wretchedness printed deep in their eyes, in their bodies and movements. These could hardly do more than creep on and moan, and shed tears and sigh. (STANLEY)

In this condition, on October 18, they came at last on the Arab settlement at a place called Ipoto:

One hour after starting on the march, we heard reports of guns in the distance, ahead of us. These we gladly answered. We felt certain that the Arabs were near, and, with newly inspired vigour, we pushed on to the brow of the hill, at which we came upon a large clearing, every inch of which was planted with corn and rice, and at the opposite border of which we sighted the longed-for Arab village. (PARKE)

*　　　*　　　*

Stanley has this to say about the people among whom the Expedition now found itself:

This community of ivory hunters established at Ipoto had arrived, five months previous to our coming, from the banks of the Lualaba (Upper Congo). . . . The journey had occupied them seven-and-a-half months, and they had seen neither grass nor open country, nor even heard of them during their wanderings. They had halted a month at Kinnena on the Lindi, and had built a station-house for their Chief Kilonga-Longa,[32] who, when he had joined them with the main body, sent on about 200 guns and 200 slave carriers to strike further in a north-easterly direction, to discover some other prosperous settlement far in advance of him, whence they could sally out in bands to destroy, burn and enslave natives in exchange for ivory.[33] On reaching the Lenda River (a tributary of the Aruwimi/

152

Ituri) they had heard of the settlements of Ugarrowa, and sheered off the limits of his raiding circle to obtain a centre of their own, and, crossing the Lenda, they succeeded in reaching the south bank of the Ituri, about south of their present settlement at Ipoto.

As the natives would not assist them over the river to the north bank, they cut down a big tree and with axe and fire hollowed it into a sizeable canoe which conveyed them across to the north bank to Ipoto. Since that date they had launched out on one of the most sanguinary and destructive careers to which even Tippu-Tib's or Tagamoyo's[34] career offers but poor comparison. Towards the Lenda and Ihuru rivers, they had levelled into black ashes every settlement, their rage for destruction had even been vented on the plantain groves, every canoe on the river had been split into pieces, every island had been searched, and into the darkest recesses, whither a slight track could be traced, they had penetrated with only one dominating passion, which was to kill as many of the men and capture as many of the women and children as craft and cruelty would enable them. However far northward or eastward these people had reached, one said nine days' march, another fifteen days; or wherever they had gone, they had done precisely as we had seen between the Lenda River and Ipoto, and reduced the forest land to a howling wilderness, and throughout all the immense area had left scarcely a hut standing.

What these destroyers had left of groves and plantations of plantain and bananas, manioc and corn-fields, the elephant, chimpanzee and monkeys had trampled and crushed into decaying and putrid muck, and in their places had sprung up, with the swiftness of mushrooms, whole hosts of large-leafed plants native to the soil, briars, calamus and bush, which the natives had in times past suppressed with their knives, axes and hoes. With every season the bush grew more robust and taller, and a few seasons only were wanted to cover all traces of former habitation and labour.

From Ipoto to the Lenda the distance by our track is 105 miles. Assume that this is the distance eastward to which their ravages have extended, and we have something like 44,000 square miles. We know what Ugarrowa has done from the preceding pages, what he was still doing with all the vigour of his mind, and we know what the Arabs in the Stanley Falls are doing on the Lumami and what sort of devil's work Mumi Muhala,[35] and Bwana Mohamed[36] are perpetrating around Lake Ozo, the source of the Lulu, and, once we know where their centres are located, we may with a pair of compasses draw great circles round each, and park off areas of 40,000 and 50,000 square miles into which half a dozen resolute men, aided by their hundreds of bandits, have divided about three-fourths of the Great Upper Congo Forest for the sole purpose of murder, and becoming heirs to a few hundred tusks of ivory.

At the date of our arrival at Ipoto there were the Manyuema headmen, physically fine stalwart fellows, named Ismaili, Khamisi, and Sangarameni, who were responsible to Kilonga-Longa, their chief, for the followers and operations entrusted to their charge. At alternate periods each set out from Ipoto to his own special sub-district. . . . Altogether there were 150 fighting men, but only about 90 armed with guns. Kilonga-Longa was still at Kinnena and was not expected for three months yet.

The fighting men under the three leaders consisted of Bakusu, Balegga, and Basongora youths who were trained by the Manyuema as raiders in the forest region in the same manner as in 1876, Manyuema youths had been trained by Arabs and Waswahili of the east coast. We see in this extraordinary increase in number of raiders in the Upper Congo basin the fruits of the Arab policy of killing off the adult aborigines and preserving the children. The girls are distributed among the Arab, Swahili and Manyuema harems, the boys are trained to carry arms and are exercised in the use of them. When they are grown tall and strong enough they are rewarded with wives from the female servants of the harem, and then are admitted partners in these bloody ventures. So many parts of the profits are due to the great proprietors, such as Tippu-Tib or Said bin Abed,[37] a less number becomes the due of the headmen, and the remainder becomes the property of the bandits. At other times large ivories, over 35 lbs. each, become the property of the proprietor, all over 20 lbs. to 35 lbs. to the headmen, scraps, pieces and young ivory are permitted to be kept by the lucky finders. Hence every member of the caravan is inspired to do his best. The caravan is well armed and well manned by the proprietor, who stays at home on the Congo or Lualaba river indulging in rice and pilaf and the excesses of his harem, the headmen, inspired by greed and cupidity, become ferocious and stern, the bandits fling themselves upon a settlement without mercy to obtain the largest share of loot, of children, flocks, poultry, and ivory. (STANLEY)[38]

The Expedition, having arrived at Ipoto in an advanced state of moral and physical destitution, was now largely dependent on the generosity, or at least the good will, of these rapacious malefactors. Stanley's immediate concerns were, firstly, to get food for his people, and secondly, to organise a relief column to return to "Starvation Camp" for Nelson and the eighty-one loads that had been left there. Neither could be done without the co-operation of the Manyuema. But the headmen Khamisi, Sangarameni, and Ismaili were conspicuously unwilling to follow the now almost traditional pattern of hospitable helpfulness which the Arab slavers had so often shown in the past to explorers in trouble. Their outward behaviour veered unpredictably between the obsequious and the obstructive, but their basic attitude was not hard to discern: the piteous state of the Expedition aroused in them not a spirit of selfless generosity but visions of easy prey and rich pickings. Perceiving the weakness of Stanley's position, they meant to sell their help dear. For a broad hint as to the terms on which dealings would have to be conducted, the travellers need look no further than the armed guards that were placed on the fields and plantations to greet the Expedition on its arrival.

Two circumstances aggravated the weakness of Stanley's bargaining position: he dared not permit an open breach with the Manyuema since he planned to avail himself of Ipoto to dump yet another batch of the Expedition's sick; secondly, and worse, he had now almost exhausted his supply of ready cash—cloth, beads, and mitako—and so had nothing to bargain with except ammunition, which he could not afford to part with, and IOUs on Barttelot, which the Manyuema were reluctant to accept.[39]

The upshot was that the men, who had looked forward to Ipoto as to Paradise, found themselves issued with two heads of corn per man per day—the best deal Stanley could make for them. Understandably dismayed, they concluded that their leader was falling down on his duty, and proceeded to remedy the situation as best they could by bartering their pathetic possessions for food. When some of them, in desperation, went so far as to sell their rifles, Stanley reacted sharply. He had all those found without arms flogged, and a man who had stolen the rifles of two of his comrades hanged.

Stairs, Parke and Jephson had also been reduced to selling their meagre belongings—empty bottles, needles, old clothes, and the like— in a buyer's market. This was particularly hard on Parke who had already lost nearly everything he owned by the desertion of the porter who had charge of his clothes. Both Jephson and Parke expressed their indignation at Stanley's thus leaving them to fend for themselves, especially as the terms of their engagement specifically made the Expedition responsible for feeding them. (The same, indeed, was true of the Zanzibaris.) Whether Stanley's refusal to part with what remained of his trade goods was the product—as Parke and Jephson supposed—of meanness and indifference, or whether he was ruled by the desire not to appear before Emin penniless, is a matter for speculation.

For the officers an additional worry was the possibility of being left behind at Ipoto, "stranded here a dependant on the charity of slaves", as Jephson put it. Stanley's first intention had, in fact, been to leave Jephson behind with Nelson and the sick, but later he changed his mind, deputed the care of the sick to Parke, and told Jephson off to relieve Nelson and then rejoin the main column. The Manyuema had promised eighty porters for the relief party but kept putting off their departure on various pretexts. It was not until October 26, when the Expedition had already been a week at Ipoto, that a relief column was finally got together. Of the eighty men promised, only thirty materialised. Stanley made the number up to seventy with his Zanzibaris. By way of supplies Jephson received for himself and the Zanzibaris "one hundred and ten heads of Indian corn . . . but half of these were so small and unripe that the number might be put down at half".[40] For Nelson himself there were "a good sized plateful of coarse hard flour and one small chicken". For the men left with Nelson there was nothing at all. Jephson adds:

> When this was brought in he (Stanley) remarked that it was an ample allowance for that time. I said nothing but I think my face must have expressed the disgust I felt at the scandalous smallness & meanness of the allowance for a few minutes after the food was taken away to my hut he sent another small chicken for me to take on.

Thus sumptuously equipped, Jephson led the relief column out of Ipoto on October 26. The next day Stanley set out with the main column in the opposite direction. Before leaving he presented Parke with a set of written orders, which constitute a most peculiar document. As often happens when Stanley is ostensibly explaining his intentions, the explanations are in themselves so confused and even totally irrational as to give the impression that he is trying to conceal what he purports to be trying to clarify. Part of the orders deals with the method of storing the loads that are to be left behind, and gives details of particular items that are to be sent with the main column. The remainder is as follows:

Arab village, Oct. 24th, 1887.
My dear Doctor Parke,
I am so reduced in numbers now that I have not men sufficient to carry what is indispensable I should do to appear before Emin Pasha with any appearance of success. This morning it came near to being a question whether I could take one officer with me, for the volunteers number only 103. Fortunately the Arabs here were persuaded to use forceful words and menaces to the lazy loons who prefer living on two ears of corn daily than walk for wages with me to the lake, which gave me 43 indifferent men more. Therefore I see my way to take Lieut. Stairs along, also Mr. Jephson, on condition they reduce their baggage. They have two boys each, and each boy is capable on emergency, which may come yet, to carry a load. The two officers must have one small medicine chest. . . . They must have 25 lbs. of bedding, and 25 lbs. weight of clothing each, and one box of European provisions between them. There are four loads already. I take the large tent with me, which will house us all. It makes seven loads. Were I alone, I should take a small tent (three loads), and leave the large tent behind. This gives eight loads to carry for the sake of two officers. I have been in the habit of taking 20 per cent of the entire force as supernumary. I now take 50 per cent to save loss of goods on the road. The condition of the people compels this as I have only 144 carriers. I dare take only 72 loads, 40 of which must be Remingtons (sc.—ammunition). Now if you compute tent, Winchesters, brass rods, medicine chests, chronometers, instruments, officers' baggage, &c., you will see how hard driven we are.

We have a great number of people yet, but they are scattered along the long track. Total No. 546. Therefore (sic) it is necessary that you should stay at this place, and look after the sick, and assist Capt. Nelson in keeping on friendly terms our men and the Arab men. . . . It may be that I shall send a caravan for your goods if I can have aid of any carriers from Emin Pasha. If so, then one of you two officers should accompany the column. If I bring the caravan, both of you may be able to go and stay with Emin Pasha. But by letter or personally I can explain this better later. . . . Good-bye, take care of yourself, and Nelson, and our sick people. Keep by all means on good terms with the Arabs, and it is most likely that we may all meet within a few months.

Yours faithfully,
Henry M. Stanley.[41]

Parke's comments on this farrago are, unfortunately, not recorded. The implication that the value of the officers to the Expedition was calculable solely in terms of how many porters were needed for their effects can hardly have been very flattering. And Stanley's apparent casualness regarding future arrangements for the rescue of the officers and men he was deserting may well have filled Parke with the gloomiest of forebodings. (These were to be amply realised.) Strangest of all is the statement that Stanley took on with him only "volunteers", and the implied corollary that he was prepared—if unwillingly—to allow the men to decide for themselves whether they would continue to follow him. That Stanley was capable of such an attitude is simply not believable. His own account contains no reference to anything of the kind. Why he should take the trouble of making such strange statements to Parke baffles conjecture.

Twenty-nine sick men were to be left at Ipoto, together with the boat, the Maxim gun, forty-seven rifles, and a tent full of miscellaneous loads, mostly ammunition. Before leaving, Stanley made, or claimed to have made, a written agreement with the Manyuema chiefs for the feeding of Parke, Nelson and the sick men. These services were to be paid for in cloth on the arrival of Barttelot's column. Though he must have known that the Manyuema were as likely to renege on the agreement as not, Stanley neglected the elementary precaution of having Parke present when the agreement was made, and failed even to apprise him in detail of its terms. This left Parke, as he himself put it with characteristic understatement, "in an exceedingly awkward position".

The main column left Ipoto on the morning of October 27. It consisted of Stanley, Stairs and one hundred and forty-six men. Parke noted that "almost all of these men were loaded"—a fact which would appear to make nonsense of the laborious calculations in Stanley's orders. Stanley did not say goodbye to Parke.

158

Twelve days' marching now lay between them and the furthest limits of Manyuema territory. The forest beyond Ipoto was inhabited partly by pygmies, whose camps (always deserted) occurred at intervals along the route, and partly by a tribe named Balessé. The latter practised a type of shifting cultivation which involved felling large trees to form a clearing open to the sunlight and then planting corn and bananas among the debris of fallen wood:

Another peculiarity of the Balessé is the condition of their clearings, and some of these are very extensive, quite a mile and a half in diameter, and the whole strewn with the relics, debris, and timber of the primeval forest. Indeed I cannot compare a Balessé clearing to anything better than a mighty abattis surrounding the principal village, and over this abattis the traveller has to find his way. As one steps out of the shadow of the forest, the path is at first, may be along the trunk of a great tree for 100 feet, it then turns at right angles along a great branch for a few feet; he takes a few paces on the soil, then finds himself in front of a massive prostrate tree-stem 3 feet in diameter or so; he climbs over that, and presently finds himself facing the out-spreading limbs of another giant, amongst which he must creep, and twist, and crawl to get footing on a branch, then from the branch to the trunk, he takes a half turn to the right, walks along the tree from which, increasing in thickness, he must soon climb on top of another that has fallen across and atop of it, when after taking a half-turn to the left, he must follow, ascending it until he is 20 feet above the ground. When he has got among the branches at this dizzy height, he needs judgment, and to be proof against nervousness. After tender, delicate balancing, he places his foot on a branch—at last descends cautiously along the steep slope until he is 6 feet from the ground from which he must jump on to another tapering branch, and follow that to another height of 20 feet, then along the monster tree, then down to the ground, and so on for hours, the hot, burning sun, and the close, steamy atmosphere of the clearing forcing the perspiration in streams from his body. I have narrowly escaped death three times during these frightful gymnastic exercises. One man died where he fell. . . . We have often congratulated ourselves on coming to a clearing at the near approach to camping-time, but it has frequently occupied us one hour and a half to reach the village. It is a most curious sight to see a caravan laden with heavy burdens walking over this wreck of a forest, and timbered clearing. Streams, swamps, watercourses, ditches are often twenty to twenty-five feet below a tapering slippery tree, which crosses them bridge-like. Some men are falling, some are tottering, one or two have already fallen, some are twenty feet above the ground, others are on the ground creeping under logs. Many are wandering among a maze of branches, thirty or more may be standing on one delicate and straight shaft, a few may be posted like sentries on a branch, perplexed which way to move. All this, however, is made much harder, and more dangerous, when, from a hundred points, the deadly arrows are flying from concealed natives, which, thank heaven, were not common. We have been too cautious for this kind of work to happen often, though we have seldom been able to leave one of those awful clearings without having some man's foot skewered, or some one lamed. . . . Never were such a series of clearings as those around Mambungu, and the neighbouring settlement of Njalis. The trees were of the largest size, and timber enough had been cut to build a navy; and these lay, in all imaginable confusion, tree upon tree, log above log, branches rising in hills above hills; and amongst all this wild ruin of woods grew in profusion upon profusion bananas, plantains, vines, parasites; ivy-like plants, palms, calamus, convolvuli, etc., through which the poor column had to burrow, struggle and sweat, while creeping, crawling, and climbing, in, through, and over obstacles and entanglements that baffle description. (STANLEY)

The villages through which they passed had been raided but not destroyed. The Manyuema had so far contented themselves with extorting tribute of food and livestock (and of course ivory) from the inhabitants, whose villages then had to fly a flag as sign of submission to the raiders' rule. The Expedition therefore managed occasionally to supplement their diet of berries and fungi with a few heads of corn or a handful of half ripe bananas per man.

On November 9, seventy-nine miles from Ipoto, they reached a complex of villages named Ibwiri. Here they realised they had reached the outer limit of the circle of death and destruction through which their path had lain for the last two hunded and fifty miles:

This was one of the richest and finest clearings we had seen since leaving Yambuya, though had the Expedition been despatched eight months earlier,[42] we should have found scores in the same prosperous condition. Here was a clearing three miles in diameter abounding in native produce, and hitherto unvisited by the Manyuema.[43] Almost every plantain stalk bore an enormous branch of fruit, with from fifty to one hundred and forty plantains attached. Some specimens of this fruit were twenty-two inches long, two and a half inches in diameter, and nearly eight inches round. . . . There was an odour of ripe fruit pervading the air, and as we climbed over the logs and felt our way gingerly along the prostrate timber, I was often asked by the delighted people to note the bunches of mellow fruit hanging temptingly before their eyes. . . . This was a great day. Since August 31st not one follower of the Expedition had enjoyed a full meal, but now bananas, plantains ripe and green, potatoes, herbs, yams, beans, sugar-cane, corn, melons in such quantities were given them that were they so many elephants they could not have exhausted the stock provided for them in less than ten days. (STANLEY)

Here the Expedition rested. The men addressed themselves single-mindedly to the business of cramming three months' eating into as many days, while Stanley waited for Jephson to rejoin with his detachment plus any men he might have been able to salvage from Nelson's party.

Jephson reached Ibwiri on November 16. He found Stanley's men already grown sleek, but Jephson, after travelling one hunded and seventy miles in just three weeks in a state of near starvation and with sick, famished and mutinous men, was near the limit of endurance. After leaving Ipoto he had marched back along the Expedition's track and found it scattered with the rotting, ant-eaten bodies of the men who had failed to reach Ipoto. In four days he had covered the distance which had taken the Main Column twelve.

As we were hurrying along within half a mile of Nelson's camp we suddenly came on a half starved man wearily searching for fruit or fungus, he was one of the sick men left with Nelson. In great excitement I plied him with questions & learned that Nelson was alive but in great straits for food & was much pulled down from hunger. Without waiting to hear more I pushed on & soon got to the camp. As I entered it not a sound was to be heard except the groans of two men dying in a hut close by, the whole place looked woebegone and deserted. I came quietly round the tent & found

Nelson sitting there—he started up with an exclamation of astonishment, we clasped hands & then poor old chap he turned away & sobbed like a child & muttered something about being very weak, twenty two days of hunger & torturing anxiety with the suspicion that we had abandoned him had brought him down in body & mind—as for me with an hysterical gulpy feeling I rushed off & began to prepare some food & after putting it down to the fire I returned to the tent to hear Nelson's experiences during the 22 days he had been left. Seventeen men had died. . . . Others had deserted at different times & out of 56 men left with Nelson only 6 men were left, two of whom were in a dying state & the other four so reduced by illness and hunger that only two would be able to drag themselves after me to the Arab camp. (JEPHSON)

Jephson succeeded in getting Nelson back to Ipoto, and left him there in the care of Surgeon Parke. He then hurried in Stanley's wake. He took with him written reports from Parke and Nelson which gave a clear picture of the sort of treatment, or rather mistreatment, Parke and Nelson could look forward to at the hands of the Manyuema. Already the slavers had embarked on a systematic attempt to starve the white men into a state where either they would be willing to trade weapons and ammunition for food, or would no longer be capable of defending the stores left in their charge. After receiving these reports at Jephson's hands, Stanley could hardly claim ignorance of the unpleasant situation in which he had left his two officers, and in which he proposed to leave them for a further indefinite period. Since the Expedition's arrival at Ibwiri, the condition of the Zanzibaris had so greatly improved that it would not have been a great matter to extricate Parke and Nelson from Ipoto. Granted that the shortage of porters was the governing factor, the men and loads could still have been transferred to a camp outside the limits of the Manyuema raiding circle. The thing could have been accomplished in two weeks, or three at the most. And quite apart from humanitarian considerations, leaving the steel boat at Ipoto proved to be a major miscalculation which added four months to the Expedition and, arguably, radically affected the whole course of future events.

But Stanley, as always, had no time for and no interest in what lay behind him. He waited a few more days at Ibwiri feeding and resting the men and waiting for the last stragglers from Jephson's column to come in. Then, on November 24, the Expedition set out on the last stage of its journey to the Lake:

> We were all in good spirits & the men are in splendid condition for going. They had large supplies of flour, corn, bananas, sweet potatoes etc, enough to last them 5 or 6 days. We did a march of 9 miles. . . . (JEPHSON)

For another week they marched through broken but still thickly wooded country, covering about nine miles a day. At last, on December 4, after one hundred and fifty-nine days in the forest and a march of six hundred and twenty miles, they emerged into open country. Quite suddenly the encircling trees fell away from them and—

> A hundred square miles of glorious country opened to our view .... Leagues upon leagues of bright green pasture land undulated in gentle waves . . . and far away to the east rose some frowning ranges of mountains beyond which we were certain slept in its deep gulf the blue Albert. (STANLEY)

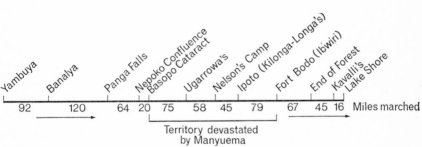

Fig. 1: The March from Yambuya to Lake Albert.

It was a rich and rolling country, watered by many streams. Game and cattle fed on the young grass. Here and there were villages surrounded by maize and millet plots and plantain groves. But while it seemed a paradise to men so long accustomed to the constricting gloom of the grassless and stifling forest, their presence did not go long unchallenged. The quiet country reacted to their arrival by bursting into angry life like a wasps' nest poked with a stick. By the third day after the Expedition's emergence from the forest, the hills along the line of march were swarming with crowds of armed and angry natives waving their weapons and shouting defiance.

On December 9 the Expedition camped on a hilltop in a strong

M   163

position, which they fortified with a thorn boma. Local agitation had now reached such a pitch that—

Stanley determined not to move until either the natives made friends with us or we gave them a good licking. (JEPHSON)

Peace negotiations were started through the medium of a Zanzibari who understood the local language. These overtures appeared to have no effect on the angry mood of the inhabitants. A punitive sortie was decided on:

The companies were mustered, and fifty rifles were led out by Lieutenant Stairs towards these obstinate and fierce fellows on the other side of the Ituri branch. A party of thirty rifles were sent under Mr. Jephson to skirmish up the slopes to the left; and twenty picked men were sent with Uledi to make a demonstration to the right. Rashid was ordered with ten men to the top of Nzera-Kum to guard against surprise from that quarter. . . . In a few minutes Stairs' company was hotly engaged. The natives received our men with cool determination for a few minutes, and shot their arrows in literal showers; but the Lieutenant, perceiving that their coolness rose from the knowledge that there was a considerable stream between them and his company, cheered his men to charge across the river. His men obeyed him, and as they ascended the opposite bank opened a withering fire which in a few seconds broke up the nest of refractory and turbulent fellows who had cried out so loudly for war. The village was taken with a rush and the banana plantations scoured. The natives broke out into the open on a run, and fled far northward. Lieutenant Stairs then collected his men, set fire to the village, and proceeded to the assault of other settlements, rattling volleys from the company announcing resistance they met.

Meanwhile, Uledi's party of chosen men had discovered a path leading up the mountain along a spur, and after ascending 500 feet, (he) led his men up into view on the right flank of the mob observing and cheering their countrymen in the valley. The Winchesters were worked most handsomely. At the same time Mr. Jephson's party came out of the left ravine, and together they had such a disastrous effect on the nerves of the natives that they fled furiously up the slopes, Uledi and his men chasing them.

Mr. Jephson, after seeing them in full flight, faced eastward, and pushed on for two miles, clearing every inhabitant out. By 1 P.M. all our men were in camp, with only one man slightly wounded. Every man had behaved wonderfully well. . . . (STANLEY)

The "lesson", as Stanley called it, was repeated that afternoon, and again the next day, till, on the evening of December 11—

. . . a native stood on a high hill above our position after all had reached camp, and announced that he had been sent by Mazamboni[44] to say that he had received our gifts, but that he had been prevented from visiting us according to his promise by the clamour of his young men, who insisted on fighting. But now, as many of them had been killed, he was ready to pay tribute, and be a true friend in future.[45]

Two days having passed in this type of intercourse, the Expedition marched out of camp unmolested at dawn on December 12. But by late morning they found they were once more being dogged by bands of yelling warriors whose numbers were constantly increasing:

. . . the natives as before gathered on the hills & shouted and jeered at us. They were very afraid of our guns especially as Stanley killed a man on the hills at a distance of full 600 yards, but they followed closely on the rearguard & began to get very bold. Stanley moved the column rapidly across a deep ravine &, ordering the men to put down their loads, turned on them suddenly & having driven them away to some distance burned all the huts round & so quieted them. We then marched on & camped in a small village at the top of a hill & got a cheerful view of the huts burning below. (JEPHSON)

The next day (December 13) the column travelled through the morning accompanied as before by groups of armed tribesmen expressing noisy hostility from just out of rifle range. In the afternoon they were marching across flat and open country:

We could see nothing before us but a mile or so of smooth plain with small "doddered" bushes dotted about & then it suddenly seemed to end in the clouds—Stanley turned round to me &

nodded his head. In ten minutes cheer after cheer burst from the men ahead & several of them rushed madly up & down shouting out "Nyanza Nyanza, cheer for Bula Matari." On coming up we found we were on a table-land, & there 2500 feet below us lay the Lake glittering like silver in the sun. (JEPHSON)

NOTES AND REFERENCES

CHAPTER 4   YAMBUYA TO LAKE ALBERT

1   The *Stanley* had started back to the Pool on June 20.

2   I.e. Tippu-Tib would provide their ammunition and Stanley would reimburse him either in money or in kind. (BARTTELOT pp. 108–109.)

3   D.A. I pp. 121–122; BARTTELOT p. 108 and p. 113n.

4   This is, in fact, the nearest Stanley comes to an explanation. See D.A. I pp. 103–104 and pp. 109–110.

5   Printed in *The Times*, June 17, 1887.

6   H. WARD p. 24. Troup was not informed either. Indeed, both were misinformed. The letters of instruction Stanley sent down by the steamer to Troup and Ward created—in a manner which cannot have been accidental—the impression that Stanley was waiting for them at Yambuya. To Ward he wrote:". . . believe me anxious for your early arrival here as my lieutenant". To Troup: "When you join us we shall be all heartily glad, and you need have no fear of separation afterwards." This deliberate dishonesty can only be explained as an attempt to guard against Troup and Ward leaving the Expedition in disgust without bothering to go up to Yambuya, an action which Stanley presumably supposed them capable of had they known in advance that they were to be left behind.

7   BARTTELOT (June 23): "I had a long talk with Stanley in the afternoon and he gave me permission to move on eastward directly Ward and Troup, etc., were up."

8   Stanley's version (D.A. I pp. 117–126) is too obviously fictionalised and for too obvious a reason for it to be of much use in elucidating the nature of his arrangements with Barttelot. At one point in the conversation Stanley gives himself the lines: "I don't like the word 'Kudos'. The kudos impulse is like the pop of a ginger-beer bottle, good for a V.C. or an Albert Medal, but it effervesces in a month in Africa. It is a damp squib." It is barely conceivable that Stanley may actually have said this. It is totally inconceivable that he should expect either Barttelot, or the readers of his book, to believe him capable of a sentiment which his whole career flatly contradicts.

9   "It (the letter) is clear on every point, but as regards our relations with Tippu-Tib's people, I think we might have been told more on this subject." (JAMESON) Prophetic words.

10 Stanley gives the figure of 330 geographical miles (= approximately 380 statute miles), a calculation based on a comparison of the known longitudes of Yambuya and Lake Albert.

11   D.A. I p. 34. Confirmed by Parke (p. 72), but contradicted by Barttelot (p. 116): "He said to me, 'Good-bye, Major; shall find you here in October, when I return.'"

12   Swamps were regarded with particular aversion as being the source of fever-production miasmas (a notion at least as old as Galen). At this period the gases emanating from decaying vegetable matter were still generally supposed to be the causative agent of malaria (whence the name). Sir Ronald Ross's identification of the mosquito as the disease vector was still some years in the future (1895–8). However, some travellers—Emin among them—had noticed that the use of a mosquito net conferred a degree of immunity. And Lugard, writing in 1893, cites researches by a Dr. Clark which positively assert the existence of a mosquito-malaria connection. (LUGARD I p. 390 and refs.)

13   *Tunga penetrans.* The female buries itself under the skin and proceeds to expand until it reaches the size of a small pea. Eggs are then laid from the ovipositor which has remained protruding from the skin of the host. After egg-laying, the female dies *in situ*. If the host takes no remedial action, the consequences are first intense irritation, and then infection in the form of ulcerous sores. This pest was introduced into the African continent from South America (probably in Portuguese ships) and was first observed in Africa (Angola) in 1872.

14   "I was greatly disappointed, as it was a nice case for ligature, and his life could easily have been saved." (PARKE) He could as easily have not been shot in the first place.

15   In fact they had deserted, and actually succeeded in getting back to Yambuya.

16   Parke (pp. 207–209) gives a detailed account of these ulcers in medical terms. Some of the sores, it seems, were so deep and spread so rapidly that rats crawled bodily into the cavities while the victim was asleep and gnawed the mortifying flesh.

17   At the confluence of the Aruwimi and Nepoko rivers.

18   Both flags were red, but the Egyptian bore a white crescent and star, the Sultan's was plain.

19   Ugarrowa had started his career as a tent-boy in the service of Speke and Grant on their 1860 expedition.

20   "In London Stanley said he would reach Wadelai by Aug 15th—it is much more likely that Nov 15th would have been nearer the mark." (JEPHSON, entry for Sept. 1.) The column did not reach the Lake until December 13, and, as will be seen, never got to Wadelai at all.

21   Parke was possibly wiser than he knew. A frequent side-effect of cannabis-smoking is a ravenous appetite.

22   Swahili term for the natives of the interior.

23   Oil-bearing palm, *elaeis guineensis.*

24 Such destruction was at times a deliberate policy, dictated by precisely the same deranged logic that produced the "free-fire zones" in Vietnam. Ugarrowa subsequently explained to Stanley that "near each (*Arab*) settlement was a waste, as it was not his policy to permit such 'murderous pagans' to exist near them, otherwise he and his people's lives were not safe". (D.A. I p. 197.) It must be conceded that, considering the limited manpower and unsophisticated hardware at their disposal, Ugarrowa and his men did a remarkably thorough job.

25 "It had salt in it which was a great treat." (JEPHSON) Subsequent gifts of food from Ugarrowa to Stanley were not shared out. The officers were reduced, like the Zanzibaris, to bartering their clothes and possessions for food. Jephson's diary at this period contains several bitter allusions to Stanley's failure to share his own ample supplies with his officers. (See entries for Sept. 18, 19, 22; Oct. 9, 10, 13.) These references are eloquent of the strain on personal relationships among the Europeans imposed by persistent near-starvation. Though Stanley maintained (*Autobiography* pp. 390–391) that the ordeal in the Forest ultimately had the effect of creating a powerful bond of sympathy between himself and his officers.

26 The Expedition was now entering a pygmy-inhabited region, the Ituri Rain Forest (the Aruwimi is known as the Ituri above this point).

27 Stanley adds that, after the hanging, "A rattan (*i.e. a length of creeper*) was substituted in place of our rope, the body was secured to the tree, and within fifteen minutes the camp was abandoned." The rattan is a nice touch of economy.

28 Impelled by motives beyond conjecture, he returned the following day.

29 Bula Matari—"Rock Breaker"—name given to Stanley by the natives on the Congo, much to his pleasure. (It is carved on his tombstone.) Stanley's account of the hanging, and more especially of its sequel, bears all the marks of one of his carefully written-up set-pieces. The versions of Jephson and Parke confirm the broad outline, but are notably more reserved than Stanley regarding the dramatic effects of the leader's oratory. "(*Stanley*) gave the men a long oration," is all Jephson has to say. And Parke merely notes: "Our leader took the opportunity of making a violent and impressive speech to the men." It may be relevant that Jephson and Parke still had only a rudimentary knowledge of Swahili, the language in which Stanley addressed the Zanzibaris.

30 It is highly illuminating that, speaking (in his *Autobiography*) of the two great generals of the American Civil War—Grant and Lee—Stanley expressed a greater admiration for Grant. Perhaps Grant's outstanding characteristic as a strategist was a deliberate willingness to accept horrifying losses in exchange for precisely-calculated gains; he can even be said to have invented the war of attrition.

31 Six days earlier Parke had recorded: "I proposed to Mr. Stanley to kill the donkeys, but he said, 'Wait.'" There is something very impressive in this monosyllabic reply.

32 Kilonga-Longa in turn was the subordinate of the Arab Abed bin Selim. (D.A. I p. 338.)

33 A popular technique was to capture the inhabitants of a given village and then ransom them for ivory, a system which minimised both capital outlay and expenditure of effort. It was later copied by the Belgians as a handy method of collecting rubber.

34 Tagamoyo (Mtagamoyo)—one of the leaders of the Arab penetration of the Central Forest region and, incidentally, first of the Coast Arabs to make contact with the Pygmies.

35 Mumi Muhala—Stanley presumably means Muni (or Muini, Muinyi, etc.) Mohara, whose headquarters were at Nyangwe. He was killed by the Belgians in 1892.

36 Bwana Mohamed—must refer to Tippu-Tib's cousin and trading partner Mohammed bin Said, known as Bwana Nzigé ("Boss Locust"). It was he and his son Rashid who had led the attack on the Stanley Falls stations in 1886.

37 Said bin Abed—son of Kilonga-Longa's superior Abed bin Selim.

38 After further expatiating on the iniquity of the Arabs' behaviour, Stanley goes on to suggest a remedy: that the European powers should combine to deny the Arabs the gunpowder which was the key to their domination of the natives of the interior. This proposal, whatever its merits, comes oddly from a man who has just bought the services of two Arab chiefs (Tippu-Tib and Ugarrowa) with the very commodity he proposes to ban.

39 Stanley comments, with all the seriousness of a man coining a platitude: ". . . with these people a present possession is better than a prospective one."

40 Far from putting it down at half, Stanley gives the figure as one thousand. (D.A. I p. 257.)

41 The orders do not appear in D.A., but Parke prints them on pp. 130–131 of his account.

42 I.e. before the arival of the Arabs on the Aruwimi.

43 Stanley had brought Manyuema guides with him from Ipoto. The agreement was that they would conduct him to the edge of their territory. At Ibwiri they turned back.

44 The paramount chief of the district.

45 He kept his word and was later of very great service to the Expedition.

5

THE CONVERGENCE OF THE TWAIN
December 1887 - April 1888

... the strange dead stop to that hopefulness which had hitherto animated us ...

STANLEY

If Stanley comes ...

EMIN

The elation felt by officers and men, standing on the plateau's edge with the Lake at their feet, was short-lived. The sense of triumph at having reached (as they thought) their goal after so long a struggle against unimaginable hardships burst like a bubble against the sharp reality of the question: What next? The mere fact of their arrival here marked, beyond doubt, an achievement of courage, determination and endurance as real and as admirable as anything of the kind which history records. But, as now became embarrassingly clear, it was an achievement which did nothing whatever to advance the stated aim of the Expedition—the Relief of Emin Pasha.

The events of the next few days were to make painfully evident the weakness that had been inherent in Stanley's position since the moment of the fatal decision to divide the Expedition. From the moment he marched out of Yambuya leaving behind half his men and most of his stores, it mattered little how soon he reached the Lake or whether he reached it at all, since his arrival could bring no material improvement to Emin's situation. However, Stanley was not, for the immediate present, concerned with the teleology of his own actions; the first problem now was to open communication with Emin. So when the Expedition descended from the plateau and marched across the few miles of open plain which separated the tableland from the Lake shore, it was with two immediate objects in view: (1) to ascertain whether the natives knew anything of Emin's present whereabouts; (2) to replace the steel boat left at Ipoto by a canoe—begged, borrowed or stolen—in which a party could be sent out on the Lake. Stanley had no way of knowing if Emin had ever received the letter sent from Zanzibar which set out the Expedition's plans and gave their estimated time and place of arrival. But if Emin had learnt from this or any other source of Stanley's approach and route, he might well have made arrangements with the natives at the south end of the Lake for contacting the Expedition on its arrival. Failing this, Stanley intended sending a party across to Kibiro on the north-west shore of the Lake. From here they should be able to contact Casati in Unyoro, and through him Emin.

Stanley's contingency planning does not appear to have included the possibility of a direct approach to Wadelai. A possible reason for this surprising omission will be suggested presently.

Two days (December 14 and 15) were spent in a futile quest for news of, or transport towards, the elusive Pasha. Inquiries and negotiations among two separate lakeside communities yielded the following meagre result: a white man had indeed been seen at the southern end of the Lake, but so long ago that (Stanley concluded) the description could only have fitted Mason Bey making his survey in 1876.[1] There were canoes in the villages but they were not for sale, and not worth seizing, as they were small two-man affairs with no chance of weathering a storm on the open Lake, where the weather was unpredictable and could be violent.

This intelligence left the Expedition in an awkward, even a ridiculous, situation. The obvious solution to the transport problem—to build a canoe—was ruled out by a freak of local geography: there were no trees either on the lake plain or the neighbouring plateau of a size or shape from which a suitable vessel could be made. And the lack of transport was not the only difficulty; food also promised to be a problem. The small lacustrine communities in this area lived by fishing and by trade with the natives of Unyoro across the Lake. They had no agriculture of their own. There was, it was true, food in plenty, both cattle and crops, on the plateau above, but this would have to be fought for.

In Stanley's view, therefore, the Expedition could neither go on nor stay where it was. In which case they would have to go, by inescapable logic, back.

On the evening of December 15 a "shauri" was held:[2]

... we resolved to adopt the only sensible course left us—that is, to return to Ibwiri, eighteen days' journey from here, and there build a strong stockade, then to send a strong party to Ipoto to bring up the boat, goods, officers, and convalescents to our stockade, and after leaving fifty rifles there under three or four officers, hurry on to Ugarrowa's settlement, and send the convalescents from there back to Ibwiri, and afterwards continue our journey in search of the Major and the rear column before he and it was a wreck, or marched into that wilderness whence we so narrowly escaped, and then, all united again, march on to this place (*the Lake shore*) with the boat, and finish the mission thoroughly, with no anxieties in the rear bewildering or enfeebling us. (STANLEY)

Put in other words, Stanley's proposal amounted to this: that instead of prosecuting its mission of relief the Expedition should now turn its attention to the strictly negative activity of undoing the harm that had been done by the Yambuya decision. In this view, Stanley's assertion that a return to Ibwiri was "the only sensible course left us" can be taken at its face value (a pleasant rarity). On the other hand, if the division at Yambuya was *not* a mistake (and this, presumably, was Stanley's view) then the question must be asked whether there really were insuperable obstacles to prevent the Advance Guard's now fulfilling its original programme of making contact with Emin. Was a return to Ibwiri really the only feasible course? There are a number of considerations which Stanley's explanation of the position brushes aside in far too cavalier a manner.

In the first place it is difficult to believe that some form of lake-worthy transport could not have been devised if there had existed a genuine and earnest desire to overcome the problem. Stanley's energy and resourcefulness, backed by the enthusiasm of Jephson[3] and the engineering skills of Stairs could surely have contrived some kind of vessel—boat, out-rigger, or even raft—from the materials at hand, however scanty and unsuitable.

In the second place, the absence of cultivation on the Lake plain was not as formidable a difficulty as Stanley would have had it sound. On his own evidence, the plain was teeming with game. A single, even moderately competent hunter, working full time, could have supplied the Expedition with fresh meat for an indefinite period.

Finally, even granted that sending a party across the Lake while the remainder waited on the Lake plain was, or seemed, hopelessly difficult, what were the objections to an overland march to Wadelai? Stanley advances only one, and that shaky in the extreme:

Since we entered the grass-land we had expended five cases of cartridges. There remained forty-seven cases with us, besides those at Ipoto in charge of Captain Nelson and Dr. Parke. Wadelai was distant twenty-five days' journey by land.[4] . . . If we travelled northward by land, it was most likely we should expend twenty-five cases in fighting to reach Wadelai, assuming that the tribes were similar to those in the south. On reaching Emin Pasha we should then only have twenty-two left. If we then left twelve cases only with him, we should have only ten to return by a route upon which we had fired thirty cases. Ten would be quite as an inadequate supply for us as twelve would be for Emin. (STANLEY)

Whether or not these highly questionable deductions can be considered a sufficient reason for not pressing on to Wadelai, this is a most interesting statement; it practically constitutes an admission that the Expedition—or at least that part of it which had reached the Lake— was frankly wasting its time, since it could not carry enough ammunition for its own needs and still be of service to Emin.

In the light of these considerations the decision to return to Ibwiri fails to make sense. But, as with other decisions made by Stanley in the course of the Expedition, the logic of it becomes apparent if the possibility of a further—unstated—motive is taken into account. In the present case the hidden motive can only have been Stanley's realisation of the absurdity of showing himself to Emin with the Expedition in its present state. Any resemblance to "the most perfectly organised expedition ever to enter Africa" had long ago vanished beyond recall. The tattered and penurious remnant of a once-powerful caravan that now stood irresolutely on the shores of Lake Albert was unlikely to impress the Governor of Equatoria as the answer to his prayers. Whatever Emin's conception of "relief" may have been, it cannot have been this. Over eight hundred men had left Zanzibar. One hundred and sixty-nine had reached the Lake. Of three hundred and eighty-nine who had filed out of Yambuya camp with flags and bugles, more than half were gone: for every one hundred men who had begun that terrible journey, forty-five had come through; desertion, fighting, starvation, and sickness had taken the rest. Of the stores it was their mission to carry, only a tiny fraction remained—forty-seven cases of ammunition and a few bundles of oddments. For the rest, what was not still three hundred miles away at Yambuya was rotting in the jungle or lying at the bottom of the Aruwimi River. Whether the

Expedition was at any time, even in the days of its conception, capable of effecting the relief of Equatoria, may remain, perhaps, an open question. But for the Expedition as it appeared in December 1887, there can be no doubt whatever: there was no point in their going on to Wadelai, as there was nothing useful they could do when they got there.

They turned their faces away from the Lake towards which they had struggled so bravely for so many months, and marched back on their tracks, up the escarpment, on to the plateau and across the grassland. On December 29 the forest closed once more around them, and on January 7, 1888, after a march of one hundred and forty miles, they were back at Ibwiri, where less than two months earlier they had rested and feasted after their escape from Manyuema territory:

> ... but alas for our fond hopes of rendering the village comfortable for occupation, the natives had set fire to their own dwellings.[5] Fortunately for us they had taken the precaution to pick out the finest boards, and had stacked them in the bush. The large stores of Indian corn[6] had been hastily removed into temporary huts built within the recesses of the impervious bush. We set to at once to collect the corn as well as the boards, and before night we had begun the construction of the future Fort Bodo, or the "Peaceful Fort". (STANLEY)

The Expedition had thus returned, if not to square one, at least to square two or three. Stanley's dash to the Lake had achieved precisely nothing beyond an irreparable and pointless loss of goods and life. The frustration Stanley must have felt at this stage is readily understandable. But in the circumstances—he had, after all, merely rushed headlong into a pit of his own digging—it was ungenerous of Stanley to blame Emin for the impasse, as he now proceeded to do. The Expedition had made, Stanley said—

> ... the direct and earnest march to the Albert Lake, to serve a Governor who had cried to the world, "Help us quickly, or we perish." For the sake of this, Major Barttelot had been allowed to bring up the rear column, the sick had been housed at Ugarrowa's and Kilonga-Longa's stations, the extra goods had been buried in a sandy cache at Nelson's starvation camp or stored at Ipoto, the boat "Advance" and been disconnected and hidden in the bush, and

Nelson and Surgeon Parke had been boarded with the Manyuema, and everything that had threatened to impede, delay or thwart the march had been thrust aside, or eluded in some way.

But now that the Governor, who had been the cynosure of our imaginations and the subject of our daily arguments, had either departed homeward, or could, or would not assist in his own relief, the various matters thrust aside for his sake required immediate attention. So I catalogued our impending duties thus:

To extricate Nelson and Parke from the clutches of the Manyuema, also to bring up the convalescents,[7] the "Advance" steel boat, Maxim machine gun, and 116 loads stored at Ipoto.[8]

To construct Fort Bodo, to securely house a garrison; make a clearing; plant corn, beans, tobacco, that the defenders may be secure, fed, and comforted.

To communicate with Major Barttelot by couriers, or proceed myself to him; to escort the convalescents at Ugarrowa's.

If the boat was stolen or destroyed, then to make a canoe for transport to the Nyanza.

If Barttelot was reported to be advancing, to hasten supplies of corn and carriers to his assistance. (STANLEY)

It was certainly a full and varied programme. The reader might even be forgiven for overlooking the fact that none of it would have been necessary if Stanley had not divided the Expedition in the first place.

The fort was to consist of a strong stockade enclosing huts for the garrison, and surrounded by a wide stretch of ground cleared for the cultivation of rice, corn and beans. The clearing itself was surrounded by extensive groves of banana and plantain:

A hundred men had been cutting tall poles, and bearing them to those who had sunk a narrow trench outlining the area of the fort, to plant firmly and closely in line. Three rows of cross poles were bound by strong vines and rattan creepers to the uprights. Outside the poles, again, had been fixed the planking, so that while the garrison might be merry-making by firelight at night, no vicious dwarf, or ferocious aborigine might creep up, and shoot a poisoned arrow into a throng, and turn joy to grief. At three angles of the fort, a tower sixteen feet high had been erected, fenced, and boarded, in like manner, for sentries by night and day to observe securely any movement in the future fields; a banquette rose against the stockade for the defenders to command a greater view. For during the months that we should be employed in realising our stated tasks, the Manyuema might possibly unite to assault the fort, and its defence therefore required to be bullet-proof as well as arrow-proof. (STANLEY)

By January 18 the heaviest and most urgent part of the work—the stockade—was completed and the next phase of Stanley's plans was put into effect. While Stanley, Jephson and sixty-eight men continued the work on the fort, Stairs was to march with the remaining men back to Ipoto to relieve Nelson and Parke and bring up the boat and other goods left there. His orders were to preserve the semblance of friendliness with the Manyuema as long as their mistreatment of Parke had not gone beyond "general niggardliness and sulkiness". But if—

. . . blood has been shed by violence, and any white or black man has been a victim, or if the boat has been destroyed, then consult with the surviving whites and blacks, think over your plans leisurely, and let the results be what they ought to be, full and final retaliation. (STANLEY)

Stairs and ninety-seven men set off for Ipoto on January 19. The men were strong now from the beef on which they had feasted in the grasslands and the ample supplies of corn at the Fort, and they marched well. But it is a measure of the deterioration in the Expedition's affairs that the number of men Stairs took with him was quite inadequate to its allotted task since there were one hundred and sixteen loads at Ipoto not counting the boat (forty-four loads), the Maxim gun, and any sick who might have to be carried. Stanley's concern seems to have been only for the boat and not at all for the loads which might have to be left behind. This is curious since, by his own admission, his recent failure (or refusal) to make contact with Emin had been due largely if not entirely to the Expedition's material deficiencies.

After Stairs' departure, Stanley and Jephson worked on to complete the fort—building, thatching and whitewashing huts to accommodate men and stores, tending the plantations, clearing more ground for cultivation, strengthening the fortifications with a ditch, and (inexplicably) building roads.[9]

Nelson and Parke were duly rescued and reached Fort Bodo on February 8. (Stairs with the boat was a few days behind.) Their physical condition, especially in Nelson's case, was shocking. During their three and a half months with the Manyuema they had suffered horribly. To the constant miseries of hunger and disease had been added the almost intolerable mental burden imposed by the uncertainties of their situation; unlike more fortunate prisoners, their suffering had no fixed term. They had no idea when, if at all, they would be relieved. Parke, in desperation, had gone so far as to invent a date for their release:

> I had said, several times . . . to Nelson that Mr. Stanley would rescue us before the three months were ended, but Nelson did not feel quite so sanguine. I had felt the idea hover over me as a sort of prevision—? second sight—that we would be relieved within the three months from the date of Mr. Stanley's departure. A dreamy idea to this effect had encouraged me to keep up during many a weary hour of depression. (PARKE)

During the whole period, they had been absolutely at the mercy of their hosts. They were systematically kept in a state of near starvation. Attempts to steal the guns and ammunition in their charge were so persistent that one of them had to remain at all times in sight of the tent in which the goods were stored (at night Parke actually had to sleep on top of the ammunition cases) and even these precautions did not prevent losses. Their men, in order to eke out a miserable living, had been forced to work for the Arabs. Eleven of them had died or been killed.[10] Parke suspected that some had been quietly eaten, as could happen among the Manyuema:

> Last night, one of the slaves went to the river to draw water—a distance of about two hundred yards from the village. He was set on by his comrades on the way, and killed and eaten there and then. Food now seems to be really scarce, indeed! (PARKE)

The programme of harassment and humiliation which the Manyuema had directed against Nelson and Parke was carried on covertly beneath an outward show of friendliness. This double-dealing made things, if anything, more unpleasant for the white officers; denied even the satisfaction of being able to treat their enemies as enemies, they remained to the last pathetically faithful to Stanley's orders to maintain good relations with the ivory-hunters.

The accumulation of petty and often pointless cruelties which they had to suffer is symbolised by the fact that Parke's donkey (the last survivor of those that had left Zanzibar) was twice attacked and wounded during the night, once by an arrow and once by a spear. Since no attempt was made to steal the animal, the aim of these attacks must have been to mutilate it, not to eat it.

All in all, Parke's account of his stay at Ipoto makes cheerless reading. At times the combination of physical and mental sufferings with enforced idleness brought both men to a state of waking delirium. At one point, in a passage which is reminiscent of nothing so much as de Quincy's opium nightmares, Parke describes how he and Nelson—

. . . for want of a more inspiring topic of conversation, descanted upon the causation of disease. . . . From the discussion we gradually subsided into an unquiet sleep; the rest derived from which was sadly interfered with by the feverish visions of the disease generators, whose forms and functions we had been picturing to ourselves. . . . Our heated brains soon magnified the microscopic entities, to whose presence in our vessels and tissues we had been attributing our present condition, to forms of colossal dimensions. . . . The phantoms of these destructive agents assumed the forms of every malignant spirit or demon of which we had heard or read since infancy; and their united hosts were sufficient, in our disordered imaginations, to overspread not only the inhospitable Manyuema camp, but an indefinite area of the adjacent forest. . . . The visions of that night have often recurred to me since my return to the regions of civilisation and science. . . .

On arrival at Fort Bodo, Parke wrote an official report to Stanley on his stay at Ipoto. Jephson comments:

This letter is only a short and mild description of what they suffered during their stay & numberless more cases of theft, annoyance & even insult could be cited. . . . Stanley tries to make as little as possible of what Nelson & Parke suffered & talks about their expecting to find themselves in a hotel.

Stanley was sometimes better served by his subordinates than he merited. Parke's account of his stay at Ipoto does not contain a single word or even hint of reproach against the true cause of their sufferings, Stanley himself.

On February 12 Stairs returned—

> . . . with every section of the boat in good order. He had been absent for twenty-five days, and his mission had been performed with a sacred regard to his instructions and without a single flaw. (STANLEY)

The same evening a shauri was held to consider what should be done next. Stanley's original plan, at the time when they had turned back from the Lake, was to bring up the rear column before making another attempt to get through to Emin. But now that he had the boat, Stanley's impatience began once more, as it had at Yambuya, to get the better of his judgement. The plan that emerged at the council, therefore, was a compromise between his desire to get back to the Lake and his obvious duty to do something about reuniting the two halves of the Expedition (not forgetting the fragment parked at Ugarrowa's): Stairs would lead a small party on a lightning march back to Ugarrowa's village. From there a party of twenty couriers would press on downstream in an attempt to make contact with Barttelot's column, while Stairs and the remainder returned to Fort Bodo. Stanley would wait for him until March 25, on which date he would set out again for the Lake, taking Stairs with him if he were back on time. According to Stanley's calculations the journey to Ugarrowa's and back involved a march of three hundred and sixty-six miles. To cover this distance in the thirty-four days allowed him Stairs would have to average better than ten miles a day. This, as Stanley himself noted, "would be magnificent travelling, especially in the forest".

At a general muster on February 16, volunteers were called for to accompany Stairs as far as Ugarrowa's and from there to try to get through to Yambuya with letters for Barttelot. Each volunteer would receive, in the event of success, a "gratuity" of £10. When the selection had been made, the indomitable Stairs, leading a party of twenty-three men and two boys, marched away once more into the forest.

The day after Stairs' departure Stanley fell ill. His condition deteriorated rapidly to a point where Parke was seriously concerned about his chances of recovery. The main trouble (there were secondary complications such as a poisoned arm) was some form of gastric infection, apparently a recurrent one, for Stanley told Parke that the same illness had "brought him to the brink of death on each of three former occasions. . . . So he (*Stanley*) is naturally very anxious about the result." Even Jephson, who previously had recorded a number of rather acid comments on Stanley's tendency to panic when ill, was obliged to recognise that Stanley's present anxiety was well-founded. On February 26 Jephson noted:

> . . . the illness has been dangerous & Stanley will take some time to recover; to make things worse he had fever with the gastritis & his arm is still bad; two days ago it was nearly well but in one of his ungovernable fits of rage—which by the way are of very frequent occurrence—he hit his German servant across the head with a stick & it has made his arm really bad, for matter has formed among the glands & it will be an affair of many days before it gets well. Parke & I have been sitting by his bedside on alternate nights. . . .

Jephson goes on to record a conversation he had with Stanley during one of these vigils by Stanley's bed. It is of interest for the light it sheds on one highly developed trait in Stanley's character—a faculty for seeing his own faults in those around him.

> A few nights ago, by way of amusing himself he gave me a sketch of my character as he had observed it. He began by saying that my enthusiasm led me to exaggeration (perhaps that's true) & that I was full of cracks & prejudices, & in fact made me out to be a perfect fiend to all of which I listened with a smile. But the thing he laid most stress upon was my "overweening pride—pride of birth & pride of self". To the latter accusation I remarked that I did not see where my pride came in, for I had had many jobs to do since I had accompanied the Expedition, such jobs as are usually given to the very lowest & I had done them all without a word & without even thinking them derogatory. He said that perhaps I had but that in doing them I had shown pride in every movement & turn of my body though he admitted I had done them properly & well—& so on until he had contrived to paint a very nasty character. He said that at the age of eighteen had I been sent out for three years into a very tough life, say, three years before the mast in a

coasting vessel I should have bourne the impress of it all my life & it would have improved my character to a very great extent. He said I had only seen the soft side of life—there he made a very great mistake, but I did not contradict him but smilingly asked if he had any other unpleasant traits to add to my character, upon which he said No, but added from what he had seen he had very great hopes of me & thought that I should return from this expedition greatly improved, which I thought was just as impertinent as his tirade against my character. He then gave me a sketch of his own character, he told me he had been just as impetuous & rash as I am when he was my age but that time etc had taught him to curb himself & a whole lot more rubbish. He made himself out to be a St John for gentleness, a Solomon for wisdom, a Job for patience & a model of truth. Whereas I do not suppose a more impatient, a more ungentle, a more untruthful man than Stanley could exist. He is most violent in his words & actions, the slightest little thing is sufficient to work him into a frenzy of rage, his sense of what is honourable is of the haziest description & he is certainly a most untruthful character—"Oh wad some power the giftie gie us".

There is far more to be learnt about Stanley than about Jephson in this passage. His insistence on what he called Jephson's "pride" may certainly be seen as a reflection of Stanley's life-long preoccupation with his own origins. It is also interesting for what it reveals of Stanley's almost infinite capacity for self-deception. Stanley, like many another "man of action", piqued himself on his skill as a judge of men. It is ironical, therefore, that Jephson's estimate of Stanley's character should be so much more perceptive than Stanley's analysis of Jephson. Jephson saw clearly the two distinct faces of his leader's personality: on the one side "the wonderful powers of resource, the indomitable energy and strength of mind, the dogged determination to carry through to a successful issue all that he takes in hand . . ." and on the other side "all the falseness and double-dealing, the indifference to breaking his word, the meanness, brutality and greediness. . . ."

By early March Stanley was sufficiently recovered to be able to walk about a little, but was still very weak. By the 18th, the earliest possible date for Stairs' return, it began to look as though it would be possible to start for the Lake on schedule.

March 25 came and went with no sign of Stairs. A week later, despite a very natural anxiety over the many possible disasters that might have overtaken Stairs' column, Stanley decided to march for the Lake without more delay. The fort, after all, was now practically impregnable, and the crops of maize and beans were doing well.[11] Forty-five men under Nelson would be left behind as a garrison, all of whom, including Nelson himself, were more or less invalids "suffering from large ulcers, and the general effects of starvation". (STANLEY)

On April 2 Stanley, Parke, Jephson and one hundred and nineteen men began the march "with a view" (as Stanley put it) "to attempt a second time to find the Pasha, or to penetrate the silence around him".

* * *

In Equatoria the situation, ever since the departure of Dr. Junker in January 1886, had been one of uneasy stasis. Throughout 1886, while Europe made desultory plans for the relief (or rape) of the province and its Governor, and on through 1887 while Stanley's Expedition starved and struggled in the Congo Rain Forest, Emin applied himself to business-as-usual.

The withdrawal of Keremallah and the Mahdi-ist army had removed, at least for the time being, the spectre of Emin's being overtaken by the annihilation visited on Gordon, Slatin, Lupton and Hicks. There remained the possibility of gradual disintegration in a province that since its inception had teetered chronically on the verge of chaos.

After the alarms and excursions of the Mahdi-ist irruption had died away, Emin found himself, like a man who to his surprise has survived an earthquake but does not know how he has managed it, in charge of a province which was still largely intact. The heart of his empire was the chain of nine river-stations from Wadelai in the south, through Duffile, Khor-Ayu, Labore, Muggi, Kiri, Bedden and Rejaf to Lado in the north.[12] To hold these and the three or four remaining inland stations, he had at his disposal a force of some fifteen hundred regular soldiers, most of whom had been recruited locally in Equatoria, Bahr-el-Ghazal, Monbuttu and Makraka. The soldiers were divided into two battalions: the First, based on Lado, held the northern stations and consisted of some seven hundred and fifty men; the Second held the southern stations and watched the border with Unyoro. Emin's HQ was at Wadelai. From there he maintained contact by means of the steamers *Khedive* and *Nyanza* with Duffile to the north and, via the lakeside village of Kibiro, with Unyoro to the south.[13]

Emin's forces were perfectly adequate to the day-to-day tasks of maintaining a semblance of order in the Province and keeping the riverine tribes in a state of healthy subjection. The main weakness in Emin's situation was not in the number or quality of the troops but in the increasingly tenuous nature of his authority over them. This state of affairs appeared at its most acute in the embarrassing and persistent rift between the northern and the southern stations. Since Emin's flight southward from Lado in April 1884, and the subsequent refusal of the Lado garrison to comply with Emin's order to evacuate, the garrisons north of Duffile, and particularly those of Lado, Bedden and Rejaf, had been in a state of tacit mutiny. The First Battalion still acknowledged Emin as Governor and maintained the formalities of administrative correspondence with Wadelai, but on the evacuation issue they would not (literally) budge. The result was that for practical purposes Emin's writ did not run north of Duffile, and the First Battalion felt itself free to manage its own affairs and decide its own future. They failed, however, to exercise their freedom. The officers and government officials, though the plotting and counter-plotting among them rose to Byzantine proportions, were quite unable to agree on a course of action. Some wanted to join the Mahdi-ists; others were in favour of establishing themselves as independent freebooters in the Makraka district; others, doggedly refusing to believe that the Sudan had really fallen to the Mahdi, still harped on a scheme for marching north to Khartoum and safety. (The belief in the certainty of eventual relief from the north was incredibly persistent,[14] especially among the Sudanese rank and file; it is possible that their officers, whether or not they believed the story themselves, deliberately fostered the illusion as the best means of combating Emin's schemes for a retreat to the south.) With such a profusion of conflicting plans to choose from, it is hardly surprising that the northern garrisons were for the time being content simply to stay put and maintain (for as long as it was expedient) a façade of loyalty to the Governor.

Emin's loss of authority over a large part of his command was not the only factor making for instability. He had other preoccupations which added largely to his difficulties. One was the uncertainty as to what, if anything, was being done in Europe towards his relief. He had asked for help. What form would "help" take? When could he expect it? There was no way of knowing. Even after the departure of Junker and the opening of a mail route to Zanzibar through the Uganda missionaries, Emin's contacts with the outside world were both tenuous and intermittent. To spend, as Emin had to, a period of two years in almost total ignorance as to what reaction (if any) had been produced by his pleas for help, might have unbalanced many another man altogether. But in such a situation Emin's greatest weakness—his tendency to avoid positive action in the hope that any given difficulty would in time resolve itself unaided—was also his greatest strength. Waiting on events was what he did best.

From his letters and diaries during this period of waiting (1886 and 1887) it is clear that what he hoped for from Europe was first and foremost not rescue but support, not help in leaving Equatoria but help in staying. In April 1887, when he knew Stanley to be on the road, he wrote:

> I shall in no case abandon my people. We have passed dark and troublous days together, and I should consider it shameful to desert my post at this particular time. In spite of many defects, my people are good and true. We have known one another now for years, and I do not think my successor would succeed in gaining their entire confidence. So that is quite out of the question. Let England put matters in Uganda on a firm basis, make our road to the coast free and safe—that is what we want.[15]

And in a letter to Felkin dated September 1887, he reiterates his determination to stay put:

> In my last letter I stated my intention of remaining here, and that even were Stanley to provide me with ammunition and supplies, I had no intention of ever leaving my post. I am strengthened in this, my firm determination, firstly by the wish to reoccupy all the stations so far abandoned, that my people may have a safe road to communicate with the outside world, and secondly by the sympathy and approbation which my work has evidently won. It is therefore my duty to persevere with my labours as long as possible. Apart from these weighty reasons, I feel that my own scientific researches are not complete; if I ever returned to Europe—though I do not expect it—I should be ashamed of submitting such a patchwork to the public. . . . It remains to be seen whether Egypt will give up all pretensions to the province, which at present is of no use to her, or whether she will retain it and be responsible for the expenditure. When it may be taken for granted that Egypt will abandon this

province, and that England for political reasons will not annex it, the question will arise for me whether I should adopt an attitude of independence. In reality it would be easy enough. . . .[16]

Clearly, despite the unequivocal renunciation of the Province in Nubar's letter, Emin either was unwilling to accept the realities of his situation or simply could not see his situation as it must appear from the outside. How else to explain his blindness to the possibility that his remaining or otherwise might depend on factors other than his own will? This mistaken appreciation was doubly dangerous since it was shortly to come into conflict with Stanley's own and equally mistaken appreciation of the situation inside Equatoria. It was almost inevitable that such a convergence of rival mis-perceptions should result in the failure of either party to achieve its aims.

The nearest thing to an evacuation that Emin was prepared to contemplate was the return to Egypt of non-native officers and officials. Emin's desire to rid himself of the Egyptians, whom he saw as the chief cause of discord and confusion in the Province, is a recurring theme:

> Nor do I see the slightest grounds for supposing that our Soudanese officers and troops, except in a few rare cases, will consent to go to Egypt. That is why I shall be heartily glad to succeed in the difficult task of detaching the Egyptians and getting them away.

Again:

> The people won't leave . . . and the differences between Soudanese and Egyptians are becoming daily more acute. The latter, excepting the very few that enjoy a tolerable reputation, are become the objects of undisguised and outspoken hatred. And not undeservedly, for in spite of every warning the Egyptians invariably treated the Soudanese as scum.

And again:

> If I can only succeed in getting the Egyptians away, a task not devoid of difficulty, half my work will be done. . . .[17]

In the meantime Emin could do little but wait. To the divisions and disloyalty among his people he adopted a passive attitude. This infuriated Casati, but, arguably, while it did nothing to mend the situation, it prevented it getting any worse: those inclined to resist Emin's authority could find nothing to exert themselves against.

To say that Emin reacted passively to some of his more obvious problems is not, however, to say that he was idle. The routines of administration and his self-imposed burden of scientific work were maintained at full stretch. Official and private correspondence, tours of inspection, and the insatiable demands of his specimen collections, surveys and observations kept him fully and usefully occupied. He established new stations on Lake Albert at Tunguru and Msawa, and there were the old stations to be inspected, cared for and improved. There were crops to be grown, seeds and grain to be distributed. Deficiencies resulting from the Province's isolation had to be made good by local substitutes and Emin turned his attention to the manufacture of shoes, cloth, candles, soap and coffee. Extracts from his correspondence give some idea of the variety of his practical concerns:

I have made Lado into quite a respectable fortress, with deep moats, towering ramparts, bastions, drawbridges, etc. . . . Honey is our substitute for sugar, and the wax makes splendid candles. . . . Shoes are made here, very nice ones, too. . . . You would hardly recognise the "Khedive", she looks so spruce; the engine has been repaired, the deck renovated, and so on. Two large new barks are ready, a third in the course of construction. I am now taking the "Nyanza" in hand; she is to be docked, i.e. brought on shore tomorrow, to repair her keel and copper-sheathe her. So we have work on hand for some time. . . . Our broad beans have flowered at last; accordingly, I am hoping to get seeds and acclimatise them. Curiously enough neither endives nor radishes can be got to seed here; perhaps they have been kept too moist. The trees are all doing well; the bananas I brought from Mora I have had planted at once. . . . A good while ago I directed the attention of the officer in charge of this station, a consummate rascal but very intelligent, to *Hibiscus sabdariffa*, extensively cultivated by the Negroes, and the seeds of which we use as a substitute for coffee. I showed him how the threads of this plant might be made into coarse cloth. Further practice will improve the weaving. . . . A soldier in this place carves very pretty spoons of the pattern we use in the service, and, as metal spoons are getting scarce, this artificer will be of great service. I gave him an order for three dozen table spoons and one dozen kitchen spoons. Now I shall try and construct a kind of lathe, and turn coffee cups out of hippopotamus teeth.[18]

Emin's dedication to the details of day-to-day administration may be seen as wholly admirable, or, considering the underlying uncertainties of his position, as a pathetic refusal to face really serious issues.

These issues were not confined to the doubtful prospect of relief and the shaky loyalty of his men. There was a third unsettling factor in the situation—the behaviour of Kabba Rega of Unyoro. With this problem, however, it may be said that Emin did, after his fashion, grapple, though to Casati, the man on the spot in Unyoro, Emin's preference when dealing with Kabba Rega for the passive response and the indirect approach seemed of a piece with Emin's attitude to the other troubles that beset him.

The episode of Casati's residence at Kabba Rega's, since events in Unyoro bore directly on events in Equatoria at this time, may be briefly recounted here.

Casati, it will be recalled, had gone as Emin's ambassador to Unyoro after Junker had left there for Uganda and the Coast. He stayed at Kabba Rega's from May 1886 to January 1888, a period of almost two years. During this time his main function was to keep open the mail route through Uganda. This in itself was a matter of some difficulty. Not only was there hostility betweeen Uganda and Unyoro, but there were also internal disturbances in Uganda where, from the time of the murder of Bishop Hannington in October 1885 and the subsequent massacres of Christian converts, affairs had drifted rapidly into a chaos of factionalism which was to lead to the expulsion of Mackay in 1887, and to open civil war and the deposition of King Mwanga in 1888.

For Casati the main variable in the situation was the apparently capricious behaviour of the king of Unyoro.[19] The king's permission had to be obtained before anyone could enter or leave the country. Kabba Rega could, and did when he felt like it, withold this permission from couriers with mails to and from Equatoria, or from Mohammed Biri, who was Emin's only means of buying the manufactured goods such as cloth of which he was badly in need. By exerting constant pressure on the king, Casati was able to keep the road open, at least intermittently. Though much of Emin's mail—for example, Stanley's letter from Zanzibar—never reached him, and a good proportion of the precious supplies vanished in transit, enough got through during 1886 and 1887 for Emin to feel that he was not entirely cut off.[20]

But even this limited achievement was practically a full-time occupation for Casati. He had to be ready twenty-four hours a day to respond to the king's hesitations, duplicities, shifts of mood and changes of policy, and to correct the balance as necessary with a well-timed gift, a bribe to an adviser, or the local equivalent of a Stiffly-Worded Note.

During Casati's stay in Unyoro the situation there showed signs of the same slow slide into chaos that was overtaking Equatoria to the north and Uganda to the south. In Casati's judgement the principal impulse to disorder came from what he called the "War Party"—a group of irresponsible and self-seeking hangers-on at the court who were gaining an increasing ascendancy over the king. They were, indeed, such individuals as might be expected to make their appearance in the orbit of any ruler who lives by the capricious exercise of absolute power unrestrained by custom, law or policy. These men, known as "banassura" ("Wara-Sura" in Stanley) were mercenary soldiers of foreign origin—

> . . . recruited from the deserters of the Egyptian troops, from runaway slaves, and riotous youths from the bordering states; in this corps of brigands there are Waganda, Bari, Shooli, Lur, Walegga, Lango, Madi and Bongo men, by whom the Crown of Unyoro was supported, its subjects terrorised, and the main strength of its combatants obtained.[21]

Under the influence of the banassura the king decided to abandon customary procedures and dispense with the elaborate organisation of government officials which was the traditional intermediary between the king and the people. Kabba Rega had proclaimed his intention of exercising his power directly on the mass of his subjects instead of through the medium of hereditary or appointed chiefs and officers.[22] But what happened was that the banassura usurped more and more of the administrative functions that previously had belonged to the displaced officials. The result was a classic case of maximum power combined with minimum responsibility, described as follows by Casati:

The military party became preponderant in Unyoro, and the banassura were considered indispensable for the preservation and grandeur of the kingdom; their numbers were increased to three thousand. They undertook to defend the throne and enforce the laws; thus, in the end everyone's life and property were at their mercy, and their misdeeds were not only unpunished, but often even openly defended. They boldly prosecuted the guilty, and also the innocent in their eagerness to confiscate valuable property, and to perform summary executions; they were very audacious in their raids, and did not tolerate any authority except that of their worthy chiefs. They had neither feelings of honour nor love for the country in which they were strangers; in war they were rather unrestrained pillagers than brave soldiers. The king did not give them any direct recompense for their services, except supplying them with arms; but he allowed them to appropriate the goods of culprits, real or suspected. In this matter he exceeded every limit of decency; justice became a jest, impunity from punishment was sold . . . and the circle of blood that surrounded (the king) and separated him from his subjects more and more every day, increased enormously.[23]

As the king's dependence on the banassura grew, so his hostility to Equatoria became more overt and Casati saw the chances of making Kabba Rega live up to his promises of friendship to Emin dwindle. This suited the War Party, for whom the prospect of plunder and disorder was meat and drink. It gradually became clear to Casati that Kabba Rega's interest in Equatoria was strictly rapacious. The king of Unyoro was well aware that the Province was rich in ivory and guns, and was aware, too, of the weaknesses and difficulties which now beset it (or why should the Governor send an ambassador to Unyoro begging for petty favours?). With this in view, the seeming vacillations of Kabba Rega's policy become easy to follow, provided due allowance is made for the measure of paranoia normally incident to the exercise of absolute power. While maintaining an outward show of friendship, Kabba Rega began cautiously to probe Emin's defences. Casati, Emin's outwork as it were, was subjected to a progressive course of frustrations, restrictions, covert hostility, and, finally, outright humiliation—all of which was designed to undermine first his morale and then his authority. At the same time it was a means of testing the strength and resolution of the Province. Casati, realising what was afoot, continually pressed Emin to take a strong line with Kabba Rega. The king, he thought, being essentially a coward, would almost certainly have backed down before a show of firmness. But Emin, incredibly, still believed Kabba Rega to be his friend and reproached Casati with tactlessness.[24] The result was, on top of everything else, bad feeling between Casati and Emin.

Meanwhile, further to test Emin's resistance and at the same time to increase the disorder in Equatoria, Kabba Rega initiated a series of aggressive demonstrations on his northern borders. These were calculated to re-assert his suzerainty over the tribes in the disputed area along the Nile and, if possible, provoke an anti-Egyptian rising further north among the Shuli in Equatoria.

Fortunately for Emin, ninety per cent of Kabba Rega's foreign policy was mere plotting and posturing, areas in which Emin could give as good as he got. And Emin's troops were quite capable of dealing with the remaining fraction of actual aggression. In the summer of 1887, for example, an army of Wanyoro was surprised by Emin's steamers in the act of crossing to the north bank of the Nile and completely routed by shell-fire from the steamers' cannon. When it came to the pinch, the banassura (as Stanley was later to prove) had no taste for war; raiding was their business. And the generality of the Wanyoro, on Casati's testimony, were no more than lukewarm in their support for the king's militaristic projects. Thus a renewal of the war with Uganda (June 1887) saw the unedifying spectacle of an army of Waganda marching almost unopposed to the very shores of Lake Albert while Kabba Rega sought refuge in the neighbourhood of Mruli, as far as possible from the theatre of operations.

However, though Kabba Rega could make no more than a token contribution to the insecurity of Equatoria by open war, the collapse of Emin's efforts to secure a friendly southern border exerted an important indirect effect on Emin's situation. When the moment for a decision in Equatoria finally arrived, the presence of a hostile neighbour on his southern flank would be an important limiting factor on Emin's freedom of choice. Meanwhile, for Casati imprisoned in Unyoro by what he considered his duty to Emin, the king's malevolence was beginning to present a real personal threat. A mishap to Emin's ambassador had always been inherently possible, though at first the measures against Casati were of the most indirect kind. After agreeing, for instance, to lease Msawa and Tunguru to Emin for his new stations, Kabba Rega summoned the chiefs of both territories to his presence, accused them of selling out to the Turks and had them summarily executed.[25] The point was not lost on Casati.

Other annoyances, such as delaying Biri on the border, soon gave way to more open measures specifically directed against Casati himself. These soon developed from diplomatic gambits (pretending to be ill when Casati wanted an audience, returning Emin's presents with disparaging remarks) into a full-blown psychological war. The area next to Casati's house was designated a place of execution, with the result that he was kept awake night after night by the noise of malefactors having their brains beaten out. Guards, ostensibly "of honour", watched his every move. The population was forbidden to trade with him. His servants were bullied and intimidated. Finally, when Casati had succeeded in getting the local Golgotha moved elsewhere, an outbreak of mysterious prowlers about his hut robbed him of more sleep. He took to stalking about all night, gun in hand—a precaution which had "a marvellous success, for I frustrated no less than eight attempts".

By January 1888 matters had progressed to a point where Casati feared a direct attempt on his life and upon that of Biri, who at that time was sharing Casati's undeclared imprisonment. (On his way between Equatoria and Uganda, he had failed to obtain permission to leave Unyoro.) Then came an unexpected ray of hope:

> On January 3 a messenger. . . . stopped at Juaya (*Kabba Rega's capital*) for the night. He was going to Mruli, and brought news that in Lendu, on the way to the Walegga country (*west of Lake Albert*) some Europeans had appeared, followed by many armed men dressed in the Zanzibar fashion. No doubt it was Stanley with the relief expedition. Our joy caused us to forget our sad condition. We entertained new hopes. I thought that the king would perhaps postpone the execution of his nefarious projects, and I was pleased to see poor Biri smile. . . .[26]

Casati's "new hopes" were to be quickly shattered. His "sad condition" was indeed nearing its term, but not in the manner he would have wished. On the morning of January 9 he and Biri were summoned to the residence of the chief minister Guakamatera. They found the place crowded with armed men. "There is treachery," whispered Casati to Biri. There was. They were set on and tied to trees, some of Casati's and all of Biri's clothes having been first removed.

Casati naturally assumed that his last hour was near, if not come. They waited all day. The expected execution failed to take place. In the evening they were untied and dragged away in different directions. Casati never saw Biri again. He was taken to an enclosure where he found the rest of his household, also under arrest. They managed to elude their guards by crawling on hands and knees through a patch of thorn forest which formed one side of the compound. The next day and all the following week Casati and his dispirited little party were hunted ignominiously from village to village until they reached the Lake shore near Magungo.[27]

The last rays of the setting sun warned us to hasten our steps. As we descended the slope we discerned an unusual commotion among the inhabitants, who were carrying away furniture and provisions, and driving off herds of cattle. They took no notice of us. Their ferocity of the morning had vanished. We spoke to some of them, but they did not answer, and hastened their departure, anxiously exclaiming, "The steamer! the steamer!"

But the next morning there was no steamer to be seen:

The stars were still shining in the sky, but our impatience was such that already we were walking to and fro on the shore of the lake, looking anxiously for a black spot on the horizon. The sun was just emerging at our back. . . . A few timid natives in canoes were flying towards the islands. . . . If the steamer did not appear by noon, our plan was to construct an ample raft of "ambatsh" (marsh cane), and to entrust our safety to the waves—an operation easy of execution, for the frightened and fleeing natives would not have troubled us. At about nine o'clock a shrill cry interrupted the flow of thoughts that had harassed my mind. It was caused by the sight of a streak of smoke on the horizon. A little later the chimney of a steamer was discerned, and then on came the vessel herself . . . shaping her course by the signal we had hoisted on the top of a pole—the white and red handkerchief of poor Hurshid[28] . . . We saluted her by waving our flag, and our salutation was returned by the usual whistle. . . . She cast anchor at a short distance from the shore, and a boat conveyed us to her. Emin Pasha, with many of his officers and officials, had attempted our rescue in spite of its apparent hopelessness, and rather to fulfil a pious duty than with any expectation of success. Joy at our unhoped-for safety made everyone mute. . . .[29]

Casati's joy and gratitude were a little damped by a misunderstanding which soon sprang up between himself and Emin. Both during his stay in Unyoro, and before that when with Emin in Equatoria, Casati had frequently been exasperated by Emin's refusal to take this or that "energetic measure", and more especially by Emin's habit of agreeing to Casati's proposals, then not carrying them out.[30] Casati kept his annoyance as far as possible to himself but the result nonetheless was a serious strain on the friendship of the two men. Now Casati demanded, reasonably enough, instant retribution against Kabba Rega.

> . . . I proposed sending one of the steamers to Kibiro with a letter for the king, requesting him to give up, within fifteen days, Biri, the soldiers, the guns, and the ivory of the Government, which he had seized, and also my personal effects, with the threat, if he did not yield within the fixed time, the Governor would maintain his right by force and avenge the outrage.[31]

Emin demurred, saying it would be more to the point to re-establish friendly intercourse with Unyoro as soon as might be. Casati interpreted Emin's reaction as meaning that Emin blamed him for the split with Unyoro and had believed the messages Kabba Rega had been sending to Equatoria demanding Casati's recall and denouncing him as a hot-head, a spy, a trouble-maker, a traitor and a witch.[32]

Emin might have done well to adopt Casati's proposal in this instance. Swift retribution might have restored the balance of moral advantage which Emin's passivity had allowed to tip so far in Kabba Rega's favour. Failure to react at all to the expulsion of Casati could only be interpreted by the Wanyoro as weakness. The fact that Biri was not executed until several weeks after Casati's escape strongly suggests that during this time Kabba Rega was waiting to see what kind of vengeance Emin was going to exact for the manhandling of Casati. When nothing happened, Kabba Rega not only took Biri's life but proceeded to redouble his warlike manœuvres in the Magungo district.

For the moment, however, Casati's revanchist schemes were pushed into the background by the news of Stanley's (presumed) arrival in the country to the west of the Lake—news which Casati now passed on to Emin. Emin decided to investigate the rumour.

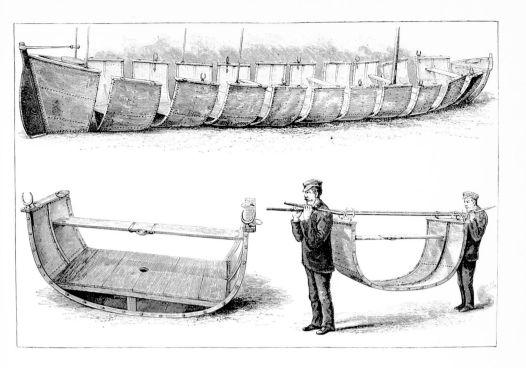

5 (i) The steel boat *Advance*

5 (ii) The march from Matadi

6 (i) STANLEY's parting with
BARTTELOT at Yambuya

6 (ii) Crossing a clearing in
the Rain Forest

At the end of January 1888 he sailed south to Tunguru and thence to Msawa. On February 25, having had no further news, he left Msawa to seek word of Stanley among the lakeside villages further south. It was now more than two months since Stanley had turned back from the Lake to Ibwiri.

The natives of the lakeside villages reacted to Emin's inquiries about Stanley in precisely the same way as they had reacted to Stanley's inquiries about Emin:

> ... the search was without success. The chiefs of the villages were very reticent in giving information, and some of them even denied altogether the presence of strangers in the adjacent districts. Others who seemed inclined to speak were prevented from doing so by their people, whilst a few asserted that the whites had been seen near Katonzi,[33] but that they had left long ago.

Casati saw in this peculiar reticence the "fatal hand" of Kabba Rega. In this he was probably correct. The area in which both Stanley and Emin had made their inquiries lay just outside the boundaries of Unyoro and was inhabited by small and defenceless communities of fisher-folk. This made it a favourite stamping-ground for Kabba Rega's banassura. Hard experience had taught the lakeside natives to make the equation stranger = danger and in consequence to adopt, when questioned by outsiders, the suspicious defensive silence of oppressed peasantries the world over.[34]

Emin returned discouraged to Msawa at the beginning of March and wrote in his diary:

> Gained some experience, lost some hopes: this is the nett result of my quest for Stanley.

But now he heard that the wife of a certain Mpigwa, chief of the lakeside district of Nyamsasi, admitted to having seen the strangers. A letter, sealed in oil cloth, was therefore despatched to Mpigwa by a chosen courier with instructions that it should be handed to the leader of the strangers if occasion offered. Having taken this rather feeble step towards contacting his rescuer, Emin felt that he had done his best and returned to Wadelai to wait upon the outcome.

The wait was to be a short one. At the end of April 1888 Stanley and Emin met.

* * *

O

Stanley's second crossing of the plains to the plateau above the Lake was made almost without fighting.[35] The column met some sporadic hostilities on the first stages of the journey, but when they reached the country nearer to the Lake which had been the scene of the three-day fight the previous December, they found the chief of that district, Mazamboni by name, willing to make peace.

> We saw no leaping or exulting warriors, nor heard a single menace or war-cry; but, as we intended to halt here a day, it was necessary to know what to expect, and we despatched our Mganda interpreter to hail the natives, who were seated afar off on the hilltops looking down upon us. At 5 P.M. after several patient efforts, they were induced to descend and approach, and they finally entered our camp. . . . We mutually exchanged views, wherein they learned that we only needed a free passage to the Lake unmolested. . . . They pleaded, as an excuse for their former behaviour, that they were assured we were Wara Sura (soldiers of Kabba Rega) who periodically visited their country, devastated their land, and carried off their cattle. (STANLEY)

From Mazamboni they had their first definite news of Emin's presence on the Lake. Stanley told Mazamboni's men—

> . . . that we were only travelling to discover a white chief, who years ago was reported to be somewhere near the sea of Unyoro. Had they ever heard of such a man? They answered eagerly, "About two moons after you passed us—when you came from the Nyanza—a white man . . . reached Katonza's in a big canoe, all of iron." . . . This was the first news we had heard of Emin Pasha, and it was with the view of this news (*i.e. of Stanley's approach*) spreading abroad, and for preparing the natives for the irruption of strangers out of the unknown west, that I had sent couriers from Zanzibar in February 1887.

This sly mention of Stanley's letter to Emin—note that Stanley speaks of "couriers" not "a letter", thereby suggesting a systematic effort to spread the news of his coming far and wide over the country— prepares the ground for what is to follow: a second attempt to shift on to Emin's weedy shoulders the blame for all the mishaps resulting from the Yambuya decision:

Had Emin, who expected us December 15th, but taken the trouble to have sent his steamers a nine-hours' steaming distance from his station of Msawa we should have met with his people December 14th, been spared five days' fighting, a four months' loss of time, and on or about the 15th of March I should have been within the palisades of Yambuya. . . .

That Emin should (apparently) have made no preparations to receive the Expedition, was a legitimate motive for grievance.[36] But it does not seem to have occurred to Stanley that he could equally well have avoided the disasters which overtook the Rear Column either by adhering to his stated intention of rejoining the Rear Column after turning back from the Lake in December, or by not deserting half the Expedition at Yambuya in the first place.[37]

After making peace with Mazamboni Stanley pushed on. Two more chiefs, Gavira and Kavalli, also made their submission. This produced a material improvement in the Expedition's situation. The three chiefs—Mazamboni, Gavira and Kavalli—between them controlled a wide area of the Lake shore, the neighbouring plateau and the grasslands to the west. Once he had secured their friendship Stanley could maintain himself and his men without fighting anywhere he chose within this region. This meant a substantial increase in his freedom of movement.

At the village of Kavalli on April 18 Emin's letter was put into Stanley's hands. The packet was wrapped in black American oilcloth. The letter inside it read:

Dear Sir,

Rumours having been afloat of white men having made their apparition somewhere south of this Lake, I have come here in quest of news. A start to the furthest end of the Lake, which I could reach by steamer, has been without success, the people being greatly afraid of Kabba Rega people, and their chiefs being under instructions to conceal whatever they know.

To-day, however, has arrived a man from Chief Mpigwa, of Nyamsassi country, who tells me that a wife of the said chief has seen you at Undussuma, her birth-place, and that his chief volunteers to send a letter of mine to you. I send, therefore, one of our allies, Chief Mogo, with the messenger to Chief Mpigwa's, requesting him to send Mogo and this letter, as well as an Arabic one, to you, or to retain Mogo and send the letter ahead.

Be pleased, if this reaches you, to rest where you are, and to inform me by letter, or one of your people, of your wishes. I could easily come to Chief Mpigwa, and my steamer and boats would bring you here. At the arrival of your letter or man, I shall start at once for Nyamsassi, and from there we could concert our further designs.

Beware of Kabba Rega's men! He has expelled Captain Casati.

Believe me, dear Sir, to be
Yours very faithfully,
Dr. Emin.

Tunguru,
25/3/88.

The Zanzibaris, when the letter was translated to them, "became mad with enthusiasm". Stanley does not say what his own reactions were.

An answer was composed and entrusted to Jephson. Escorted by Parke and a small detachment of Zanzibaris, Jephson then made his way to the Lake shore with the boat. His orders were to make for Msawa—of whose existence Stanley had now learned from the natives—and from there to make contact with Emin by whatever means presented themselves. Jephson had a boat's crew of fifteen men, and a brother of Kavalli's to act as interpreter and guide. On the morning of April 23, after two days on the Lake, they reached Emin's most southerly station, Msawa.

We started off at 6.30 with the Egyptian flag flying at the masthead, and I improvised a sail out of one of my blankets as there was a fair wind. The men pulled like madmen, and we flew along before the wind and reached M'sawa at a little before nine o'clock. A guard of honour was drawn up on the beach to receive me, and a grand salute of guns was fired, and then with flags flying and trumpets playing the Khedival Hymn, I was escorted up to the station. . . . (JEPHSON—E.P.)

From the Commandant, Shukri Aga, Jephson learnt that Emin was at the next station, Tunguru, about forty miles further north. Messengers had already left to inform the Pasha of Jephson's arrival. On Shukri Aga's advice, Jephson decided to wait where he was until Emin could get down to him in the steamer.

There followed a delay of several days. The steamer (*Khedive*) was not at Tunguru but at Wadelai and had to be recalled. Jephson, containing his impatience as best he could, took stock of his surroundings. He could not fail to be impressed by the appearance of order, industry and prosperity which the station presented.[38] Though it was an appearance in some respects only skin deep, it was nevertheless a thought-provoking contrast to the state of the dilapidated and poverty-stricken caravan Stanley now led. The scene which met Jephson's eyes hardly fitted the notion of a desperate and beleaguered colony fighting for its life.

The station stood about a quarter of a mile from the Lake shore, on a hill rising from a plain enclosed by a semi-circle of mountains:

This plain, which is watered by a fine large stream falling from the mountains in a large cascade, is very densely populated, and comprises one of the largest settlements of the Lur tribe. Large villages, with immense flocks of sheep and goats, were to be seen from the station dotted all over the plain, every acre almost of which was under cultivation. Large fields of m'tama,[39] Indian corn, sweet potatoes, and ground nuts, mingled with groves of bananas surrounded the villages. Immediately below the station were the cultivations of the soldiers and Government officials, which consisted chiefly of patches of cotton, Indian corn, m'tama, millet, sessam, balmias, Kolokasias and vegetables of different kinds.

The station was built in two separate blocks, one containing Emin's compound, divan, and strangers' houses, the other consisting of the soldiers' and officials' quarters. Each family had a small compound to itself, in which there were three, four, or more huts, according to the size of the household. Between the two blocks was a large parade ground, in the middle of which were the Government store houses, and a high staff from which flew the Egyptian flag. The entire station, bomas and huts, was built of bright yellow bamboo, in some cases plastered over with a mixture of mud and cow dung, and the houses were thatched with grass.

On the grass land between the station and the mountains was a large kraal containing some hundreds of cattle, sheep and goats. There was evidence of abundance of food of all sorts.

I saw numbers of women, boys, and even soldiers walking or standing about the station carrying large bunches of raw cotton under their left arms, from which they spun thread by rapidly twisting a little crooked distaff. When a number of bobbins of cotton thread were finished they were stretched in lengths along posts like miniature rope-walks, and were then ready for weaving.

They took me to a large open hut, at one side of which a trench had been dug, and an exceedingly primitive spindle was fitted into it, which was worked by an intelligent looking Negro lad. Several qualities of cotton cloth were made here, some remarkably fine for the women's clothes, and some of a coarser description for the men's tunics and loose Turkish trousers. The men's clothes were usually dyed a warm reddish brown colour, from a solution made by soaking the bruised bark of a wild fig-tree in water. These fig-trees grow in great numbers all though the entire country. The cloth had a slightly fluffy appearance, it was almost as warm as flannel and wonderfully strong and serviceable. (JEPHSON—E.P.)

Jephson had been four days at Msawa when Emin at last arrived aboard the Khedive:

I had quite given up hope of seeing the steamer today when they came to tell me at 5 o'clock that she was in sight. I came out to look & saw her just rounding a rocky headland about 5 miles off. The soldiers all turned out & the officers put on their best uniforms & the little cannon was got ready to fire a salute.

The guard then marched down to the shore with two Turkish flags, followed by my men marching two & two, carrying the big Egyptian flag, after a bit I went down to the shore to await the steamer's coming, my men begged me to allow them to fire a couple of salutes when Emin Pasha landed. It was almost dark before the steamer had dropped anchor & the boat was pulled ashore. As the boat touched the sand Emin Pasha leaped out & welcomed me with both hands, he kept repeating expressions of welcome and cordial greeting as he held both my hands in his; one really felt that the welcome was from the bottom of his heart. He introduced me to Captain Cassati who was with him, but, as Cassati spoke no English & did not understand French, I could only say a few words to him through Emin Pasha, he is a thick-set middle-aged man & not very prepossessing in appearance.[40] After this Emin Pasha put his hand on my shoulder & we walked up to the station together followed by all the officials. We sat outside in the bright moonlight & talked till late about many things. We remain here tomorrow & then go down in the steamer to Nyamsassie where Stanley & the people will meet us with the loads & impedimenta. (JEPHSON)

Jephson was struck from the first by Emin's charm, culture, courtesy and kindness. And Emin's insistence on making up the deficiencies in Jephson's kit was a reversal of the roles of rescuer and rescued—later to be repeated on Emin's meeting with Stanley—which must have given Jephson food for thought.

> Seeing my tattered state, clothes were brought me by Emin Pasha's orders, two coats & a pair of trousers & the tailor was called in to take my measure for four pair of knickerbockers, & the shoemaker was called to take my measure for 5 pair of shoes, whilest a quantity of red cloth was delivered over to my servants to put in my bag. Emin Pasha then sat down with his note book & insisted on my telling him my wants. With much hesitation & a good deal of shyness, at begging in this wholesale way, I told him the following things would be most acceptable, salt, soap & a note book, all of which he wrote down & gave orders that they should be put in my house, grumbling all the time at the smallness of my demand. He enumerated several things which he could give me & which I should awfully have liked to have, but I said, no I was quite ashamed of asking for anything at all, for his kindness is quite overpowering & his manner paternal, one's heart really goes out towards such a man for one feels he is really sincere. (JEPHSON)

By April 29 the steamer was wooded, and loaded with provisions and livestock till she looked like a floating farmyard. In the morning Emin, Casati and Jephson went on board. All day they steamed south down the Lake. The *Khedive*, old, heavily freighted, and towing the *Advance*, could do no better than five knots.[41] Even so, that evening, as Emin recorded in his diary:

> At 6.32 p.m. we anchored before Nyamsasi, and were not a little surprised at hearing ourselves welcomed by gunshots. It then appeared that Stanley had taken up his quarters about half an hour further south, to watch for us. I therefore had the vessel moored, and, in company of Casati and Jephson, went southward in the latter's boat. We traversed a kind of swamp; on the height, the almost frenzied Zanzibaris greeted us with their rifles, and at last I was in the presence of Stanley. It was a moment I shall never forget.

Stanley's account of the meeting gives, as one would expect, rather more circumstantial detail:

> At 9 A.M. we set out for the Lake. Two hours later we were camped about a quarter of a mile from the shore. . . . From my tent-door, at 4.30 P.M., I saw a dark object loom up on the north-east horizon of the Lake . . . and at 6.30 P.M. the steamer dropped anchor in the baylet of Nyamsassi, inshore of the island of that name. Scores of our people were on the beach in front of our camp firing guns, and waving signals, but though we were only two miles from the island, no one appeared to observe us.
>
> Ardent messengers were therefore sent along the shore to inform the party on board of our presence, and these were, unhappily, so exuberant, that as they fired their rifles to give notice, they were fired at in return by the Soudanese, who naturally enough took the wild figures for Kabba Rega's people. However, no harm was done; the boat's crew distinguished their comrades' cries, the word was passed that the people on shore were friends, and the boat was made ready to convey our visitors to the beach near the camp. At eight o'clock, amid great rejoicing, and after repeated salutes from rifles, Emin Pasha himself walked into camp, accompanied by Captain Casati and Mr. Jephson, and one of the Pasha's officers. I shook hands with all, and asked which one was Emin Pasha? Then one rather small, slight figure, wearing glasses, arrested my attention by saying in excellent English, "I owe you a thousand thanks, Mr. Stanley; I really do not know how to express my thanks to you."

To which Stanley responded (varying his formula)—

> "Ah, you are Emin Pasha. Do not mention thanks, but come in and sit down. It is so dark out here we cannot see one another."

"We cannot see one another"—the words were a prophetic summary of what relations between the two men were to become. In their meeting an object (of a kind) had been attained; but between two men so dissimilar in intellect and in temperament there was to be no meeting of minds, no sympathy, no true understanding.

It is perhaps not too far-fetched to see in this blundering and misbegotten convergence a collision between East and West. The French historian who called Stanley "the last conquistador"[42] spoke truly to the extent that there was in Stanley the same brutal and heedless energy which had already characterised three hundred years and more of European expansion. It was an energy which, secure in its consciousness of technical and (God forgive us) moral superiority, saw no need of subtlety, of finesse, no need to penetrate and understand the inner reality of the cultures with which its blind impulse to expand brought it in contact. Emin, by contrast, despite the circumstances of his life, exhibits no temperamental affinity with the historical movement of which he was part. He was of the East, not of the West, opposing an almost effeminate subtlety to Stanley's brutal vigour, passive where Stanley was active, intellectual where Stanley was animal, meticulous where Stanley was crude, indifferent to time where Stanley could be made frantic by delays. Above all, Emin was of the East in his fatalism, his readiness to submit to circumstances: Stanley was of those who write their own destiny.[43]

Now these two men, polar opposites, were called on to co-operate in deciding the fate of Equatoria. But such men are created to be opponents, not collaborators. The idea of their working together was weirdly improbable. The attempt was foredoomed, but it had to be made.

NOTES AND REFERENCES

CHAPTER 5   THE CONVERGENCE OF THE TWAIN

1   Emin had twice visited the southern end of the Lake by steamer: in August–
    October 1886 and in February 1887. Either these visits had gone unobserved by
    the natives Stanley questioned (which is unlikely), or the natives, for reasons of
    their own, were lying (which is highly probable, for reasons which will be
    referred to below).

2   Jephson noted that what he called these "rubbishing" shauris always led to the
    adoption of a plan the leader had already decided on. (JEPHSON pp. 165 and
    375.)

3   "I suggested that as a last resource we . . . march north till we were opposite
    Kibero . . . try & seize a canoe from the natives & I would go across the Lake in
    it & take my chance of reaching Kassati. Stanley said, No, it would not do. I
    said let us try anything rather than turn back when we were on the eve of
    success. However Stanley was against it, though Stairs was on my side so we
    must make up our minds to the return journey." (JEPHSON p. 213.)

4   Emin had recently built a station at Msawa, half-way down the western shore of
    the Lake. Thus, though Stanley did not know it, he was only sixty miles—say
    five days' march—from Emin's nearest outpost.

5   It often happened that a village which the Expedition had stayed in was burnt
    by the inhabitants after the intruders had moved on.

6   ". . . about 8 tons . . ." (JEPHSON)

7   Stanley persistently uses this term for the men he had left behind to die, and
    always behaved as though the system of abandoning the sick was an inevitable
    feature of African travel. An outside observer, however repugnant he finds the
    system, cannot comment on the validity of Stanley's contention. But at least one
    African traveller—Lugard—whose experience qualifies him to express an
    opinion, held views diametrically opposed to Stanley's on this question.
    (See LUGARD II p. 227: "We had 3 sick men ourselves, who were being
    carried, for I detest the system of abandoning men to the care of 'friendly
    villagers' . . . I preferred to abandon (or issue) food-loads, or make other
    arrangements, so that the sick might be carried, rather than adopt these
    methods.")

8   All the loads from Ipoto were eventually recovered, the last not until June 1888,
    when a party under Parke went there for that purpose. (See next chapter.)

9   "Our leader has a great fancy for making roads," noted Parke on his arrival
    at the fort. "When a standing camp has been made, the first thing he does is to

make a road or two in some direction which may be utilised. Two have been constructed here, the 'Avenue Nyanza' and the 'Avenue Manyema' . . ." Stanley justified his road-building programme as a make-work project to keep idle hands from devilish employments. (Cf. PARKE p. 207.)

10   The number of men rescued from Ipoto is a little difficult to disentangle. Stanley left twenty-nine men with Parke; Jephson brought up seven more from Nelson's camp; ten more of the men left with Nelson later reappeared of their own accord (January 9). Total: forty-six. Of these, eleven died or disappeared at Ipoto; at least three died on the march to Fort Bodo after their relief by Stairs; seven who had been away with a Manyuema raiding-party at the time of Stairs' arrival later returned independently to Fort Bodo; five others were too ill to leave Ipoto. Therefore the maximum number recovered by Stairs is twenty, or less than fifty per cent of the original total.

11   Maize ripened three months after planting, beans two months.

12   Lado was abandoned in March or April 1887 after a bad fire and Rejaf became the HQ of the First Battalion.

13   On the river, the steamers only operated between Wadelai and Duffile, because of the rapids; below Duffile, communcation between the stations was by land. All the river stations, including Wadelai and Duffile, were on the same (left) bank.

14   As late as June 1886 Emin was writing to Junker: ". . . they (the officers at Lado) were still somewhat dubious as to the authenticity of the news from Egypt and the Soudan, nor could I convince them, inasmuch as Nubar Pasha's letter was written in French . . ." (SCHWEITZER I p. 201.) According to Jephson, the hope of relief from the north, and the belief that the Egyptians still had a government in Khartoum, persisted right up to 1888. (See JEPHSON—E.P. pp. 109 and 116.)

15   SCHWEITZER I p. 263.

16   SCHWEITZER I pp. 263–264.

17   SCHWEITZER I p. 196, p. 198, and p. 201. Emin's anxiety to get rid of the Egyptians is better understood when it is remembered that the Egyptian officers had been, in many cases, sent to Equatoria precisely because they were malcontents, plotters and trouble-makers. Some were supporters of Arabi Pasha who had been exiled to the Southern Sudan (Egypt's Siberia) after the failure of the Arabist revolution.

18   Extracts from Emin's letters (1884–1887). SCHWEITZER I pp. 172, 173, 212, 246, 247, 250.

19   "Apparently"—because Emin, though perhaps not Casati, underestimated the extent to which xenophobic suspicion of "Turkish" intentions was consistently present in Kabba Rega's policies. (Cf. CASATI II p. 21: "But the inveterate hatred that prevailed among the Wanyoro since Baker made his armed appearance there, kept the king's mind in a state of doubt and uncertainty.")

20 Apart from Biri's two visits to Equatoria with goods and mails from Uganda (October '86 and June '87), Emin received mails from outside on at least five occasions during 1886 and 1887 (February '86, April '86, June '86, May '87, December '87).

21 CASATI II pp. 61–62.

22 CASATI II p. 26.

23 CASATI II pp. 62–63.

24 "I am somewhat anxious about Casati. I have seldom met so true and loyal a man. But to judge from his last letters, he seems to be rather at variance with Kabba Rega. The cause appears to me that Casati is too candid with the King, and expects that Kabba Rega will renounce his dodges and subterfuges and treat him honestly and straightforwardly." (Emin to Junker, January 20, 1887.)

25 Both places, being on the western shore of the Lake, were outside the confines of Unyoro proper but their inhabitants recognised the suzerainty of Unyoro and paid tribute.

26 CASATI II p. 93.

27 That Casati was neither executed nor re-arrested suggests that there was some residual reluctance on Kabba Rega's part to take this final step. Casati can hardly be said to have "escaped", since his whereabouts was apparently known at all times during his flight. His departure, in fact, had more the aspect of a rather chaotic *battue* than a serious manhunt: he was, as it were, escorted to the borders from behind. No remnant of diplomatic scruple intervened to save poor Biri; he was murdered on the King's orders a few weeks later.

28 A Circassian, one of three regular soldiers from the Equatorial troops who had formed Casati's escort during his stay in Unyoro.

29 CASATI II pp. 122–124.

30 See, for example, CASATI I pp. 307–310 and II p. 153.

31 CASATI II p. 141. The ivory was being taken to Uganda to buy goods on Emin's behalf.

32 CASATI II pp. 143–144.

33 CASATI II p. 146. Katonzi (or Katonza) was one of the villages which Stanley had visited in December.

34 Stanley records the reaction of the lakeside natives to the Expedition's arrival in December 1887: ". . . Perhaps after all we were Wara-Sura (*they thought*) or their friends, for we had guns also." Stanley adds: "We had, unknown to ourselves, incurred their suspicion by speaking too kindly of Unyoro and of Kabba Rega, who, we found later, was their mortal enemy." D.A. I p. 310.

35 One Zanzibari fell victim to purely internal dissension: "Stanley got in a great rage with the men today & as they were not working as well as they might he

fired at two of them, he just grazed the heel of one of the men & took a piece of the skin off about the size of a sixpence, a quarter of an inch more would have shattered the bone of the foot & made him lame for life; Stanley really is not responsible for what he does when he gets into these fits of passion . . ." (JEPHSON p. 235.)

36 In addition to building stations at Tunguru and Msawa on the Lake, Emin had prepared accommodation for the Expedition at Duffile. See JEPHSON—E.P. p. 83.

37 Schweitzer comments, with irony, that Stanley was "annoyed at Emin, of whom he seems to have conceived the wonderful notion that he had nothing else to do than to stand by in his steamer for months at this one particular spot." (SCHWEITZER I pp. 271–272.) This does not answer Stanley's complaint that Emin could and should have made some arrangement for contacting the Expedition through the lakeside natives. Even so, Emin's mistake does not make him responsible for Stanley's.

38 "The station . . . was exquisitely clean and neat, and all the huts were airy and cool . . . The people all looked so smart in their costumes of snowy white or brown cotton cloth, such a contrast to us, the relief party, who had arrived in rags and dirt. . . ." (JEPHSON—E.P. pp. 14–15.)

39 A kind of millet. Used locally for making beer.

40 Jephson also made the acquaintance of Vita Hassan: "There is an apothecary, a Tunisian—Signor Vitta—a very decent little fellow & very useful to Emin Pasha, he was sent out eight years ago when Emin Pasha applied for a doctor, he is now his apothecary, store keeper, general helper." (JEPHSON p. 249.)

41 It was now nearly twenty years since Baker had brought the Khedive (and her consort the Nyanza) to the Sudan. That she was still in working order is a tribute both to the skill of the Victorian engineers (Samuda brothers) who built her, and to Emin's painstaking attention to practical detail. Jephson comments: "It is wonderful that she is in such good order; Emin Pasha has taken very great care of her." Her boilers, however, were growing weak.

42 J. P. Aimot: Stanley, le dernier Conquistador.

43 Cf. STIGAND p. 175: "The Eastern side of his (Emin's) nature . . . showed itself in indecision, changing of orders, procrastination, a tendency to let things drift or obtain an object by intrigue rather than by direct means."

6

STANLEY AND EMIN
April to June 1888

I am now asked to give up everything, to abandon everything, and go away. That was not the idea I had of Stanley's expedition and its purpose.

EMIN

The day after their meeting, the two parties moved some six miles further north along the Lake shore to Nsabe and set up a combined camp.

Stanley now proceeded to relieve Emin. He handed over thirty-one cases of Remington ammunition, the Khedive's *firman*, Nubar's letter, and—

> . . . a big pack . . . containing some clothes kindly sent by the government, a packet of "Petermannscher Mitteilungen" and maps from Gotha, and a bundle of letters—all in a sorry condition owing to the continued dampness.[1]

Emin riposted with gifts of cloth, clothes, shoes, sesame, millet, honey, salt, fruit, onions, cows, sheep, goats, chickens, soap, tobacco, and sufficient Indian corn to feed all Stanley's men for a month.[2]

This exchange of merchandise introduced an element almost of farce into the situation. It raised the question of who was relieving whom to an embarrassing prominence. And it represented a painful anti-climax to Emin's years of isolation and anxious waiting, and to the Expedition's months of struggle in the unfriendly wilderness. Once Stanley had handed over the ammunition and the other tatty impedimenta, the Expedition was—as far as its publicly-stated and strictly philanthropic purpose was concerned—over. It had fulfilled its declared aim of carrying relief supplies to Emin, and could now go home. To say this is in no way to belittle the cost in human suffering of those thirty-one boxes, those ill-fitting clothes and that mildewed correspondence.[3] But the courage and devotion that had gone into the effort to get those pathetic bundles into and through the heart of Africa could not conceal the inherent futility of the gesture. Even Stanley's insistence that this was only a "first instalment" cannot, in the circumstances, have buttered very many parsnips. Only by the most determined suspension of the critical faculties could two loads of mouldy clothing be considered better than one. There was, therefore, a dangerous possibility that if Stanley were now to return home, his claim to have accomplished his mission, while in a sense true, would be greeted with embarrassment by his friends, displeasure by his employers, and by his enemies with the derision it deserved. If it were not that such an eventuality could and should have been foreseen while the Expedition was still planning, one might almost feel sorry for the great explorer. Without any doubt the delivery of the cartridges was, in view of the difficulties of the journey, a tremendous achievement. But in view of the uselessness of those cartridges, the delivery of as many boxes of left-handed golf-clubs would have been of equal value. Stanley needed, therefore, something more concrete than a walk across Africa to point to on his return to Europe. He needed a trophy, and the obvious candidate for this post was Dr. Mohammed Emin, Pasha, Governor of Equatoria. Emin must be not merely relieved, but rescued. And so that the world should see he had been rescued, he must return to Europe. If the Governor refused to abandon his province, Stanley would have precious little to show for his trouble.

In the discussions of Emin's future plans which took place over the next three weeks Stanley exerted a steady pressure to convince Emin of the impossibility of holding his ground in Equatoria. The relevant portions of Stanley's account are given below:

(April 30) This evening Emin Pasha came ashore, and we had a lengthy conversation, but after all I am unable to gather in the least what his intentions may be. . . .

I had an idea that I might have to wait about two weeks, when we would all march to the plateau and occupy a suitable spot in Undussuma, where, after seeing everything done for complete security and comfort, I could leave him to return to the assistance of the rear column. On being re-united we could resume our march within a few days for Zanzibar; but the Pasha's manner is ominous. When I propose a return to the sea to him, he has the habit of tapping his knee, and smiling in a kind of "We shall see" manner. It is evident that he finds it difficult to renounce his position in a country where he has performed viceregal functions.

After laying before him at length the reasons of the abandonment of the Equatorial Provinces by Egypt he replied, "I see clearly the difficulty Egypt is in as regards retention of these provinces, but I do not see so clearly my way of returning. The Khedive has written to me that the pay of myself, officers and men will be settled by the Paymaster General if we return to Egypt, but if we stay here we do so at our own risk and on our own responsibility, and that we cannot expect further aid from Egypt. Nubar Pasha has written to me a longer letter, but to the same effect. Now I do not call these instructions. They do not tell me that I must quit, but they leave me a free agent."

"Well, I will supplement these letters with my own positive knowledge, if you will permit me, as the Khedive and Nubar Pasha are not here to answer for themselves. Dr. Junker arrived in Egypt telling the world that you were in great distress for want of ammunition, but that you had a sufficient quantity to defend your position for a year or perhaps eighteen months, providing no determined attack was made on you, and you were not called upon to make a prolonged resistance; that you had defended the Equatorial Provinces so far successfully; that you would continue to do so to the utmost of your ability, until you should receive orders from your Government to do otherwise; that you loved the country and people greatly; that the country was in a prosperous state—quiet and contented—possessed of almost everything required to maintain it in this happy condition; that you would not like to see all your work thrown away, but that you would much prefer that Egypt should retain these provinces, or failing Egypt, some European Power able and willing to continue your work. Did Dr. Junker report you correctly, Pasha?"

"Yes, he did."

"Well, then, the first idea that occurred to the minds of the Egyptian officials upon hearing Dr. Junker's report was, that no matter what instructions you received, you would be disinclined to leave your provinces, therefore the Khedive says that if you remain here, you do so upon your own responsibility, and at your own risk, and you are not to expect further aid from Egypt. Our instructions are to carry a certain quantity of ammunition to you, and

7 The meeting with EMIN

8 (i) MAJOR EDMUND
MUSGRAVE BARTTELOT

8 (ii) JAMES S. JAMESON

say to you, upon your obtaining it, 'Now we are ready to guide and assist you out of Africa, if you are willing to accompany us, and we shall be delighted to have the pleasure of your company; but if you decline going, our mission is ended.' Let us suppose the latter, that you prefer remaining in Africa. Well, you are still young, only forty-eight; your condition is still good. Let us say you will feel the same vigour for five, ten, even fifteen years longer; but the infirmities of age will creep on you, and your strength will fade away. Then you will begin to look doubtingly upon the future prospect, and mayhap suddenly resolve to retire before it is too late. Some route will be chosen—the Monbuttu route,[4] for instance—to the sea. Say that you reach the Congo and are nearing civilisation; how will you maintain your people, for food must then be bought for money or goods? And supposing you reach the sea, what will you do then? Who will assist you to convey your people to their homes? You rejected Egypt's help when it was offered to you, and, to quote the words of the Khedive, 'You are not to expect further aid from Egypt.' If you stay here during life, what becomes of the provinces afterwards? Your men will fight among themselves for supremacy, and involve all in one common ruin. These are grave questions, not to be hastily answered. If your provinces were situated within reasonable reach of the sea, whence you could be furnished with means to maintain your position, I should be one of the last to advise you to accept the Khedive's offer, and should be most active in assisting you with suggestions as to the means of maintenance; but here, surrounded as this lake is by powerful kings and warlike peoples on all sides, by such a vast forest on the west, and by the fanatic followers of the Mahdi on the north, were I in your place, I would not hesitate one moment what to do."

"What you say is quite true," replied the Pasha, "but we have such a large number of women and children, probably 10,000 people altogether! How can they all be brought out of here? We shall want a great many carriers."

"Carriers for what?"

"For the women and children. You surely would not leave them, and they cannot travel."

"The women must walk; for such children as cannot walk, they will be carried on donkeys, of which you say you have many. Your people cannot travel far during the first months, but little by little they will get accustomed to it. Our women on my second expedition crossed Africa; your women, after a little while, will do quite as well."

"They will require a vast amount of provisions for the road."

"Well, you have a large number of cattle, some hundreds, I believe. Those will furnish beef. The countries through which we pass must furnish grain and vegetable food. And when we come to countries that will accept pay for food, we have means to pay for it, and at Msalala we have another stock of goods ready for the journey to the coast."

"Well, well. We will defer further talk of it till tomorrow."

The arguments which Stanley attributes to himself in the foregoing conversation contain scarcely a single sentence which might not be challenged as contrary to logic or to plain truth. Yet Stanley would have his readers believe that, by the next day, Emin had already bowed to the force of his logic. When the conversation was resumed—

"What you told me last night", began the Pasha, "has led me to think that it is best we should retire from Africa. The Egyptians are very willing to go I know. There are about fifty men of them besides women and children. Of those there is no doubt, and even if I stayed here I should be glad to be rid of them, because they undermine my authority, and nullify all my endeavours for retreat. When I informed them that Khartoum had fallen and Gordon Pasha was slain they always told the Nubians that the story was concocted by me, and that some day we should see the steamers ascend the river for their relief. But of the Regulars, who compose two battalions, I am extremely doubtful. They have led such a free and happy life here, that they would demur at leaving a country where they enjoy luxuries such as they cannot hope for in Egypt. They are married, and besides, each soldier has his harem; most of the Irregulars would doubtless retire and follow me. Now supposing the Regulars refused to leave, you can imagine my position would be a difficult one. Would I be right in leaving them to their fate? Would it not be consigning them all to ruin? I should have to leave them arms and ammunition, and on my retiring all recognized authority and discipline would be at an end. There would presently rise disputes and factions would be formed. The more ambitious would aspire to be chiefs by force, and from rivalries would spring hate and mutual slaughter, involving all in one common fate."

"It is a terrible picture you have drawn, Pasha," I said. "Nevertheless, bred as I have been to obey orders, no matter what may happen to others, the line of your duty, as a faithful officer to the Khedive, seems to me to be clear. All you have to do, according to my idea, is to read the Khedive's letter to your troops, and ask those willing to depart with you to stand on one side, and those preferring to remain to stand on the other, and prepare the first for immediate departure, while to the latter you can leave what ammunition and guns you can spare. If those who remain number three-fourths or four-fifths of your force, it does not at all matter to anyone what becomes of them, for it is their own choice, nor does it absolve you personally from the line of conduct duty to the Khedive directs."

"That is very true," replied the Pasha; "but supposing the men surround me and detain me by force?"

"That is unlikely, I should think, from the state of discipline I see among your men; but of course you know your own men best."

"Well, I shall send the steamer down tomorrow with the Khedive's letter, and you would oblige me greatly if you would allow one of your officers to go and show himself to the troops at Duffile. Let him speak to the men himself, and say he has come from the representative of the Government, who has been specially sent by the Khedive to bring them out, and perhaps when they have seen him, and talked with your Soudanese, they will be willing to depart with us. If the people go, I go; if they stay, I stay."

"Now supposing you resolve to stay, what of the Egyptians?"

"Oh, those I shall have to ask you to take charge of."

"Now will you be good enough to ask Captain Casati if we are to have the pleasure of his company to the coast, for we have been instructed to lend him every assistance within our power?"

Captain Casati answered through Emin Pasha.

"If the Governor Emin goes, I go; if he stays, I stay."

"Well, I see, Pasha, that in the event of your staying your responsibilities will be great, for you involve Captain Casati in your own fate."

(A laugh), and the sentence was translated to Casati, and the gallant Captain at once replied.

"Oh, I absolve Emin Pasha from all responsibility connected with me, for I am governed by my own choice entirely."

"May I suggest then, Pasha, if you elect to remain here, that you make your will?"

"Will! What for?"

"To dispose of your pay of course, which must by this time be considerable. Eight years I believe you said? Or perhaps you meditate leaving it to Nubar Pasha?"

"I give Nubar Pasha my love. Pho! There can be only about two thousand and odd pounds due. What is such a sum to a man about to be shelved? I am now forty-eight and one of my eyes is utterly gone. When I get to Egypt they will give me some fine words and bow me out. And all I have to do is to seek out some corner of Cairo or Stamboul for a final resting-place. A fine prospect truly!"

In the afternoon Emin Pasha came again to my tent, and during our conversation he said that he had resolved to leave Africa—"if his people were willing; if not, he would stay with them".

This was as near to a definite arrangement as Emin and Stanley managed to come: Emin would put the question to his people with the help of an officer delegated by Stanley, and would abide by their decision. Two days later, however, Stanley returned to the charge and—finally— to the real purpose of his mission.

(*May* 3) During a long conversation this afternoon Emin Pasha stated, "I feel convinced my people will never go to Egypt. . . . The Egyptians, of course, will go, but they are few in number, and certainly of no use to me or to any one else."

This has been the most definite answer I have received yet. I have been awaiting a positive declaration of this kind before venturing on any further proposition to him. Now, to fulfil my promise to various parties, though they appear somewhat conflicting, I have two other propositions to make. My first duty is to the Khedive, of course; and I should be glad to find the Pasha conformable, as an obedient officer who kept his post so gallantly until ordered to withdraw. By this course he would realise the ideal Governor his letters created in my mind. Nevertheless, he has but to speak positively to induce me to assist him in any way to the best of my power.

"Very well," I said, "and now pray listen, Pasha, to two other propositions I have the honour of making to you from parties who would be glad to avail themselves of your services. Added to that which comes from His Highness the Khedive, these two will make three, and I would suggest that, as there appears to be abundant time before you, that you examine each on its merits and elect for yourself. Let me repeat them. The first proposition is that you still continue to be an obedient soldier and accompany me to Egypt.[5] On arrival, yourself, your officers and men, will receive your pay up to date. Whether you will be employed by the Government in active service I do not know; I should think you would. Officers of your kind are rare, and Egypt has a frontier where such services as you could render would be valuable. In answer to this proposition you, however, say that you feel convinced your men will not depart from here, and that in the event of a declaration to that effect being given by them that you will remain with them.

"Now, my second proposition to you comes from Leopold, King of the Belgians. He has requested me to inform you that in order to prevent the lapse of the Equatorial Provinces to barbarism, and provided they can yield a reasonable revenue, the Congo State might undertake the government of them if it could be done by an expenditure of about £10,000 or £12,000 per annum; and further, that his Majesty King Leopold was willing to pay a sufficient salary to you—£1,500 as Governor, with the rank of General—in the belief that such employment agrees with your own inclination. Your duty would be to keep open the communications between the Nile and the Congo, and to maintain law and order in the Equatorial Provinces.

"My third proposition is: If you are convinced that your people will positively decline the Khedive's offer to return to Egypt, that you accompany me with such soldiers as are loyal to you to the north-east corner of Victoria Nyanza,[6] and permit me to establish you there in the name of the East African Association. We will assist you to build your fort in a locality suitable to the aims of such an association, leave our boat and such things as would be necessary for your purpose with you, and then hasten home across the Masai Land, lay the matter before the East African Association, and obtain its sanction for the act, as well as its assistance to establish you permanently in Africa. I must explain to you that I have no authority to make this last proposition, that it issues from my own goodwill to you, and with an earnest desire to save you and your men from the consequences of your determination to remain here. But I feel assured that I can obtain its hearty approval and co-operation, and that the Association will readily appreciate the value of a trained battalion or two in their new acquisition, and the services of such an administrator as yourself."

(At this point Stanley launches, for Emin's benefit, into a long disquisition on the incompetence of Egypt as a colonial power and the precise reasons why she could not hold, and would never retake, the Sudan. This leads naturally to a comparison of Egyptian colonising methods with the prudence, moderation, humanity, forethought, economic flair and administrative horse-sense that went into the making of the Congo State. Then, having enlightened his hearer on the nuts and bolts of practical colonial administration, Stanley returns to the subject of Emin's future.)

"Now every man who reflects at all will see that these Provinces of yours can never be reoccupied by Egypt. . . . Who else, then, will be so quixotic as to cast a covetous eye on these Provinces? The King of the Belgians? Well, there is a stipulation connected with this proposal, and that is, if the Provinces can 'give a reasonable revenue'. You are the best judge of this matter, and whether £10,000 or £12,000 subsidy will suffice for the support of the Government of these Provinces. The revenue, whatever it may be with this additional sum, must be sufficient to maintain about twenty stations between here and Yambuya, a distance of 650 miles or thereabouts; that is, to pay about 1,200 soldiers, about fifty or sixty officers, and a supreme Governor, furnish their equipments, the means of defence, and such transport force as may be necessary to unite the most distant part with the Congo. Failing the King of the Belgians, who else will undertake your support and maintenance, befitting your station and necessity? There are enough kind-hearted people in this world possessed of sufficient superfluous means to equip an Expedition once, say, every three years. But this is only a temporary expedient for mere subsistence, and it scarcely responds to your wishes. What then? I await your answer, Pasha, again begging to be excused for being so talkative."

"I thank you very much, Mr. Stanley, I do assure you, from my

216

heart. If I fail to express my gratitude, it is because language is insufficient. But I feel your kindness deeply, I do assure you, and will answer you frankly. Now, to the first proposition you have made me, I have already given my answer. To the second I would say that, first of all, my duty is to Egypt. While I am here, the Provinces belong to Egypt, and remain her property until I retire. When I depart they become 'no man's land'. I cannot strike my flag in such a manner, and change the red for the blue. I have served the first for thirty[7] years; the latter I never saw. Besides, may I ask you if, with your recent experience, you think it likely that communication could be kept open at reasonable cost?"

"Undoubtedly not at first. Our experiences have been too terrible to forget them soon; but we shall return to Yambuya for the rear column, I anticipate, with much less suffering. The pioneer suffers most. Those who follow us will profit by what we have learned."

"That may be, but we shall be at least two years before any news can reach us. No, I do not think that proposition, with all due gratitude to His Majesty King Leopold, can be entertained, and therefore let us turn to the last proposition. I do not think that my people would object to accompanying me to the Victoria Nyanza, as their objection, so far as I know, only applies to going to Egypt. Assuming that the people are willing, I admire the project very much. It is the best solution of the difficulty, and by far the most reasonable. For consider that three-fourths of the 8,000 people are women, children and young slaves. What would the Government do with such a mass of people? Would it feed them? Then think of the difficulty of travel with such an army of helpless people. I cannot take upon myself the responsibility of leading such a host of tender-footed people to die on the road. The journey to the Victoria is possible. It is comparatively short. Yes, by far the last proposition is the most feasible."

"There is no hurry, since you are to await the arrival of the rear column. Turn the matter over in your mind while I go to bring the Major up. You have certainly some weeks before you to consider the question thoroughly."

I then showed him the printed Foreign Office despatches furnished to me by order of Lord Iddesleigh. Among these was a copy of his (Emin's) letter to Sir John Kirk, wherein he offered the Province in 1886 to England, and stated that he would be most happy to surrender the Province to the British Government, or, in fact, any Power that would undertake to maintain the Province.

"Ah," said the Pasha, "they should never have published this letter. It was private. What will the Egyptian Government think of my conduct in venturing to treat of such a matter?"

"I cannot see the harm," I replied; "the Egyptian Government declares its inability to keep the Province, the British Government will have nothing to do with it, and I do not know of any company or body of men who would undertake the maintenance of what I regard, under all the circumstances, as a useless possession. In my opinion it is just 500 miles too far inland to be of any value, unless Uganda and Unyoro have been first brought under law; that is, if you persist in declining King Leopold's offer. If you absolutely decline to serve the King of the Belgians, and you are resolved to stay in Africa, you must trust in my promise to get a British Company to employ you and your troops, which probably has by this time been chartered with the purpose of constituting a British possession in East Africa."[8]

Throughout these discussions Stanley had to reconcile, or appear to reconcile, the conflicting aims of his three employers—the Khedive, King Leopold, and Mackinnon's Association. The Khedive, on behalf of the British Government, wanted the file on Equatoria closed; Leopold wanted a foothold on the headwaters of the Nile; Mackinnon wanted a commercial base in East Africa within reach of the sea. However, it is clear that Stanley made no real effort to present the options impartially. His own preference, quite obviously, was for Emin to return to Egypt, and nearly all his arguments are directed to this end.

Emin's preference, on the other hand, was for a quite opposite course: he longed, desperately, pathetically, to remain where he was and for things to go on as they had always done.

Thus the course that most appealed to Emin was the one that least appealed to Stanley; and the course which best suited Stanley's book was the very one Emin most wanted to avoid. In such a situation a compromise solution is the predictable outcome. Emin would not, if he could avoid it, return to Egypt; Stanley would not, if it could be helped, simply go away and leave Emin where he was. Leopold's offer and Mackinnon's offer were both available as compromise solutions.

Leopold's proposal was, of the two possibilities, the less attractive. On that Emin and Stanley appear to have been in agreement. For

Emin, the horrors of Stanley's journey up the Aruwimi were sufficient proof of the impracticability of an effective junction between Nile and Congo.[9] As for Stanley's attitude, the opinion of Casati that—

... such a proposal was rather in compliance with instructions received than from a conviction of the probability of its being feasible.

is very probably correct. Had Stanley himself leant towards this solution he would certainly have pressed harder for it, whereas, according to statements made later by Emin, Stanley himself urged Emin not to accept Leopold's offer.

The answer, then, would appear to be obvious: the best course to adopt was the one least disagreeable to both parties, or in other words, Mackinnon's scheme for the occupation of Kavirondo.[10] But if this is so, how was it that a month after the Expedition's arrival Emin appeared to be no nearer a definite decision than when the question of the future of Equatoria had first been raised three years earlier?

Emin's unwillingness to commit himself cannot simply be written down to an Oblomovian penchant for inaction, not until at least an attempt has been made to understand why the decision was such a hard one to take. And while the task of establishing Emin's motives and intentions can certainly be no easier a hundred years after the event than Stanley found it at the time, it should be possible to examine the factors bearing on Emin's decision (or indecision) with greater sympathy and detachment than Stanley brought to the task.

In the first place there is no reason to doubt the firmness and genuineness of Emin's often-stated intention: to stay at his post. Nor are there any grounds for questioning the sincerity of Emin's frequent assertions that his first duty was to his people. If they refused to leave Equatoria, he must stay. The decision, therefore, must ultimately come from them and he would abide by it.

On the other hand it must not be forgotten that Emin's idea of maintaining his position in Equatoria was premised on the supposition that a relief expedition would be so organised as to bring about a substantial improvement in his situation. He had hoped from Stanley one or more of three things: (1) the opening up of a permanently available route to the coast; (2) cloth, ammunition and other manufactured goods in sufficient quantities to offset local deficiencies; and (3) word that either Egypt or England would be willing to underwrite the maintenance of the Equatorial Province.

None of these expectations was realised. Instead, the arrival of the Expedition destroyed overnight the hopes Emin had nurtured so carefully during three long and anxious years. No new route had been opened up; Stanley had got through to Equatoria but at an impossible cost, and once there was himself as much cut off as Emin had ever been. The supplies he brought were derisory. The instructions he brought from Egypt added nothing to what Emin already knew from Nubar's letter of 1885—that Egypt washed her hands of the Province and Emin was free to decide his own future. Britain would have nothing to do with Emin's proposal of a protectorate.

Emin's disappointment must have been terrible. He hid it as best he could behind expressions of gratitude for Stanley's efforts, but this best was not good enough for Stanley who still expected Emin to hail him as a saviour. Stanley could not, or would not, understand that the arrival of the Expedition was not the answer to Emin's prayers but the death of his dearest hopes. So on a foundation of mutual incomprehension the two men began to erect a barrier of suspicion, resentment and mistrust.

If Stanley had been able to see the situation from Emin's point of view, he must have realised that the arrival of the Expedition had not merely failed to improve Emin's position but had on the contrary considerably weakened it. Stanley's bedraggled little party in no way corresponded to the sumptuous rescue expedition Emin had been led to expect and of whose forthcoming arrival he had fed such glowing stories to his people. Stories and rumours of the sufferings of Stanley's men could only increase the already powerful reluctance of Emin's men to embark on the trek away from their homeland to an unknown destination.[11] Moreover, anything which tended, as did Stanley's arrival, to increase the mood of suspicion and uncertainty among Emin's followers must inescapably have the simultaneous effect of weakening Emin's already tenuous hold on their loyalty and obedience. And without that loyalty and obedience Emin's future was bleak indeed.

The fact that Stanley did not actually enter Equatoria and show himself to Emin's men was a further source of future trouble. While Stanley held aloof at Nsabe, his arrival and his intentions could be known inside Equatoria only by rumour and second-hand reports, whose effect would certainly be to increase rather than lessen the prevailing unease. Emin was aware of this and pressed Stanley to enter the Province, talk to the men, explain the situation to them and bring the influence of his personality to bear. This Stanley refused to do, though what his reasons were can only be matter for speculation. He kept them to himself.[12]

Emin's inviting Stanley to tour the Province gives the lie to Stanley's later insinuation that Emin had deliberately tried to conceal from him the true state of affairs there. Casati tells how he begged Emin to explain to Stanley the full extent of the dissensions and disobedience among the troops, and that Emin promised to do so but "only threw out vague hints". This was true, but the explanation lay not in a Machiavellian design on Emin's part to bamboozle his rescuer, but in a simple human weakness, pride. Casati himself gives the reason when he says that Emin remained silent because—

> To confess his own powerlessness, and censure his own errors, was repugnant to his proud mind.[13]

Here Casati touched on a factor which is important in any assessment of Emin's situation during the period after Stanley's arrival. Arguably, Emin's pride was the greatest single obstacle to his accepting a withdrawal from Equatoria; it was unquestionably at the root of his reluctance to return to Egypt. To leave Equatoria was to admit himself beaten, to abandon his life's work half finished, and to give up his Province to the chaos from which he had tried so long and so hard to preserve it. It was also to exchange a position of power and authority for the likelihood of an obscure retirement as the pensioner of an ungrateful government. Worse still, perhaps, it would mean an end to his scientific labours and to the reputation his researches had begun to earn him in the museums, learned societies and universities of Europe. In a passage already quoted Emin speaks of being ashamed to return to Europe while his scientific researches were still in a condition he describes as "patchwork".[14] There is every reason to suppose that Emin here means exactly what he says. Certainly his reputation as a scientist meant more to him than his reputation as Gordon's successor in the Sudan. Why else would he have made the mistake of supposing that it was to rescue Emin the Scientist rather than Emin the Governor that the Relief Expedition was sent? It was this notion that caused Emin to suppose a connection between the specimens he had sent to the British Museum and the arrival of Stanley, and to boast to Casati:

> Thus my scientific labours have borne good fruit. Who would have thought that a bird and a butterfly would have proved so useful to me and my people?[15]

Only if due weight is given to this vein of pride—it might even be called vanity—in Emin's character is it possible to explain the paradox that, though he remained conspicuously unwilling to return to Egypt, he accepted with comparative alacrity the idea of abandoning the Province once a solution was proposed that did not involve a return to private life. Stanley's suggestion that Emin should move to Kavirondo and govern it for Mackinnon's Association seemed the perfect compromise. It would allow Emin to abandon Equatoria without at the same time abandoning everything that gave his life meaning. His scientific work could continue; his authority and responsibility would be undiminished; he would retain the security which derived from the backing of an outside power; finally, Stanley would be satisfied and would cease to nag him to return to Egypt. So attractive did Emin find these advantages that his enthusiasm led him to overlook or at least to underrate a major obstacle—the unwillingness of the Sudanese to change either their allegiance or their habitat. It was precisely this objection which had counted so heavily against the evacuation of the Province or the acceptance of a Belgian protectorate. Casati describes Emin's reactions to the scheme as follows:

> This project, so flattering in appearance, made Emin forget the material and moral difficulties that opposed the realisation of it, and rendered Stanley still more fervent in his efforts to strengthen the British undertaking, and gain for it (if possible) the military force that served under Emin. And Emin, forgetful of the most elementary prudence, boasted of this arrangement to his people, thus engendering, later on, a mistrust in their minds and the fear of being sold and torn away from their brothers in religion. When with firm conviction he hinted at his strong sympathy for the British nation and with great satisfaction praised himself for such faith, he believed the solution of the difficult problem was near. . . . Emin did not hesitate, and, with due reserve for the rights of the Egyptian Government and the duty that bound him to it, manifested his full adhesion to the project of establishing himself on the Victoria Lake, declaring that that might be effected, both on account of the shortness of the journey and the undoubted consent of his people. He was deceiving himself, and the delusion that it shortly after proved shed bitterness in his heart.

The satisfaction with which Emin related these conversations with Stanley,[16] caused me sad reflection, and I did not cease encouraging my friend to seriously consider the political situation of the Province and to recall the true position of it to his mind.

"Stanley's coming," I added, "augments your weakness instead of increasing your authority. The matters discussed here at the end of the lake, and beyond the Province, between you and Stanley, without witnesses, will excite mistrust and lead to disorders. The Expedition cannot return (*from bringing up the Rear Column*) under eight months, everything being favourable. The enterprise may still fail, and then what way of escape will be left us?"

And having fired these arrows of gloomy good sense into the balloon of Emin's hopes, Casati went into another of his Achillean periods of withdrawal:

On May 16, 1888, I took leave of Stanley and returned to Tunguru.

Emin stayed on at Nsabe finalising the arrangements he had made with Stanley. Stanley was now to return to Yambuya to make contact with Barttelot's detachment and bring it up to the Lake. From there the reunited Expedition would begin the homeward march for the East Coast and Zanzibar.[17] Emin in the meantime would tour the Province to sound out opinion among the soldiers. They would be read the Khedive's *firman* and asked to decide whether to stay where they were or to leave under Stanley's conduct. Emin's own choice would be determined by that of the soldiers. All those who wished to leave were to congregate at the south end of the Lake, ready to leave as soon as Stanley should return from Yambuya. A small station would be set up at Nsabe, built and manned by Emin's troops, ready to receive the Expedition on its return. Finally, at Jephson's suggestion, it was agreed that, time permitting, the men and loads from Fort Bodo would be brought down to the station at the Lake.

To help matters along Stanley left behind with Emin one of his officers—Jephson—and the three surviving Sudanese soldiers. Their task was to bear living witness to the genuineness of Stanley's mission. (It is permissible to suppose that Jephson's orders also included a commission from Stanley to do whatever he could to prod Emin into decisive action.)

Jephson was furnished with a proclamation drawn up by Stanley in his best heroic style. It read:

Soldiers of Emin Pasha,

After a long journey from Zanzibar, I have at last reached your Nyanza, and seen your Pasha. I have come expressly at the command of the Khedive Tewfik, to lead you out of this country and show you the way to Egypt. For you must know that the river el Abiad is closed, that Khartoum is in the hands of the followers of Mohammed Achmet, that the great Pasha Gordon and all his people were killed over three years ago, and that the country and river between Wady Halfa and the Bahr Ghazal is occuped by your enemies and by the rebels.

Four times have the Khedive and your friends made attempts to help you. First Gordon Pasha was sent to Khartoum to bring you all home, but before he could safely leave Khartoum, that city was taken and he himself killed.

Next, the English soldiers came near to Khartoum to try and help Gordon Pasha, but they were four days too late, for Gordon was dead and Khartoum was lost.

Next came Dr. Fischer, by way of the Nyanza of Uganda, but he found too many enemies in the path, and returned home and died.

Next came Dr. Lenz, by way of the Congo, but he could not find men enough to carry his goods, and he also went home.

I tell you these things to prove to you that you have not been forgotten in Egypt. No, the Khedive and his vizier Nubar Pasha have always kept you in mind though they could not reach you. They have heard from your Pasha, by way of Uganda, how bravely you have held to your posts, and how staunch you have been to your duties as soldiers.

Therefore they sent me to tell you this, and to say to you that you are well remembered and that your reward is awaiting you. At the same time, the Khedive says that if you think the road is too long, or are afraid of the journey, that you may stay here, but if you do so you are no longer his soldiers, and that your pay stops at once, and that if any trouble befall you hereafter you are not to expect any help from him. Should you decide to obey him and follow me to Egypt, I am to show you the way to Zanzibar, and there put you on board a steamer, and take you to Suez, and thence to Cairo, and that your pay continues until you arrive in Egypt, and that all promotions made here will be secured to you, and all rewards promised you here will be paid in full.

I send one of my officers, Mr. Jephson, to read to you this

message, and that you may know that he comes from me I lend him my sword. I now go back a little way to collect all my people and goods, and bring them here. After a few months—Inshallah—I shall return to hear what you have to say. If you say, "Let us go to Egypt," I will then show you a safe road, and will accompany you and not leave you until you stand before the Khedive. If you say, "We shall not leave this country," then I will bid you farewell and return to Egypt with my own people, and give the Khedive your answer.

May God have you in his safe keeping.

This is from your good friend,

STANLEY.

It will be noticed that Stanley's proclamation makes no mention of the plan to settle in Kavirondo. The omission is understandable. When it was seen how many soldiers, if any, were prepared to leave would be time enough to unveil the Kavirondo scheme. Unfortunately, however, no direct information exists as to what precisely had been agreed between Stanley and Emin on this point.[18]

Altogether, the month Stanley spent at Nsabe was a trying time for both parties. For Emin there was the shock of disappointment to be got over. For Stanley there was the frustration of finding that the man whom he had half expected to find packed and ready to leave had in fact made no decision whatever about his future movements, and that even after Stanley had had a whole month to force Emin to a decision, the most Emin would commit himself to was that he would see what his men said. And if Emin's indecision was incomprehensible to Stanley, Stanley's impatience was no less incomprehensible to the fatalistic Emin. Stanley quite failed to realise that the arrival of the Expedition had not only demolished Emin's hopes of better days but had brought about a completely new situation in Equatoria which dated from Stanley's arrival and to which Emin had had not three years, but a matter of weeks to adjust.

Even so, when they parted (May 24, 1888) relations between the two men were still cordial. As far as anyone knew there had been no actual friction. But if there was as yet no obvious divergence, the lack of convergence between the ideas and attitudes of the two men was equally conspicuous. Whether they would, or could, ever walk the same road, remained to be seen.

*   *   *

May 23 was the last day of the halt at Nsabe.

> The Zanzibaris entertained the Pasha and his officers to-night with a farewell dance. Though they are quite well aware of the dangers and fatigue of the journey before them, which will commence tomorrow, there are no symptoms of misgiving in any of them. But it is certain that some of them will take their last look of the Pasha tomorrow. (STANLEY)

The march began the next day (the Queen's birthday as Parke noted loyally). As a kind of parting present Emin had supplied Stanley with one hundred and thirty Madi carriers. The irony of Emin's having to supply not only provisions but also porters to the Expedition sent to rescue him appears to have been lost on the Expedition's leader.

> Emin Pasha marched a company along our new road[19] at dawn this morning, and halted it about two miles from the Lake. Having arranged the Madi carriers in their place in the column, the advance guard issued out from camp and took the road towards the west at 6.15 A.M. In half an hour we found the Pasha's Soudanese drawn up in line on one side of the road. They saluted us as we passed on, and the Pasha fervently thanked us and bade us good-bye. At the end of our new road twenty-one of the Madis broke from the line of the column and disappeared towards the north rapidly.[20] . . . About a mile from the village there was another stampede, and eighty-nine Madis deserted in a body, but not without sending a shower of arrows among the rear guard. The doctor, believing that this was preliminary to an attack on his small detachment, fired his rifle, and dropped a Madi dead, which precipitated the flight of the deserters. The remaining nineteen out of the 130 were secured. (STANLEY)

This untimely withdrawal of labour was at once reported back to Emin who promptly despatched a steamer to Msawa for a fresh supply. On May 26, eighty-two more Madis, under an escort of Emin's soldiers, duly presented themselves in Stanley's camp at the foot of the plateau. The march resumed.

The composition of the force which now ascended the escarpment and began to cross the grassland is given by Stanley as—

> . . . 111 Zanzibaris, 3 whites,[21] 6 cooks and boys, 101 Madis, and

3 soldiers belonging to the Pasha—total 224, exclusive of a few dozen natives who voluntarily follow us.

One incident of note marked the return to Fort Bodo. This occurred on May 24, the day the march began. Stanley records it thus:

When about five miles from Nsabe camp . . . my eyes were directed by a boy to a mountain said to be covered with salt, and I saw a peculiar shaped cloud of a most beautiful silver colour, which assumed the proportions and appearance of a vast mountain covered with snow. Following its form downward, I became struck with the deep blue-black colour of its base, and wondered if it portended another tornado; then . . . I became for the first time conscious that what I gazed upon was not the image or semblance of a vast mountain, but the solid substance of a real one, with its summit covered with snow. I ordered a halt and examined it carefully with a field-glass, then took a compass bearing of the centre of it, and found it bear 215° magnetic. It now dawned on me that this must be the Ruwenzori, which was said to be covered with a white metal. . . . This great mountain continued to be in sight most distinctly for two hours, but as we drew nearer to Badzwa at the foot of the plateau, the lofty wall of the plateau hid it from view.

The discovery was one of considerable geographical interest: the mountain Stanley had just observed supplied the one piece until that moment still missing from the complex jigsaw puzzle of the Nile sources. Until Speke's discovery of Lake Victoria all accounts of the Nile headwaters had been based on legend, myth or remote hearsay. But these accounts, however fanciful, tended to be consistent in certain respects; there was general agreement that the Nile sources comprised two associated geographical features—a system of lakes, and a range of snow-capped mountains, the so-called Mountains of the Moon. By the efforts of Burton, Speke, Baker, Stanley and others, the lakes of legend had become solid geographical facts. But no mountains had so far been found. The snow-capped peaks of Kenya, first reported by the German missionaries Krapf and Rebmann, had proved the possibility of snow-peaks at the Equator. But demonstrably these mountains were no part of the Nile system. It was only with the discovery of the Ruwenzori that the last element of the puzzle fell into place. Here at last were the Mountains of the Moon.

After recounting his sighting Stanley goes on to wonder why so conspicuous an object had escaped the notice of all previous visitors to the Lake. Baker had not seen it, nor had Gessi, nor had Mason; nor indeed had Emin, though in 1886 he had explored up the mouth of the Semliki River and so had come nearer than any other European visitor to the foot of the range.

> It will be evident (*Stanley concluded*) that it requires a peculiar condition of the atmosphere to enable one to see the mountain. . . . Near objects . . . an ordinarily clear atmosphere may enable us to distinguish; but in such a humid region as this is,[22] on a bright day such a quantity of vapour is exhaled from the heated earth, that at 30 miles it would be intensified into a haze which no eyesight could penetrate. But at certain times wind-currents clear the haze, and expose to the view objects which we wonder we have not seen before.

In fact someone *had* seen the Ruwenzori before, and for Stanley to claim this important discovery as his own was both dishonourable and disingenuous. The honour of the discovery—the most significant geographical result of the entire Expedition—belongs jointly to Parke and Jephson. They had glimpsed the same mountain on April 20 when on their way to the Lake with the boat. Parke's entry for this day reads:

> On the march we distinctly saw *snow* on the top of a huge mountain situated to the south-west of our position. As this was a curious and unexpected sight, we halted the caravan to have a good view. Some of the Zanzibaris tried to persuade us that the white covering which decorated this mountain was *salt*; but Jephson and myself were satisfied that it was snow.

They later reported their discovery to Stanley. According to Parke, "He was a good deal interested," though Jephson says that Stanley "had laughed at me and pooh poohed the idea".[23] Stanley's account does, indeed, refer to the report he had had from Jephson and Parke, but in a way that somehow contrives to suggest either that his officers were mistaken or that they had seen a different mountain. Such petty meanness accords ill with the stature of a man whose geographical discoveries had brought him sufficient fame and honour to satisfy ten normal men. He had no need to add to his triumphs by stealing from his subordinates.

A note was sent back to Emin informing him of Stanley's sighting. In his reply Emin said—

> Allow me to be the first to congratulate you on your most splendid discovery of a snow-clad mountain. We will take it as a good omen for further directions on our road to Victoria.

With this bogus bonus under his belt Stanley brought the column back to Fort Bodo on June 8.

At the fort he found all well. During Stanley's absence Stairs had returned safely from Ugarrowa's, where he had gone to recover the invalids left there. He found thirty of the original fifty-six still alive and of these he had managed to get fourteen back to Fort Bodo.

With this addition the composition and numbers of the Advance Column was now as follows:

At Fort Bodo:

Stanley, Parke, Nelson, Stairs, Hoffman	5
Zanzibaris able to march	119
Sick....................................	57
Madis	98
Emin's soldiers	4
TOTAL	283

With Emin:

Jephson, 3 Sudanese, servant	5

Couriers:

(En route for Yambuya with letters)	20
TOTAL	308

Subtracting from this total Emin's Sudanese and the Madis, we are left with two hundred and six survivors of the original three hundred and eighty-nine in the Advance Column, a loss of nearly fifty per cent. Stanley now proposed to make a two-way journey over the ground which, on a one-way journey, had already cost him the lives of nearly half his force. This time he had, it is true, some advantages: he knew the ground; the men would be travelling light on the first half of the round trip, carrying only their own rations; and behind them they now had a secure base, amply supplied. Even so, any man might have been forgiven for refusing to face again that awful forest.

A week was spent in mustering the companies and preparing rations for the march. Each man ground and packed a twenty-five-days' ration of Indian corn and prepared as much plantain flour as he could carry. All the fit men would travel with Stanley. The sick would remain in the Fort. A small party would travel with the main column as far as Ipoto, pick up the remaining loads stored there and return to Fort Bodo. Reasoning that Nelson was still an invalid, that Stairs deserved a rest, and that Parke would be needed to look after the sick, Stanley decided to leave all the officers behind on the dash through the forest. Accordingly, the two hundred and eighty-three men in Fort Bodo were now divided into three groups:

Main column:
    Stanley and 213 men 214

Ipoto Party:
    14 of the strongest invalids under Parke 15

Garrison:
    Nelson, Stairs, 52 men 54

                            TOTAL 283

When everything was ready——

> On the 16th of June, in the early morning we set out for Yambuya in excellent spirits loudly cheered by the garrison and with the best wishes of the officers. (STANLEY)

For the moment Emin and the problems of Equatoria were forgotten. A more urgent question now occupied Stanley's attention: What would he find when he reached Yambuya?

NOTES AND REFERENCES

CHAPTER 6   STANLEY AND EMIN

1   Emin (diary). Petermann's *Mitteilung*—journal published in Gotha, covering matters of geographical interest. Emin was one of its correspondents, as he was of similar periodicals such as the Italian *L'Esploratore*, whose editor, Manfredo Camperio, was instrumental in sending Casati to the Sudan.

2   Parke was as impressed as Jephson had been by Emin's generosity. (PARKE pp. 225 and 232.) Stanley saw it as evidence of Emin's duplicity (or that of his European supporters, Felkin and Junker) in representing Emin's need of supplies as more urgent than it actually was. (D.A. I p. 398; SCHWEITZER I p. 274).

3   Some uniforms had been made for Emin in Cairo. The legs of the trousers were six inches too long, apparently because Junker had, according to Stanley, described Emin as "a tall man of six feet or thereabouts, but in reality Emin Pasha does not exceed 5 feet 7 inches in height". Clearly this was another piece of duplicity on the part of Emin's friends. As for the ammunition, it was of doubtful quality even before it left Egypt (D.A. I p. 56), and 31 boxes represented at best 10 rounds a man for Emin's 1,500 troops (or, more accurately, 20 rounds a man for half of Emin's troops, since only 750 were armed with Remingtons and the remainder with muzzle-loading percussion-cap muskets).

4   Favoured by Casati. (CASATI II p. 153).

5   The insinuation that by remaining in Equatoria Emin would be *disobeying* the Khedive (as impertinent as it is false) is a nice example of Stanley's discursive method. Emin could not, of course, disobey in the absence of an order.

6   The area known as Kavirondo.

7   Stanley must mean thirteen; Emin had come to the Sudan in 1875.

8   Mackinnon set up the "British East Africa Association" in 1887 merely as a kind of steering committee for what became in September 1888 the "Imperial British East Africa Company".

9   "The fate of the Relief Expedition was so eloquent as to render any reply needless." (CASATI)

10 The point may be illustrated quantitatively by the process known in the Orwellian jargon of Games Theory as "assigning utilities to outcomes". The possible courses of action are rated numerically according to (a) Stanley's evaluation, and (b) Emin's. Thus—

	a	b	TOTAL
Status quo	o	3	3
Belgian protectorate	1	1	2
Kavirondo scheme	2	2	4
Return to Egypt	3	o	3

It will be seen that Mackinnon's is the highest-scoring proposal and therefore, "logically", the best course to follow.

11 "... already the people who had come with us (to Nsabe) looked with wonder, eyes wide open and dubious hearts, at this remnant of the Expedition, of which the Governor had sung so many praises, and which he had taught them to consider a fount of comfort. . . . Emin felt profoundly the sad impression that must be produced by the description of the miseries suffered, and the difficulties of the road, that the soldiers and Zanzibaris would not have failed to give to our people . . ." (CASATI II pp. 158–159). See also SCHWEITZER I p. 283.

12 There is no evidence for the tempting supposition that Stanley kept out of the Province because he knew that by so doing he increased the instability of Emin's position.

13 CASATI II p. 159.

14 For confirmation, see also Emin to Felkin, May 5, 1886. (Qu. Felkin in his Introduction, SCHWEITZER p. xxviii.)

15 CASATI II p. 161. See also JEPHSON—E.P. p. 34: "None of the letters we had brought him gave him such pleasure as those relating to his scientific researches. There was one from the British Museum announcing the safe arrival of several boxes of skulls, skins, birds, and bugs, which he had sent off some months before. He talked delightedly of the letter for days. Several of the chief scientific societies had written telling him that his name was enrolled among their members. All these letters gave him the keenest pleasure and satisfaction."

16 "I think this is perhaps the most memorable day of my life", wrote Emin in his diary for May 4, after recording the conversation in which Stanley had laid before him the proposals of Mackinnon and King Leopold.

17 As already noted, Stanley's objections to the East Coast routes are no more heard of once he had decided to return that way. For Casati's comments on this phenomenon, see CASATI II p. 155 and p. 157.

18 Another interesting point on which we have no information is whether the question of ivory was raised in the discussions between the two men. The idea must have been present in Stanley's mind that if Emin decided to stay in Equatoria, he might wish to keep some or all of his ivory with him.

19 Stanley had again been indulging his fancy for civil engineering during the halt at Nsabe. Detachments under Jephson and Parke had cleared a three-mile stretch of road leading away from the Lake towards the foot of the plateau.

20 I.e. homewards. Their tribal lands were around Duffile.

21 Stanley, Parke and Hoffman.

22 Between the mountains and the south end of the Lake—as Stanley was later to discover—lay forty miles of swamp formed by the Semliki River.

23 JEPHSON—entry for May 26, 1888.

THE REAR GUARD
June 1887—August 1888

Good God! will these porters never come? Must all of us lie down and
rot and die?

WARD

Sœur Anne, sœur Anne, ne vois-tu rien qui radine?

SAN-ANTONIO

There were five Europeans at Yambuya with the Rear Guard: Barttelot,
Jameson, Troup, Ward and Bonny. All except Bonny left published
accounts—largely in the form of diaries and letters—of their experiences in the service of the Emin Pasha Relief Expedition. Two of these
accounts, those of Barttelot and Jameson, were published post-
humously, as their authors never returned from Africa. Collectively
the four stories make as depressing a piece of reading as can be found
anywhere in the annals of African exploration. The reason lies not
simply in the squalid miseries their authors suffered at Yambuya,
nor even in the intensity of their sufferings, but in that those sufferings,
endured without complaint, were in the last analysis absolutely futile
and absolutely unnecessary. They suffered without glory, without
purpose and without hope. And their only reward was to be viciously
calumniated by the man at whose orders and in whose service they
had endured so much, so uselessly, and for so long.

*   *   *

When the Advance Guard marched out of Yambuya on June 28
1887, Ward and Bonny were still at Bolobo with one hundred and
twenty-five men, and Troup was even further down-river at Stanley
Pool with the remaining loads. Six weeks later, on August 14, the
Stanley brought both Ward's and Troup's contingents up to Yambuya.
The united Rear Guard now consisted of:

Europeans	5
Zanzibaris	200
Sudanese	44
Somalis	2
TOTAL[1]	251

These men were the flotsam of the Expedition: the weaklings, the laggers, the trouble-makers and hard characters, or (like Barttelot and the Sudanese) simply those for whom Stanley had formed an aversion. When from the total of two hundred and fifty-one were subtracted the sick, the officers, the boys, and the soldiers, Barttelot was left with only one hundred and sixty-five men able to carry loads. And there were six hundred and sixty loads in the camp—one hundred and sixty-seven left by Stanley and four hundred and ninety-three brought up by Troup.

One hundred and sixty-five carriers and six hundred and sixty loads: there were exactly four times as many loads as men to carry them. This simple sum was the central fact of existence at Yambuya camp.

One further fact, and one unanswerable question completed the grim picture.

There were extensive plantations of manioc in the immediate vicinity of the camp. These represented the only substantial source of food available to Barttelot and his men.[2]

The besetting question, on the answer to which the Rear Guard's whole future depended, was: How soon would Tippu-Tib send the porters he had promised?

Barttelot had three courses of action to choose from: to remain where he was until Stanley returned; to wait for the porters from Tippu-Tib and then move off on Stanley's track; or to move off with only the porters he had, making short stages many times over on a relay system. The crucial problem was that of deciding how long to wait for Tippu-Tib. If he waited too long there was every chance that his force would be so weakened by sickness and malnutrition that movement of any kind would become impossible. Every day he waited would bring the arrival of the promised porters and/or Stanley's return one day nearer. But it also took his camp one more stage along the road of slow deterioration which would inevitably turn it, first

235

into a hospital, and ultimately into a charnel-house. The Rear Guard was in a trap.

*   *   *

Arguably, Barttelot was the worst possible man Stanley could have chosen to command at Yambuya. His courage and his military ability were never in question. His service in the Sudan campaign had proved his energy, determination and organising ability, and he had come to the Expedition with recommendations from Wolseley and from Sir Redvers Buller. On the other hand, he was a disciplinarian with a rigidity of mind which made it impossible for him to adapt the habits and methods of the regular army to the handling of Zanzibari porters, and he lacked the flexibility and subtlety required for dealing with the Arabs. He also lacked the inner resources which made it easier for some men than others to cope with the demoralising frustration of prolonged inaction. There is something frightening in Ward's casual observation that, while the other officers spent their free time sketching, collecting, talking or reading, Major Barttelot spent his *"walking up and down"*. His temper was short and sometimes violent. Finally, he laboured under a disadvantage which, one would have thought, should have debarred him altogether from partici-pating in an African exploring expedition:

> . . . he had an intense hatred of anything in the shape of a black man, for he made no disguise of this, but frequently mentioned the fact. His hatred was so marked that I was seized with great misgivings concerning his future dealings with them. . . . (TROUP)

Ward, too, was of the opinion that Barttelot's temperament unfitted him for command in Africa:

> Somehow or another from the very start Barttelot and I failed to "hit it off". We viewed things in different lights: he through the strict, stern, rigid spectacles of discipline and with the autocratic manner of a British officer; while I, who had roughed it all the world over, had the influence upon me which came of much adventure, and that cosmopolitanism which results from being vis-à-vis to every phase of life. In a word, he was a soldier come to rescue Emin Pasha; I had joined the explorer in the hope of stirring adventure with gun and pencil. He was a stranger to African

236

manners and speech, with ever-present suspicion of everyone and everything which this disadvantage must always excite. I had an acquaintance with two or three of the languages, and that knowledge of native methods which could only be acquired by residence among the people. As a consequence of all this, the black people with whom he was brought into contact were to Barttelot an unknown quantity, and the contempt and disdain natural to the highly strung young officer who believed nothing was equal to the British soldier, gained full and unfortunate sway.

In the situation in which the Rear Guard found itself placed, the question of morale was of towering importance. The combination of enforced idleness, bad health, worse food and an inhospitable environment was bad enough by itself. With harsh discipline and unsympathetic leadership thrown in for good measure, the resulting mixture was lethal to the morale of the men. The full extent of the deterioration, indeed, might not be immediately apparent, especially while the Rear Guard remained idle at Yambuya. But if and when the time came for action, the hidden damage to the morale of the men, combined with almost insuperable organisational problems, could be enough to nullify the efforts even of a man who had Stanley's abilities as a leader. For Barttelot, incapable of inspiring either respect or admiration in his men, it was to prove fatal.

*   *   *

In late June Tippu-Tib had promised to be at Yambuya with the porters in ten days. In mid-August, when Troup and Ward arrived, over six weeks had already passed and Tippu-Tib had given no sign. On August 17 Jameson confided to his diary:

> We have almost given up hope of Tippu-Tib's men, and are already talking about how we shall employ our time until November.

November, of course, was the anticipated date of Stanley's return. On this point Ward commented significantly:

> Stanley . . . had roughly calculated that, even if we were compelled to remain at Yambuya till his return, our stay there would not extend beyond the month of November. The period, however, was

fixed rather by inference than by plain statement of fact, the inference resting on the postscript in his letter of instructions to Barttelot, directing that one brass rod (to buy fish) and six cowrie shells should be given to each man per week for five months.[3]

For the officers, life in the camp soon resolved itself into the dreary business of supervising a futile, make-work routine, bouts of wasting sickness, and a constant, demoralising, preoccupation with food. Meanwhile, before their eyes was the ever-present spectacle of scores of poor wretches, for whom nothing could be done, weakening and dying daily of starvation and disease. If the men of the Advance Guard suffered as much and more from the same afflictions, they at least had the idea of an attainable goal to give meaning to their struggles. The men at Yambuya had to suffer and die where they stood, waiting on events in miserable uncertainty.

On August 15, the day after the arrival of the *Stanley*, they had the first intimation that they were not the only strangers abroad in the forest. A group of Manyuema under an Arab chief attacked the native settlement across the river from the camp. This event—

> . . . was noteworthy because of the impression it gave us, that they were the advanced guard of the men promised us by Tippoo Tib. . . . We found later on, however, that we were quite in error, and that, as regards our idea of these men being connected in some way with our porters, the wish was only unfortunately father to the thought. (WARD)

The Manyuema, it turned out, were indeed from Stanley Falls, but their presence at Yambuya had nothing to do with the Expedition; it represented merely an extension of the raiding circle of the Falls Arabs. From the Expedition's point of view their arrival was simply an added unpleasantness in an already less than rosy situation. Its main practical result was to cut off the trickle of food—mainly fish and palm oil—which had been coming into the camp from the native villages. The Arabs terrorised the villagers, forbade them to sell food to the Expedition's men, and arrogated to themselves whatever meagre surplus the unfortunate natives had.

The headman of the raiders soon presented himself in the camp:

> He was interviewed by Major Barttelot in presence of us all. From him we learnt that Tippoo Tib had sent about 500 men to us in

canoes, but they had encountered such hostility from the natives, and were so done up after paddling six days against the stream without finding any indication of our whereabouts, that they had eventually disbanded, small bands of Manyemas being sent out in different directions in order to discover us, if possible. . . . A further reason for the disbanding of the men was, we were told, that their ammunition had given out, and the natives had proved too strong for them.[4] . . . (He) urged that, as Stanley Falls was only a few days' journey off, we should go ourselves and see Tippoo Tib personally on the subject. . . . After consultation together, Major Barttelot decided to send Jameson and myself. . . . (WARD)

Jameson and Ward set out on August 23 and reached the Falls five days later after a miserable journey over swampy forest trails to the Congo and then up-river by canoe.

On our arrival at Stanley Falls we found Tippoo Tib, bland, courteous, and accommodating in every way. We handed him a letter from Major Barttelot, which had been translated into Arabic by Assad Farran the interpreter, explaining the mistake his men had made, telling him that Mr. Stanley had gone on, and saying we were still awaiting the promised 600 men. The letter concluded by informing Tippoo Tib that the powder promised him by Mr. Stanley had arrived at Yambuya, and that the agreement made at Zanzibar held good. (WARD)

In reply Tippu-Tib repeated the story they had already heard from the headman at Yambuya of the five hundred men who had tried and failed to reach the Expedition's camp:

To make a long story short, Tippoo Tib professed friendliness in a marked degree, and we left with the understanding that he would immediately send us as many men as he could, but he feared he would not be able to make up the large number he had originally got together. (WARD)

With this answer the envoys had to be content and returned to Yambuya. Jameson got back a few days after Ward. With him came Selim bin Mohammed, nephew of Tippu-Tib,[5] who had come to take over as headman of the Arab encampment at Yambuya.

The waiting went on.

Ward collapsed on his return. For five weeks he lay in his tent between life and death. When he emerged again, in mid-October—

Matters appeared to be precisely as they were when I had been taken ill. The expected porters had not arrived from Tippoo Tib, there was no news from Mr. Stanley, and all in camp were still waiting on events. Sickness and disease had thinned our ranks, while Troup, Bonny and Jameson had had more or less severe touches of fever.

At the beginning of October, however, Barttelot had decided to have another try at getting Tippu-Tib to fulfil his contract. This time he had gone in person to the Falls, taking Troup with him.

Tippu-Tib was now fully occupied with projects of his own in the Falls district, on the Aruwimi, and on the Lomami (which joins the Congo about half-way between Stanley Falls and the Aruwimi confluence). He told Barttelot that the men would be found, but because of the heavy calls on his manpower, the new porters would have to come from Kasongo, a month's journey up-river and the real centre of Tippu-Tib's empire.

My impression of Tippu-Tib and the Falls (wrote Troup) is this. He has very few men here really of his own, though there are several native villages under his control. The great part of his own men are away after ivory, &c., all over the country. A large body are at the Lomami under Raschid, trying to settle down there among the natives for trading purposes. . . . Then a lot are scattered over the district Stanley has traversed as well as elsewhere. His son, Sefu, who reigns at Kasongo, has plenty of men, and it is from there they say they will get our carriers, but I don't put much faith in their story.

Once again Barttelot had to be content with promises. At the beginning of November he and Troup returned to Yambuya accompanied by a mixed herd of goats and chickens they had acquired at the Falls.

Their neighbours in the Arab encampment at Yambuya were now beginning to present something of a headache. Not only had the Arabs prevented the natives selling food to Barttelot's men, but the contacts between Zanzibaris and Manyuema were giving rise to anxieties of a different kind.

. . . friendly relations were soon established between our men and these wanderers of the forest. All this was very much against our wish, and boded very badly for us. The free, unrestrained life of the Arabs stood out in marked contrast to the discipline and methodical procedure we found it absolutely necessary to maintain, and a sense of grievance naturally took possession of our men . . . but, worse than this, the stories which our men told of discipline and difficulty, obtained wide circulation through the Arabs, and undoubtedly acted as a strong deterrent to our getting the porters for whom we so anxiously waited and watched. (WARD)

Discipline in the camp went far beyond "methodical procedure". Floggings for such offences as stealing, desertion, and sleeping on sentry-go were almost daily occurrences.[6] One man, a Zanzibari named John Henry, died after receiving an exceptionally heavy punishment of three hundred lashes. Another man, a Sudanese deserter, was executed by a firing squad. On the latter case Jameson observed:

. . . there is no doubt that it ought to have a good effect upon the others; but when one thinks what a miserable poor wretch he is, and from what a miserable existence he tried to escape, one cannot help pitying him.

Ward was now ordered to Stanley Falls to complain about the behaviour of the Arabs at Yambuya and ask that they should be compelled to make their camp further away from the Expedition's. Bwana Nzige received Ward at the Falls with the news that Tippu-Tib had left for Kasongo a few days earlier. In a limited way this was good news since it meant that the possibility of extra porters being obtained from Kasongo was brought one step closer to realisation. Ward also obtained the promise of stricter control over the Manyuema at Yambuya.

It was the end of November when he returned:

I arrived back in camp to find all my comrades, like myself, suffering from illness. Rheumatism, fever, and biliousness was the order of the day. By December 5 there were thirty-one deaths among the blacks. Each morning a miserable sight met our eyes as, crowding round Bonny's hut, their number growing each day, a mass of suffering Zanzibaris and Soudanese sought relief and medicine, from the scanty store he had at his disposal. The wet weather, the wretched food, and the weary, miserable existence we were forced to lead was telling on us all, but with most deadly effect on these poor creatures, whose uncared-for flesh broke into festering sores of the most painful character.

Still there was no sign from Stanley, no word from him. Jameson wrote:

> This waiting here in utter darkness is sickening, and the men are dying off like rotten sheep.

Christmas came. Still no porters. Still Stanley did not return. Some of his deserters had filtered back to the Falls Region. They told fantastic and contradictory stories of battles and starvation. These garbled accounts were no help to Barttelot in his dilemma, which grew each day more acute. If Stanley had simply been delayed on the road by difficulties of one kind or another then Barttelot's best course was to stay put, as each day automatically brought nearer the day of Stanley's return. But if, as now began to appear possible, the Advance Column had met with a mishap to prevent it ever returning or even communicating with the Rear Guard, then Barttelot had every interest in making a move before his force was so reduced as to make positive action impossible. There was even—in Barttelot's mind, at least—a possibility that Stanley had "relieved" Emin and marched straight on to Zanzibar.

Troup, the transport specialist, raised his voice against attempting to leave Yambuya without extra porters:

> The idea of our moving out with the bulk of the loads with the Zanzibaris only . . . would have been in my opinion perfectly insane. . . . With about a hundred Zanzibaris—all that would have been fit to carry—with five hundred loads (supposing we had dispensed with two hundred), it would have taken us twelve days to get all these loads one day's march of four miles. At this rate we could not have gone far before we met Stanley coming back.

It seemed better to wait a little longer. Barttelot, however, was now approaching a state of something like desperation. The strain produced on him by the joint effects of prolonged inactivity and continual uncertainty was beginning to show. Certainly, he of all the officers must have found the waiting hardest to bear, both by reason of the responsibility he bore as commander, and because of his impatient nature. He must do something. For the want of a better idea, he decided on yet another—the fourth—expedition to Stanley Falls. Taking with him Jameson and the Sudanese interpreter Assad Farran, he set out on February 14. At the Falls they found Bwana Nzige still in charge. Tippu-Tib would not be back for another month. Barttelot decided, instead of simply waiting for Tippu-Tib's return, to send Jameson down to Kasongo to try to get the porters.

At first sight this decision was strange since there were now signs that things were at last moving in the direction Barttelot wished. On the way to the Falls they had met a party of one hundred and fifty men just sent up from Kasongo and had been informed that this was the first instalment of the promised carriers. While Barttelot was at the Falls, another fifty came in. Moreover, Troup, in temporary command at Yambuya, sent a letter announcing that a further fifty had reached Yambuya. Barttelot, incomprehensibly, was so far from excited by this last intelligence that he sent off a brusquely-worded note to Troup ordering him to refrain from further frivolous communications and restrict himself to important messages "such as news of Stanley or any trouble in the camp". Jameson would go to Kasongo as planned. His orders were to place before Tippu-Tib a new set of proposals whereby, in addition to the six hundred carriers already agreed on, the Arab leader was asked to provide a force of four hundred "fighting men". As Barttelot explained in his report to the Relief Committee:

> The reason for my taking 400 fighting men is that I consider it useless to try and relieve Mr. Stanley, if he be in a fix, with a force as small as he started with . . . and we cannot help thinking otherwise, as we can get no news of him either from Tippu-Tib or other sources.[7]

On March 18 Barttelot and Jameson parted. Jameson, with Assad Farran, set off up-river for Kasongo. Barttelot, though ill, started back to Yambuya. "Shattered and weak" (his own words) he got back to camp on March 25. Immediately on his return he took another step the rationale of which is not immediately apparent: he told Ward to get ready for a trip to the coast carrying a telegram addressed to the Relief Committee. It read as follows:

No news of Stanley since writing last October. Tippo Tib went Kassongo November sixteenth, but up to March has only got us two hundred and fifty men; more are coming, but in uncertain numbers and at uncertain times. Presuming Stanley in trouble, absurd for me to start with less numbers than he did, I carrying more loads and minus "Maxim" gun; therefore have sent Jameson Kassongo to hasten Tippo in regard to remainder of originally promised six hundred men, and to obtain from him as many fighting men as possible up to four hundred; to make most advantageous terms he can as regards service and payment of men, he and I guaranteeing money in name of Expedition. Jameson will return about May fourteenth, but earliest date to start will be June first. When I start, propose leaving officer with all loads not absolutely wanted at Stanley Falls. Ward carries this message. Please obtain wire from King Belgians to Administrator "Free State", to place carriers at his disposal, and have steamer in readiness to convey him Yambuya. If men come before his arrival (we will) start without him. He should return about July first. Wire advice and opinion. Officers all well. Ward awaits reply.

Ward was to make his way by canoe to Bangala, escorted by thirty Zanzibaris and five Sudanese. There he would leave his escort, hire canoes and paddlers from the Belgian commandant, and follow the river down to Stanley Pool. From there he would travel on foot to the coast and then take a steamer to either St. Tomé or St. Paul de Loanda, both of which were terminals on the undersea telegraph cable. Such a journey could under no circumstances take less than two months either way and was so hazardous (particularly the first stage to Bangala, through unsubdued territory) as to present a strong probability of Ward's not getting through at all. Were such a risk and such an expenditure of time, effort and money justified by the sending of a cable which merely reported what Barttelot intended to do? It would hardly seem so. It may therefore be asked whether Barttelot had some additional reason for sending Ward off to the coast with a telegram which might never reach its destination, and the answer to which (a) could have no material effect on Barttelot's situation, and (b) might never reach him, since he proposed to leave Yambuya before Ward's return.

Various explanations offer themselves, though in no case is the evidence sufficient to permit of certainty. Barttelot's biographer explains Ward's mission by saying:

> The reason is simple. There are two sides to the African Continent, and Major Barttelot expected the Committee might have news of Stanley from Zanzibar. Major Barttelot was quite prepared to hear that the relief had been effected, and to receive a telegram of recall.[8]

The actual contents of the telegram hardly bear out this interpretation, though the idea that he expected a recall is supported by the instructions he sent to Ward when the latter was returning from the coast. Another explanation is that Barttelot's mental state, and hence his judgement, were beginning to show adverse effects from the strain he was under. In this case Ward's mission to the coast, like Jameson's to Kasongo, can be interpreted as displacement activities— outlets for the frustration imposed by the simultaneous presence of two conflicting drives. Faced with the absolute necessity for action, and, at the same time with the impossibility of carrying out that action, Barttelot endeavoured to resolve the contradiction by actions which were unrelated to his real position and his real needs.

A third possibility, not as outrageous as it might at first appear, is that Barttelot sent Ward to the coast to get rid of him. We already know, on Ward's evidence, that he and Barttelot did not "hit it off", though no specific instances of friction are recorded by either party. However, Barttelot's diary shows that, on his return from the Falls, he learnt (or thought he learnt) that the other officers had been misbehaving in his absence. The nature of their misdeeds is not stated but it seems that the offence was some form of dishonesty, that Ward was supposed to be the chief or only culprit, that Barttelot's informant was Bonny, and finally, that Barttelot kept his suspicions to himself and made no open accusations.[9] There are plain hints of all this in Barttelot's diary. Thus on March 25, the day after his return from the Falls:

> I was prostrate, and that opportunity was taken to play me false.

The next day:

> I find they have been playing the mischief since I have been away.

And on March 27, the day before Ward's departure:

> I am much upset at what I find. . . .[10]

The likelihood that Barttelot's suspicions were strictly delusory is strong. His mood at this time showed a strange and unhealthy agitation, which the others supposed a symptom of his fever but which may well have been what is politely termed a "nervous" disorder. "Poor Barttelot", remarked Ward in his diary, "is almost beside himself with his fever, weakness, and the preparation of letters for me." To Troup, Barttelot confided a suspicion that his illness arose from an attempt to poison him by the Arabs at the Falls. It is clear, however, from Jameson's account of their visit, that the Arabs had treated them with the same courtesy and hospitality they invariably showed to the Expedition's officers. Barttelot himself had written to Troup from the Falls:

> Our treatment here, since our arrival, has been that of favoured guests, and Nzige has done everything in his power for us, as regards the Expedition, and our own personal comfort and amusement.

Troup also records that Barttelot at this time was "much upset", "very excited", "distressed in mind" and "disturbed". These are terms which, like Ward's "beside himself", clearly refer to mental rather than physical disorder.

Ward and Troup set out together on March 28. Troup had been detailed to buy goats at the Lomami River settlement and would keep Ward company for the first few days' journey. On April 2 they were overtaken by a canoe bringing a letter from Barttelot to Ward. It read:

> WARD—I am sending this to warn you to be very careful in the manner you behave below—I mean as regards pecuniary matters. I shall require at your hands a receipted bill for everything you spend, and should you be unable to purchase the champagne and the watch, you will not draw that £20. The slightest attempt at any

246

nonsense I shall be down upon you for. I have given you a position of trust, so see that you do not abuse it. You will send me a receipt of this letter. EDMUND M. BARTTELOT, Major.[11]

Ward was clearly astounded. This was certainly the first intimation he had had of Barttelot's paranoid suspicions. He noted in his diary:

Have replied: consider letter gross insult, and will demand explanation and satisfaction on my return.

It is not difficult to guess what had prompted this astonishing epistle, since Barttelot's diary for March 30, the day on which the letter was written, contains the significant entry:

More disclosures were made to me. . . .

Again the gentlemanly reticence of Barttelot's biographer denies us details of these revelations, but one thing is clear: they can only have come from Bonny since he and Barttelot were now the only officers in the camp, and there are entries elsewhere in Barttelot's diaries which show that he was willing to listen to Bonny's gossip about the other officers.[12]

When Barttelot's amazing missive reached them, Ward and Troup had, in Troup's words—

. . . a long talk together regarding his (*Ward's*) arduous journey and the causes for it. We were both of the opinion that it would not be of much benefit to the Expedition, only causing a deal of trouble and expense, because the Committee could only reply, "Carry out Stanley's instructions."

Such scraps of information as are on record do not justify any solid conclusions either about the reasons for Barttelot's odd behaviour or about his mental state at this time. His treatment of Ward, how-ever, is on its own sufficiently eccentric to arouse some misgivings about the soundness of the Major's judgement, and from this time on, the question of his mental health has to be kept in view.

Towards April Barttelot became convinced that the Arabs at Yambuya were planning an attack on his camp. There had been a

247

number of petty disputes between the Expedition's men and Selim bin Mohammed's Manyuema. Barttelot supposed these to be the opening moves in an Arab campaign which was to culminate in open fighting and an attempt on the Expedition's stores. His diary for the beginning of April, in which he records the "incidents" which had excited his apprehension, is interspersed with remarks like: "Salem means mischief", "Things look black", and "Perhaps my days are numbered". The threat was certainly more imaginary than real. There can be little doubt that it had its origins in Barttelot's chronic mistrust not only of the Arabs but also of the Zanzibaris, Sudanese, the natives, and even his own officers. This generalised suspicion led him to behave in ways that were, to say the least, quirky. Thus, having now decided to make yet another pilgrimage to the Falls—this time to enlist Bwana Nzige's support in the coming confrontation with Selim— Barttelot's orders to Bonny included the amazing injunction:

> Should the natives prove aggressive, inform and place yourself in the hands of Salem Mohammed.

Barttelot reached the Falls on April 10.

> I had a palaver with Nzige, and told him what had been happening at the camp, and that if he wished the loads to be safe, Salem Mohammed had better move his camp a mile . . .

The next day—

> About 11 a.m. Nzige and Naribo ben Sulieman came, and told me their decision, that Salem Mohammed be recalled.

Satisfied with this answer Barttelot left immediately to return to Yambuya. On the way back he met Troup returning (goatless) from the Lomami. Troup describes the encounter:

> I was amazed to meet Barttelot looking terribly ill and very disturbed. . . . He was evidently much excited over the recent events in camp, and could not give me a clear statement of what had taken place.

Arriving back at the camp Barttelot found the treacherous onslaught he expected had not materialised. Bonny was able to recount a number of dangerous-seeming moments that had occurred, though these show every sign of having arisen from simple misunderstandings rather than hostile intent. It is possible that they were deliberately over-dramatised in the retelling by Bonny either to add glamour to his own brief tenure of command or even to pander to Barttelot's fantasies.

In one respect Barttelot's fears were justifiable: the garrison was in no position to resist even the most half-hearted assault. By the end of March the number of deaths in the camp had risen to around seventy. These losses, plus the general weakness of the men and the detachment of an escort for Ward, had reduced Barttelot's effectives to a mere handful. On the other hand, the very fact of the garrison's weakness makes it all the more certain that there was no Arab plot against them, since, as Troup observed—

Had Salim-bin-Mohammed or Tippu-Tib been treacherous, our lives were not worth a day's purchase.

And again:

... had the Arabs in anger taken matters into their own hands, they could have quickly made an end of our portion of the Expedition, either by starving us out or by an attack on our not-too-strongly fortified and none-too-well-garrisoned camp.

There was no attack. On April 18 Barttelot noted:

Salem Mohammed came to see me, and told me he was going away down river.

And added cautiously:

This may be a blind. I have sent men out to watch him.

The next day Selim Mohammed left.

May came in, a season of despair. There had been no news from Jameson, none from Ward, none from Stanley. Troup took to his bed. His health had collapsed completely and he was assumed to be dying. No more had been seen or heard of the two hundred and fifty

Kasongo men whose arrival had caused a momentary optimism earlier in the year. Nothing moved, nothing changed—except the number of graves in the cemetery at Yambuya camp.

Had Barttelot but known it, however, his long wait was nearly at an end.

On May 8 there was an unexpected visit. The steamer *A.I.A.* appeared suddenly at Yambuya. On board were Lt. van Kerckhoven (Commissaire de District at Bangala) and the steamer's engineer, a man named Werner.[13] They had with them the escort Ward had left at Bangala, less one Sudanese who had died there. This unlooked-for event marked a sudden re-awakening of Belgian interest in affairs on the Upper Congo. It was also the first of a series of comings and goings at the camp which, compared to the dreary months of hopeless waiting which had gone before, seemed a whirlwind of purposeful activity.

The *A.I.A.* stayed three days at Yambuya before steaming off in the direction of Stanley Falls. A few days later Barttelot, too, left for the Falls, meaning to wait there for Jameson's return. His timing was good. On May 22 Jameson, in company with Tippu-Tib, got back from Kasongo to find Barttelot waiting for him:

> At 4 p.m. I heard that Tippu-Tib and Jameson had come, and canoed over to see them, and found it true. Dear old Jameson, whom I was right glad to see, and was very fit, told me Tippu-Tib had promised him about 800 men. I made my salaams to Tippu-Tib, and we came over and dined, and Van Kerkhoven gave us champagne, the first I have tasted for fourteen months. . . . Next day I had a palaver with Tippu-Tib. He then said he had got 400 men for me, but no more; that out of these 300 were to carry 40 lb., the others only 20 lb. Jameson reminded him of what he had said at Kasongo about the 800 men, and he said it was nothing of the sort—that 400 men were all he could spare us; every available man he had was wanted. . . . We have to pay, or, rather, guarantee, £1,000 to a big Arab (Muni Somai), who is to come as the commander of the 400 Manyuema, and is to see us through this business, being responsible for all loads and men.

To see half his eight hundred porters suddenly snatched from his grasp in this way was a bad shock for Barttelot. The next day[14] the mysterious diminution was explained:

Tippu came over early to see us, and after a palaver Van Kerkhoven asked Jameson and self to leave the room, and he had a tremendous palaver with Tippu. After that we knew why we had only got 400 instead of 800 men; for Van Kerkhoven had told Tippu of the Ubangi River,[15] and asked him to send men there, for the double purpose of diverting him from Bangala, and of preventing anybody else from getting possession.

Barttelot may or may not have been correct in asserting that Van Kerckhoven's proposal was the limiting factor on the number of porters Tippu-Tib was prepared to supply to the Expedition. But nothing is more probable than that Van Kerckhoven used the occasion of his meeting with Tippu-Tib to interest him in the possibility of expansion towards the north. The Belgians' fear of an Arab descent on Bangala (which would have forestalled Belgian occupation of the as yet "unpacified" zone between Bangala and the Aruwimi) was real enough. And since the Belgians themselves later tried to occupy the Welle valley with the aim of linking the Congo to the Nile headwaters via Monbuttu, the thinking behind Van Kerckhoven's proposal is quite clear. By giving Tippu-Tib, as Jameson put it, "a protectorate over all the Aruwimi and up to the Welle" two birds could be killed with one stone: Arab expansion westward would be checked, thus permitting Belgian expansion to the east; and the Belgians, at no cost to themselves, would be able to estimate the practicability of using the Welle valley to communicate with Equatoria. That the notion should have appealed to Tippu-Tib is also inherently probable since, during the past year, the Arabs had already manifested their interest in the area by pushing parties north from Yambuya into the untapped territory between there and the Welle.

Whatever the nature of Tippu-Tib's arrangement with Van Kerck-hoven, and whatever the precise facts of his previous arrangement with Jameson at Kasongo, the four hundred porters now offered were a solid fact and Barttelot wisely decided to be content with the bird in hand.

By June 4 Barttelot, Jameson, Tippu-Tib, the headman Muni Somai, and the A.I.A. were all back at Yambuya. So too was a second Belgian steamer, the *Stanley*, bringing the long-awaited Belgian Resident who was to "assist" Tippu-Tib in his gubernatorial duties.[16]

In the next week Jameson and Barttelot got through a Herculean quantity of work in preparation for their departure.

Jameson's main concern was arranging the loads, a task which devolved on him through Troup's continued illness. At the beginning of May there were six hundred and thirteen loads in camp. It was decided to send down to Bangala one hundred and forty loads that could not be carried. This left four hundred and seventy full loads of 60 to 65 lbs. each. Most of these now had to be reduced to 40 lbs. in accordance with the new contract. The cloth, powder, beads and ammunition discarded by this process went to Tippu-Tib and Muni Somai as advances on their fees.[17]

While Jameson, helped by Werner the engineer, laboured at organising the loads, Barttelot produced tens of thousands of words of letters, reports, orders, copies of agreements, lists of loads, etc., most of which were destined for the Relief Committee in London. He arranged with the Belgians that Troup, the interpreter Assad Farran, and one of the Sudanese soldiers, all of whom were being invalided home, should be evacuated on the steamer which took the loads to Bangala. Twenty-nine Zanzibaris and four Sudanese, deemed unfit to proceed, were entrusted to Tippu-Tib who undertook to get them to Zanzibar.

Between June 4 and June 10 Barttelot produced a long report for Mackinnon detailing events at Yambuya since May, explaining his present arrangements with the Arabs and setting out his hopes and plans for the future course of the Expedition. The extracts below give a picture of events in camp during the week which preceded the beginning of the Rear Guard's march:

(June 5) I had another palaver with Tippu-Tib, asking him where were the two hundred and fifty men already sent. He explained to me that they had been dispersed, and on trying to collect them they refused to come, owing to the bad reports brought in by deserters, and that as they were subjects, and not slaves, he could not force them. That was the reason why he had brought 400 entirely fresh men from Kasongo for us. However, Tippu said he could let me have 30 more men of Muni Somai. This, as I was so terribly short of men, I agreed to. . . .

(June 8) This morning I had the loads for Tippu-Tib's and Muni Somai's men stacked, and Tippu-Tib himself came down to see them prior to issuing. However, he took exception to the loads, said they were too heavy (the heaviest was 45 lb.), and his men could not carry them. Two days before he had expressed his approbation of the weight of the very same loads he refused today. I pointed out to him that he, as well as I, knew the difficulty of getting any load other than a bale to scale the exact weight, and that the loads his men carried were far above the prescribed weight of 60 lb. We were to have started tomorrow, so we shall not now start till June 11 or 12, as I am going to make all his loads weigh exactly 40 lb. . . .[18]

(June 9) We shall easily be able to start by the 11th, but I am sorry to say our loss of ammunition by the lightening of the loads—for it was the ammunition they particularly took notice of—is something enormous. Both the *A.I.A.* and the *Stanley* left this morning for Stanley Falls, but Tippu-Tib and his Belgian secretary remain behind, also four ships' carpenters, whom Captain Van Gèle and M. Van Kirkhoven left with us to help us. The Belgians have behaved with very great kindness to us, and helped us on our way enormously. . . .[19]

(June 10) The loads have been weighed and handed over—powder and caps issued to the Manyuema force,[20] and we are all ready to start, which we shall do tomorrow morning. I have told you of all now I can think of, but I would bring finally to your notice that Tippu-Tib has broken faith with us. The man Muni Somai, I think, means business, and therefore I trust all will be well.

In the same report Barttelot explains his plans as follows:

My intentions on leaving this camp are to make the best of my way along the same route taken by Mr. Stanley; should I get no tidings of him along the road, to proceed as far as Kavalli, and then, if I hear nothing there, to proceed to Kibero. If I can ascertain either at Kavalli or Kibero his whereabouts, no matter how far it may be, I will endeavour to reach him. Should he be in a fix, I will do my utmost to relieve him. . . . Rumour is always rife, and is seldom correct, concerning Mr. Stanley. I can hear no news whatever, though my labours in that direction have been most strenuous. He is not dead, to the best of my belief nor of the Arabs here or at Kasongo. . . . I deem it my bounden duty to proceed on this business, in which I am fully upheld by both Mr. Jameson and Mr. Bonny: to wait longer would be both useless and culpable, as Tippu-Tib has not the remotest intention of helping us any more,[21] and to withdraw would be pusillanimous, and, I am certain, entirely contrary to your wishes and those of the Committee.

I calculate it will take me from three to four months to reach the lakes, and from seven to nine more to reach the coast.

By the evening of July 10 everything was ready for a start the next day. The composition of the column was as follows:

Europeans	3	
Zanzibaris	115	
Sudanese	22	
Somalis	1	
TOTAL	141[22]	loads: 70
Muni Somai and Manyuema	431	loads: 380
TOTAL	572[23]	loads: 430

On the eve of departure, Barttelot wrote, in a letter to his sister:

We leave this June 11, 1888, for abomination, desolation, and vexation, but I hope in the end success.

*   *   *

The march was a shambles from the word go. The Manyuema behaved exactly as they pleased. Groups of them wandered about as the fancy took them, firing off their guns. They stopped where and when they felt like it. They broke into the loads. No one seemed to have any clear idea of the road to be followed and the column became hopelessly confused as different parties followed their noses along different trails. For Barttelot and Jameson to try to control the unruly horde was out of the question, it having been understood all along that the purpose of hiring Muni Somai was to perform that office. It was now made painfully clear that the task was too much even for him. Meanwhile, to add to the general unpleasantness, smallpox had broken out among the Manyuema.

The indiscipline of the porters and the incompetence of Muni Somai was not the end of Barttelot's troubles: almost from the first day, the Zanzibaris began to desert. The number of absentees had soon reached twenty-two, a dangerously high proportion of the total force. These desertions brought all Barttelot's suspicious hatred of the

Zanzibaris boiling up. On June 23 a crisis was reached when Barttelot's own servant, for whom he had a special affection, deserted.

> I was told that many others intended to desert. I fell them all in, and took away all the arms from the Zanzibaris, and their ammunition. The Sudanese are faithful.

Barttelot's next action was so surprising that it would seem to justify the opinion of one contemporary writer that Barttelot "had by this time fallen into such a state of feverish excitement that he was no longer responsible for his actions".[24]

> I told Bonny I should go to the Falls the next day and get some chains, and that I would not return the rifles to the Zanzibaris for some lengthened period. He thought it good.

The next day Barttelot proceeded to put this weird decision into effect and set out for the Falls with an escort of fourteen Zanzibaris and three Sudanese. Jameson, unfortunately, was not present, or he might have been able to persuade Barttelot that, as commander, his time might be more usefully employed than in dashing off to the Falls in search of gyves and fetters. The two men had separated, Barttelot leading with the Zanzibaris and Sudanese, Jameson following with Muni Somai and the Manyuema. They were never to meet again.

Before leaving, Barttelot issued orders to Bonny and Jameson to concentrate the column at the village of Banalya (some ninety-five miles' march from Yambuya) and hold it there till his return. He then made a dash back to the Falls, where he arrived on July 1, having covered, by his own estimate, three hundred miles in eight days.[25]

Tippu-Tib's feelings on witnessing the hot-foot return of the bugbear he imagined hundreds of miles away, are not too hard to guess. Exactly what passed between them is not recorded; Barttelot's diary ceases at this point. It appears, however, that in addition to the wherewithal for forming the Zanzibaris into a chain gang, Barttelot asked for sixty extra men to act as guards over the errant porters. Tippu-Tib consented and gave Barttelot a draft for the extra men on Abdulla Koroni, the Arab headman at Banalya.[26] Barttelot was evidently satisfied; he wrote to his father from the Falls (July 5):

Our march altogether up to the present has not been a success, but I think I have now so arranged matters that I shall have no more stoppage.

From this point the only information regarding Barttelot's movements comes from Bonny, who had reached Banalya with the head of the column on July 15. Jameson, at the rear, was still five days behind —a fact which provides an index of the prevailing disorganisation of the march. On July 17 Barttelot appeared at Banalya and presented Abdulla with his request for sixty men. These were refused. What followed is thus reconstructed by Barttelot's brother from Bonny's statements:

Soon after this the Manyuema, to annoy them, began firing off their guns, and Muni Somai refused to stop them. Major Barttelot and Mr. Bonny, while sitting later on in the back of Mr. Bonny's house, were startled by a shot, which passed over their heads and lodged in the roof. Major Barttelot caught the man and punished him severely.

July 18—Major Barttelot continued to press Abdulla for the carriers, apparently without success. About 10 p.m. drums were heard and singing, and Barttelot sent his boy to stop it. The noise ceased.

July 19—Early this morning a Manyuema woman commenced beating a drum and singing. Major Barttelot sent his boy, Sudi, to stop this;[27] loud and angry voices were heard, followed by two shots. The Major then ordered some Soudanese to find the men who were firing, and at the same time he got up from bed and took his revolvers from the case. He said, "I will shoot the first man I catch firing." He went out, revolver in hand, to where the Soudanese were. They told him they could not find the men who were firing. The Major then pushed aside some Manyuema, and passed through them towards the woman who was beating the drum and singing, and ordered her to desist. Just then a shot was fired through a loophole in a house opposite by Sanga, the husband of the woman. The shot passed through Major Barttelot's body below the heart, and lodged in a post supporting the veranda, under which he fell. Mr Bonny went and, with one Somali and one Soudanese, found the body, and carried it to the house.[28]

The immediate result of the murder was a general panic. Bonny, in his written report to Stanley, stated:

From the screaming, I thought a general massacre had commenced, for I had not seen a single Zanzibari. They were either hiding within their houses or joining in the general stampede which followed. . . . I now sent my men to collect what goods they could, and before long I recovered 299 porter loads. They had been scattered all over the place, some in the forest, in the rice field, and in the village huts hidden away within and without, in fact everywhere. Some of the bead sacks and ammunition boxes had already been ripped or broken open, and the whole of their contents, or in part, gone. After counting up I found I was forty-eight loads short. The inhabitants of the village numbered about 200 or 300 people. I had arrived with about 100 men; Muni Sumai, the chief headman of the Manyuema, with 430 carriers and about 200 followers, making a total of about 1000 people, of whom 900 were cannibals, all confined within an area 165 yards by 25 yards. You can therefore better judge than I can describe the scene when the general stampede commenced, the screaming, firing, shouting, looting our stores, &c., &c. I regret to say that the Soudanese and Zanzibaris without exception joined in the looting, but in my turn I raided their houses and haunts and captured a quantity of cloth, beads, rice, &c. I had to punish severely before I succeeded in stopping it. I now wrote to Mr. Jameson, who was about four days off bringing up the remaining loads. I also wrote to Mons. Baert, a Congo State officer, and secretary to Tippu-Tib at Stanley Falls, explaining what had taken place, how I was situated, and asking him to use all his tact with Tippu-Tib to get him to come here or send some chief to replace Muini Sumai, who had been one of the first to abscond. . . . I then buried the Major, after sewing the body up in a blanket. I dug a grave just within the forest, placing leaves as a cushion within the bottom of the grave, and covered the body with the same. I then read the church service from our Prayer-Book over the body, and this brought the terrible day to a close.[29]

Two days after the murder Jameson had a note from Bonny "shorter than a telegram ought to have been" telling him that Barttelot was shot and that Muni Somai and the Manyuema had "left". The next day Jameson reached Banalya:

On my arrival I found all quiet, only Bonny and the Zanzibaris with the Soudanese occupying the village, and two or three of the head muniaparas of the Manyemas, with their men, camped outside the village. Bonny had done all that a man could do under very trying circumstances. He had recovered about three hundred of the loads carried by the Manyemas, and had succeeded in quieting those of them who remained.

Jameson spent two days making an inventory of the goods that remained, repacking the loads that had been broken open, sorting through Barttelot's papers and talking to the Manyuema headmen. From the latter he learned that both Muni Somai and Sanga, Barttelot's assassin, had fled to Stanley Falls. Jameson therefore told Bonny to stay put, and set out himself for the Falls with the double purpose of finding a replacement for Muni Somai and obtaining the arrest and punishment of Sanga.

At the Falls Jameson asked at first for Bwana Nzige's son Rashid to command the Manyuema. Tippu-Tib made no objection, but Rashid politely declined saying he had other fish to fry.[30] Tippu-Tib then suggested Selim bin Mohammed. Jameson, mindful of the past year's difficulties with the Yambuya Arabs, was unenthusiastic. Tippu-Tib then "jumped up out of his chair and said, 'Give me £20,000 and I and my people will go with you, find Mr. Stanley, and relieve Emin Bey'".[31]

On the face of it the proposal was absurd, but Jameson was desperate. Without someone of sufficient authority to control the Manyuema, the Expedition was wrecked. Apart from Rashid and Selim, the only other man of the requisite stature among the Falls Arabs was Tippu-Tib's own son, Sef, and he was away in Zanzibar. The more Jameson thought about it, the more clearly it appeared to him that it was Tippu-Tib or nothing. Would Tippu-Tib reduce his price? Tippu-Tib would not. Jameson clutched at the straw held out to him. But he could hardly agree on his own authority to such a staggering fee, as much again as the entire cost of the Expedition. If he did so and the Committee repudiated the agreement, Jameson would be a very ruined man indeed.

With this in mind, Jameson decided on a compromise. He had heard from Van Kerckhoven that Ward had reached Bangala with the Committee's reply to Barttelot's telegram. But no one except Ward knew what instructions the telegram contained, and there was no way of finding out short of actually going down to Bangala in person. The reason for this anomalous, not to say stupid, situation was that Ward, ascending the river, had met the invalid Troup coming down and received an extraordinary written order from Barttelot which forbade him to advance beyond Bangala and strictly enjoined him to make no effort to communicate with the Rear Column unless the Committee's reply contained Barttelot's recall. Jameson therefore informed Tippu-Tib that, before deciding on his offer, he would go himself to Bangala to ascertain the contents of the Committee's telegram:

If I find the reply from the Committee to be "go on at all hazards", I will return at once and start with your men myself. If I find that it does not tell me to go on at all hazards, I will send Mr Ward. with a telegram to Banana stating my present position, your proposals, and asking for orders. . . . He agreed to find me canoes and men to go to Bangala. (JAMESON)

Meanwhile justice had been done on the trigger-happy Sanga, though in a manner which, to a critical eye, might seem a little hazy in its regard for the niceties of judicial procedure:

. . . Sanga was tried before Mons. Haneuse, three other Belgian officers, and Tippu-Tib. Sanga was first asked what he had to say. He told a rambling story about Major Barttelot coming to his house where his women were drumming and singing, and that Kapranga came too; that Major Barttelot kicked him; and that when Kapranga, the Major and he were outside, some one fired a shot from behind him, and shot the Major dead, the ball going in at his back, but that he had not done it. Here Tippu-Tib stated that Sanga had told him, on arrival here, that he was in bed at the time the Major was shot. Mons. Haneuse asked him what made him run away and come here. He said that many people had accused him of having done it, and so he ran away. I then made the statement which Mr. Bonny had given me . . . and further stated that all the muni-aparas of the Manyema had assured me that Sanga had shot Major Barttelot. Sanga was asked if he had anything further to say. He repeated that he had not done it. . . . Voting papers were then given to Tippu-Tib, Mons. Haneuse, and the three other Belgian officers, to mark with a cross, if they considered him guilty, and to leave blank if innocent. All five papers were found crossed, so Mons. Haneuse told Sanga that he had been found guilty and would be shot. He laughingly replied "Well, do it quick." He was chained to a large log, and when carried outside said again with a laugh, "It is all right; the white man is dead, I am going to die too." He was carried down to the rocks on the shore, where a firing party of six Houssas, at six paces, fired at him and did not kill him; then one of the Belgian officers ran up with a revolver, and fired two shots into his head. Only four bullets had hit him, two in the right breast, one in the knee, and one in the throat, besides the two from the revolver. After the first discharge, when he was hit by some of the bullets, the look he gave us was the most horrible I think I ever saw on a man's face.

We then had lunch. . . . (JAMESON)

On August 9 Jameson left by canoe for Bangala, having first written to Bonny to let him know what he was doing. On the 10th he reached Rashid's camp on the Lomami.

(*August 10*) . . . I was frightfully seedy, having caught cold inside after a big dose of medicine. One of the canoes I bought from Tippu-Tib leaked so much I had to exchange it for one from Rachid. A great quantity of ivory arrived for him, and he could attend to nothing. Had two canoes lashed together at last and four days' food on board, and started early in the afternoon.

(*August 11*)—After a long night's work found ourselves past the Aruwimi in the morning. The natives told us today . . . that the Tamba-Tambas[32] had killed a tremendous number of them on the south bank. This is where Rachid's enormous lot of ivory came from that I saw arrive yesterday. I had the greatest difficulty all day in quieting the natives, who thought we were more Tamba-Tambas, and had to sit in the sun all day to let them see me, and speak with them. They are perfectly mad.

(*August 12*)—Got through the worst of the natives during the night. One very curious scene. Shot out of an open reach—fine clear night—into a dark narrow channel, not more than forty yards wide. All at once it became lit up with dozens of fires on both sides, throwing a bright light back into the forest and across the water. We glided on without a sound from us but the zip-zip of the paddles, drums beating, horns blowing, shouts and cries on every side, the white loin-cloths of our men showing plainly who they were. Down this lane of fires and noise we went for nearly half a mile, when suddenly it opened out into a grand open reach of the river on our right, the fires, drums, &c., going on for more than a mile away down on our left. I don't think I ever heard such a noise before. We shot out away to our right, and soon left all the tumult behind. . . .

After August 12 there are no more entries in Jameson's diary.

* * *

The journey Ward had made to the coast and back was an exploit beyond praise. Though believing himself to be engaged on a futile errand, he had driven himself to the limit over the fourteen-hundred-mile journey to Matadi, arriving there just thirty-one days after leaving Yambuya. At the coast he had taken a steamer to the cable station at Loanda, sent his telegram, and, on May 6, received Mackinnon's reply:

> Committee refer you to Stanley's orders of June 24, 1887. If you cannot march in accordance with these orders then stay where you are, awaiting his arrival or until you receive fresh instructions from Stanley. Committee do not authorise engagement of fighting men. News has been received from Emin Pasha, via Zanzibar, dated Wadelai, November 2. Stanley was not then heard of. Emin Pasha is well, and is in no immediate want of supplies, and goes to south-west of lake to watch for Stanley. Letters have been posted regularly via East.

On June 11, the day the Rear Column left Yambuya, Ward was back at Stanley Pool. Here he caught the steamer *En Avant* which was making the trip up-river. On July 3, much to his surprise, he met Troup on his way down from Yambuya in the *Stanley*. Troup was so ill, however, that Ward was only able to gather a confused and sketchy account of what had taken place in the camp since his departure in March. Even more surprising was the letter of instructions from Barttelot which was handed to Ward by the captain of the steamer:

> SIR—On arrival at Bangala you will report yourself to the chief of the station, and take over the stores from him belonging to the

Expedition. You will remain at Bangala till you receive orders from the Committee concerning yourself and the loads. . . . On no account will you leave Bangala while you remain in the service of the Expedition, till you receive orders from home. . . . Should you bring a telegram of recall for me, you will make arrangements with the chief of Bangala to forward it to the Falls, where a messenger awaits it. You will not, however, send any other message after me, nor will you on any account leave Bangala station unless you receive orders to that effect from the Committee—

EDMUND M. BARTTELOT.

Ward's astonishment may be imagined at this inexplicable loss of interest in the telegram which had involved him in a journey of nearly four thousand miles. No less great than his astonishment was his chagrin at finding himself suddenly and without explanation debarred from further participation in the Expedition at the very moment when the weary months of waiting had at last given way to action.

This letter appeared to me the unkindest act which had been done me since I had been with the Expedition, and, on the impulse of the moment, I felt inclined to throw everything up and return home.

Ward nevertheless went on to Bangala and loyally accepted the meaningless task of watching over the surplus loads that had been sent down from Yambuya. There followed what he called "an unpleasant period of waiting" lasting nearly a month. Then came a letter from Jameson announcing Barttelot's death and telling Ward to stay put "as I might have to employ you at any moment relative to either telegrams or loads".

This letter was not the last of Ward's unpleasant surprises. Since it said nothing of Jameson's coming down to Bangala in person,[33] Ward had another shock waiting for him when, on August 16—

. . . a boy came rushing into my room, saying in Kiswahili that a white man had just come down from the Falls in a canoe. I rushed to the beach, and there saw a deathlike figure lying back in the men's arms, insensible. I jumped into the canoe, and, great Heavens! it was poor Jameson.

Jameson died the next evening. Ward was standing by Jameson's bed when suddenly drums began to beat—the signal to knock off work in the station:

> He opened his eyes and stared at me, clutching my hands and saying with a husky voice, "Ward, Ward! they're coming! listen!" And the drums continued to rumble in the distance. "Yes, they're coming! Now let's stand together!". . . . As I supported him to administer brandy with a spoon, he drew a long breath, and his pulse stopped.

From Jameson's papers Ward was able to get a reasonably clear picture of the state in which the Rear Column had been left by Barttelot's death. He therefore decided to prosecute Jameson's intention of submitting Tippu-Tib's offer to the Committee. He wrote to Bonny, telling him of Jameson's death and his own intention of cabling the Committee for further instructions. Then, though himself ill with fever, he set out once more for the coast. From St. Paul de Loanda he telegraphed Mackinnon:

> Barttelot's death broke up Expedition; Manyemas disbanded. Jameson coming Bangala died there August 17 fever. He reported Tippoo Tib only man competent command Manyemas; his unalterable terms £20,000 sterling unconditionally, irrespective Manyemas' pay, but returns if opposed without forfeiting above terms.[34] Route, Nyangwe, Kibero, Unyoro. Bonny and remaining loads Yarrocombi, close Stanley Falls. Many men and loads missing. Awaiting reply Loanda. WARD.

It was October 4 before Ward received definite instructions from the Committee:

> Return Stanley Falls; leave powder, Remington cartridges and portion of goods in charge officers there in case communication with Emin opened. Sell remainder goods to State. See Governor about this. Bring Bonny, all men Expedition, all Barttelot's and Jameson's effects and collections Banana; ship them England, care Gray, Dawes & Co. If help wanted engage and take back Casement. Wire if these instructions understood.

Ward duly acknowledged and once more turned his face up-river to put his orders into effect.

He was already several months too late. On August 17, the very day Jameson had died in Ward's arms, Stanley and the Advance Column, in a fleet of canoes, had reached Bonny's camp at Banalya.

*   *   *

Stanley's trip had been a fast one. He had covered the four hundred and sixty miles from Fort Bodo to Banalya in just two months—half the time it had taken to cover the same ground on the outward journey the previous year. Travelling light, and making the best use of canoes and a favourable current, the Column had made an uneventful crossing of the forest with relatively little loss of life.[35] At Ugarrowa's, where Stanley had hoped to have news of the Rear Guard, he found that nothing had been heard from Barttelot and his men. Stanley's two letters—the one he had entrusted to Ugarrowa the previous September, and the one sent down with Stairs' couriers in February—were now handed back to the sender. The messengers in both cases claimed they had been unable to get through in the face of hostility from the natives.

With his anxiety about Barttelot's fate sharpened by this total lack of news, Stanley pushed on till, in mid-August, he was some one hundred miles from Yambuya. The villages in this district were ruined and the country deserted. This was a further motive for disquiet, though Stanley put the destruction down to inter-village wars and missed the real reason, that the Arabs had moved up on his tracks from Yambuya. On August 17 the flotilla came in sight of Banalya and—

> . . . about half past nine we saw one village, a great way down through the light mist of the morning, still standing. . . . Presently white dresses were seen, and quickly taking up my field glass, I discovered a red flag hoisted. A suspicion of the truth crept into my mind. A light puff of wind unrolled the flag for an instant, and the white crescent and star were revealed. I sprang to my feet and cried out, "The Major, boys! Pull away bravely." A vociferous shouting and hurrahing followed, and every canoe shot forward at racing speed.
>
> About 200 yards from the village we stopped paddling and as I saw a great number of strangers on the shore, I asked, "Whose

men are you?" "We are Stanley's men," was the answer delivered in mainland Swahili. But assured by this, and still more so as we recognised a European near the gate, we paddled ashore. The European on a nearer view turned out to be Mr. William Bonny, who had been engaged as doctor's assistant to the Expedition.

Pressing his hand, I said, "Well, Bonny, how are you? Where is the Major? Sick, I suppose?"

"The Major is dead, sir."

"Dead? Good God! How dead? Fever?"

"No, sir, he was shot."

"By whom?"

"By the Manyuema—Tippu-Tib's people."

"Good heavens! Well, where is Jameson?"

"At Stanley Falls."[36]

"What is he doing there, in the name of goodness?"

"He went to obtain more carriers."

"Well then, where is Mr. Ward, or Mr. Troup?"

"Mr. Ward is at Bangala."

"Bangala! Bangala! what can he be doing there?"

"Yes, sir, he is at Bangala, and Mr. Troup has been invalided home some months ago."

These queries, rapidly put and answered as we stood by the gate at the water side, prepared me to hear as deplorable a story as could be rendered of one of the most remarkable series of derangements that an organised body of men could possibly be plunged into. (STANLEY)

Shorn of the jumbled rhetoric with which Stanley invests his account of it, the situation of the Rear Guard on August 17 was as follows:

—Of the original two hundred Zanzibaris, there remained seventy-five at Banalya.
—Of forty-four Sudanese there remained twenty-two.
—Of two Somalis there remained one.
—Of five officers there remained one.

This meant that, with a total of one hundred (excluding the Manyuema) present at Banalya, the Rear Guard's losses from all causes (including such items as ten Zanzibaris at the Falls with Jameson) amounted to one hundred and fifty-eight since the departure of Stanley's column the year before. Since leaving Yambuya in June the Rear Guard had lost forty-one men.[37]

The physical condition of many of the survivors was very bad indeed. A year's subsistence on an exclusive regime of manioc (often eaten raw) had reduced nearly half of them to stinking, saucer-eyed skeletons. The presence of smallpox[38] among the Manyuema did nothing to improve the picture, though the Zanzibaris and Sudanese were not infected, thanks to Parke's thorough prophylactic measures at the beginning of the Expedition. There were six bodies of smallpox victims lying unburied in the camp, and (in Stanley's lapidary phrase) "the smitten living with their festers lounged in front of us by the dozen".

If the Rear Guard's losses in men were frighteningly high, their material losses were as high, and even more dangerous to the functioning of the Expedition. Men could be replaced. Remington cartridges could not.

There were six hundred and sixty loads originally stored at Yambuya. By May 1888 current consumption had reduced these to six hundred and thirteen, a perfectly acceptable figure. It was during the preparations for departure from Yambuya that the real damage had been done. One hundred and thirty loads for which there were no carriers had been sent down to Bangala. The reduction in weight of the remaining loads and payments to Tippu-Tib and Muni Somai had meant a further reduction of approximately one-third. Finally there had come the losses incurred on the march and in the stampede after Barttelot's murder. Thus there remained at Banalya on Stanley's arrival two hundred and ninety-eight light loads, or approximately two hundred full loads. The Rear Guard's total loss of goods over the period since June 1887 therefore amounted to over sixty per cent.[39]

To summarise: between June 1887 and August 1888 the Rear Guard had lost all but one of its officers, sixty per cent of its men, and sixty per cent of its goods. It had moved ninety-five miles nearer to the Lake and it had suffered a complete breakdown in morale. These facts are adequate justification for Stanley's referring to the column he found at Banalya as a "wreck" and to the whole episode of the Rear Guard as a "disaster".

Nothing could more clearly illustrate the two sides of Stanley's nature than his reactions to the situation which met him on his arrival at Bonny's camp. The speed and energy with which he transformed the Rear Guard from a wreck into a going concern are wholly admirable.

His utter refusal to accept any part of the responsibility for the disaster, and the casual disregard for decency and truth which he displayed in his attacks on the conduct of the Rear Guard's officers, are less easy to stomach.

After the Expedition's return to England, Stanley's quarrel with the Rear Guard officers developed into a full-blown public controversy with scandalous overtones, carried on vigorously in books, newspapers, lecture halls and solicitors' offices. An account of this sordid episode may conveniently be deferred, on chronological grounds, until the end of the story. For the present it suffices to give here a brief account of Stanley's actions after reaching Banalya.

After inspecting the camp and hearing Bonny's version of the Rear Guard's ordeal, Stanley decided to move away from what he called the "charnel-house" of Banalya and carry out his reorganisation in a healthier spot. He ordered a general move to an island six miles distant up-river.

The unruliness of the Manyuema—it took them three days to make this short march—convinced Stanley that he would be better off without them. He therefore issued an ultimatum:

"If you decline the journey it is well, if you proceed with me it is well also. Exercise your own free will. I do not need you, but if you like to follow me I can make use of you, and will pay you according to the number of loads you carry." Some of them understood this as implying leave to proceed upon their own business—that of ravaging and marauding—but three head men volunteered to accompany me. I engaged them on the condition that if they followed me of their own will for thirty days I would after that time trust them with loads. (STANLEY)

By this means Stanley reduced the number of Manyuema carriers to sixty-one. At the same time, the manner in which he laid down the terms of their engagement subtly but firmly asserted his authority over them.

A message in similar terms was sent to Tippu-Tib inviting him to participate in the Expedition and/or to present himself at Banalya for a palaver.[40]

Stanley's first action on arrival at the island was to distribute cloth, beads, cowries and mitako to the value of £1,000 among the Zanzibaris and Sudanese. This measure was intended partly to improve morale and partly to enable the men to buy food from the Arabs on the return journey to Fort Bodo.

A few more days were spent in writing reports and correspondence for despatch down-river, listening to the windy complaints of the Yambuya men against their officers, preparing the loads and mustering the men. The reorganised column was now composed as follows:

Zanzibaris capable of carrying loads	165
Madis „ „ „ „	57
Manyuema „ „ „ „	61
Sudanese	21
Sick	45
Somalis	1
Emin's soldiers	4
Manyuema chiefs, women, and slaves	108
Europeans	3
TOTAL	465

(283 porters)

There were two hundred and seventy-five loads to be carried, all of which, together with the sick, could be accommodated in the canoes during the first stages of the journey. The march would be made, as before, in two columns, one by land and one by water, until the point was reached where river navigation became too difficult.

On August 29, no reply having been received from Tippu-Tib, and Jameson (who had now been dead twelve days) having failed to present himself, orders were given for a start to be made the next day.

On the march which followed, the Expedition suffered once more all the miseries which had afflicted it on the journey to the Lake the previous year. There were even some additional refinements such as the rapid spread of smallpox among the Madis. On the later stages of the journey the difficulty of finding food was so great that at one point there was a serious possibility of the Expedition's becoming a total loss; while the stronger men were despatched on a desperate search for food, Stanley kept one hundred and thirty of the remainder alive for a week by the daily distribution of a "broth" consisting of a pot of butter and a pot of milk mixed with a vast amount of water. When the column marched into Fort Bodo on December 20, it had lost one hundred and six men from exhaustion, disease, native attacks, and starvation.

Now, for the first time since leaving Stanley Pool, the entire Expedition (excepting only Jephson's little party and the much-wandering Ward) was gathered together in one place. In this situation, the full extent of their losses was hideously apparent. More than seven hundred men had set out from Zanzibar to follow Stanley across Africa. Less than half that number now remained, and between them and their homeland stood another thirteen hundred miles' march.

On December 22 Stanley mustered the remnants of his Expedition. There were present in Fort Bodo:

Europeans	6
Zanzibaris	209
Sudanese	17
Somalis	1
Madis	26
Manyuema and followers	151
TOTAL	410

Stairs handed Stanley a report on his six months' tenure of command. The garrison's main business had been the care of the sick, and the energetic patrolling necessary to protect the plantations from the depredations of hungry natives and marauding elephants. But during those six months life at the fort had been lived under a dark cloud of doubt growing each day larger and more disturbing: at the end of July Jephson should have been at Fort Bodo to conduct the garrison and stores to the Lake. Not only had he failed to appear, there had been no word from him to explain his absence. The conclusion was inescapable: something had gone badly wrong in Equatoria. But what? The only way to find out was to get back to the Lake with as little delay as possible.

On December 23 the entire column packed its belongings and marched away to the east, leaving Fort Bodo in flames behind it.

NOTES AND REFERENCES

CHAPTER 7   THE REAR GUARD

1   BARTTELOT p. 148; WARD p. 35; TROUP p. 138 and p. 147. There were 7 deaths at Yambuya between the departure of Stanley and the arrival of Troup and Ward, so the total number of men left behind by Stanley was 258 (and not 271 as he later stated).

2   "After digging up the roots they usually ate them raw." (TROUP p. 145.) The danger of eating manioc improperly prepared has already been mentioned.

3   In the letter of instructions as printed in D.A., the postscript is omitted.

4   What had happened was that on reaching a spot near the Aruwimi mouth where, a year or so earlier, an Arab column from the Falls had been massacred by the natives, Tippu-Tib's men had undertaken a (? spontaneous) punitive raid, blazed away all their powder, and gone home. Whether they had ever intended, or been intended, to reach Yambuya and join the Expedition, there is no knowing.

5   Tippu-Tib's cousin Bwana Nzige had two sons, Rashid and Selim. Rashid had been at the Falls since before its capture. Selim had come out from Zanzibar with Tippu-Tib and the Expedition.

6   Cf. Jameson's diary for July 7: "No sentries asleep, so no floggings this morning, thank goodness."

7   Barttelot to Mackinnon, March 27, 1888.

8   BARTTELOT pp. 288–289.

9   It later transpired that Ward was suspected of stealing brass rods (WARD p. 149 and pp. 159–161). A telling comment on the small choice of vices available to men cut off from civilisation.

10 A row of dots in the printed text of Barttelot's diary suggests that the editor (Barttelot's brother) has, with regrettable delicacy, suppressed what can only have been a specification of the officers' offences.

11 The letter only appears in WARD. Troup refers to its arrival but not to its contents.

12 BARTTELOT pp. 169–170 (entries for Nov. 29 and 30), and p. 232 (entries for April 30 and May 1). It is not difficult to imagine Bonny playing on the fact that both he and Barttelot were regular army men, in order to develop a

special relationship. Bonny's actions and motives will be considered in more detail below.

13   Werner subsequently published a book comprehensively entitled: *A visit to Stanley's Rear Guard at Major Barttelot's camp on the Aruwimi with an account of river life on the Congo.*

14   May 24, the day Stanley parted from Emin to return to Yambuya. Like Parke, Barttelot noted in his diary: "The Queen's birthday; we drank her health in champagne."

15   I.e. the Mobangi-Welle.

16   Tippu-Tib had pointed to the non-arrival of the promised Belgian official as further evidence of Stanley's sloppy attitude to contracts. In fact, two Residents had been detailed to the Falls since Tippu-Tib's appointment, but neither had reached there: one had died *en route*, and the other been invalided home.

17   Muni Somai got goods to the value of £128, Tippu-Tib £836.

18   "The loads could not be reduced to the required weight without an immense amount of trouble, as the powder and cartridges were in air-tight, soldered tins, weighing about 15 lb. each. Three of these tins, packed in a wooden case of from 10 to 12 lb. weight, formed a load. Thus when one tin was taken out, each load, including the case, would weigh 41 or 42 lb. To reduce this, the tins would have to be opened and soldered up again." (WERNER p. 271.)

19   Barttelot arranged, at his own expense, for silver goblets to be presented to Van Kerckhoven and to Liebriechts, inscribed: "In remembrance of many kindnesses and aid rendered to the Emin Pasha Relief Expedition."

20   "Nearly all the caps turn out to be bad. When packing them on board the S.S. *Madura*, I tried some of them, and told Mr. Stanley they were bad, but he would not listen to me; the consequence is, we have had to buy 40,000 from Tippu-Tib." (JAMESON p. 306.)

21   Barttelot realised a fact too often overlooked—that one of the main obstacles to Tippu-Tib's helping the Expedition was the opposition of the other Arab sheikhs to such help being given. (See BARTTELOT p. 279 and p. 308.)

22   If to this figure are added: Ward (1), Troup (1), and the other invalids (35), the total number of survivors at June 10 is 178. The original strength of the Rear Column was 258. Therefore Barttelot's losses by death or desertion up to leaving Yambuya amount to 80, or roughly 30 per cent in just under a year.

23   This total does not include a horde of women and children, camp followers of the Manyuema, which brought the real numbers of the column up to something like 800. Nor does it include 15 slaves Barttelot bought from Tippu-Tib in exchange for a 500-express rifle. (JAMESON p. 305.)

24   FOX-BOURNE p. 130. Fox-Bourne was not hostile to Barttelot, though he was

violently anti-Stanley on humanitarian grounds. Like Casement, he later played
an important part in exposing Belgian abuses on the Congo.

25 He left his escort two days behind. Barttelot was proud of his ability to outwalk
all comers, which may account for a slight exaggeration here. Even allowing
for the tortuousness of forest paths, the distance cannot have been much over
200 miles.

26 BARTTELOT p. 350, based on Bonny's statements.

27 Sudi, the deserter, had been recaptured on June 25. "I did not punish him, as it
was partly my fault that he ran away, and the boy is not a bad one."
(BARTTELOT)

28 BARTTELOT pp. 350–351.

29 Qu. (in a "revised" form) by Stanley, D.A. I pp. 490–491.

30 "Developing" the Lomami River.

31 JAMESON p. 359.

32 I.e. Manyuema raiders.

33 He had not formed this intention at the time of writing (August 4) as he still
hoped to get the services of Rashid. He told Ward he would be leaving the Falls
"in two or three days at the most" to continue the march eastward, "and then
we shall go as fast as we can leg it". But he asked that all mails should be sent
up from Bangala "on the faint chance of their reaching us".

34 Tippu-Tib reserved the right to turn back if the column met serious native
opposition.

35 Except among the unfortunate Madis, of whom only 57 (out of 98) reached
Banalya. Stanley attributed this mortality to their own fecklessness in throwing
away their provisions to lighten their loads. (D.A. I p. 447.) three Zanzibaris
were lost: two by drowning, and one by desertion "in a fit of spleen".

36 Jameson's letter, informing Bonny of his intention to go down to Bangala,
did not reach Banalya until August 20.

37 On August 17, Bonny drew up, at Stanley's request, a comprehensive account
of the Rear Guard's losses since June 28, 1887. (D.A. I pp. 476–477.) Bonny's
figures are confusing as they give the original strength of the Rear Guard as
271. This total is accepted by Stanley although it conflicts with all other
estimates including figures quoted earlier by Stanley himself. (D.A. I p. 131.) By
adding 11 deserters picked up from the Advance Column, Bonny brings the
total up to 282. If these 11 deserters are included among those present at
Banalya (Bonny's returns are not clear on this point) then Barttelot's losses must
be considered as 169 out of 269, rather than 158 out of 258.

38 Referred to by Stanley in a baffling periphrasis as "the nameless scourge of
barbarians".

39 In the crucial item of Remington ammunition, the loss was only about fifty per cent., though in other classes of ammunition it was higher. Stanley gives the following figures:

		powder	Remgtn.	Winchr.	Maxim
	at Yambuya (15/8/87)	100	158	38	24
No. of loads	at Banalya (29/8/88)	37	83	11	9

(D.A. I p. 519 and II p. 14; cf. BARTTELOT pp. 251–252.)

40 See WARD pp. 138–139.

8

COLLAPSE IN EQUATORIA
May to December 1888

I was getting terribly sceptical about these people.

JEPHSON

... they proved themselves an excitable, frivolous, untrustworthy, and criminal race.

STANLEY

When Stanley, like young Lochinvar reversing his course, had vanished into the west, Jephson and Emin went north by steamer to Msawa, the first stage on their tour of the Province.

Here there was a short delay while Emin organised a belated punitive expedition against Unyoro. A detachment of soldiers crossed by steamer to Kibiro, burnt the town, massacred such of the population as failed to escape in time, and returned with a vast stock of looted salt cakes (a valuable commodity). Emin reproached the soldiers on their return for the brutality and licentiousness of their proceedings. He would have done better not to have sent them in the first place. The venture was militarily useless: it came too late to undo the harm done by Emin's failure to punish Kabba Rega for his treatment of Casati, and far from cowing Kabba Rega merely aggravated his hostility.

From Msawa Emin and Jephson moved north to Tunguru. Jephson addressed the garrison, read them Stanley's proclamation, the Khedive's firman and Nubar Pasha's letter, and asked them what they wanted to do. The answer was unanimous, if non-committal: if Emin stayed, they would stay; if he went, they would go. To Jephson it seemed that this reply was motivated more by complaisance than anything else; behind it, he felt, was a fundamental and general reluctance to leave their homes for a country most of them had never seen. Later events confirmed Jephson's judgement.

The chief of the station, Suliman Aga, was touching in his protestations of loyalty to Emin:

He said, "Where the Pasha goes, my soldiers and I follow"; he put his two hands together so as to form a circle, and said, "These are my soldiers, and the Pasha goes in the middle, that is the way we will travel, by whatever route the Pasha wishes."[1]

Casati, left behind at Tunguru when Emin and Jephson moved on to Wadelai, was in a good position to judge the real value of Suliman Aga's protestations. As soon as the Governor's back was turned, the same Suliman—

> . . . a man of narrow mind but quick in action, openly threw off the mask, and, having called together the officers and officials of that station, preached resistance to the Christians.[2]

In fact Suliman, acting on the suspicions aroused by the arrival of Stanley's Expedition, set himself to fan the smouldering discontent into open disaffection among the hitherto loyal garrisons of the southern stations. He entered into a seditious correspondence with Fadl el-Mulla Aga, the commander of Fabbo station,[3] urging immediate action to forestall the evacuation of the Province and the possibility of a treacherous attempt on Emin's part to sell his people into the hands of the British. These overtures found a ready response. Soon a regular mutiny was a-brewing.

Emin, meanwhile, was at Wadelai, preparing to accompany Jephson to the northern stations. Though warned by Casati, he and Jephson—

> . . . ignored the machinations which were in the course of organisation, and were deaf to the advice already given by me that they should use moderation and political prudence.[4]

The probable reason for Emin's ignoring Casati's advice on this occasion is that the two men had just had another quarrel. After Stanley's departure, Emin had learned that two Egyptians (an officer and a clerk—both former Arabists) had been secretly to Stanley with complaints and accusations against Emin. Stanley had very properly sent them packing, but, perhaps unwisely, had said nothing of the incident to Emin. The discomfited pair had returned to Tunguru (though not before they had told the Madi carriers destined for the Expedition that Stanley meant to kill them—hence the desertions). Emin soon heard of the affair and was forgivably piqued. On his return to Tunguru he had punished the guilty officer (and several others whose loyalty he suspected) with a reduction in rank. The offending clerk was sent to Duffile in irons. At the same time, according to Casati, Emin had arranged with the Egyptian officer commanding at Duffile, Hawashi Effendi, for "a secret inquiry intended to strike at mutineers and malcontents". Casati had protested energetically against what he called these "proscriptions" and urged, for once, "a more conciliatory policy". Emin rejected Casati's advice. As a result, when Emin left Tunguru, he and Casati were no longer on speaking terms.[5]

Emin and Jephson reached Wadelai early in July. Here Jephson made the acquaintance of another European sharing Emin's exile in Equatoria, a Greek merchant named Markos[6] "who came up to trade some years ago but is now an enforced resident here . . . he is not at all dark-coloured and seems a very decent old fellow" (Jephson). Also at Wadelai was Emin's four-year-old daughter Farida. Some years earlier Emin had married an Abyssinian woman who had borne him two children, a boy (who had died soon after his birth) and little Farida. Emin's wife had herself died of "bilious fever" in March 1887.[7] There appears to have subsisted a strong bond of tenderness and affection between father and daughter. Parke, who met her later, described Farida as: ". . . of an olive complexion, with beautiful dark eyes, eyebrows, and eye-lashes". He added: "She is constantly running about without boots. . . . Her great delight appears to be in catching beetles for her father."[8]

The day after the arrival of Emin and Jephson there was another, unlooked-for, arrival at Wadelai in the form of a deputation from the mutinous First Battalion at Rejaf. It was led by the senior officer of the Rejaf men, Hamid Aga. The mood of the ambassadors was submissive, even contrite. It may safely be assumed that the true purpose of their visit was to report on the likely implications of Stanley's arrival, but Emin seems to have overlooked this obvious possibility under the influence of his delight at what looked like a return of the lost sheep to the fold. Flattered, his spirits borne up by one of the surges of optimism to which he was periodically subject, he accepted their protestations at face value and agreed, after a suitable display of unforgiving coldness, to go to Rejaf, speak to the troops there, and accept their submission in person.

Jephson now addressed a parade of the Wadelai garrison and asked them for their decision. The answer was the same as it had been at Tunguru: "We will follow the Governor; if he goes, we go; if he

stays, we stay." After this answer had been given, the chief of the
station came forward privately with the suggestion that, if their
position in Equatoria was no longer tenable, why could they not—
instead of returning to Egypt—march to some country in closer
touch with the coast and establish themselves there? This notion
coincided startlingly with the Kavirondo scheme, which neither
Stanley nor Emin had made public. The coincidence was the more
striking to Jephson in that he had already had the same suggestion
put to him by two other individuals, Suliman Aga at Tunguru, and
Hamid Aga at Wadelai:

> I again, therefore, had the Soudanese officers and non-commissioned
> officers up before me, and, speaking to them said, "From what I
> have heard from certain officers, I understand that it is not your
> wish and that of the soldiers to go to Egypt, but to follow us with
> your Governor to a country somewhat nearer the sea, and there to
> settle down. Is this your wish?" I was greeted by a deafening
> "Aywah" from all. This answer was conclusive. The feeling was
> evidently against going to Egypt.

As yet Jephson had seen nothing in the outwardly well-ordered
stations of Msawa, Tunguru and Wadelai that might have shown him
how near the Province was to collapse. He had heard from Emin of
the mutiny in the First Battalion, and wondered why neither Emin nor
Junker had said anything of it in their published letters to Europe.
He had heard, too, of the scheming of the Egyptian officers and, more
especially, the Egyptian clerks. But he had seen nothing with his own
eyes which bespoke a breakdown of discipline—either actual or
impending—beyond the occasional surprising spectacle of a
subordinate arguing with the Governor about his orders. This would
have been all the more startling to one trained, as Jephson was, in
Stanley's school of instant-obedience-or-else. Emin clearly saw nothing
odd in it.

With these reservations, everything seemed to be going well, and it
was with a relatively easy mind that Jephson boarded the steamer with
Emin, Hamid Aga, and Vita Hassan, and set out for Duffile.

Duffile, founded by Gordon in 1874, was the most impressive
station Jephson had so far seen. It had brick buildings, engineering
shops, steamer wharves, a mosque, extensive gardens and orchards,
and was surrounded by earthworks and a moat. Its garrison consisted of

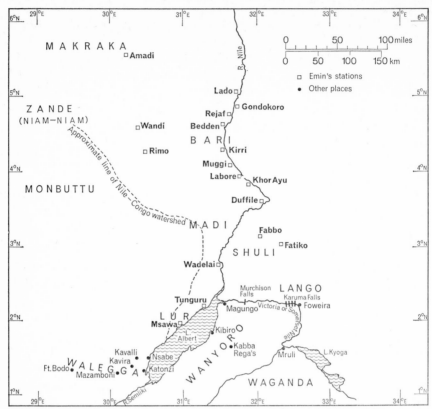

4   Equatoria and Lake Albert, showing Emin's stations and main tribal districts

200 men and two mountain guns. The Commander, Hawashi Effendi,[9] was a man noted for his self-seeking rapacity, though he lacked neither charm nor ability. He had originally been sent to Equatoria "for selling Government stores to the enemy in the war against Abyssinia" (Jephson). Since then he had unscrupulously made use of his position to fill his pockets, and his grasping and high-handed ways made him generally disliked and envied. Emin, however, found him indispensable; Hawashi was one of the few officers in the Province to whom work could safely be delegated, since he had the combination (rare locally) of intelligence to see the necessity for a given course of action, and energy to see it carried through.

Hawashi organised a feast in honour of Emin and his guest. In the course of the evening he proceeded, somewhat gratuitously, to denounce his own countrymen as treacherous blackguards, generously making no exception of himself.[10] He warned Jephson:

278

"If a Soudanese comes at you with scowls on his face and a loaded gun, whilst on the other hand an Egyptian comes to you with a carpet and a friendly greeting, turn to the Soudanese, he with his loaded gun will do you less harm than the Egyptian with his smiles and his carpet."[11]

Events were shortly to prove him wrong. The Sudanese were about to take the bit between their teeth in Equatoria.

Emin and his party stayed only one night at Duffile (during which Jephson suffered direly from over-indulgence in Hawashi Effendi's hospitality) and then set off overland for Rejaf. In quick succession they passed through the stations of Khor Ayu, Labore, and Muggi and on July 20 reached Kirri. At this point only one station, Bedden, lay between them and the rebel stronghold of Rejaf. Emin, warned by Hawashi against putting his head too readily into what might well be a noose, was smitten with caution. He decided to stay where he was until he had sounded the mood of the soldiers at Rejaf. Hamid Aga and his deputation went on ahead with orders to send the rebel soldiers down to Kirri. There they were to make their submission and hand over their ringleaders as a sign of good faith. If they complied, they would be forgiven. If they refused, the stations between them and Duffile would be evacuated and the men at Rejaf and Bedden left to fend for themselves.

In due course the answer arrived from Hamid Aga at Rejaf that the men were unwilling to take any decision until they had consulted with their comrades in Makraka. This was a reference to a splinter-group of the northern garrisons, who, under the leadership of Ali Aga Djabor, had established themselves as independent marauders in Makraka country to the east on the borders of Bahr-el-Ghazal. This Ali Aga had taken a leading part in fomenting the original mutiny and defying the Governor's attempts to re-establish his authority. Emin, against Jephson's advice, decided to wait for Ali Aga's arrival. Encouraged by his supposed success in bringing Hamid Aga to heel, he was confident that he could talk Ali Aga, too, into submission.

Meanwhile Jephson had addressed the garrison at Kirri, painting a black picture of their future if they stayed where they were and neglected the opportunity that was being offered them to fall back towards civilisation and safety. They declared their readiness to retire.

Further news now arrived from Hamid Aga. In a letter smuggled out of Rejaf he warned Emin that the garrison there intended treachery.

They had formed a plot, which Hamid Aga declared himself powerless to prevent, to seize Emin if he appeared there, and then "to start by way of Gondokoro to rejoin their Government, which they are convinced still exists at Khartoum".[12]

This was sufficient to make Emin change his mind about waiting any longer at Kirri. His present situation reminded him too closely of his near-capture at the same spot and under the same circumstances when on a tour of inspection the previous December.[13] On that occasion a timely warning of impending treachery at Rejaf had caused him to beat a rather undignified retreat, a tactic which he now decided to repeat.

Before leaving Kirri, he ordered that, as a first step in the proposed evacuation, the ammunition should be removed from the magazines and sent down to Muggi. Then, without waiting to see the order carried out, he and Jephson started south on the return journey. They had not gone far before they were overtaken by a messenger from the Commander of the Kirri garrison to say that the soldiers, suspecting a trick, had refused to allow the ammunition to leave the station.

If it is possible to isolate a moment at which Emin ceased to be Governor of Equatoria, this was the moment. The situation was a precise replica of that in which Emin had lost a great part of his authority three years previously. Then, having given orders for the abandonment of Lado, he had started south and been overtaken on the road by the refusal of the garrison to carry out his instructions. Instead of returning to confront the rebels, he had merely continued on his way to Wadelai. Now, in the same situation, he reacted in the same way. Even to a newcomer like Jephson it was obvious that at this juncture any successful resistance to Emin's will could mean the end of his authority among the hitherto loyal portion of his troops. It was therefore urgent that Emin should return at once to Kirri, calm the fears of the soldiers, and insist on his orders being carried out.

Emin did not return and did not insist. He merely sent off to Kirri a written repetition of the original order and then—as on the previous, fatal, occasion—continued on his way. That evening, at Muggi, he had a further message from Kirri to say that the men still refused to release the ammunition. "The soldiers had now", wrote Jephson, "defied his orders, and he could look no longer for obedience from them."

Events now began a rapid slide into almost farcical confusion.

At Muggi Jephson addressed the garrison—ninety strong under a loyal and capable commander, Abdul Aga Manzal.[14] Emin had high hopes of their setting a good example to the other garrisons north of Duffile by consenting to a prompt and orderly withdrawal. But at this point Emin, whose mercurial temper was now tacking almost hourly between cheery optimism and black despair, received another blow to his morale: news came in that the Kirri men had thrown in their lot with the mutineers at Rejaf, and that the Rejaf men had sent a party down to Kirri to appropriate the disputed ammunition. On Jephson's advice Emin sent a countervailing party from Muggi to talk the Kirri men over and bring south as many as were willing to join the withdrawal. When the Muggi men returned, they brought with them, not the garrison of Kirri or any part thereof, but a second deputation from Rejaf loudly protesting their loyalty, obedience and good faith. Emin's spirits rose. The Rejaf men were sent back to spread the gospel of submission among their comrades of the First Battalion and lead them down to Duffile. "Emin thought all would yet be well." (Jephson)

The next news, however, was not of a kind to sustain Emin's optimism. It came from Hawashi Effendi, who wrote to announce that an armed band of "Khartoum people" had appeared in the country north-east of Lado and were fighting with the Latuka who inhabited that region. Hawashi added: "I trust in God they are people from our Government in Khartoum." Emin, unable to share this touching belief that Khartoum was still in Egyptian hands, realised that the news, if true, was bad. The strangers might be only a Danagla raiding party; but it was by no means impossible that they represented something far more ominous—the advance guard of a second Mahdi-ist invasion force. The latter suspicion added a touch of urgency to the situation. Emin decided to wait no longer on the outcome at Rejaf. The evacuation of Muggi was proceeding smoothly. The ammunition had already gone down to Duffile, and parties of women, children, cattle and baggage were leaving daily. On August 12, Emin and Jephson moved to Labore, the next station on their route.

The commandant here was Selim Aga Matera, a giant Sudanese described by Jephson as "a great easy-going fellow, with a good-natured, cherubic face, and . . . a little shrew of a wife who kept him in splendid order". He was an old soldier, grown grey in the Khedive's service, and had been Commandant at Mruli under Gordon. Of his loyalty Emin was reasonably sure, but his second in command, Surur Aga, was a doubtful quantity. Selim told Emin he had already spoken to his people and they had agreed to go south. But the next day, when they were fallen in to hear the letters from Stanley, Nubar and the Khedive, Jephson—

. . . noticed that the soldiers were not as attentive as was generally the case, and that there was a good deal of whispering going on amongst them. A large crowd of people, too, men, women, and children, had gathered in dense masses on a little bluff, above the place where the soldiers were drawn up in line, and there was an uneasy stir amongst them, as if something unusual was going to happen.

After I had finished speaking, Emin, as was his custom, added a few words to what I had said. Whilst he was speaking, a big, bull-headed, sullen-looking Soudanese stepped out of the ranks and exclaimed, "All you have been telling us is a lie, and the letter you have read out is a forgery, for if it had come from Effendina (the Khedive) he would have commanded us to come, and not have told us we might do as we pleased. You do not come from Egypt, we know of only one road to Egypt, and that is by Khartoum, we will either go by that road, or will live and die in this country."

Emin instantly sprang forward and seized him, and trying to wrench the gun out of his hand, shouted to his four orderlies to arrest the man, and carry him off to prison. A struggle then ensued, and the mutineer shouted to his companions to help him. There arose a scene of confusion and uproar which is impossible to describe. The soldiers, breaking from the ranks, dashed at Emin and me with loaded guns, and surrounded us. Shouts of hate and execration were hurled at us as the mutineers hemmed us in with guns pointed at us. Emin drew his sword and dared them to come on. It was a horrible moment as we saw ourselves surrounded by the infuriated soldiery, their fingers moving uneasily on the triggers of their loaded guns, while they cursed us, with their brutal faces distorted with fury, and their eyes gleaming with hatred. For a second it seemed to me that this was to be the ending of all our long struggle to rescue Emin Pasha, and the thought of Stanley and my companions far away, flashed vividly through my mind. At this moment, someone called out that my orderlies[15] were going to seize the powder magazine, and with one of those sudden changes of purpose so characteristic of the Negro character, the soldiers wrenched their companion from the grasp of Emin's orderlies, and rushed off to the magazine, bearing their comrade with them with shouts of defiance and contempt. Emin and I were left standing almost alone, for nearly all our followers had run away in terror at the first outbreak. Selim Aga and the other officers had done what they could to quiet the soldiers, but they might as well have tried to still the ocean, for their voices were drowned in the uproar and confusion.[16]

Finally Jephson persuaded Emin to retire to his house. Then, almost alone and showing the greatest coolness, Jephson went among the soldiers, talked to them, and managed to calm them to the point of getting them to state their grievances rationally. He insisted that no one had any intention of getting them to leave the Province against their will, and that they were free agents. It was agreed that he would meet them again the next day to hear what they had decided to do.

> Emin was dreadfully excited all the evening, and feared the soldiers would attack us that night, but I felt certain they would not do that. After a while I sent for Selim Aga and the officers of the station, who came down and had a long talk with us. They all expressed themselves horrified at what had happened, and deplored the conduct of the soldiers. However, from what he said, or perhaps more from his manner when he spoke, I felt a great distrust of Surore Aga. . . . It transpired many days afterwards, that the mutineer who stepped out of the ranks and defied Emin was Surore Aga's orderly, and had been instigated by him to do it. Surore Aga, we eventually heard, had, ever since Stanley's arrival at the lake, been in constant communication with the rebels at Rejaf. I spoke in the evening to Emin's and my orderlies, and commended them for their conduct during the outbreak that afternoon. They had behaved with great courage, and they, together with my servant Binza, had helped me greatly in quieting the soldiers.[17]

The next day the men paraded and Jephson confronted them alone (though not unarmed—he had prudently put a revolver in his pocket). They expressed contrition for their behaviour of the day before. Jephson heard them out and, having repeated that they were perfectly free to take part in the evacuation or not, left them. That day he and Emin (leaving yet another unresolved crisis in their rear) moved on to the next station, Khor Ayu. Here a letter reached them from Hamid Aga to say that Ali Aga Djabor had arrived at Rejaf. Emin still persisted in the belief that the Rejaf garrison, hearing that the stations to the south of them were being abandoned, would join the movement, especially if they had also heard of the arrival of the Danagla to the north of them. Emin's optimism was unfounded. Ali Aga had all along been one of the most resolute and *jusqu'auboutiste* of the mutineers and would hardly return to the fold at this late date; while Hamid Aga, their nominal commander, though a well-intentioned man, had comparatively little influence with the soldiers. Ali Aga's position should have been clear enough from the message he sent via Hamid Aga—that if there was to be any discussion, Emin must come to Rejaf.

Matters were at this pass—open defiance from Rejaf, total confusion at Kirri, a barely-quelled mutiny at Labore, and the threat of a possible invasion hanging over them from the north—when the final blow fell.

> Late on the evening of August 18th, a letter came in from Hawashi Effendi, saying that rebellion had broken out in Duffile, and he had been made a prisoner. Three officers (led by) Fadl el Mulla Aga . . . with 60 soldiers, had that day arrived from Fabbo station and had seized the government store-houses and powder magazine. They then addressed the soldiers and told them that they were fools to listen to what the Pasha, Stanley and I had told them, that the road we wished to take them by did not lead to Egypt, the only road to which lay through Khartoum. The letters we had brought with us were forgeries, they were convinced that we had not come from Egypt, and had positive proof that we wished only to take the people out of the country and hand them, their wives and children over as slaves to the English. These words spread like wildfire amongst the ignorant people, and the soldiers readily joined the mutineers. All the officers in Duffile joined them also, and elected Fadl-el-Mulla as their chief.[18]

Emin and Jephson were caught in a trap with mutinous garrisons both north and south of them. Emin took a decision which, though it testified to his personal courage, was unlikely to redress the balance in his favour: he decided to go to Duffile and confront the rebels. On August 20, accompanied by Jephson and Vita Hassan, he marched straight into the station, passed through a jeering mob of drunken and unruly soldiers and entered the Governor's compound. No sooner were Emin and his party inside than a guard of Fadl el-Mulla's men took up

284

their posts outside the gate and the Governor's compound became the Governor's prison.

Fadl el-Mulla now summoned a general assembly of officers and officials from both the northern and southern stations. They formed themselves into a provisional council to govern the Province. The chief movers of this august assembly were the Sudanese officers Fadl el-Mulla and Ali Aga Djabor, but nearly all the senior officers except Hawashi Effendi took part in what followed with varying degrees of enthusiasm. Some, such as Hamid Aga and Selim Aga—both of whom seem to have joined the mutineers less out of conviction than for lack of a viable alternative—formed a moderate group in the council. The noisiest section was formed by the civilian employees (mostly Egyptian clerks), but these clerks lived and moved in so contorted an atmosphere of fevered plotting and counterplotting that they were quite unable to combine in steady pursuit of any agreed objective, and in the last resort their influence on affairs was negligible. Alone of the Sudanese officers, Shukri Aga, from his isolated position at Msawa, managed to remain unequivocally loyal to Emin throughout the rebellion. Even Hawashi Effendi, imprisoned at the start of the outbreak, failed to keep his hands clean, since at one point he attempted to secure his release by giving false testimony against Emin.

The coup had been bloodless, sudden, and completely successful. Perhaps its very success took its perpetrators by surprise. They certainly had no clear idea of where to go next. Instead, they proceeded to fritter their time away in pointless attacks on an already defeated enemy—that is, on Emin and his supporters. An attempt to prove Jephson an impostor, and his letters forgeries, failed when the signatures on the Khedive's and Nubar's letters were found on inspection to be genuine. An attempt to impeach Emin on grounds of corruption and mismanagement failed, too, for lack of evidence—an outcome which must have caused considerable surprise, since an official who neither accepted presents, nor fudged his accounts, nor misappropriated government property, was an animal as rare as the Phoenix.

In late August rumours of Stanley's return reached Duffile. This prospect caused the rebels some uneasiness, as Stanley was an unknown but menacing factor in their calculations. It was decided to send a deputation (of which Jephson would form part) to call on Stanley in the hope of finding out which way that particular wind was likely to blow. Jephson was taken down by steamer as far as Tunguru, where he saw Casati.[19] When Casati heard how things stood at Duffile, he readily agreed to sink his differences with Emin and stand by his friend.

The rumour of Stanley's arrival had by now been found to be false. Jephson stayed at Tunguru while the rebel deputation went down to Msawa. Shukri Aga prudently arranged to be absent on a tax-collecting tour. The rebels helped themselves to the "relief" ammunition which had been stored at Msawa, then turned back. By mid-September Jephson and Casati were back at Duffile to share Emin's confinement.

The rebel council now gave itself up day after day to endless, futile, and tortuous discussion, and night after night to orgies of drunkenness and over-eating. The lack of a single clear motive behind the rebellion—beyond a generalised feeling of suspicious apprehension—plus the absence of a commanding personality among the rebels, rendered abortive their half-hearted attempts to reorganise the government of the Province. As they lacked either an agreed leader or an agreed aim, everything they did served only to increase the prevailing confusion. The soldiers, meanwhile, began to regret the good old days of Emin's governorship, became fractious, and refused to obey orders. And since the rebel officers also refused to obey orders from any of their fellow rebels, the breakdown in discipline was general.

For lack of a better occupation the council embarked on a programme of confiscation and extortion aimed at Emin's supporters. First Hawashi Effendi, then Vita Hassan, and finally Emin himself had their houses ransacked and their goods stolen. These measures found a degree of popular favour and served as a local and temporary ersatz for actual government.

Another—though hardly more constructive—measure was forced through by the clerks after much bickering in the council. This was nothing less than Emin's formal deposition. As it was felt that such a measure needed ratification by the highest possible authority, a document embodying the decision was drawn up in due form and presented to Emin for his signature. On Casati's advice, Emin meekly complied.

This last occasion was nearly fatal to one of Emin's senior Egyptian officials, Osman Latif Effendi, the Vakil or Vice-Governor. This unhappy man had until then been trying desperately to keep a foot in both camps. But his secret communications with Emin became known to the rebel officers, who upbraided him for covertly supporting the deposed Governor.

The rogue, at once perceiving the gravity of the situation, and pretending to be driven mad by the infamous calumny, was seized with a wild impulse to throw himself into the river. Some humane persons took him out, still trembling with convulsions, and brought him into the presence of the chief of the rebels, who said, in a tone of irony and contempt, "You should have left this carrion to be drowned. What was the use of saving him?" I was afterwards assured that Osman would not have been drowned, even had he remained all day in the river, for at the place he had selected, and where he threw himself on his knees, the water only reached his chin.[20]

All this time Emin remained a close prisoner. Jephson and Casati were allowed a limited freedom of movement about the station, a freedom which they employed in vain attempts to sort out from the welter of gossip, rumour, and evanescent intentions, the probable future actions of the rebels. Emin, forbidden to leave his compound, sank deeper and deeper into dejection. He was bitterly hurt and terribly shaken by what had occurred, not so much on account of the depth and extent of the disloyalty which became daily more apparent, but more by what he saw as ingratitude on the part of a people he had served unstintingly for so many years.

Jephson's account shows Emin in an advanced stage of demoralisation:

At this time he gave way entirely. It was not, of course, to be wondered at after all those years of strain. . . . I told him that the people would go on talking and talking for weeks to come and would settle nothing; but it was of no use, the slightest rumour against him was sufficient to plunge him into the deepest dejection. The suspense and uncertainty were indeed terrible. . . . Fear he had none; such a thing was not in his composition. But it was the nervousness from want of appetite and sleep, which caused his hand to shake and made him start at every sound.[21]

Apart from the nervous strain, the mere physical confinement was irksome and depressing to an active man:

During those days of our imprisonment, cooped up in a small yard, closed in by a high thick boma, and surrounded by a noisy station, Emin longed for a glimpse of trees and green grass once more. I discovered that by standing on a chair, we could just see a small patch of green grass with five or six Borassus palms growing on it, some mile and a half from the station. We used, therefore, frequently to mount on our chairs, and stand gazing at this small picture.[22]

In the middle of October came an event which, while it did nothing to lessen the prevailing chaos, profoundly affected the whole situation of the Province. A soldier from Rejaf came into Duffile on October 15. He brought news that a Mahdi-ist army had arrived at Lado and was preparing to move south.

* * *

The arrival of Stanley's Expedition, by bringing to a head the suspicion and uncertainty prevalent among Emin's followers, was without doubt the stimulus which released the mutiny at Duffile. The renewal of the Mahdi-ist attack on the Province, which completed the work of destruction that the mutiny had begun, may be traced to the same source.[23] Reports of Stanley's arrival at the south end of the Lake had made their way to Khartoum and to the ears of the Khalifa Abdullah, the Mahdi's successor. These reports decided him to extirpate the last vestiges of "Turkish" rule in the Sudan. In the summer of 1888, therefore, he ordered the invasion of Equatoria. On June 11, a force of fifteen hundred men under the emir Omar Saleh embarked in a flotilla of three steamers and six barges and left Khartoum bound for the upper river. They had a difficult passage; the steamers were overloaded and the engines of one of them were so unserviceable that it had to be towed. They did not reach Lado until October 11, 1888.[24] They found the station deserted (as it had been for over a year). Letters were promptly sent to the garrison at Rejaf and to Emin at Duffile demanding instant surrender to the will of God. As soon as this formality had been carried out, Omar Saleh advanced and laid siege to Rejaf.

The garrison of Rejaf, though deprived of their leaders (who were away at Duffile, politicking), refused to surrender and prepared to fight it out. On October 19 they sallied out and attacked the besiegers but were beaten back by a counter-attack which ended with the Mahdi-ists forcing their way into the station. In half an hour resistance was at an end. Those of the garrison who failed to escape south to Duffile or west to Makraka were killed or made prisoner. Omar Saleh reported his own losses as ninety-six (killed, wounded and missing). The booty included five hundred slaves.

Among the loot which Omar Saleh sent north to the Khalifa after the battle was the copy of the Khedive's firman which Jephson had sent up to Rejaf in July. The Khalifa forwarded it, together with a copy of Omar Saleh's report, to Osman Digna, who in turn sent both documents together with a covering letter to General Grenfell, the Sirdar (C-in-C) of the Egyptian Army. Omar Saleh's despatch contained the news that Emin and "a traveller who was with him" had been made prisoner by the Equatorial troops. Osman Digna misinterpreted this intelligence as meaning that Emin and his whole province were now in the hands of the Mahdi-ists and stated as much in his letter to General Grenfell. Thus, in December 1888, the rumour spread through Europe that Emin and his province, and Stanley with him, were now in the Khalifa's power. The fact that the Khedive's firman, entrusted to Stanley, had been captured by the Mahdi-ists seemed confirmation of this interpretation. No authentic news of Stanley had reached Europe since his last despatch before leaving Yambuya. This had arrived in September 1887. Then, for fifteen months, nothing. There had been rumours a-plenty—mostly involving reports of Stanley's death or capture. The news from Suakin, therefore, fell on ears already attuned to tales of disaster; and since the authentication of the story appeared complete, the idea that Stanley and Emin were prisoners of the Khalifa found ready acceptance, though a careful reading of Omar Saleh's despatch should at least have thrown doubt on the story.[25] But it was the arrival, in late December, only weeks after the news from Suakin, of Stanley's despatches from Banalya which proved the news of his capture to be false. The civilised world (doubtless) breathed again.

Meanwhile, at Duffile, the rebel officers had quite lost whatever slight grip on affairs they may once have had. The first news of the steamers' arrival had caused a last pathetic upsurge in the hope of relief from the north. This baseless optimism had finally been quenched by the arrival of three Peacock Dervishes bearing Omar Saleh's surrender demand. The terms offered were, as always, an unalluring choice between instant surrender and instant destruction. The Emir wrote:

... the whole Sudan and its dependencies accepted the Mahdi's rule, and submitted to the Imam, the Mahdi, and gave themselves to him with their children and possesssions, and became his followers, and whoever opposed him was killed by God, and his children and property became the prey of the Moslems. ... So now we have come in three steamers, and in sandals and nuggars, filled with soldiers from God's army ... and we bring you such news as will ensure your welfare in this world and the next, and to tell you what God wishes, He and His Prophet, and to assure you of a free pardon, to you and to whomsoever is with you, and protection for your children and property, from God and His Prophet, on condition that you submit to God.[26]

The letter had been received, not by Emin, but by the officers of the council. Dismayed, they promptly repaired to Emin's compound, read him the letter, and asked what was to be done. This, if ever, was Emin's chance to recover his authority, but pettishly he refused to take it:

He ... told them as they had put him aside, and had brought the country to this pass, they must now manage the affair themselves.[27]

He did, however, consent to give his advice: surrender was not to be thought of; instead, the northern stations should be evacuated at once, burned, and their garrisons concentrated at Duffile to cover a further retreat of non-combatants to Wadelai. It was good advice, but it was not taken. Emin, fatalistically, did not insist, though not only his Province, but his life, was now at stake.

The Rejaf officers, including Ali Aga Djabor and Hamid Aga, marched north the same day with sixty men, intending to bring in their detachments from Makraka, and give battle to the invaders. This action, though futile (Rejaf fell long before the proposed concentration could be put into effect), at least had the merit that it was founded on the desire to do *something*. The same could not be said of Fadl el-Mulla and the other officers remaining at Duffile, who seemed to have as much trouble as ever in devising constructive ways to occupy their time. They reverted, *faute de mieux*, to their normal routine of discussion, bickering and orgies. By way of diversion the dervishes who had brought Omar Saleh's letter were tortured (in a rather desultory and haphazard fashion) for information concerning the enemy's strength.

9 (i) JOHN ROSE TROUP

9 (ii) SERGEANT WILLIAM BONNY

9 (iii) HERBERT WARD. Photograph
taken at Loanda in May 1888

10 (i) On the Congo, 1889. WARD is in the canoe

10 (ii) The Mutiny at Labore

They bore the tortures with such utter stoicism that their tormentors became discouraged and desisted.

On October 22 came the news of the fall of Rejaf.

This dolorous intelligence was not without effect at Duffile: it stimulated a sudden frenzied concern for the manufacture of silver bullets, the Mahdi-ists being supposed immune to baser metals.[28] Fortunately there was a good supply of silver to hand in the several thousand dollars that Hawashi Effendi had disgorged—though with the utmost reluctance and in small lots—after his impeachment.

The steamers began ferrying refugees from Duffile to Wadelai. Jephson was asked to report on ways to strengthen the defences of Duffile. He did so, but his advice was not acted on. Day followed day of vacillation, disorder, and endless contradictory rumours until, on November 16, came the news that an attempt by the survivors of the First Battalion to retake Rejaf had ended in a crushing defeat at the hands of the Mahdi-ists. The Sudanese troops had been routed, the chief officers—among them Hamid Aga and Ali Aga Djabor[29]— killed, and the Bari, rising against their oppressors, had joined in the pursuit of the defeated army and made hay among the stragglers.

From Emin's point of view the rout in the north at least had the merit of eliminating at a stroke a good half of the ringleaders of the mutiny. Leadership now devolved on two of the senior officers left at Duffile: Selim Aga, a responsible officer but not a very forceful personality; and Fadl el-Mulla, one of the most determinedly self-interested (and therefore consistent) of the mutineers. The differences between the two men were soon to become a matter of some importance in the brief remainder of the Province's existence. At the moment, feeling among the rank and file was running against Fadl el-Mulla, who had conspicuously failed to give a lead in the crisis. By general consent[30] Selim Aga was given charge of affairs. His first action was to persuade the rump of the rebel council to set Emin, Jephson and Casati at liberty and send them down to Wadelai. Emin consented to what was, in effect, as much a dismissal as a release, but not before he had given (at Fadl el-Mulla's insistence) an assurance that he would refrain from interference in the running of the Province:

. . . Fadl el-Mulla Aga begged he would not conspire with people who would no doubt come to him to turn things upside down, the Pasha said he would not, for after what had happened he wished to have nothing to do with the affairs of the country.[31]

The following day, November 17, Emin left Duffile to an impressive ceremonial send-off:

> The farewell the Pasha received was a triumph over his enemies. The soldiers were marched down to the landing-place & the Khedival hymn was played, they were all drawn up in two lines & saluted as the Pasha passed between them; salutes were fired by the mountain guns & the whole station, with the exception of the five clerks, turned out "en masse" to greet the Pasha & wish him God speed. Everyone seems to breathe more freely now. . . .[32]

It was the reaction of a host who, after hours of moody and grudging hospitality to an unwanted guest, over-compensates with a last-minute burst of hearty geniality when his visitor has taken his hat to leave and been safely steered as far as the doorstep.

Wadelai seemed genuinely glad at Emin's return. He was received on all sides with effusive declarations of loyalty.

> . . . the whole station nearly was assembled & the soldiers were all dressed in white & drawn up for saluting. When we were made fast all the officers clerks, civil servants & artisans flocked on board to greet the Pasha & escorted him with joyful acclamations up to his house. . . . Every one seems glad to have him back & the utmost contentment prevails, the faithfuls who have stuck to him, in spite of threats etc from the rebels, go about with grinning faces, showing the height of their delight that the bad days are over. The Pasha's return here is decidedly triumphant.[33]

Emin, however, was unmoved in his decision to let affairs take their course, even if it meant that he was to be, like Hamlet, a mere "spectator in his own tragedy". He made no attempt to reassert his own authority. In the days that followed he busied himself with his medical duties (there was an epidemic in progress at Wadelai) and with the highly congenial task of sorting through his beloved collection. Jephson went duck-shooting. Casati took to his bed with a rheumatic complaint.

At the beginning of December, when Emin had been over a fortnight at Wadelai, rumours began to come in thick and fast of fresh disasters in the north and an impending attack on Wadelai itself. The soldiers, led by the non-commissioned officers, paraded before

Emin's residence and petitioned him to resume command of the Province. Still Emin refused, but in a characteristic attempt to satisfy both sides, he tempered his refusal with assurances that he was ready to support his people with "advice". This brought both Jephson and Casati to despair, for they saw it as prefiguring a return to Emin's bad old temporising habits. Jephson was now pressing for Emin to abandon without further ceremony the people who had betrayed him, and to accept Stanley's conduct to the coast.[34] Casati went about muttering darkly against Emin's readiness, under pressure, to promise what he had neither the means nor the intention to perform. Both wanted Emin to tell the people point blank to expect nothing further from him and then to go his own way.

Two days after Emin's address to the soldiers, matters came suddenly to a head. Wadelai had now been waiting anxiously for some time for a steamer with news from Duffile. No steamer had appeared. This was ominous, since Duffile was presumed to be threatened, if not actually under attack.

Into this rather fraught atmosphere there came, on December 4, a party of refugees from Bora, a village mid-way between Wadelai and Duffile, with news which seemed to confirm Emin's worst fears. They reported that Omar Saleh's men had taken and burnt all the northern stations, that Duffile was under siege, that Fabbo had been attacked and taken, and that the Shuli had risen against the Turks.

The officers at Wadelai met hastily to discuss the news. Emin was asked for his advice. He recommended instant evacuation on the grounds that Wadelai was indefensible. And, on the assumption that Duffile, if attacked, would inevitably share the fate of Rejaf and the other stations, the turn of Wadelai could not be far away. It was decided to fall back immediately on Tunguru:

> The funeral bell was tolling. Most probably Dufile had already fallen into the hands of the enemy, and availing himself of the two steamers, he might appear before Wadelai much sooner than we wished. The station was not sufficiently fortified for defence against a serious attack; the surrounding land was not suited for successful combats; the storehouses were deficient in corn; water had to be brought from the river; there was no choice: we had to give up every idea of resistance and march to Tunguru, keeping on the heights.

The proposal of retreat was confusedly voted, with the usual unwilling and stupid protestations of sacrifice from those who (as it always happens) would have been the first to set the example of flight.[35]

The next day (December 5) the retreat began. It had been decided on in panic and was carried out in chaos. The Madi living about the station would no longer obey orders and so there were practically no carriers to be had. Nearly everything had to be abandoned—Emin's collections, books, scientific and medical instruments; Jephson's luggage; the steel boat *Advance*; and all the contents of the government storehouses and magazines. The ivory and the station's cannon were thrown into the river. At the last moment the soldiers refused to leave, but "it was no time for waiting and we started off without them" (Jephson).

The column consisted of a large number of women, children and slaves from Wadelai and the northern stations, plus Emin and a cosmopolitan coterie comprising his daughter Farida (in a hammock made by Jephson from an old blanket), Casati, Jephson (carrying his precious journal wrapped in a towel), Markos, Vita Hassan, Osman Latif, Hawashi Effendi, and a handful of soldiers, officers and clerks.

We got off by seven o'clock, and as we left the station we could see a confused straggling line of women and children, goats, cattle and sheep, donkeys, and baggage stretching ahead for three miles. All was utter confusion and noise. . . . Some of the people took the queerest things with them. I saw one man carrying in his load four immensely heavy carved legs of a bedstead, while another had a great bunch of ostrich feathers, which he told me he had heard were valuable in Europe. Another was carrying a sledge hammer, a basin, and a heavy cross-cut saw. . . . Several people took their parrots, one woman had three, and I saw one man carrying a cat in a basket. Two soldiers had the tubes of Emin's thermometers hanging to their belts, they were under the impression that they were a sort of clock by which they could tell the time. I could have laughed, only that I felt so much more inclined to do the other thing. It was so awfully pathetic to see these poor half-savage people with their loads stuffed full of all sorts of useless rubbish, under the weight of which they were staggering along, carrying or dragging their poor unfortunate little children after them. . . . At one place we had to cross a broad shallow river, with steep sloping banks on either side.

Here a scene of the utmost confusion prevailed. The high bank was soon churned into a black slippery mud, in which the women and children sank up their knees, and were continually falling. The press on the further bank was terrible, and when some unfortunate child or woman fell, the dense mass of donkeys and people behind swept over them and trampled them under foot. . . . Nothing makes people so cruel as fear, and the terror that the Donagla were following us made these people merciless. . . . After one of the most trying and painful marches I have ever made, we camped at three o'clock, having done only ten miles. . . . From the last stragglers who reached camp we heard that great numbers of people, being tired on the march, had returned to Wadelai, so that our caravan was reduced to one fourth of its original number. We were now in all about 400 souls. There was a rumour that as the last of the column left the station the smoke of the steamers coming up river was seen in the distance. . . . If it is the Donagla, they will probably come on us in the night.[36]

All in all the evacuation of Wadelai was a performance so ill thought-out and so woefully mismanaged as to make the worst of Stanley's marches the previous year look like a Sovereign's Parade at Sandhurst. Fortunately, this unedifying trek was not of long duration. The next day the column was overtaken by a steamer. Jephson "thought it was all up with us", but the steamer turned out to contain not the advance guard of a dervish horde, but a load of refugees from Duffile. Their news was surprising. Duffile had been surrounded and attacked by Omar Saleh's army. But it had not fallen. Not only had the garrison beaten off the Mahdi-ist attack, but in doing so they had given such a good account of themselves that the enemy had lifted the siege and fallen back on Rejaf. As in 1885, the soldiers, once cornered, had resisted fiercely and to good effect; and, as on the previous occasion, the result was an unexpected reprieve from the total disaster which had seemed imminent and inevitable. True, successs had been born out of confusion in a manner and at a moment that had so little to do with planning as to seem almost inadvertent. The defence of Rejaf was a most curious blend of cowardice and courage, competence and confusion. The fort had been entered by a party of the enemy at a place which Jephson had specifically pointed to as a weak spot, but which nothing had been done to strengthen.[37] Selim Aga, who had led the rally and counter-attack against this incursion, was also responsible for having left the weak spot undefended. Suliman Aga, the Commander from Tunguru, received wounds from which he later died; it was reliably reported that he had been shot by his own men, though whether from malice or mischance no one cared to inquire too closely. And the same soldiers whose fierce resistance had caused the Mahdi-ists to apply the spurs of panic to the horses of retreat, had themselves, at one stage, been observed flying about the station in groups like stampeding sheep. Before his death, Suliman Aga told Jephson—

> . . . that he saw sixty soldiers armed with Remington rifles flying before one of the Donagla armed with a sword and spear only. It was not until three or four of them had been cut down with the sword that it suddenly seemed to strike them that they had guns. They then halted, and fired a volley at their pursuer, which riddled him with bullets.[38]

On the other hand, Suliman Aga—

> . . . spoke in admiration of the conduct of Selim Aga, Abdul Aga Manzal, Bachit Aga (*Commandant of Kirri*), and three or four other officers, who, during the panic, had fought splendidly, and at length induced the soldiers to rally. He said it was entirely owing to these officers that the station had been saved.[39]

No one knew, however, how long a reprieve the victory had earned them. In any case, it had come too late to check the internal dissolution of the Province. The retreat went on. Emin and his party continued to Tunguru. Duffile was evacuated and burnt and its defenders fell back on Wadelai.

Equatoria now consisted of three stations. In the south was Msawa under Shukri Aga, still unswervingly loyal to Emin. In the north was Wadelai occupied by the mutinous troops under divided leadership— Selim arguing for evacuation under Stanley's escort, Fadl el-Mulla determined to stay in Equatoria come what might. At Tunguru, poised awkwardly between the loyal and the mutinous stations, was Emin, who, having come so far, was now (to the despair of Jephson) showing signs of wanting to go back, lest it should be thought he had "abandoned his people". To add to Emin's difficulties, the Lur, who lived around Tunguru, had become infected with the unrest which had spread progressively among the tribes from Lado southwards keeping pace with the collapse of Egyptian rule. Finally, Kabba Rega from across the Lake was making hostile demonstrations which might develop into an attack on the Lake stations at any time.

But while Emin hesitated, plagued by doubts and scruples, his mind—as so often happened on these occasions—was made up for him by the march of events. At the end of January 1889, Stanley reappeared on the scene.

NOTES AND REFERENCES

CHAPTER 8   COLLAPSE IN EQUATORIA

1   JEPHSON—E.P. p. 45.

2   CASATI II p. 171.

3   Fadl el-Mulla was of the Dinka tribe. Suliman Aga may have been his brother, though Casati merely calls them "compatriots".

4   CASATI II p. 173.

5   A certain petulance in Casati's references to Jephson's influence over Emin suggests that simple jealousy on Casati's part may have had something to do with the coldness between himself and Emin.

6   Usually referred to by the Italianised appellation "Signore Marco". Stanley at one points calls him "Marco Polo", implying (unless it is a joke) that his name may have been Markopoulos.

7   Emin to Junker, March 7, 1887.

8   JEPHSON—E.P. pp. 75–76.

9   The senior officer of the Second Battalion, as Hamid Aga was of the First.

10 "The Pasha remarked 'And you?' 'Oh' said Hawashi Effendi, 'I'm the biggest scoundrel of them all.'" (JEPHSON p. 271.)

11 JEPHSON—E.P. p. 86.

12 JEPHSON—E.P. p. 107.

13 SCHWEITZER I p. 251.

14 Jephson remarked that this officer not only enjoyed the respect and obedience of his troops (a thing far from common) but also the friendship and confidence of the local tribesmen (rarer still). (JEPHSON—E.P. p. 123.)

15 I.e. the Sudanese soldiers Stanley had left with Jephson as an escort.

16 JEPHSON—E.P. pp. 145–147.

17 JEPHSON—E.P. pp. 149–150.

18 JEPHSON—E.P. pp. 154–155.

19 Jephson noted disapprovingly that Casati "had quite given up European habits and lived almost like an Oriental . . . He sat in his house all day and smoked; he had no books and kept no journal; I never could understand how he managed to pass the time . . ." (JEPHSON—E.P. p. 196.)

20 CASATI II p. 223. For a more sympathetic account of Osman's brush with death, cf. JEPHSON—E.P. p. 223. Though nominally Vice-Governor, Osman Latif was out of office at the time of the rebellion. Emin had to dismiss him from his post (for plotting) on at least two occasions. If it is surprising that Emin should have continued to employ a man of proven unreliability, it must be remembered that Equatoria was virtually a closed system. It was as difficult for Emin to "lose" one of his Egyptian subordinates, however troublesome, as it was for him to recruit new ones.

21 JEPHSON—E.P. p. 222.

22 JEPHSON—E.P. p. 216.

23 COLLINS p. 55.

24 Jephson (E.P. p. 242) identifies Omar Saleh's army with the Danagla whose presence had been reported in Latuka country in July, and states that Omar Saleh would have been at Rejaf four months earlier if he had not turned aside at Bor to attack the Latuka and suffered a reverse at their hands. Collins (pp. 59–60) doubts whether the men who fought the Latuka could have been Omar Saleh's since his despatches to the Khalifa make no mention of any such operations and report no casualties until the attack on Rejaf.

25 See COLLINS p. 61n and WAUTERS Ch. XIII. Stanley prints both Osman Digna's letter and Omar Saleh's report for the weirdly idiosyncratic reason that they constitute "criminating proofs that intercourse with the enemy was maintained by the rebel officers". (See D.A. pp. 228–229.)

26 Extracted from Omar Saleh's letter, the full text of which can be found in JEPHSON—E.P. pp. 245–251.

27 JEPHSON—E.P. p. 253.

28 JEPHSON p. 286: "It seems rather queer that such beliefs should hold in the nineteenth century, but when one comes to think of it, it was not so long ago that the belief held in Scotland, I believe Claverhouse was considered proof against bullets & was finally supposed to have been killed by a silver button used as a bullet . . . The belief in the efficacy of silver bullets holds, I am told, over the whole Orient, even to this day." The same story—of death caused by a waistcoat button used as a bullet—is told of Charles XII of Sweden, whose imperviousness to lead was attested by the number of bullets he used to tip out of his wide-topped boots after a day's fighting. And Lady Hester Stanhope, speaking to Kinglake about Ibrahim Pasha (the adopted son of Mohammed Ali of Egypt) said "that Ibrahim's life was charmed against balls and steel, and that after a battle he loosened the folds of his shawl, and shook out the bullets like dust". (Eothen Ch. VIII.)

29 Jephson (E.P. p. 286) pays a little tribute to Hamid Aga, who, Jephson believed, was at heart "a firm friend of Emin in fair and foul weather". He wrote: "I was sorry for Hamid Aga's death. He was a thoroughly good, honest, straightforward old fellow . . . At the taking of Rejaf some weeks before, all

his wives and children were captured by the Donagla, and he seemed, from all accounts, to have become reckless in consequence . . . I felt really grieved that I should not again see his kind old face."

30 JEPHSON—E.P. p. 287. The word "general" should perhaps be understood rather loosely in view of the confused and conflicting interests which animated the soldiery.

31 JEPHSON p. 301.

32 JEPHSON pp. 301–302. The "five clerks" were a diehard splinter-group that made a last-minute effort to prevent Emin's release.

33 JEPHSON p. 302.

34 The Kavirondo scheme was now, of course, out of the question since Emin no longer commanded the armed force which was indispensable to its execution.

35 CASATI II pp. 187–198.

36 JEPHSON—E.P. pp. 323–326.

37 See JEPHSON—E.P. pp. 268–269.

38 JEPHSON—E.P. p. 352.

39 JEPHSON—E.P. pp. 352–353. From the same source (Suliman Aga) Jephson learnt that the three unfortunate dervishes, still being held at Duffile when the siege began, had been beaten to death with clubs by the Equatorial soldiers.

9

FLIGHT
January to December 1889

Emin . . . helplessly chained to Stanley's triumphal car . . .

SCHWEITZER

Stanley marched eastward from Fort Bodo until he came into Mazamboni's country. Here, on January 16, 1889, "one long day's march from the Lake", he received the letters which had been sent by Emin and Jephson from Tunguru a month before. Jephson's outlined events in the Province since Stanley's departure. Emin's added a warning to Stanley not to advance beyond Kavalli's until the situation in Equatoria had resolved itself.

Stanley's reaction to the news of the rebellion, Emin's imprisonment, and the Mahdi-ist invasion, was to lose his temper. Any man might be forgiven for displaying some mortification at such disastrous and unlooked-for complications; Stanley, however, insisted on regarding them simply as perverse and malicious interference with his own plans—a height of egocentricity that few other men, one suspects, could have risen to. That Emin's men had mutinied and imprisoned their lawful governor, and that half the Province had already fallen to the Mahdi-ist army, were facts of less importance to Stanley than that Jephson had broken his promises and failed to carry out his instructions.

He replied to Jephson's letter as follows:[1]

Camp at Gavira's.
January 17th, 1889.

My dear Jephson—Your letter of Nov. 7th, 1888, with two post-scripts, one dated Nov. 24, the other dated Dec. 18th, is to hand, and its contents noted.

I will not criticise your letter, nor discuss any of its contents.

I wish to be brief and promptly act. With that view I present you with a precis of events connected with our journey.

We separated from the Pasha on the 23rd May last, with the understanding that in about two months you, with or without the Pasha, would start for Fort Bodo with sufficient porters to take the goods at the Fort, and convey them to the Nyanza. The Pasha expressed himself anxious to see Mount Pisgah,[2] and if words may be relied on, he was anxious to assist us in his own relief. We some-what doubted if his affairs would permit the Pasha's absence, but we were assured you would not remain inactive. It was also understood that the Pasha would erect a small station on Nyam-sassie Island as a provision depot, in order that our Expedition might find means of subsistence on our arrival at the lake.

Eight months have elapsed, and not one single promise has been performed.

On the other hand, we, faithful to our promises, departed from the Nyanza plain, May 25th, arrived at Fort Bodo June 8th, fifteen days from the Nyanza. Conveying to Lieutenant Stairs and Captain Nelson your comforting assurances that you would be there in two months, and giving Stairs and Nelson orders to evacuate the Fort, and accompany you to the Nyanza with the garrison, which with the Pasha's soldiers would have made a strong depot of Nyamsassie Island, I set out from Fort Bodo on 16th June, to hunt up the Major and his column, alone, unaccompanied by any officers. On the 10th August we overtook our couriers who had left Fort Bodo on the 15th February with Stairs. Of the twenty couriers, three had been killed, two were so debilitated by the effects of arrow poison that they eventually died, fifteen were left, but only one has carried. On the morning of August 17th, at 10 a.m., we sighted the rear column at Banalya, ninety English miles from Yambuya, 592 miles from the Nyanza, on the 63rd day from Fort Bodo, and the 85th day from the Nyanza Plain. The rear column, which on our departure from Yambuya numbered 271 all told, was a mere wreck. Major Barttelot was dead, had been shot with a gun by one of Tippu Tib's Manyuema, on the morning of the 21st of July. Mr Jameson had departed on the 23rd July for Stanley Falls, and a letter dated August 12th, five days before my arrival at Banalya, states that he was about descending the Congo River for Bangala; but the couriers who brought his letter to us stoutly asserted his last intentions were to go down to Banana Point. Mr Herbert Ward had been sent to Banagla, and finally to St. Paul de Loanda. He had returned, and reached reached Bangala with letters, and instructions from the committee, but was detained there by order of Major Barttelot! Mr. John Rose Troup had been invalided home in June, 1888. So no one was left with the wreck of the rear column except William Bonny, who is now with me in this camp. One hundred Soudanese, Zanzibaris, and Somalis had been buried at Yambuya; thirty-three men were left at Yambuya helpless and dying, and fourteen of these died later on; twenty-six deserted. So that when I saw Bonny and his people, the rear column, Zanzibaris, Somalis, and Soudanese, numbered 102 all told, out of 271, and only one officer out of five! Besides this deplorable record, the condition of the stores was just as bad. Out of 660 loads—65 lbs. each—there remained only 230 loads, of 65 lbs. weight. All my personal clothing, except hats, boots, one flannel jacket, a cap, and three pairs of drawers, had been sent down to Bangala, because rumour had stated that I was dead, and the advance party gone to the dogs; a remnant of thirty, however, had managed to escape to Ujiji ! ! !³

I sent my despatches to Stanley Falls, and thence to Europe, and on 31st August commenced my return towards the Nyanza. Two days before the date stated I was at Fort Bodo, December 20th. On December 24th we moved from Fort Bodo towards the Ituri Ferry. But as your non-arrival at Fort Bodo had left us with a larger number of goods than our force could carry at one time, we had to make double journeys to Fort Bodo and back to the Ituri Ferry, but by the 10th January all that remained of the Expedition, with all its effects, were on the east side of the Ituri River, encamped half a mile from the Ferry, with abundance of food assured for months. On the 12th January, I left Stairs, Nelson, Parke, and my servant, at the Ituri Ferry camp, with 150 people,⁴ and started for the lake with 210 people all told, to obtain news of the Pasha and yourself. Your absence from the Fort, and the absolute silence respecting you, all made us suspect that serious trouble had broken out. Yesterday your letter, as above stated, came to hand, and its contents explained the trouble.

The difficulties I met at Banalya are repeated today near the Albert Lake, and nothing can save us now from being overwhelmed by them but a calm and clear decision. If I had hesitated at Banalya, very likely I should still be there waiting for Jameson and Ward, with my own men dying by dozens from sheer inanition. I should have found my strength, stores, and men exhausted.

Are the Pasha, Casati, and yourself to share the same fate? If you are still the victims of indecision, then a long good night to you all, but while I retain my senses, I must save my Expedition. You may be saved also if you are wise.

In the "High Order" of the Khedive, dated February 1st, 1887, No. 3, to Emin Pasha, a translation of which was handed to me, I find the following words:

"And since it is our sincerest desire to relieve you with your officers and soldiers from the difficult position you are in, our Government have made up their mind about the manner by which relief from these troubles may be obtained.

"A mission for the relief has been formed, and the command of it given to Mr. Stanley, the famous, etc., etc., and as he intends to set out on it, with all necessary provisions to you, so that he may bring you with your officers and men to Cairo by the route he may think proper to take.

"Consequently we have issued this 'High Order' to you, and it is sent to you by the hand of Mr. Stanley, to let you know what has been done. As soon as it reaches you, convey my best wishes to the officers and men. And you are at full liberty with regard to your leaving for Cairo or your stay(ing) there with officers and men.

"Our Government has given a decision for paying your salaries with that of the officers and men.

"Those who wish to stay there of the officers and men do so on their own responsibility, and they may not expect any assistance from the Government.

"Try to understand the contents well, and make them well known to all the officers and men, that they may be fully aware of what they are going to do."

It is precisely what the Khedive says, that I wish to say to you. Try and understand all this thoroughly, that you may be saved from the effects of indiscretion, which will be fatal to you all if unheeded.

The first instalment of relief was handed to Emin Pasha on or about May 1st, 1888. The second final instalment of relief is at this camp with us, ready for delivery at any place the Pasha designates, or to any person charged by the Pasha to receive it. If the Pasha fails to receive it, or to decide what shall be done with it, I must then decide briefly what I must do.

Our second object in coming here was to receive such at our camp as were disposed to leave Africa; our Expedition has no further business in these regions, and will at once retire.

Try and understand what all this means. Try and see the utter, and final abandonment of all further relief, and the bitter end and fate of those obstinate and misguided people, who decline assistance when tendered to them. From May 1st, 1888, to January 1889, are nine months, so long a time to consider a simple proposition of leaving Africa or staying here!

Therefore, in the official and formal letter accompanying this explanatory note to you, I designate Kavalli's village as the rendez-vous, where I am willing to receive those desirous of leaving Africa, subject, of course, to any new light thrown upon the complication by a personal interview, or a second letter from you.

And now I address myself to you personally. If you consider yourself still a member of the Expedition, subject to my orders, then, upon receipt of this letter, you will at once leave for Kavalli's with such of my men, Binza, and the three Soudanese, as are willing to obey you, and bring me the final decision of Emin Pasha, and Signor Casati, respecting their personal intentions. If I am not at Kavalli's then stay there, and send word by letter by Kavalli's messengers to M'pinga, chief of Gavira's, who will transmit the same to Mazamboni, where probably I shall receive it.

You will understand that it will be a severe strain on Kavalli's resources to maintain us with provisions for longer than six days, and if you are longer than this period we must retire to Mazamboni's, and finally to our camp on the Ituri Ferry, otherwise we must seize provisions by force, and any act of violence would cut off and close native communication, this difficulty might have been avoided had the Pasha followed my suggestion of making a depot at Nyamsassie. The fact that there are provisions at Msawa does not help us at all. There are provisions in Europe also, but unfortunately they are as inaccessible as those of Msawa. We have no boat now to communicate by lake, and you do not mention what has become of the steamers, the 'Khedive' and 'Nyanza'.

I understand that the Pasha has been deposed, and is a prisoner. Who then is to communicate with me respecting what is to be done? I have no authority to receive communications from officers, mutineers. It was Emin Pasha and people I was supposed to relieve. If Emin Pasha were dead, then to his lawful successor in authority. Emin Pasha being alive, I can receive no communications from any other person unless he be designated by the Pasha. Therefore, the Pasha, if he be unable to come in person to meet me at Kavalli's, with a sufficient escort of faithful men, or be able to appoint some person authorised to receive this relief, it will remain for me to destroy the ammunition, so laboriously brought here, and return home.

You must understand that my people are only porters. They have performed their contract with me with a fidelity unexampled, and having brought the boat and goods here, their duty is ended. You have been pleased to destroy the boat and have injured us irreparably by doing so. I presume the two cases of Winchester ammunition left with the Pasha are lost also.

I ought to mention also that the people at the Ituri Ferry camp are almost all sick, and will be unable to move for at least a month.

And also I have brought with me about 100 Manyuema, with forty-two of whom I have contracted to pay a tusk of ivory to each, for forty-two loads they have brought here for Emin Pasha. Therefore, to satisfy them, I require forty-two tusks of ivory to pay them. Please consider how this can be done to their satisfaction. Also consider how we are to be supplied with food, pending the termination of this eventful part of our journey, if we have to return to the neighbourhood of Kavalli's or the Lake, to await this long deferred decision on the part of the Pasha and his men.

Finally, if the Pasha's people are desirous of leaving this part of Africa, and settle in some country not far remote from here, or anywhere bordering the Nyanza (Victoria), or along the route to Zanzibar, I am perfectly ready to assist, besides escorting those who wish to go home to Cairo safely. But I must have clear and definite assertions, followed by promptitude, according to such orders as I shall give for effecting this purpose; or a clear and definite refusal, as we cannot stay here all our lives awaiting people who seem to be not very clear as to what they wish.

Give my best wishes to the Pasha and Signor Casati, and I hope and pray wisdom may guide them both before it is too late. I long to see you, my dear fellow, and hear from your own lips your story.

Yours very sincerely,

HENRY M. STANLEY.

This letter was meant for Emin as much as for Jephson. To it Stanley appended a postscript for Jephson's eyes only and marked "STRICTLY PERSONAL". In the main it merely repeats, in a more conversational tone, the orders and advice given in the letter, though it also contains a vicious sneer at the unfortunate officers of the Rear Column:

306

11 (i) Carrying goods from
the Lake shore to the plateau

11 (ii) STANLEY haranguing
the "rebel" officers at Kavalli's

12 (i) CASATI, VITA HASSAN, JUNKER. Photograph taken
at Cairo in 1890. Emin's picture is on the table

12 (ii) STANLEY and his officers, 1890. *Standing, left to
right*: Captain Robert H. Nelson, Lt. William G. Stairs.
Sitting, left to right: Surgeon Parke, Henry M. Stanley,
A. J. M. Jephson

Jameson paid a thousand pounds to accompany us. Well, you see, he disobeyed orders and we left him to ponder on the things he had done. Ward, you know, was very eager to accompany us, but he disobeyed orders and was left at Bangala, a victim to his craving for novel adventures. Barttelot, poor fellow, was mad for Kudos, but he has lost his life and all—a victim to perverseness. Now don't you be perverse, but obey, and set my order to you as a frontlet between the eyes, and all, with God's gracious help, will end well.

Stanley's letter to Emin was businesslike to the point of brusqueness. It amounted to an ultimatum.

SIR,

I have the honour to inform you that the second instalment of relief which this Expedition was ordered to convey to you is now in this camp, ready for delivery to any person charged to receive it by you. If you prefer that we should deposit it at Kavalli or Kyya Nkondo's, on the Lake, we shall be ready to do so on receipt of your instructions.

This second instalment of relief consists of sixty-three cases Remington cartridges, twenty-six cases of gunpowder, each 45 lbs. weight; four cases of percussion caps, four bales of goods, one bale of goods for Signor Casati—a gift from myself; two pieces of blue serge, writing paper, envelopes, blank books, &c.[5]

Having after great difficulty—greater than was anticipated— brought relief to you, I am constrained to officially demand from you receipts for the above goods and relief brought to you, and also a definite answer to the question if you propose to accept our escort and assistance to reach Zanzibar, or if Signor Casati proposes to do so, or whether there are any officers or men disposed to accept our safe conduct to the sea. In the latter event, I would be obliged to you if you would kindly state how those persons desirous of leaving Africa can be communicated with. I would respectfully suggest that all persons desirous of leaving with me should proceed to and form camp either at Nsabe or at Kyya Nkondo's on the Lake, with sufficient stores of grain, &c., to support them one month, and that a note should be sent to me informing me of the same via Kavalli, whence I soon may receive it. The person in charge of the people at this camp will inform me definitely whether the people are ready to accept our safe conduct, and, upon being thus informed, I shall be pleased to assume all further charge of them. . . .[6]

If, at the end of twenty days, no news has been heard from you or Mr. Jephson, I cannot hold myself responsible for what may happen. We should be glad to stay at Kavalli's if we were assured of food, but a large following cannot be maintained there except by exacting contributions by force, which would entirely close our intercourse with the natives, and prevent us from being able to communicate with you.

If grain could be landed at Kyya Nkondo's by steamer, and left in charge of six or seven of your men, I could, upon being informed of the fact, send a detachment of men to convey it to the plateau. It is only the question of food that creates anxiety. Hence you will perceive that I am under the necessity of requesting you to be very definite and prompt, if you have the power.[7]

If within this period of twenty days you will be able to communicate with me, and inform or suggest to me any way I can make myself useful, or lend effective aid, I promise to strain every effort to perform service to you. Meantime, awaiting your steamer with anxiety.

I am, your obedient servant,
HENRY M. STANLEY,
Commanding Relief Expedition.

Kavalli provided messengers and the letters were despatched on January 20. They reached Emin and Jephson at Tunguru on January 26. After reading them, Jephson recorded his comments in his diary:

These are the letters; of the letter to the Pasha I say nothing—it is merely an official letter. But his letter to me is in many ways greatly wanting in common sense & I think the way he speaks about the officers of the rear guard is not very pleasant. He seems to forget he told them he would be away at the outside 6 months & in point of fact was gone 14 months, meanwhile these people were left encumbered with loads, unable to move, & the men, from his description dying like flies, they could have hardly anything moreover to eat. However I reserve my judgement of the whole until I hear the story from Bonny, the sole remaining European of the rear guard. Stanley's stories are never very just in matters of this kind & I suspect there is a good deal more in the real story than meets the eye in his letters. . . . Poor Barttelot's death is most tragic & sad, & will create a profound sensation at home where he is fairly well known. Poor fellow he was so bright & full of life & go— indeed the whole story is a very dark one, as dark as any of the many dark stories connected with African travel.

It is instructive to compare Jephson's reflections on Barttelot's fate with the remarks of Stanley quoted above. Such a comparison suggests that the quality in which Stanley was deficient was not so much common sense as common humanity; and a mere pinch of that quality would go very far to forgive his arrogance, untruthfulness, egotism, insensitivity, and apparently boundless capacity for hypocritical self-delusion.

Although resenting, and justly, Stanley's misconceived and wrong-headed reproaches, Jephson reacted as if electrified to Stanley's injunction to return to the fold. Like a chained dog responding to his master's whistle, he exerted himself frantically to break free of the cloying morass of indecision which surrounded him at Tunguru. He made a last desperate attempt to persuade Emin to leave with him. Emin refused, shying away instinctively from a step so (as he saw it) hasty, and so irrevocable. Jephson would wait no longer. On February 6, only ten days after receiving Stanley's letter, he rejoined his chief at Kavalli's.

On arrival he handed Stanley Emin's reply to the twenty-day ultimatum:

> Tunguru.
> January 27, 1889.
>
> Sir—
>
> I have the honour to acknowledge receipt of your note of January 17th, which came to hand yesterday afternoon. I beg at the same time to be allowed to express my sincere congratulations to you and to your party for the work you performed.
>
> I take note of your offer to deliver to me, or any person appointed by me, the second instalment of goods brought by you, consisting of sixty-three cases of Remington cartridges, twenty-six cases of gunpowder, each 45 lbs. weight, four cases percussion caps, four bales of goods, one bale of goods for Signor Casati—a gift from yourself; two pieces of serge, writing-paper, envelopes, blank books, &c. As soon as the officers I am awaiting from Wadelai

come here, I shall appoint one of them to take charge of these goods, and I shall at the same time instruct him to give you formal receipt for them.

The thirty-one cases of Remington cartridges, which formed the first instalment of goods, have been duly deposited in Government stores.

Concerning your question if Signor Casati and myself propose to accept your escort and assistance to reach Zanzibar, and if there are any officers and men disposed to accept of your safe-conduct to the sea, I have to state that not only Signor Casati and myself would gladly avail us of your help, but that there are lots of people desirous of going out from the far Egypt (sic), as well as for any other convenient place. As these people have been delayed by the deplorable events which have happened during your absence, and as only from a few days they begin to come in, I should entreat you to kindly assist them. I propose to send them to Nyamsassi, and a first party start today with Mr. Jephson. Every one of them has pro-visions enough to last at least for a month.

I beg to tender my thanks for the statement of your movements. As from the day you fixed your movements until the arrival of your letter elapsed nine days; the remainder of the time you kindly gave us, viz., eleven days, will scarcely be sufficient. I cannot, therefore, but thank you for your good intentions, and those of the people who sent you, and I must leave it to you if you can await us, and prefer to start after the twenty days have elapsed.

I fully understand the difficulties of getting food and provisions for your people, and I am very sorry that the short time you have to give me will not be sufficient to send you stores from here.

As Mr. Jephson starts by this steamer, and has kindly promised to hand you this note, I avail myself of the occasion to bear witness to the great help and assistance his presence afforded to me. Under the most trying circumstances he has shown so splendid courage, such unfaltering kindness and patience, that I cannot but wish him every success in life, and thank him for all his forbearance. As probably I shall not see you any more, you will be pleased to inform his relations of my thanks to him and them.

Before concluding, I beg to be permitted to tender anew my most heartfelt thanks to you and to your officers and men, and to ask you to transmit my everlasting gratitude to the kind people who sent you to help us. May God protect you and your party, and give you a happy and speedy homeward march.

I am, Sir,
Your obedient servant,
Dr. EMIN PASHA.

Attempting to assess Emin's motives and intentions is at the best of times like trying to build on quicksand; no one can know—he may not have known himself—whether he wanted or expected Stanley to take his pathetic renunciation of further aid at face value.[8] Once he had received this answer, however, there was absolutely nothing to prevent Stanley leaving at once for the coast and leaving Equatoria to its fate. Certainly Stanley was by now heartily sick of Emin, Equatoria and the whole messy business—and with good reason. Why then did he not accept Emin's invitation and wash his hands of it? The answer is not far to seek.

Stanley's immediate reaction to Emin's reply was to begin drawing up a whole series of plans for rescuing Emin by force[9] (the very thing his letter to Jephson had stated that he could not and would not do). It is clear that, come what might, Stanley meant to take Emin with him to the coast. It would be charitable to suppose that simple humanity dictated this imperative. But everything that is known of Stanley's life and character make it clear that disinterested kindness was a factor of no particular weight in deciding his behaviour. Therefore his refusal to accept the opportunity he had been offered to slip his cables and run for home only makes sense in the light of his desire, already referred to, not to return to Europe empty-handed. He still wanted his trophy— more so than ever, in fact, since the Kavirondo scheme had gone by the board. Possession of Emin (there is no other word for it) was necessary to retrieve the fortunes of an Expedition which so far had nothing to show but bungling, confusion, disappointment and disaster.

There was, inevitably, a catch. Emin's delicate conscience would not permit him to leave alone. Unless he took with him all those who wished to be evacuated, he would not go. But not only might the sorting out and transporting to Nsabe of these putative refugees take a very long time, it was also possible that their number might turn out to be very large. And whereas a real live Pasha delivered in good condition to Europe or even Egypt was a prize worth struggling for, the addition of a ragged and unruly mob of Egyptian civilians and Sudanese slaves had no publicity value whatever. Indeed, the appearance of such a horde at Zanzibar might well prove counter-productive, as it would tend to give the Expedition more the air of a third-rate slave caravan than of a rescue expedition.[10]

Stanley's problem, then, was to persuade Emin to leave, even if it meant removing him by force from the bosom of his turbulent subjects, and at the same time to keep to a minimum the number of refugees that were the price of the Pasha's voluntary departure. Since Emin showed no signs of renouncing his intention to abide by the decision of a majority of his people, enough refugees would have to be admitted to the Expedition to lend colour to the notion that Emin was not abandoning his people but accompanying them.

Stanley's handling of this delicate balancing trick was masterly, though it is true that both Emin and his followers played into Stanley's hands. Good general that he was, Stanley knew how to turn his opponents' mistakes to his own advantage.

The game began on February 13 with the arrival of a letter from Emin:

February 13, 1889.

Sir—

In answer to your letter of the 7th instant,[11] for which I beg to tender my best thanks, I have the honour to inform you that yesterday, at 3 p.m., I arrived here (at the southern end of the Lake, near Nsabe) with my two steamers, carrying a first lot of people desirous to leave this country under your escort. As soon as I have arranged for cover of my people, the steamships have to start for Msawa station, to bring on another lot of people awaiting transport.

With me there are some twelve officers anxious to see you, and only forty soldiers. They have come under my orders to request you to give them some time to bring their brothers—at least, such as are willing to leave—from Wadelai, and I promised them to do my best to assist them. Things having to some extent now changed, you will be able to make them undergo whatever conditions you see fit to impose on them. To arrange these I shall start from here with the officers for your camp, after having provided for the camp, and if you send carriers I could avail me of some of them.

I hope sincerely that the great difficulties you have had to undergo, and the great sacrifices made by your Expedition in its way to assist us, may be rewarded by a full success in bringing out my people. The wave of insanity which overran the country has subsided, and of such people as are now coming with me, we may be sure.

Signor Casati requests me to give his best thanks for your kind remembrance of him.

Permit me to express to you once more my cordial thanks for whatever you have done for us until now, and believe me to be,

Yours very faithfully,

DR. EMIN.

Emin's unexpected arrival at Nsabe enabled Stanley to drop his plans for a cutting-out party. Jephson was sent down to the Lake to escort the Pasha up to Kavalli's. He found Emin encamped on the Lake shore with a large party of refugees including Farida, Casati, Markos, Vita Hassan, Hawashi Effendi and Osman Latif. He had brought with him the ivory Stanley had demanded,[12] the *Advance* (rescued from Wadelai), and two hundred loads of provisions (sesame, salt, millet). The steamers had returned to Msawa to bring on more refugees.

On February 17 Emin marched into Stanley's camp.

Since the party Emin had brought south consisted of two distinct groups—the officers' deputation led by Selim Aga,[13] and the refugees— the question naturally arose as to which group Emin belonged to. By his own assertion he had come as sponsor and interpreter to Selim's deputation. On the other hand, he, Casati, Markos and Vita had all brought away with them their entire worldly possessions, a thing they would hardly have done if they had intended to return. But even so, if Stanley was led for a moment to assume that Emin had made a final decision to abandon the Province, the assumption was premature.

Selim and his fellow officers were granted an audience. Emin acted as interpreter, but took no other part in the proceedings. The deputation gave Stanley to understand that the people were unanimous in their desire to leave the Province and only begged for sufficient time to complete their arrangements for the evacuation. As earnest of their intentions, a letter was presented from the officers at Wadelai. It read:

To His Excellency the Envoy of our Great
Government, Mr. Stanley.

When Selim Bey Mator, commander of the troops of this province, came here and told us of the news of your coming, we were greatly

rejoiced to learn of your safe arrival in this Province, and our desire
to reach our Government has been greatly augmented, and therefore
we hope, with the help of God, to be very soon with you, and to
inform you of this we have written this letter.

It was signed with the names of thirty-six officers, including that of
Fadl el-Mulla.

Selim was assured that the offer of safe-conduct to Egypt still held
good for all who cared to avail themselves of it; the Expedition
would remain where it was for a "reasonable" (but unspecified) time
to allow intending refugees to make their way to the south of the
Lake. This decision was embodied in a letter to the officers at Wadelai.
Armed with this document, Selim left, promising to set the evacuation
in motion immediately on his return to Wadelai.

Meanwhile the Zanzibaris, with auxiliary porters from the Plateau
tribes, were busy ferrying Emin's baggage from the Lake shore to
Kavalli. Friction soon arose between the Expedition's men and the
refugees. There were two causes. The Egyptians and Sudanese, both
officers and civilians, were so used to lording it over a native population they treated as slaves, that they deemed it beneath them to lift a
finger in their own behalf. True products of a slave-oriented economy,
they measured their status by how little work they did. Their lofty disdain of manual labour, combined with their tendency to treat Stanley's
Zanzibaris as slaves, not only provoked ill-feeling between the two
groups, but led to mutinous discontent among the Expedition's
porters. The second cause of the trouble was that Stanley's strict
instructions to the evacuees not to burden themselves with unnecessary luggage had been completely ignored. Casati had brought
eighty loads, Markos sixty, Vita Hassan forty. Hawashi Effendi, as
befitted his station, had outdone them all with a magnificent ninety-
four. Their conception of an irreducible minimum embraced not
merely a vast amount of rubbish, but also items which, though useful
in their way, could only by the most generous stretch of the imagination be considered portable. Thus the travelling-kit of the refugees was
found to include such items as ten-gallon jars for making raki,
wooden bedsteads, twenty-gallon copper cooking pots, and grinding
stones weighing up to eighty pounds a piece. The work of carrying
these impedimenta fell largely on the shoulders, or rather heads, of
the Zanzibaris, who spent weeks toiling up and down the steep
escarpment with load after load of gear which they well knew to be as

useless as it was bulky. Disenchantment with this duty brought them nearer to open mutiny than they had been at any other time in the whole course of the Expedition.

The disillusion of the Zanzibaris, and their contempt for the people on whose behalf they were making these insane exertions, were shared by the Expedition's officers. These feelings are clearly reflected in the diaries of Jephson and Parke.

These people are awfully selfish and helpless. . . . Some of the loads were enormously too heavy, others were absurdly light, they are so lazy they will not take the trouble to equalise them. One sees a great load of pots kettles & pans heavy enough for two men to carry, & another basket containing only a lantern & a pipe. . . . The officers all looked on me with surprise when they saw me giving out the loads to each man with my own hands, they made no attempt whatever to assist me & I felt with an amused feeling that I had fallen 50 per cent in their estimation by doing so—had I sat still & deputed somebody else to do my work they would have respected me. . . . It was now that one felt so indignant when one saw one of our hard worked, patient, faithful Zanzibaris toiling in the sun up the mountain side staggering under the weight of a load belonging to some of these worthless people, & loads of rubbish which will have to be thrown away when we make our final start. . . . (JEPHSON)

The Pasha says that each of his people can, at a single sitting, drink one or two quart bottles of a clear-coloured, intoxicating liquor, distilled from corn—somewhat after the manner, although not quite of the quality, of our Irish poteen at home. The physique of his officers entirely corroborates this statement; some of them can be impartially described as licentious, indolent, overfed, bloated, congested masses of human flesh. I never saw a more loathsome set of wretches in my life. . . . (PARKE)

Of the Egyptians who had accompanied Emin, Parke wrote:

It must also be remembered that many of them are criminals, and almost all are bad characters—having been connected with Arabi's rebellion, or been convicted of crime in Egypt, and then transported here to the Equatorial Province, to fulfil their terms of penal servitude. They certainly do look like a party of midnight assassins;

and thoroughly represent what might be expected to be the appearance of the denizens of the 'Botany Bay' of Egypt. His (Emin's) confidential clerks were of this class, and all are enfeebled by disease which has been aggravated by intemperance or other vice, or by misconduct. . . . Of those who are really ill, most are syphilitic. . . .[14]

Parke shared Jephson's feeling that it was unjust to make the long-suffering Zanzibaris work so hard and so uselessly on behalf of such ignoble wretches as Emin's followers:

> Every individual in the Pasha's camp, even the servants, have several loads to be transported for him, or her. . . . Half the loads were simply rubbish, and I am really surprised that Mr. Stanley allows this kind of thing to go on; it actually went to my heart to load our men, who have already endured so many indispensable hardships, with such enormous loads of rubbishy articles, and all for so contemptible a people, who do not seem disposed to lift a hand to assist themselves.

Mr. Stanley, who did little or nothing without good reason, knew exactly what he was doing in allowing "this kind of thing to go on". He could have stopped the trouble at its source simply by ordering the "rubbish" to be left on the Lake shore.[15] The loads would have to be sorted, sooner or later, into those which could and those which could not be taken along on the march to the coast. Clearly it was in everybody's interest that the sorting-out should have taken place on the Lake shore rather than on the Plateau. But Stanley gave no such order. On the contrary, he watched the growing discontent among his officers and men with Machiavellian satisfaction. The ill-feeling between his own and Emin's men was a factor which had a calculated role to play in his plans for the immediate future, and while he did nothing to promote it, he did nothing to lessen it. When the officers protested against the work the men were being put to, he replied blandly, that his hands were tied:

> "I am aware of what is going on. But what can we do? These people are our guests. We are bound to help them as much as possible. We indeed came here for that purpose."[16]

And when at last a group of Zanzibaris rebelled and refused to make another trip to the Lake, Stanley reacted sharply. He disarmed the whole group. Then the ringleaders were flogged and tied to the flag-staff in the centre of the camp, and the remainder of the party was sternly sent back to its duty.

Stanley's unsympathetic attitude was incomprehensible to the officers, the more so as they knew (to their cost) that Stanley normally took the part of the Zanzibaris in any dispute, even against his own officers. But in the present case Stanley knew very well what he was about. He had a use in mind for the fund of resentment against the Sudanese and Egyptians that was building up in his men; that resentment represented a source of stored energy which he intended before very long to release and direct towards a precisely calculated end.

At the same time, while the work of transporting the refugees and their mountains of gear up to the Plateau was going forward, Stanley was preparing the second prong of his attack. He put it about that the Sudanese and Egyptians were hatching a plot (or plots) against the Expedition. The Wadelai men were planning, he asserted, to—

. . . curry favour with the Khalif by betraying their would be rescuers and their former Pasha and his white companions into his hands. . . . For the machine guns, repeating rifles and Remingtons, and a batch of white prisoners, the Khalif would reward them handsomely, and promote those chiefly concerned in their delivery to him to honourable and lucrative offices, and endow them with robes of honour. . . . Once in the stranger's camp we may see for ourselves what further can be done, and if we then agree to capture the gang of whites and their followers, nothing will be easier, for all white men are soft-headed duffers. At any rate, it is wise to have two ways from which to choose. If the Khalif is relentless . . . and the door to his mercy is closed, we can fall back upon the camp of the white men, and by apparent obedience disarm all suspicion, make use of them to find us a land of plenty, and suddenly possess ourselves of their arms and ammunition, and either send them adrift as beggars, or slay the whites and make their followers our slaves.[17]

There is no shred of evidence that this imaginative and enterprising conspiracy existed anywhere but in Stanley's mind. It was the product of a few scraps of camp gossip picked up from sources such as Osman Latif[18] and embroidered by the exercise of Stanley's inventive faculties into a full-blown strategic plan. The materials of which it was made were of the kind which, had he not *chosen* to believe, he would normally have treated with a proper contempt. While it is not possible to know exactly how much credence Stanley gave to the rumours he heard in the camp, it can be asserted with some confidence that he was by and large a man to believe what it suited him to believe. It is therefore safe to assume that there was more calculation than paranoia behind Stanley's version of the supposed conspiracy. Treacherous intentions—real or imagined—on the part of the Wadelai men were exactly the justification Stanley needed for getting away from Equatoria with a minimum of delay and a minimum of encumbrance. He had no intention of waiting for Selim Bey and the remainder of the soldiers and people from Wadelai. The idea of a conspiracy to disarm the Expedition was the perfect tool for his purpose: if he left Equatoria without Selim, he was still covered against possible future accusations of deserting the people he had come to help; and if by some miracle Selim actually managed to get a substantial group of people as far as Kavalli's, Stanley had a ready-made reason for refusing to take them along.

The motive behind Stanley's calculations presents no puzzle. Once he had Emin Pasha as living proof of the success of his mission, anyone extra was merely an encumbrance. The miserable refugees now collecting at Kavalli's had a nuisance value as high as their publicity value was low. The five hundred or so people Emin had brought out were, besides, sufficient to strain the resources of the Expedition to their furthest limit. The prospect of several thousand more lazy, disputatious and unruly evacuees, all burdened with mountains of useless luggage, all requiring porters, medical attention, food, protection, and policing, was simply unthinkable.

Stanley need not, as it turned out, have been quite so thorough in protecting his rear. He had underestimated the crippling inability to decide on a common line of action which had from the start nullified the efforts of the mutineers. When Selim returned to Wadelai it was to find that a palace revolution had occurred in his absence and all bets were, as a consequence, off. With his main rival conveniently away on business, the wily Fadl el-Mulla had improved the shining hour to such purpose that he had succeeded in once more swinging a majority behind his anti-evacuation policy. Having regained control of the hearts and minds of the troops, he had lost no time in clearing out the magazines, promoting himself to the rank of Bey, and then taking to the hills followed by a majority of the soldiers.[19] For good measure, perhaps the better to emphasise the final passing of the *ancien régime*, Fadl el-Mulla had Emin, Casati and Selim sentenced to death (*in absentia*) by court-martial. "This", commented Stanley with aristocratic disapproval, "is quite in Jack Cade's style."

Now that Fadl el-Mulla had, as Stanley saw it, shown his true colours, he could effectively be discounted in all future calculations (except to the extent that Stanley may genuinely have believed in a possible intention to attack the Expedition's camp at Kavalli's). Selim Bey retained a small group of followers and was still committed to joining the evacuation. But Fadl el-Mulla's coup, combined with the natural indolence for which the obese and easy-going Selim was noted, left him paralysed. With the followers that remained to him he established himself at Tunguru and there, for the time being, stuck.

This left Stanley free to concentrate on matters nearer to hand. His first priority was to get Emin to agree to a date on which, come what may, the homeward march would begin. Emin and Stanley had in fact already settled the date—April 10. But now, to Stanley's horror, Emin was beginning to hedge, and plead for more time. Stanley resolved to take a firm line. He had already invested a good deal of effort in the endeavour to persuade Emin that the rest of the people had no intention of leaving the country, and if they came down to Kavalli's it would only be to carry out their diabolical designs on the munitions of the Expedition and the life and liberties of its personnel.[20] In spite of all Stanley could do, however, Emin clung stubbornly to his belief that the people would see reason and needed only time. In this he was supported by Casati, whose attitude was, and had been since the time of Stanley's first arrival, that if Emin was to retreat from Equatoria, he could and should do it under his own steam rather than consent to become a helpless nonentity attached to Stanley's travelling circus.[21] This argument was a powerful one in that it acted on Emin's most sensitive area—his pride. And since it was an attitude based on pride, it was unassailable by reason.

Temporarily baffled in his attempts to win Emin round, Stanley decided to fall back on superior numbers. On March 26 he summoned a meeting of the officers in Emin's presence and addressed them:

"Gentlemen ... Shukri Aga, the chief of the Msawa Station ... paid us a visit here in the middle of March. He was informed on the 16th of March, the day that he departed, that our departure for Zanzibar would positively begin on the 10th of April. He took with him urgent letters for Selim Bey, announcing that fact in unmistakable terms. Eight days later we hear that Shukri Aga is still at Msawa, having only sent a few women and children to the Nyanza Camp; yet he and his people might have been here by this if they intended to accompany us.

"Thirty days ago Selim Bey left us with a promise of reasonable time. The Pasha thought once that twenty days would be a reasonable time. However, we have extended it to forty-four days. Judging by the length of time Selim Bey has already taken, only reaching Tunguru with one-sixteenth of the expected force, I personally am quite prepared to give the Pasha my decision. For you must know, gentlemen, that the Pasha having heard from Selim Bey 'intelligence so encouraging', wishes to know my decision, but I have preferred to call you to answer for me. . . ."

After this introduction, there could be no doubt in the officers' minds what conclusion the meeting was expected to reach. Stanley then reverted to the conspiracy-bogey:

"Remembering the three revolts which these same officers have inspired, their pronounced intentions against this Expedition, their plots and counterplots, the life of conspiracy and smiling treachery they have led, we may well pause to consider what object principally animates them now—that from being ungovernably rebellious against all constituted authority, they have suddenly become obedient and loyal soldiers of the Khedive and his 'Great Government'. You must be aware that, exclusive of the thirty-one boxes of ammunition delivered to the Pasha by us in May, 1888, the rebels possess ammunition of the Provincial Government equal to twenty of our cases. We are bound to credit them with intelligence enough to perceive that such a small supply would be fired in an hour's fighting among so many rifles,[22] and that only a show of submission and apparent loyalty will ensure a further supply from us. Though the Pasha brightens up each time he obtains a plausible letter from these people, strangers like we are may also be forgiven for not readily trusting those men whom they have such good cause to mistrust. . . . Can we be certain . . . that if we admit them into this camp as good friends and loyal soldiers of Egypt, they will not rise up some night and possess themselves of all the ammunition, and so deprive us of the power of returning to Zanzibar? It would be a very easy matter for them to do so, after they had acquired the knowledge of the rules of the camp. With our minds filled with Mr. Jephson's extraordinary revelations of what has been going on in the Province since the closing of the Nile route, beholding the Pasha here before my very eyes, who was lately supposed to have several thousand people under him, but now without any important following, and bearing in mind the 'cajoling' and 'wiles' by which we were to be entrapped, I ask you, would we be wise in extending the time of delay beyond the date fixed, that is, the 10th of April?"

The officers one after another replied in the negative.

"There, Pasha," I said, "you have your answer. We march on the 10th of April."

The Pasha then asked if we could "in our conscience acquit him of having abandoned his people", supposing they had not arrived by the 10th of April. We replied, "Most certainly."[23]

This extraordinary performance provides a further illustration of Stanley's total indifference to logical argument once he knew the conclusion he wanted to reach. His hearers must surely have wondered why, if it was so unthinkably risky to admit the Wadelai men to the camp, it should be necessary to wait until the 10th of April for them to arrive.[24] The explanation, of course, was that Stanley knew full well they neither would nor could get to Kavalli's by that time. Nevertheless, he went through the pantomime of serving final notice on Selim Bey that the march was to begin on the date agreed, and that there would be no further prolongation. The same ultimatum was given to Shukri Aga.

This council cannot have been a pleasant experience for Emin. He had already had to put up with a good deal of private hectoring from Stanley, and it was painful to him at any time to hear "his people" unkindly spoken of.[25] But to have to sit still and listen while Stanley, with the sensitivity of a crocodile in a bullet-proof waistcoat, lectured his young officers on the Pasha's fallen fortunes, the Pasha's gullibility, the Pasha's incompetence, and the worthlessness of the Pasha's people, was an experience not every man would be capable of sitting through at all. Emin bore the humiliation as meekly as he accepted the decision forced upon him. But inwardly he burned with resentment and his already much-wounded vanity received a blow from which it never recovered. Relations between Emin and Stanley deteriorated steadily from now on. Stanley noted the deterioration, but had the gall to maintain that he was totally unable to account for it.

By the end of March the transfer of goods from the Lake shore was complete. In six weeks, one thousand three hundred and fifty-five loads had been carried up to Kavalli's, and there were now estimated to be between five and six hundred refugees in the camp. Plainly, if it had taken six weeks to move the refugees' belongings the distance of a two days' march, then the march to the Coast would have to be reckoned in years. This problem, however, would solve itself simply enough when the time came.

On April 1 an advance party under Stairs was despatched to Mazamboni's to form a depot for the collection of stores against the homeward march. He had with him three or four Egyptians with their families and dependants, and most of the Expedition's ammunition.

Stanley's attention was now devoted to two other important preliminaries to the resumption of the march. One was the necessity of overcoming once and for all the inconvenient and incredibly persistent scruples which Emin still suffered as to the propriety of abandoning his people. The second was the equally imperative necessity of Stanley's asserting once and for all his authority over Emin's followers.

Under March 31 Stanley records a long discussion which began with Emin coming to Stanley's tent with the news that Casati objected to Emin's leaving the Province. Emin begged Stanley to talk to Casati and overcome his objections. Stanley agreed to try. Emin acted as interpreter. (The only language Stanley and Casati had in common was very bad French.) In Stanley's version of what followed the discussion takes the form—commonly used by Stanley in writing up his set-piece conversations—of a Socratic dialogue, with Stanley in the title role and the other participants confined to agreeing on cue with his remorseless logic. In Casati's version the cut and thrust of the colloquy is more evenly shared, and it emerges that the main point at issue was: whether Emin was still bound by his acceptance, at Msawa the preceding February, of the submission of Selim and his fellow officers. Casati's view was that Emin's accepting the officers' submission bound him to stick by them even if they failed to join the Expedition in time. Emin, it seems, had abandoned this rigorous interpretation and, in asking Stanley to speak to Casati, was rather seeking reassurance for himself than trying to allay Casati's doubts. Casati remained unconvinced (as even Stanley admits). Emin continued to agonise between the two views.[26]

The details of the discussion are less important than the effect on Stanley of the realisation that, in spite of all he could say or do, Emin was still wavering and that Casati was busily stoking the boilers of Emin's indecision. Perhaps it was only now that Stanley realised the importance of Casati's role in sustaining Emin's efforts to retain some shreds of capacity for independent action.

It was this pathetic vestige of independent authority and independent decision that Stanley now set himself to demolish. Once again the tool he selected was the nebulous phantasm of a plot to seize the Expedition's weapons, but with the difference that this particular plot was supposed to have its origins inside the camp itself.

The day selected for crushing the monstrous conspiracy was April 5.

It is instructive to compare three different accounts of that day's events: those of Parke, Casati, and finally Stanley himself. Taking Parke's account first, we see only the tip of the iceberg. For he, like everyone else in the camp (including, perhaps, the conspirators themselves) was unaware of the evil that was hatching beneath the calm exterior of the daily routine, and saw what took place with the objective but uncomprehending eye of the loyal subordinate who is not fully in the picture:

This morning, Mr Stanley came suddenly out of his tent, about 10 a.m., blew his whistle, and in a very determined way ordered each of us to fall in with our respective companies—also to have our fire-arms ready in case they were wanted. It was very evident from his appearance and gesticulations that something was up; none of us had, however, the faintest idea what was the matter. . . . All our companies were in their places in five minutes. Grasping his rifle with energy and resolution he roared to the men that he was *Bula Matari* to-day, ordered them to have the tents struck and all things packed up at once. He then asked the Pasha to assemble his people in the square, whereupon the latter sounded the *assemblée*; and, after a little dawdling, all his officers, soldiers and clerks appeared on the square. Mr. Stanley then told them in a loud voice—using the Pasha as interpreter, that all who wished to follow him were to fall in on one side, and those who would not follow were to fall in on the other side. The immediate result was, that they all fell in on the side of following us—thereby announcing their intention of accompanying us to Egypt. These trembling, feeble, procrastinating, useless villains, really did appear to have been stirred up to reason by the promptitude of Mr. Stanley's action: they have, at all events, given a definite answer; and, probably, for the first time in their lives. Some of the Pasha's soldiers were afterwards made prisoners for refusing to lay down their arms when ordered; a few of these men are the Pasha's own servants. . . . When this was all over, our tents were repitched, and everything was quiet again. In the evening, I spoke to Mr. Stanley, who seemed to think that he had done a good day's work. . . .

The background to the day's work contains much that is obscure, thanks partly to Stanley's taking great pains to explain the whole matter in detail. The exercise Parke had witnessed was, as Parke was later told, stimulated by the necessity of scotching the plot afore-mentioned. The evidence for this conspiracy, despite the length of Stanley's explanations, is more than a little tenuous, and sadly lacking in circumstantial detail. It boils down to three items:[27] (1) Stanley's perception (intuitive) of a "general feeling in the camp that something is about to happen"; (2) the fact that Emin's people were given to the insidious and guilty practice of sitting about in groups, talking; (3) the equally sinister fact that many of Emin's people in the camp had been exchanging letters with their relatives and friends in Wadelai. These personal observations were reinforced by reports from Stanley's private intelligence system, that is, by camp-gossip relayed to him by his boy Sali, whom he calls, not without a touch of pardonable pride, "the cleverest spy in the camp".[28] On the morning of April 5,

> . . . Sali reported to me that the Zanzibaris were talking of several attempts having been made, in various parts of the camp, to steal rifles from their huts, but that on each occasion the attempt was thwarted by the prompt wakefulness of the people.

Stanley responded to this dreadful revelation as if he had just received certain information that the sky was falling. He showed no interest in the accidentals of the case—details such as how many Zanzibaris had not been robbed of their rifles, how many assailants had not robbed them, &c. He wasted no time on checking the story at first hand. He did not pause to identify, let alone to congratulate, the men whose "prompt wakefulness" had foiled the horrid plot. Instead, he dashed off to Emin's tent, informed the startled Pasha that a bloody massacre was only minutes away, and that only he (Emin) could prevent it. Emin was forced to admit that he had no plan ready for such a contingency. Stanley, fortunately, happened to have not one but two plans ready, and lost no time in putting them forward.

As he did so, two interesting points became apparent. The first was that the massacre in question was not something the plotters had prepared for Stanley's men, but the fate Stanley had in store for the plotters should they fail to abandon their designs when called on to do so. The second interesting feature of the case was a degree of confusion that apparently existed in Stanley's mind as to whether the occasion of the uproar and shenanigans was the plot to disarm the Expedition, or something else entirely—a suspicion that some or all of Emin's men were secretly planning to stay behind when the march began. Emin might have been forgiven his evident perplexity at being called on to make an instant decision between two actions, neither of which he could see the necessity for, but which, he was told, were his only hope of avoiding an instant and general bloodletting. In Casati's account[29] Stanley presented the dilemma as follows:

"I have two proposals to make to you; it is for you to choose, and that without delay. Tomorrow morning I mean to make the round of my Zanzibaris and to tell them of our immediate departure. In case of any resistance or attempt at refusal, I am prepared to use force, and then start with you and the few who remain faithful to you. Should these strong measures not suit you, then I propose that you should start with a trustworthy escort at once, unknown to every one; I would soon rejoin you. Choose, Pasha; decide."

"I cannot accede to your proposals. The first I will not discuss; as for the second, you will understand that I cannot abandon Casati, Vita and Marco."

"Do not think of them. As soon as I have encamped in a favourable position, I shall come and take them (by force if necessary) from the hands of the Egyptians."

"But I do not think there will be any necessity for employing such means. We shall depart on the 10th."

Stanley's anger rose to its highest pitch. He stamped his foot upon the ground and said in a convulsed voice:

". . .! I leave you to God, and the blood which will now flow must fall upon your own head!"

He rushed out and whistled the signal of alarm, and entered his tent, leaving it again almost immediately, gun in hand and his cartridge pouch on his belt.

The Zanzibaris assembled in the square, part occupying the exit of the camp; the tents were taken down, exposing heaps of merchandise and cases of ammunition. From the door of my house I could observe an unusual bustle of armed men. I thought it meant a drill to prepare them for the approaching departure. I asked some of the passers by, but none knew the reason of the commotion. I sent my boy to ask Emin, and he quickly returned telling me that the Pasha was making preparations for an immediate departure.

I went to see the Pasha: he was pale with rage and indignation.

"We are going," said he to me with a trembling voice. "Today, for the first time in my life, I have been covered with insults. Stanley has passed every limit of courtesy, but I have promised not to speak, so can say no more."[30]

. . . In the meantime, Emin's officers, employés, soldiers and servants were assembled in the square, stupefied by the great agitation—a sure sign of some calamity. Emin and I arrived at last.

"If you have the courage, point your guns at my breast," cried Stanley addressing them. "I am here alone and unarmed.."

Blind fury made him forget that he held a Winchester rifle in his hand, and that there was a wall of about a hundred armed Zanzibari behind him.

"My orders are to be obeyed here, and whoever resists I will kill him with this gun, and trample him under my feet. Whoever intends to start and follow me, let him pass to this side."

In a moment every one moved, and all was changed; the terrible conspirators became as quiet as lambs. The reputed chiefs of the opposition, being called into Stanley's presence, were ordered to be disarmed and cast into prison.

"Will you start with me?" he said.

"Yes," they all answered.

"Will you obey my orders implicitly?"

"Yes, we promise," they hastened to say, simultaneously.

"I will conduct you to safety and will supply your needs during the journey. You have my promise; but I warn you that, as sure as

my name is Stanley, I shall not tolerate any renewal of the disturbances of Duffile or Wadelai. Bear in mind that the departure is
irrevocably fixed for the 10th."

From that day the encampment had the appearance of a village
which had been placed under martial law. The guards were
doubled, patrols were continually on the move during the night,
all were forbidden to leave their dwellings under pain of being
placed under arrest.

It does not emerge from Casati's story, any more than it does from
that of Parke, exactly what Stanley thought he had achieved by this
comedy, why he should have felt it to be "a good day's work". The
point becomes clearer when it is noticed that in Stanley's account, a
great deal is made of a point which Casati and Parke only touch on in
passing—the way in which the Zanzibaris were used to cow and
humiliate Emin's men. Stanley describes himself as standing in the
square, which was surrounded on three sides by his men, when
Emin came out of his tent. Emin had apparently decided to go along
with Stanley's pantomime of a sudden departure since Parke describes
him as "with his long field boots on, and ready to march". Stanley
asked him to muster his men in the square:

"It is too late, Pasha, to adopt the pacific course I suggested to you.
The alarm is general now, and therefore I propose to discover for
myself this danger, and face it here. Sound the signal, please, for
muster of your Arabs before me."

"Very good," replied the Pasha, and gave the order to his
trumpeter.

We waited ten minutes in silence. Then, perceiving that not much
attention was paid to the signal, I requested Mr. Jephson to take
No. 1 company, arm the men with clubs and sticks, and drive every
Arab, Egyptian, and Soudanese into the square, without regard to
rank, to search every house, and drag out every male found within.

The Zanzibaris were deployed across the camp, and, advancing
on the run, began to shower blows upon every laggard and dawdler
they came across, until the most sceptical was constrained to admit
that, when commanded, the Zanzibaris were fit for something
better than working as a hamal[31] for a lazy Egyptian and his slave.

For the first time the Egyptians and Soudanese formed a decent
line. Not until they had formed it with military exactitude and

precision was a word said to them. It was most amusing to see an ordinary Zanzibari carrier straighten with his staff—which he flourished with a grim face—the line of Majors, Vakeels, captains, lieutenants, clerks and storekeepers.

When the line was satisfactory, I stepped up to them and informed them that I heard they wished to fight, that they were eager to try what kind of men the Zanzibaris were. They had seen how well they could work; it would be a pity if they were not able to see how well they could fight.

The Vakeel (*Osman Latrif*) . . . replied, "But we don't wish to fight."[32]

The clear implication is that, from Stanley's point of view, the significance of the exercise lay largely in the role played by the Zanzibaris. What Parke saw as a kind of drill, Emin as a calculated insult, and Casati as an autocratic display of temper, was for Stanley a display of his power over his own men, and through his men, over Emin's. He had brought into play, at precisely the right moment, the long-restrained resentment which the Zanzibaris felt for their mistreatment at the hands of Emin's people. The result was, for Stanley, highly satisfactory. Not only had he established that degree of control over Emin's people which was indispensable to the proper conduct of the coming march, but at the same time he had kicked away the last prop to the crumbling façade of Emin's authority. When he forced Emin's men to make a public declaration of their willingness to follow Stanley to the Coast, Emin's last hope of avoiding such a move, or of exercising a degree of control over its execution, was gone for ever.

The next day a census was taken of Emin's followers:

. . . each had his loads and people in front of his house in spite of the heavy rain which was falling. We went round to each family & took the numbers of people & loads and general particulars. It was piteous to see some families, nothing but little bright eyed children with their fathers being killed in the war there was no one but the negro mother & slaves to look after them, there was one family of 7 small children whose father was dead; little yellow weazened up children with faces like little old women, how they will ever get along is an enigma; there will be some awful scenes on the way, just as there were in our flight from Wadelai, only that this will be such a long journey that the women & children will fall like flies on the road. One wretched looking Egyptian soldier whose wife had run away from him & left him with their little child was standing by himself with one poor load before him holding his little baby in his arms which was reduced to skin & bone through the desertion of its mother he was trying to protect it from the weather by holding a tattered cloth over its head, there he stood, a forlorn looking figure in the fast falling rain, his worldly possessions representing one small basket & a half starved baby, as we came up to ask of what his household consisted a sense of his utterly forlorn & deserted position seemed to come over him & he could only answer with such a passion of sobbing that one felt an utter brute for even asking him the question; one's heart ached for him. . . . It does not do to see such sights as these, if one sees them it must be with unseeing eyes. . . . I dread the road on account of the heartbreaking scenes we shall have to go through. . . . (JEPHSON)

The census yielded the following result:

Emin, Casati, Vita, Markos	4
Officers, soldiers, clerks	60
Wives of the above.	84
"Followers" (men)	130
"Followers" (women)	187
Children	109
TOTAL	574

Loads	448
Guns.	40[33]

When this was done, the preliminaries were over. The march began on schedule:

At daybreak on April 10, 1889, the well-known whistle was heard; the signal for departure. Stanley kept his word; the caravan fell into marching order, and at seven o'clock began to move, leaving behind it a dense column of smoke and the crackling flames of the burning camp. (CASATI)[34]

329

The approximate composition of the column was as follows:

Expedition	230
Emin and people	600
Auxiliaries:	
Manyuema	130
From Kavalli's, etc.	550

$$\text{TOTAL} \quad 1{,}510^{35}$$

The caravan looked a tremendous length winding along over the plain, & our cattle greatly added to the length as they straggled a good deal, the caravan was very gay with flags, & the coloured clothes of Zanzibaris & Egyptian women added to the general brightness, there were over 1,400 people including the native carriers & the whole caravan must have been three miles long,— Raschid my head chief said it was like the story of the flight from Egypt under Moschi (Moses) as they read in the Khoran. Children, donkeys, goats, women, Zanzibaris, Egyptians, Circassians, Greeks, Jews & Nubians all mixed up together. . . . (JEPHSON)

For the first two days everything went well, as even the pessimistic and disgruntled Casati was forced to admit. On April 12 the main column overtook Stairs' advance party waiting for them at Mazamboni's, and here they were joined by Shukri Aga and half a dozen followers. He brought news of chaos in the Province and reported that Selim Bey, despite repeated urgings from Shukri Aga, was apparently no nearer to departure than he had been a month before.

The next day Stanley fell ill. His symptoms resembled those which had laid him low at Fort Bodo, and once again Parke was seriously worried for him. The crisis passed, however, in a few days, but Stanley was too ill to continue the journey. The column remained at Mazamboni's for four weeks. Supplies began to be a problem and raids were made on the surrounding tribes. The unfortunate natives who were singled out for these attacks were those who had not joined Mazamboni and Kavalli in allying themselves with Stanley, and Stanley was thus able to justify his depredations in some measure by referring to the victims as "allies of Kabba Rega". On some of these raids prisoners were taken for use as carriers—a practice hard to justify on any grounds. Jephson, in the privacy of his diary, called these prisoners what they were—slaves:

> *April* 20th. This morning Stanley told us to count over the slaves, chiefly women and children, whom our people had caught & hand half of them over to the Pasha to give to his people. This Stairs & I did & handed him over 20. We brought them over to the Pasha's house, upon my word it was a most shameful scene & was as bad every bit as the open slave markets that existed in the East till virtuous England set her back up. Orders are however orders & we must obey them in spite of the heartrending scenes & shameless brutality we see in these raids.[36]

While Stanley, under the combined ministrations of Emin and Parke, was convalescing, the length of the halt enabled a number of Emin's followers—perhaps disillusioned by their first taste of marching under Stanley—to make good their escape back to the Lake. Stanley was anxious to put a stop to this retrograde movement by a salutary example. A party was sent out to recapture the fugitives and succeeded in apprehending several. They were brought back to camp. One of them, a young soldier of Emin's named Rehan, was sentenced to death. He was considered particularly dangerous as he was among the four soldiers from Emin's troops who had been with Stanley on the march in search of the Rear Guard, and the horrifying stories he had to tell of his experiences had enabled him to induce a number of his companions to desert. It was decided to hang him. Stanley, on his feet for the first time since his illness, read the sentence to the people. In his excitement he collapsed, overbalanced by his own wild gesticulations.

Parke's conduct on this occasion exhibited a touch of that morbid curiosity about death which has since grown into the vampire-haunted folklore of Victorian medical science:

> The rope used had become so rotten, from exposure to wet and damp, that it broke when the culprit had been hoisted to a height of about a foot from the ground. Four plies were then plaited together, and he was drawn up to a height of fourteen feet from the ground, in which position the body was left suspended for the night. . . . When the rope had broken, and the culprit Rehan had fallen to the ground, I talked to him, as I was interested to observe

what was his mental state in the wretched position in which he was then placed. I found him utterly indifferent and apathetic. . . .

During the halt at Mazamboni's, while Stanley was slowly recovering his strength, relations between him and Emin deteriorated to the point where neither would meet the other face to face. They confined themselves to the exchange of quarrelsome messages through intermediaries. Even Jephson was thoroughly out of patience with Emin:

> The people . . . are constantly coming to Stanley to complain of the Pasha, which in his state of health irritates him almost to madness, the result is that unpleasant messages are daily passing between them, & we officers are made the carriers of these messages. Stanley is rude to us because he knows we do not deliver the messages as he gives them—we cannot—& the Pasha is very rude to us in his turn when we deliver the messages in a milder form & I really think he believes we add to the rudeness instead of doing all we can to soften Stanley's messages. It is an awfully unpleasant position for us all & we get blamed &, I may say, insulted for doing our best to prevent a regular row.

From this point, until the Expedition reached the Coast, relations between Stanley and Emin never again improved beyond a strained and conventional politeness.

By the end of the first week in May Stanley was well enough to go on, though carried at first in a litter. Before leaving Mazamboni's, Stairs, on Stanley's orders, secretly buried twenty-five cases of ammunition for which there were not enough porters.[37] It was a fit comment on the futility of the whole Expedition: to get those precious boxes so far had cost two years of suffering and struggle; now, become an embarrassment, they were to end their career furtively entombed beneath the mud floor of a grass hut in the middle of nowhere. And yet, considering the number of lives its transport had cost, it is possible that no other ammunition in history had dealt such death and devastation without a round of it having so much as seen the breech of a rifle.

When the march resumed on May 8, the question of Selim Bey had still not been settled. It looked, however, as if he were at last on the move. Letters had arrived from him at Mazamboni's, and the day after leaving, the column was overtaken by a deputation from Selim.

Their news was that he and his followers had reached Msawa and now begged to be allowed time to join the Expedition. It seemed to Stanley, probably with justice, that the real reason for Selim's sudden display of near-energy was less his desire to leave for Egypt than a last-minute panic at finding himself left behind, almost alone and almost defenceless. (He had only four cases of ammunition.) The terms of Stanley's answer to the deputation are in dispute. He himself says that he returned a friendly message urging Selim to do his best to overtake the column, and promising to wait for several days at the north end of the Ruwenzori range.[38] According to Jephson, however, Stanley was furious with the deputation and told them (amongst other things) that—

> . . . they had behaved like savages & madmen & now he would not give them a cartridge or wait an hour for them, he would go on marching day by day & if they liked to follow him & try & catch him up they might do so, but he would not alter his plans in the slightest degree for them.[39]

Whether the tenor of Stanley's answer to Selim was friendly or abusive, Jephson's account is certainly the one which gives the most accurate reflection of the attitude of Stanley and the officers at this time. They had one and all had enough of procrastination and prevarication. They wanted only to get home. Parke's comment on the news of the deputation's approach sums up their mood:

> The news made us all feel anxious; as we thought that we might now again be delayed by these wretched, helpless, thoughtless Egyptians.

Their anxiety to be off on the homeward journey is easy to understand and to sympathise with. Yet it is to be noted that, even at this late date, Stanley was still energetically flogging the never very lively horse of a conspiracy (this time between Selim and the refugees already with the Expedition).[40] It is therefore difficult to avoid the conclusion that Selim's foot-dragging was simply a convenient pretext for justifying what to some observers looked like the deliberate abandonment of people who were genuinely anxious to join in the evacuation. Schweitzer is only slightly overstating his case when he writes:

Stanley was anxious to be rid of Emin's associates and soldiers, hence this bugbear of conspiracy against the expedition, to which he referred everything that happened, and so palpably that it is impossible not to discern the motive. Emin, on the other hand, was saddened by the thought that his associates were being betrayed and deserted, in order that he alone, the only object of the expedition that was still of some value, might promptly be "saved" and brought to the coast.[41]

Casati, an equally hostile critic, went so far as to suggest that, after leaving Mazamboni's, Stanley deliberately chose a difficult route in order to make it hard for Selim to follow. He says that Stanley, pointing to the peaks of Ruwenzori, declared:

"When I have put between me and them . . . such a series of obstacles, the Expedition will no longer have any cause for fear."[42]

Stanley need not have worried, if worried he really was. To overtake the caravan would have demanded a sustained and co-ordinated effort quite beyond the easy-going Selim and his fractious followers. Stanley never saw him again.

*   *   *

The march from Mazamboni's to the coast, a distance of some fifteen hundred miles, took seven months.

A contemporary account of the Expedition compared the flight from Equatoria with the exploit of Xenophon's Ten Thousand.[43] The comparison shows an exemplary generosity of spirit in its author, but, as even he had to admit, there were differences. Indeed, the retreat from Moscow (which somewhat surprisingly also finds its way into this chronicler's eulogies) would be a more apt analogy in many respects. The truth, though, lies between the two. It was neither a triumph nor a disaster, but a long, hard, dogged and nasty plod, relieved neither by dramatic sufferings, nor desperate dangers, nor brilliant discoveries. There was no lack of the "heartbreaking scenes" that Jephson had foreseen, nor of the other, by now familiar hardships of African travel—hunger, disease, exhaustion, and death. But these made up an accumulation of personal, private sufferings, of small tragedies, against the background of a march which went inexorably

334

on day after dreary day, as if the caravan had a life of its own, independent of, and indifferent to, the fate of the individuals which composed it.

Throughout the journey Emin confined himself strictly to the role of passenger. At the head of the caravan strode Stanley, a pipe in his mouth, a stick in his hand, grim and aloof like a rock in motion, maintaining by his presence, his will-power and his whistle the energy and cohesion of the whole:

The march was opened by Stanley, preceded by a vanguard of Zanzibaris with native guides; the company under Jephson's command followed; then Emin with his people, escorted by another company. The families of the officials, servants, carriers, and the Manyema, enrolled at Yambuya, were in the rear. The long column was protected by a company who served as the rear-guard, under the alternate command of Captain Nelson and Lieutenant Stairs.

The march began at sunrise, and was continued until eleven o'clock A.M., without halts. Generally in that lapse of time, and often before it ended, the head of the caravan had reached the place where we were to pass the night; but the greater part of the people—the porters especially—used to drop in by groups, or singly, so that the camp could not be said to be complete till three or four in the afternoon. The nature of the route—the difficulties of mountain passes—the slackening of the pace—and the necessity of short stoppages for the porters to rest—soon lengthened the column, in which long intervals were to be seen, breaking the compactness of the march. Later . . . frequent cases of fever occurred in the ranks, and many, especially the Egyptians, were afflicted with painful sores on their feet. The assiduous cares of Dr. Parke, always ready and courteous, were not sufficient to meet the requirements; sick people from time to time begged for some days' rest; the Pasha used to advise them to apply to Stanley, and he, in his turn . . . asked Emin for advice—whose decision always was that, a few days being insufficient to ensure recovery, the best thing to do was to continue the journey. And those poor suffering creatures dragged themselves along, cursing in their heart the moment in which they had listened to the promising offer of relief.

It was a daily occurrence for people to fall and be abandoned on the road, or to go astray; and every day the losses we sustained increased the labour of the survivors.[44]

335

Leaving Mazamboni's, they moved south into the valley of the Semliki, the river which joins Lakes Albert and Albert Edward. They crossed the river and moved parallel with it along the western flank of the Ruwenzori range. This brought them in mid June to the northern end of Lake Edward.

This route enabled Stanley to inspect the new-found Mountains of the Moon, to chart the Semliki valley, and to take a close look at the previously unvisited Lake Edward, which until then existed on the maps only by virtue of a distant glimpse Stanley had had of it in 1876. These investigations, though performed very much en passant, were the main geographical fruits of the Expedition and were of considerable importance. The significance of the Mountains of the Moon to the history of the discovery of the Nile sources has already been alluded to. The discovery that the Semliki linked a third component to the system formed by Lakes Albert and Victoria was of no less importance in completing the work which Speke and Baker had begun and which Stanley had done more than any other man to finish.

An additional advantage of Stanley's choice of route was that it put the Ruwenzori between the Expedition and the hostile armies of Unyoro. There were skirmishes with banassura war-bands at both the northern and southern ends of the range. But at no time was the Expedition seriously threatened by a sustained attack from Kabba Rega's men, as it might well have been if it had been forced to pass directly through his territory.

No more was it threatened, when it turned south-east through Nkole, by the warrior hordes which had loomed so large in Stanley's imagination when the Expedition was being planned.

From Nkole they held on south-east through Karagwe, which in Speke's day had been a formidable subsidiary of Uganda, and at the end of August reached the southern end of Lake Victoria.

Here they stayed for three weeks at the mission of the indomitable Mackay. After being forced to flee from Uganda by persecutions of King Mwanga, Mackay had made his headquarters at Msalala where he had taken charge of the goods Stanley had ordered during his stay in Zanzibar. Also awaiting the Expedition were mails and news from Europe,[45] and from here Stanley and Emin sent back to the coast the first news of the evacuation and their impending arrival in Zanzibar.

Beyond Msalala they were moving along the well-trodden Uganda–Zanzibar trade route. Even so, it was here that the Expedition met the most serious and sustained hostilities it had had to face since the fighting with Mazamboni's people on the first approach to Lake Albert. The Wasukuma, through whose territory they were passing, harried the line of march for five days in succession. So near to home, Stanley was in no mood to waste time on argument, and at one point the Maxim gun was brought into play to secure a passage.[46]

At the end of October they had their first direct intimation that they were approaching civilisation. In the middle of a patch of thorn forest they came suddenly on a native caravan travelling in the opposite direction, whose porters greeted them with cheerful cries of "Guten Morgen!" and travesties of Germany military salutes. The meaning of this extraordinary apparition became clear when the leader of the caravan put into Emin's hands a letter from the German traveller von Wissmann, no longer a simple explorer but proudly signing himself "Imperial German Commissioner for East Africa".

Since the Expedition had left Zanzibar at the beginning of 1887, the Germans had built up a powerful presence—military and naval units as well as traders and settlers—on "their" portion of the coastal strip, and were pressing on with plans for a determined expansion inland towards the Lakes. This had led to armed conflict with the Arabs, naturally alarmed at the threat to their trade hegemony. The suppression of this "rebellion", as he called it, was the reason for von Wissmann's presence in the area, a task in which (as he modestly wrote to Emin) "I succeeded sooner than I thought".[47] He added that he hoped to be at Bagamoyo on Emin's arrival to greet him in person.

There was further evidence, not merely of German activities in East Africa, but of German interest in Emin, when the Expedition reached Mpwapwa on November 10 and found it held by a German-led garrison under Lt. Rochus Schmidt. He made them welcome with champagne, brandy and cigars. Emin wrote in his diary: "I am quite at home here." The remark is significant in the light of what was to follow.

When the Expedition moved on from Mpwapwa, Schmidt attached himself to the column as escort.

Suddenly a new dimension had been added to the tangled relationships between Emin and Stanley—that of German-British rivalry in the field of colonial enterprise. The marks of attention and respect which Emin now received in increasing numbers from the countrymen he had turned his back on nearly twenty-five years before, and by whom he

337

had supposed himself forgotten, flattered and charmed him. His ego, wilted and battered by the treatment it had had from Stanley, blossomed anew like a flower opening to the sun. Almost overnight, Emin, who had worn the fez all his working life, became a German.

Stanley saw what was happening and disliked what he saw. Emin's sudden transformation represented a threat of the most obvious kind to his proprietary interest in Emin.

Entries from Emin's diary[48] during the last days of the march clearly reflect the apocalyptic reawakening of Emin's sense of national identity:

(November 25) On the whole, and in spite of all English opposition, German influence appears to be slowly but surely taking deeper root, and I only hope an advanced column will be sent out as soon as possible towards Lake Victoria, and that eventually Uganda will be occupied before it is too late. It is curious to observe how little Stanley can rid himself of his English prejudices. He is fond of acting the cosmopolitan; and therefore, in speaking to us, approves of the extension of German domination, but in unguarded moments, when we are alone, he reproaches me with my German proclivities. The officers of the Expedition are superlatively English, and look down upon us Germans from a sublime altitude. Lieutenant Stairs, for example, only the other day expressed the opinion that it would be wrong to make use of Wissmann's German steamers for the passage to Zanzibar; that ours was an English expedition, and should terminate as such! And then people talk about German narrow-mindedness and particularism!

(November 29) . . . At noon we were joined by Freiherr von Gravenreuth, Lieutenant Langheld, Herr Weidmann, Messrs. Mariano, Vizetelly, and Stevens:[49] splendid people. Seven letters from Wissmann, with seven cases of delicacies, cigars, etc. He intends to come to meet us. The officers and the two correspondents vie with one another in affability. One Herr Gasch, of Zanzibar, has sent me the German illustrated papers. What have I done to deserve all this?

(November 30) We are still here because Stanley is waiting for his caravan; which, indeed, is far inferior to the German one.[50] Telegram of welcome from Colonel Euan Smith, the English Consul-General at Zanzibar. . . . Wissmann has even sent cattle for us. The day passed quickly, and in the evening we were all together chatting over a bottle of wine. Gravenreuth is most excellent company, and speaks English well. All the Germans are pleasant people. Vizetelly sent off three messengers today to the coast, each with a bulky letter. However, as he is not yet sober, he cannot surely have written them himself, and the solution of the problem is—as Dr. Parke tells me—simply that Stanley had the correspondence ready and knocked it down to the highest bidder—Vizetelly, i.e. Gordon Bennett—and quite right, too.

The long march was now over.

The evening of December 3rd (*wrote Stanley*), as we were conversing in the moonlight, the sound of a cannon was heard. It was the evening gun at Zanzibar, and the Zanzibaris set up ear-piercing cries of joy at that which announced to them that the long journey across the Continent was drawing near its close, and the Egyptians and their followers echoed the shouts as the conviction dawned on them that within the next twenty-four hours they should see the ocean, on which with all comfort and leisure they would be borne to the land of Egypt and to their future homes.

Oh! the deep relief I felt that this was the end of that continual rising in the morning with a hundred moaning and despairing invalids wailing their helplessness and imploring for help, of those daily scenes of disease, suffering, and unmitigable misery, and of the diurnal torture to which the long-enduring caravan had been subjected during what seemed now to have been an age of hideous troubles far beyond the range of anything we had anticipated when we so lightheartedly accepted the mission of relieving the Governor of Equatoria.

On arriving at the ferry of the Kingani River, Major Wissman came across to meet us. . . . On reaching the right bank of the Kingani we found some horses saddled, and turning over the command of the column to Lieut. Stairs, Emin Pasha and myself were conducted by Major Wissman and Lieut. Schmidt to Bagamoyo. Within the coast town we found the streets decorated handsomely with palm branches, and received the congratulations of Banian and Hindu citizens, and of many a brave German officer who had shared the fatigues and dangers of the arduous campaign, which Wissman was prosecuting with such well-deserved success, against the Arab malcontents of German East Africa.

Presently rounding the corner of the street we came in view of

z

the battery square in front of Wissman's headquarters, and on our left, close at hand, was the softly undulating Indian Sea, one great expanse of purified blue.

"There, Pasha," I said. "We are at home!"

"Yes, thank God," he replied.

At the same time the battery thundered the salute in his honour, and announced to the war-ships at anchor that Emin, the Governor of Equatoria, had arrived at Bagamoyo.

NOTES AND REFERENCES

1   Jephson received the letter on January 26 and at once copied it into his diary. (JEPHSON pp. 321–327.) This version corresponds with that in Jephson's *Emin Pasha* (pp. 388–400). Stanley's version of the letter (D.A. II pp. 114–118) has been edited and shows both additions and excisions; Jephson's version has therefore been followed here. Italicised passages are those omitted from Stanley's version.

2   Near Fort Bodo.

3   The loss of part of his wardrobe became something of an obsession with Stanley, and the charge that Barttelot had "left him naked" came to assume pride of place in the long catalogue of his complaints and accusations against the officers of the Rear Column. In sending part of Stanley's kit (there were 15 loads of it at Yambuya) down to Bangala, Barttelot was merely following Stanley's instructions (q.v.) as to what to discard if there were not enough porters. Rumours of Stanley's death were not believed at Yambuya and had, of course, nothing to do with Barttelot's decision as to which parts of Stanley's baggage to discard and which to keep.

4   They rejoined Stanley at Kavalli's on February 18.

5   It would be interesting to know just what is subsumed under this enigmatic "etc."—buttons? paper-clips? pen-wipers?

6   Omitted is a table of Stanley's expected movements during the period January 18 to February 6.

7   Stanley may have been exaggerating his anxieties over supplies in order to use them as a goad to prod Emin with. In the event, he was able to maintain a force which eventually numbered about a thousand at Kavalli's until the second week in April.

8   Casati certainly had some influence on Emin's decision not to leave with Jephson. "He (*Jephson*) had left us with the firm conviction that we should never meet again. To the last moment he had insisted on Emin accompanying him; but this time I was gratified to see my advice accepted . . . that the word he had given, that he would not move until he had conferred with the officers who were to arrive from Wadelai, must be kept. 'It will be a matter of a few days, but I promise you to take the Pasha to Stanley,' I said to Jephson at his departure." (CASATI II pp. 216–217). Jephson, of course, had no way of knowing what this promise was worth.

9   D.A. II pp. 129–131.

10 Emin himself seems to have been aware all along of the poor impression his people would create on arrival in civilisation, and this consideration may have influenced his original reluctance to evacuate. See SCHWEITZER I p. 201: "The sudden appearance at the coast of such a throng of women, girls, boys, etc., could only tend to the discredit of the Government, and there is no need for Egypt to lay itself open afresh to the charge of encouraging slavery." (Emin to Junker, June 5, 1886.)

11 Stanley does not print this letter, though he takes a page to explain how diplomatically and cunningly it was written. Apparently it renewed his offer of aid and suggested several schemes for Emin's escape, or rescue, from Tunguru. (D.A. II pp. 130–131.)

12 Emin had brought sixty tusks. In fact not even this modest amount left Equatoria: the Manyuema finally opted to take their payment in goods, and most of the tusks, being too large to carry easily, were left at the Lake-shore camp. (D.A. II p. 165.)

13 Now Selim Bey. Emin had promoted him for his defence of Duffile.

14 Jephson states that syphilis was common amongst the Bari, who practised innoculation against it, "but with no good results". (E.P. p. 140.)

15 Emin would very probably have supported Stanley in this: Jephson reported (D.A. II pp. 136–137) that Emin was angry with Casati for demanding 80 carriers and "remonstrated" with him "for taking all his grinding-stones, earthen jars, bedsteads for his boys and women, &c.".

16 D.A. II p. 151.

17 D.A. II pp. 133–134.

18 The people who had come out with Emin—especially Vita Hassan, Osman Latif, and Hawashi Effendi—were those who were identified with Emin in the minds of the rebels, and whose lives would be at risk if they stayed in the Province and Emin did not. Fear of the rebels may have led these people to encourage the belief that the Wadelai men intended treachery. They were simply afraid of finding themselves in the same camp as Fadl el-Mulla and company. (Cf. CASATI II p. 247.)

19 It is not clear why Fadl el-Mulla abandoned Wadelai. His decision might have resulted from the desire to make a clean break with Emin and all his works, as well as with Selim and the "moderates"; or he might have feared a renewal of the Mahdi-ist attack. The second possibility need not have concerned him, not immediately, anyhow: after the repulse at Duffile, Omar Saleh had fallen back on Rejaf, which then became his base for expeditions to subdue the tribes east and west of the river. (He found this task no easier than his predecessors had done.) Fadl el-Mulla, finding it too difficult to supply his force in the hills, eventually returned to Wadelai. (COLLINS pp. 70–71.)

20 D.A. II p. 161.

21   Cf., for example, CASATI II pp. 153, 238 and 247.

22   Did Stanley credit his hearers with sufficient intelligence to perceive that, by the same calculation, the total of 94 cases delivered to Emin would be fired in 282 minutes' fighting?

23   The whole speech appears in D.A. (II pp. 161–163).

24   The point did, apparently, occur to Parke (PARKE p. 393), who states that Stanley intended to disarm the Wadelai men on their arrival.

25   PARKE p. 381.

26   Compare CASATI II pp. 239–240 with D.A. II pp. 168–171.

27   D.A. II p. 180.

28   D.A. II p. 169.

29   Casati was not present. His account must derive from Emin. (CASATI II pp. 248–249.) Emin's only reference to the scene is a note in his diary that Stanley had insulted him in his own house. (SCHWEITZER I p. 206.)

30   Stanley had made a special point of Emin's not telling Casati what was afoot, presumably because he feared that once Emin and Casati put their heads together, all chance of getting a decision out of Emin was gone.

31   Porter (Arabic).

32   D.A. II pp. 183–184. Stanley also gives Stairs a part in these proceedings. This must be a mistake, as Stairs was not in the camp, but ahead with the advance party. Stanley must have been confusing him with Nelson.

33   JEPHSON p. 343; PARKE p. 406; D.A. II pp. 186–187. The totals should have been somewhat higher, partly because some of Emin's people evaded or ignored the census, partly because Stairs' advance party was not included. The figure for "loads" represents the number Stanley was prepared to carry, not the total of loads in the camp, since the figure is smaller by two-thirds than the number brought up from the Lake.

34   "When all had cleared out of camp, Nelson returned with a party of men, searched all the huts, and afterwards burnt them. The camp was strewn all over with pots, bedsteads, tin baths, chairs, and all sorts of rubbish in the basket line; grinding-stones, and one enormous copper pot, were also included in the non-transferable material." (PARKE p. 409.)

35   D.A. II p. 192.

36   In fairness to Stanley, it must be pointed out that Emin's men were the worst culprits in the slave-taking. (JEPHSON pp. 350–351.)

37   The porters from Kavalli's apparently only accompanied the Expedition to the borders of their country.

38   D.A. II p. 206. Confirmed by Casati (II p. 262), who, however, puts a different construction on Stanley's promise to wait for several days.

39 JEPHSON p. 353.

40 PARKE pp. 420–421; JEPHSON pp. 351–352.

41 The evident hostility to Stanley of Emin's biographer was a more or less chauvinistic reaction to German-British rivalry in E. Africa. (See next chapter.) For Schweitzer, Stanley was identified 100 per cent with the British interest. The real position was not so clear-cut, thanks to Stanley's involvement with Leopold and the Belgians.

42 CASATI II p. 264.

43 WAUTERS pp. 347–348.

44 CASATI II pp. 258–259.

45 Among the news were the first reactions to the Rear Guard disaster. Some of the comment was critical of Stanley and even blamed him for Barttelot's death. From this point on, therefore, Stanley must have been preparing his side of the story, siting his batteries for an all-out attack on Barttelot and the others at the first opportunity.

46 This appears to have been the only occasion on which it was fired in anger. Stanley says it killed nobody, but effectively frightened off the attackers. (D.A. II pp. 399–400.) In his first report of the incident he also made the surprising assertion that the hostility of the Wasukuma was caused by their taking exception to the blackness of the skins of the Sudanese. (C.5906 p. 15.) The real cause of the dispute is more likely to have been Stanley's impatience with demands for "hongo" (tax levied on caravans—a universal practice between Lake Tanganyika and the Coast).

47 One of the porters met in the forest had shouted to Emin, "Arab Bagamoyo kaputt!"

48 Qu. SCHWEITZER I pp. 328–329.

49 Vizetelly and Stevens were the correspondents of the New York Herald (Stanley's old paper) and the New York World respectively.

50 "Stanley's" caravan bore 170 loads of goods—clothes and provisions— addressed to the Expedition by Mackinnon's East Africa Company. It arrived on December 2, so how Emin knew it to be inferior on November 30 is a puzzle.

AFTERMATH

Heureux qui comme Ulysse a fait un beau voyage.

JOACHIM DU BELLAY

Something had been achieved. No one knew what. But the cost was horribly clear. Over seven hundred men of the Expedition had sailed from Zanzibar three years before. Of these, two hundred and forty-three now marched with Stanley into Bagamoyo; the continent had swallowed the rest. And of the six hundred-odd refugees who had set out on the trek from Kavalli's to the coast, only two hundred and ninety ever reached the sea; of the others "probably eighty perished from ulcers, fevers, fatigue, and debility". The remainder, unable to keep up with the march, had simply been left behind to fend for themselves, or rather, in Stanley's delicate phrase, had been "cared for" by the natives through whose territory the Expedition had passed.[1]

These figures tell their own story. Indeed, they tell two: on the one hand they are testimony to the almost miraculous courage and endurance of the survivors in the face of unbelievable hardship over six thousand miles of river, swamp, jungle, mountain and plain; on the other hand they bespeak an appalling and futile waste of time, money, effort and human life in pursuit of a goal that was unrealisable even before the Expedition set out.

Neither the ostensible nor the secret aims of the Expedition had been realised in any point. Indeed, they were in every case further from realisation than they had been before the Expedition set out. Emin had looked for aid which would have made his Province secure against threatened dissolution; instead he had seen it pushed over the brink into total anarchy. Leopold had hoped for the extension of his possessions to the headwaters of the Nile; he was disappointed. Mackinnon and his friends had stumped up £10,000 for a ready-made empire; they got nothing for their money. The Khedive—perhaps the most nearly disinterested of all the participants—found himself with nearly three hundred exhausted, suffering, bewildered and quite useless refugees commended to his care. The newspapers got their stories, the public something to talk about. No one got any ivory. Stanley's hair had turned white.

The Expedition's sole visible asset, the only tangible reward for its years of suffering and struggle, was one Egyptian Government official, middle-aged, crotchety and half-blind, who, if his own wishes had been consulted, would now still be a thousand miles away in the interior of Africa happily engaged in collecting birds.

Even this doubtful gain was about to slip from Stanley's hands.

The night of the entry into Bagamoyo, Wissmann held a banquet in honour of the heroes' return. The guests included Stanley and his officers, Emin, Casati, the German and British Consuls, representatives of the two East Africa Companies, and the captains of the German naval squadron at that time energetically showing the flag in East African waters. The distinguished company sat down to dinner in an upper room. One of the German ships provided an orchestra (judged "somewhat mediocre" by their commander, Captain Hirschberg). There were toasts and speeches. Emin, who to his delight had just received a personal telegram of congratulation from the Kaiser, countersigned by Bismarck, and been awarded the Order of the Crown (Second Class, with Star), proposed the health of the German Emperor. Wissmann proposed Stanley's health. Stanley proposed Wissmann's. No one proposed Emin's. Unnoticed, Emin left the table and went into the next room. There, mistaking a low window for a door, he made a sudden and unplanned descent into the street fifteen feet below.[2] This ludicrous and lamentable accident might easily have been fatal had not his fall been partly broken by a steep lean-to roof below the window. A message brought Lieut. Schmidt hurrying down. He found Emin unconscious, badly bruised, and bleeding from the ears. Having failed to rouse Emin by pouring cold water over him, Schmidt sent for a stretcher party. Upstairs, the festivities went on. Emin's accident, like his absence, had passed unremarked. By the time the company learned of the accident, Emin was already installed in the German hospital with severe concussion and a suspected fracture of the skull.

The Pasha's Unhappy Fall solved, in a manner as unlooked for as it was drastic, a crucial problem in the relationship between Emin and Stanley. Stanley had not been slow to recognise and to resist the implications of the Germans' attentions to Emin. Ever since, at Mpwapwa, the Expedition had found itself in an area of active German influence, a covert battle had been going on between Stanley and Wissmann. The purpose of this undeclared conflict was to decide who should enjoy Emin's future services, Germany or England. The flattering notice that was being taken of Emin by, as it seemed, the entire German nation from the Kaiser downwards, was of itself sufficiently alarming. Emin's susceptibility to this treatment was even more so. Stanley had therefore, after practically ignoring Emin throughout the whole trek from Kavalli's to the Coast, begun to manifest a sudden renewal of interest in Emin's plans for the future. As early as November 16, Emin recorded the following conversation with Stanley:

> Quite suddenly he questioned me as to what I intended to do with my Madi-Irigwe, suggesting that the very best thing to do would be to hand them over to the English East Africa Company, since all this time they had been fed at Mackinnon's expense. Of course it was merely a "hint", and I should do as I liked; after all, being a German at heart, I might perhaps desire to transfer the people to the Germans, to which he had no objection. Only I ought to bear in mind that England sent the Expedition, whilst Germany had not thought of me till the eleventh hour. . . . I told him that I reserved to myself the disposal of my servants.[3]

Stanley confirms, if indirectly, that he had been putting pressure on Emin, hoping to maintain a lien on his future loyalties by appealing to his sense of gratitude:

> Emin Pasha, who breathed a cosmopolitan spirit while he was in the Interior, and who professed broad views, became different in a few days. Only one day before we reached Bagamoyo I had said to him, "Within a short time, Pasha, you will be among your countrymen; but while you glow with pride and pleasure at being once more amongst them, do not forget that they were English people who first heard your cries in the days of gloom; that it was English money which enabled these young English gentlemen to rescue you from Khartoum."[4]

What might have been the outcome of this tug-of-war, had it been allowed to run its course, can only be matter for speculation. What is certain is that Emin's accident decided the issue at a stroke, and the result was point, game, set and match to the Germans. With Emin settled in a German hospital, under German doctors, surrounded by fellow Germans professing themselves his admiring friends, and in no state to make decisions for himself, Stanley might kiss goodbye to his hard-won trophy.

Stanley did not surrender without a struggle. He at once demanded that Emin should be transferred to Zanzibar on a British man-of-war. But when the demand was turned down on medical grounds, he had shot his bolt and took his leave with the best grace he could muster. The most he could do to maintain his stake in Emin was to leave Parke behind at Bagamoyo while the remainder of the Expedition embarked, on December 6, in a flotilla of German and English ships for the triumphal crossing to Zanzibar. Parke, however, himself fell sick. Messengers from Stanley were denied access to Emin, and the Germans managed to maintain an efficient quarantine to shield their patient from pernicious British influences. Jephson and the other officers of the Expedition interpreted the Pasha's sudden isolation as cold and deliberate ingratitude and were both puzzled and hurt by it.[5] The British press put the same construction on the rupture between Emin and Stanley. Jephson, who before leaving Zanzibar for Egypt made a last unsuccessful attempt to get Emin to accompany him, believed that Emin was unaware of what the Germans at Bagamoyo had done and were doing to prevent contact between himself and the Expedition. At any rate the two parted friends:

> In parting he held my hand in both his, and told me how deeply grateful he was for what we had done for him. He said, "You I shall never forget, for you have been my companion and friend through those months of our imprisonment together, those months which were the worst of my life."
>
> It seemed as if he were taking a long goodbye, and profoundly touched by the inexpressible sadness of his tone, I once more urged him to come with us. Again he shook his head and said it was impossible. . . .[6]

He never saw Emin again, and when Emin did leave Bagamoyo it was not to return to Egypt or to Europe, but to retrace his steps, at the head of a German Expedition, back into the interior of the inhospitable continent from which he had been with such pain extracted.

At Zanzibar, meanwhile, Emin's people were embarked on the

Egyptian steamer *Mansourah* for transport to Suez. The survivors of
the Zanzibaris were paid off. A sum of 10,000 rupees was distributed
among the widows and orphans of the dead.

At the same time telegrams of congratulation were flooding in.[7]
Queen Victoria's contribution to Stanley's fan-mail read:

> STANLEY, Zanzibar. My thoughts are often with you and your brave
> followers, whose dangers and hardships are now at an end. Once
> more I heartily congratulate all, including the survivors of the
> gallant Zanzibaris who displayed such devotion and fortitude during
> your marvellous Expedition. Trust Emin progresses favourably.
>
> V.R.I.

The Kaiser's telegram managed to get in a discreet but pointed
reference to the New Order in East Africa:

> . . . that your way home led you through territories placed under
> my flag, gives me great satisfaction. . . .
>
> WILHELM IMPERATOR REX.

Stanley's reception by the European community in Zanzibar was as
generous and enthusiastic as had been his reception in Bagamoyo.
This, and the congratulatory messages from half the crowned heads
and nearly all the Geographic Societies of the civilised world, served
to whet his appetite for the welcome awaiting him in Europe. He was
anxious to be gone.

However, as had happened with his previous exploits, acclamation
and acrimony followed hand-in-hand. Stanley's brief stay at Zanzibar
saw the opening of the series of disputes, polemics and litigations
which were to be the principal fruits of the Expedition.

The first broadside was directed against Tippu-Tib, well below
the waterline. Stanley learnt that one of the Indian merchants who
acted as bankers to the Zanzibar Arabs held over £10,000 in gold,
paid him by the Congo State for the credit of Tippu-Tib in exchange for
ivory bought by the Belgians. Stanley made a rapid calculation of what
Tippu-Tib owed him for breach of contract, favours received and not
reciprocated, damages, and a few other little matters, and found—to no
one's surprise—that the bill came to just £10,000. It was more than
a nice round figure; it had the added merit that it would almost
completely reimburse the Emin Relief Committee for their outlay on

the Expedition, a most gratifying outcome if it could be managed. Since the Indian in question was a British subject, Stanley was able to apply to the consular court in Zanzibar for an injunction forbidding the transfer of the funds to Tippu-Tib until "an English court should decide whether the Emin Relief Committee was not entitled in equity to have these expenses and moneys refunded . . . a consummation devoutly to be wished". The injunction was granted pending further litigation and Stanley, pleased at the chance fate had given him to stab his old enemy so neatly in the back, embarked for Egypt with his officers.[8]

They reached Cairo on January 16 and handed over two hundred and sixty refugees to the Egyptian authorities. (The remainder—Emin's personal servants and their families—had remained in Bagamoyo.) If Stanley then promptly lost interest in the fate of the people he had so summarily rescued, he can hardly be blamed.

His next action was to shut himself up in a house in Cairo, the Villa Victoria, to catch up on his correspondence and write his account of the Expedition. These two tasks occupied him for exactly fifty days. In that time he wrote over a hundred telegrams, four hundred letters, and the nine hundred and three pages of foolscap manuscript that were shortly to become the solid twin volumes of In Darkest Africa; or, The Quest, Rescue and Retreat of Emin, Governor of Equatoria.[9]

He then embarked for Europe and the final stages of his triumphal homecoming.

*　　　*　　　*

Nothing was lacking in the welcome that awaited Stanley and his officers. While Emin lay slowly recovering in the hospital at Bagamoyo, Stanley was being fêted, lionised, banqueted, decorated, interviewed, reported, audienced, invited to lecture, and showered with honorary doctorates and freedoms-of-the-city from all over Europe. But underlying at first, and in the end overshadowing, the initial euphoria was the fact that the Expedition had ended with its original object unrealised, and with Stanley barely on speaking terms with the man he had set out to save. These facts were not perhaps of great moment, at least to the general public, unconcerned with the political niceties of the Expedition. But Stanley's quarrel with the officers of the Rear Guard, charged as it was with overtones of scandal and hints of dark doings too horrible and too African to be admitted to the daylight of civilised Europe, was another matter. For the sad fact was that Stanley was not content with the purely disciplinary allegations he made against the officers of the Rear Guard—allegations principally of incompetence and disobedience—but also saw fit to lend countenance to a number of sordid rumours that had begun to circulate respecting the personal conduct and morality of the Europeans left at Yambuya.

These stories had their origins in two sources, both tainted. One was the Sudanese interpreter Assad Farran, the other Sergeant William Bonny.

Assad Farran had been left with the Rear Guard at Yambuya, had accompanied Jameson on his trip to Kasongo, and had finally been invalided home before the march to Banalya. In fact, though, his separation from the Expedition had been less due to bad health than to laziness, dishonesty and incompetence. To these qualities must be added a generous dash of malice, since his first act on going down-river was to denounce his late employers in a letter addressed to the Belgian authorities and containing what Barttelot, who heard about it during his last visit to the Falls, called "the most abominable stories about us". The most sensational of these stories was the accusation that Jameson had sponsored, if not actually participated in, cannibal orgies, and had paid a group of Manyuema to kill and eat a human being in his presence. This slander was the more dangerous in that it contained a germ of truth; it was a distorted version of an incident which actually took place while Jameson was returning with Tippu-Tib from Kasongo. Here is Jameson's account of it from his diary:

(Tippu-Tib) then told me, amongst other stories, that long ago, when fighting near Malela, they killed a great many of the enemy. The natives who were with him were cannibals, and not a body could be found next morning. He tells me that two men will easily eat one man in a night. He sent for water in the night to wash his hands and to drink, the water there being in a well. When it was brought, he could not make out why it stuck to his hands, and was so oily and bad to drink. Next day he and several Arabs went up to see what was the matter with the water, and there they saw a most horrible sight. The top of the water was all covered with a thick layer of yellow fat, which was running over the side, and he found out that his natives had taken all the human meat to the well to wash it before eating. At the next place he camped by a stream, and made the natives camp below him. I told him that people at home generally believed that these were only "travellers' tales", as they are called in our country, or, in other words, lies. He then said something to an Arab called Ali, seated next him, who turned round to me and said, "Give me a bit of cloth, and see." I sent my boy for six handkerchiefs, thinking it was all a joke, and that they were not in earnest, but presently a man appeared, leading a young girl of about ten years old by the hand, and I then witnessed the most horribly sickening sight I am ever likely to see in my life. He plunged a knife quickly into her breast twice, and she fell on her face, turning over on her side. Three men then ran forward, and began to cut up the body of the girl; finally her head was cut off, and not a particle remained, each man taking his piece away down to the river to wash it. The most extraordinary thing was that the girl never uttered a sound, nor struggled, until she fell. Until the last moment I could not believe that they were in earnest. I have heard many stories of this kind since I have been in this country, but never could believe them, and I never would have been such a beast as to witness this, but I could not bring myself to believe that it was anything save a ruse to get money out of me, until the last moment.[10]

This account has an obvious frankness which makes it difficult to believe in Jameson's culpability. Parke's judgement of the affair seems as reasonable as it is humane:

I entirely disbelieve that James Sligo Jameson was capable of any act of deliberate cruelty. Although his own letter is compromising, yet its candour is significant. It is a maxim to speak only well of the dead and to leave untouched all that is unpleasant concerning them; but of Jameson I never knew but good.[11]

The story against Jameson was repeated by Bonny,[12] who, however, concentrated most of his venom on Barttelot—ironically the only European in the Expedition who had any time for him. Bonny's contributions to the disparagement of the Rear Guard officers are harder to assess because uncorroborated by anything except the vague hints, already referred to, of abnormalities in Barttelot's behaviour. His motives appear to have been partly the desire to ingratiate himself with Stanley after the disaster at Yambuya, and partly his resentment (referred to in several accounts) at being treated as an inferior by the other officers. References in Jephson's diary to Bonny's behaviour after rejoining the Advance Guard make it clear that Jephson and the other officers both disliked and distrusted Bonny:

> The officers are not pleased with Bonny's story of events which happened in the rear guard & do not give credence to a good deal of what he relates, it is certainly peculiar that when he tells his story one is struck by the fact that any grain of sense which is shown in the many senseless councils they (*the Rear Guard officers*) held should have invariably come from Bonny—according to his own account—he was never very remarkable for common sense, so one is rather inclined to distrust his evidence. He has stocked his outfit with numbers of things belonging to the other officers. . . . & we do not . . . think it is likely that the officers would have given him their things in the way he said they did. Even the Zanzibaris speak about it & say he came with only two small loads & now he has eight. Stanley & the officers are terribly down on him & speak out plainly about him, I myself hardly know what to think. . . . The thing which is so bad is that Bonny seems to take such a pleasure in telling all the most dark & disreputable stories of the officers & he has certainly done his best to blacken their character as much as possible, for even were all the stories true—which we all of us doubt—still there is no necessity to repeat them with such pleasure. He says he thinks Barttelot became insane, & he tells a story of his running after a woman & seizing her by the cheek with his teeth, & relates a story of Jameson having bought a slave woman & handed her over to the Manyuema on condition that they would kill & eat her before him. Stories like these are incredible.[13]

Elsewhere, Jephson relates a discreditable quarrel between Bonny and Nelson after Nelson had reported Bonny for neglecting his duty:

> Bonny was very angry at being reported & a furious scene took place in which he said all sorts of evil things about Nelson in a sort of shrill scream—whether true or not I can't say—& finally called Nelson a liar, upon which Nelson struck him & a rather disgraceful struggle took place.

Jephson adds—

> Bonny is a most exasperating, low sort of fellow, he is just a sergeant with all the feelings, ideas, & loafing propensities of a

typical "Tommy Atkins" added to this he has an overweening conceit which is quite wonderful seeing that he has absolutely nothing to be conceited about; he has done nothing for the Expedition & is despised by the men . . . he is a man none of us have ever liked or trusted, for he is simply dishonest.[14]

But if Jephson was troubled by the unpleasant nature of Bonny's stories, and suspicious of Bonny's motives, Stanley had no such scruples. With such piquant additions as these, Stanley now had at his disposal a whole arsenal of weapons with which to fight off any attempt to put the blame for the Rear Guard disaster where it belonged. He could, and did, accuse Tippu-Tib. Alternatively he could shift the blame to Emin for not being at the Lake to meet the Expedition on its first arrival there, an omission which Stanley bluntly asserts, "cost us the life of a gallant Englishman, and the lives of over a hundred of our brave and faithful followers".[15] Finally he could put the blame on the officers of the Rear Guard; and if his condemnation of their professional conduct lacked force, the allegations could be helped to stick by a generous application of mud. That these three explanations were mutually contradictory bothered Stanley not at all. Shifting his ground with lightning speed from one target to another, varying his complaints and insinuations up and down a gamut of supposed misdemeanours from cannibalism to carelessness and from disobedience to mental derangement, and showing throughout a lordly disregard for the restraints either of decency or of common sense, Stanley was an adversary hard to defeat. He had, too, a valuable advantage over his subordinates—the clause in their contracts which forbade them to publish anything in their own defence until six months after the appearance of the "official" account, by which time any damage would be hard to undo. Troup was already in England (and, somewhat to his surprise, still alive) when Stanley's first inaccurate reports of the Yambuya affair began to appear in April 1889. Troup at once tried to publish his own account in an effort to set the record straight. He was restrained by a court injunction obtained by Stanley's agents in London. In due course, however, the accounts of the remaining officers appeared. The defences made by Ward and Troup, and the efforts made by the editors of Jameson's and Barttelot's diaries and letters to vindicate the honour of the dead, are as remarkable for their dignity, reason and restraint as were Stanley's attacks for the lack of these qualities.

However, during the first few months after the Expedition's return, Stanley did not immediately avail himself of the sordid rumours about the behaviour of the Rear Guard officers as weapons of character-assassination.[16] By the publication of In Darkest Africa, with its lavish diatribes against the faithlessness of Tippu-Tib, the "extraordinary vacillation" of Emin Pasha, the treachery of the Sudanese and Egyptians, and the "irresolution . . . neglect of their promises and indifference to their written orders" among the officers of the Rear Guard, Stanley imagined that he had disposed thoroughly and permanently of any suggestion that he himself should bear a portion of the blame for the tragedy at Yambuya. But in the autumn of 1890, when, after the legally-prescribed lapse of time, the accounts of the Rear Guard officers began to appear, Stanley realised with a shock of indignation that the people concerned were perfectly capable *even when dead* of rebutting each and every one of his allegations against their professional conduct. In particular, it was the appearance of Barttelot's posthumous memoirs that aroused Stanley's indignation and brought home to him that he still had a fight on his hands. Clearly, it was going to require arguments of a new and more potent kind to stifle this unlooked-for resistance. With this in mind Stanley, who did nothing by halves, threw himself whole-heartedly into the business of mud, threat and smears.

Barttelot and Jameson were the principal targets.

The course of the battle that ensued can be followed in the columns of The Times for the months of November and December 1890. It opened on November 8 with a long statement delivered by Stanley to reporters in New York (where he was at the time on a lecture-tour). This set the tone for what ensued. That the tone was, from the start, pitched pretty low, will be readily apparent from the following sample:

I was told (Stanley declared) that Major Barttelot had expressed great curiosity to learn the probable effect of a dose of cyanide of potassium, and at one time was caught tasting it on his tongue in order to ascertain whether its taste would be likely to be detected in a cup of coffee. I was at the same time told that the person for whom this dose was intended was Selim Mohammed, the nephew of Tippoo-Tib. I was also told that Major Barttelot's life was twice saved by Mr. Bonny, once when Major Barttelot had suddenly seized a woman and fastened his teeth in her shoulder. I was told that frequently Major Barttelot would cause his black followers to shrink from before him by standing in their path in front of the advancing natives and grinning like a fiend—that is the expression that was used. I was told that with a steel-pointed cypress staff he had run about the camp prodding his people with it, and then flourishing the stick and hitting about him indiscriminately. And all this without apparent cause. A Manyuema chief, a comrade of the man Sanga, reported that he had been prodded 17 times in one day. . . . I am informed that Major Barttelot told Mr. Bonny that he had recommended his brother Mr. Walter Barttelot to look after Lieutenant Troup on the arrival of the latter in England, in order that Troup might not be tempted to disclose what was going on at Yambuya with the rear column. I am further told that when the deserters from the advance column reached Yambuya, and told Major Barttelot a graphic tale about my having been killed, he exclaimed: "Thank God! I shall be made a colonel now. . . ."

And so on, and so on. There is more, and worse: Barttelot took a sadistic delight in punishing his men; he had native women kidnapped for his sexual gratification; he gave his boy Sudi a kick from which Sudi later died; he refused medicine to the sick; he was insane; he antagonised the Manyuema; he sent Stanley's wardrobe down-river; etc.

In short—a right rotter.

The fact that the whole diatribe is simply a hotch-potch of second- or third-hand gleanings from camp gossip, covering a spectrum from the scurrilous to the plain silly, troubles Stanley not at all. "I was told" is all the authority he needs, and one gathers the impression that he coolly expected his audience to share his majestic indifference to the laws of evidence, not to say of logic.

Needless to say, Jameson comes in for his fair share of insinuation, misrepresentation and abuse, the cannibalism story being duly trotted out with suitable embellishments and its proper quota of "I-was-tolds". And so that Troup and Ward shall not feel left out they are accused of conniving at Barttelot's crimes by wilfully ignoring their plain duty of putting him under restraint and shipping him home.

Characteristically, in the heat of the moment, Stanley manages at one point completely to demolish his own case against Barttelot when he observes, in speaking of the opinion he had formed of the Major *before* parting from him at Yambuya—

My view of his case was this. Major Barttelot had no special aptitude for anything beyond being useful in case a fight should occur. In the meantime he could exist as a member of the Expedition, and as my nominal second-in-command, until he should develop meritorious qualities.

Clearly, if this was Stanley's true opinion, to have engaged such a man for the Expedition bespeaks a lamentable want of judgement, while to have appointed him to the crucial post of commander of the Rear Guard was nothing less than an act of criminal folly. There could be no more damning exposure of Stanley's defects as a leader, or, by implication, a more thorough exoneration of the man he is attacking.

The slanderous farrago concludes with a lip-service nod towards the dimly-perceived conventions of decency, truth and common-sense:

I have told these facts (sic) as they were told me. Whether every one of them is true or not, I have no means of knowing from personal knowledge. Some are attested by affidavits, others are stated in official reports, which I, being bent upon saving the Expedition from scandal, tried to suppress. . . .[17]

The hare which Stanley had started with his statement of November 8, turned out a really lovely runner. In the weeks which followed, the argument in the sedate columns of The Times raged vigorously around the absorbing question of whether two rather ordinary young Englishmen were, or were not, insane, brutal and perverted sadists. In the ding-dong, one, and only one, small voice was raised in an attempt to bring some sense into the insane controversy: on November 19, Ward published a letter in which he pointed out that the furor about the public and private morals of Messrs. Jameson and Barttelot had strictly nothing to do with the matter in hand; the real issue was whether Stanley or Barttelot was ultimately responsible for the fate of the Yambuya garrison.

Ward's attempt to bring the discussion back to basics was a failure. The argument raged on unchecked until the end of December, by which time both sides were beginning to repeat themselves and, in certain cases, had already been doing so for some time. A stalemate was tacitly declared and the participants retired to nurse their resentments.

However successful it may have been as a smoke-screen, the undignified nature of Stanley's quarrel with his dead subordinates, not to mention his disputes with Tippu-Tib and with Emin himself, undoubtedly did much to detract from the real worth of his exploit. In the same way, the desperate shifts and expedients to which he resorted in order to avoid admitting the possibility that he could have made a mistake, went far to diminish his qualities as a man. And the pity of it was that the whole business was as unnecessary as it was sordid. The welcome he received on his return to Europe was proof enough that Stanley's reputation was by now unassailably that of the greatest explorer of his time. To have taken at least part of the blame for the disaster upon himself could have done him no real harm. Certainly it would have done him less harm than the tactics he took to evade the responsibility. The strengths and virtues of his character were, and are, well known and beyond dispute; they make it easy to excuse a lack of humility in his make-up. Humility is not a quality the world finds indispensable in its Great Men. But such a gross and glaring lack of magnanimity is a very different pair of shoes.

It is true that Stanley was constitutionally incapable of believing himself to blame for the mistakes and disasters of the Expedition. Thus the deception he practised in his account of the affair was less a calculated attempt to confuse and conceal the real facts, than an act of self-deception. On this self-deception he may fittingly be judged in his own words: at the very outset of the venture, when on the way from Suez to Zanzibar, the Expedition's steamer put in at Lamu on the East African Coast, and here Stanley recorded the following in his journal:

> Soon after (our arrival) S.S. *Baghdad* came in with Dr. Lenz, the Austrian traveller, who had started to proceed to Emin Bey, but failing, came across to Zanzibar instead. Having failed in his purpose, he will blame Africa and abuse the Congo especially. It is natural with all classes to shift the blame on others, and I feel assured Lenz will be no exception.

This utterance is of a type familiar enough in Stanley's writing—a cheap sneer lacking either the easy virtue of truth or the feeble justification of necessity. When applied to Stanley's own affairs, it has, besides, a quality of sublime, prophetic blindness that would not be unworthy of a Greek tragedy.

*   *   *

Stanley's petty disputes with his subordinates and associates, which so marred the Expedition's return, were carried on against the background of a much larger dispute, the rivalry between Germany and England over the dismemberment of the territories formerly claimed by the Sultans of Zanzibar. This in its turn formed part of a more widespread scramble among the colonial powers for the portions of Africa still unoccupied or unclaimed. These larger themes cannot be treated in detail here. But the story of the Emin Pasha Relief Expedition did not end with the arrival at Bagamoyo of Stanley and his dilapidated caravan. The Expedition, and particularly the events in Equatoria which its arrival had precipitated, had resolved nothing, but had merely unlocked a situation, releasing forces which still had to work themselves out. To carry the story through to its end, therefore, it is necessary to consider briefly at least one aspect of the territorial carve-up, namely the subsequent attempts of Stanley's employers, Leopold and Mackinnon, to further their designs on Emin's territory after the failure of the Expedition to accomplish their hopes. And since Germany was by now committed to schemes of her own in East Africa, these must be taken into consideration, at least in so far as they impinged on the projects of the other interested parties.

The Anglo-German map-making game in East Africa was carried on very much in the manner of a modern arms race: the moves of each side were not actions but reactions, made not in furtherance of distinctly-perceived goals but rather out of suspicious ignorance regarding the aims and motives of the other party. Neither Bismarck on the German side, nor the governments of Gladstone and Salisbury on the British, at any time conceived the acquisition of new territories in Africa as a worthwhile goal. On the other hand, there were in both countries private individuals deeply committed to the doctrines of economic imperialism. Thus the history of the partition of East Africa is as much concerned with the relations of the colony-enthusiasts (men like Mackinnon and Peters) with their respective governments, as it is with relations between the governments themselves.

Germany's first official move in East Africa had been the recognition of the "treaties" with native chiefs in the Sultan's dominions made by Peters on his flag-hoisting expedition of 1884. In this Bismarck was not motivated by colonial ambitions but by the desire to embarrass Britain by forcing her to embroil herself in Africa. Britain dutifully responded, to the extent of negotiating the treaty of 1886, delimiting Anglo-German spheres of influence in the Sultan of Zanzibar's

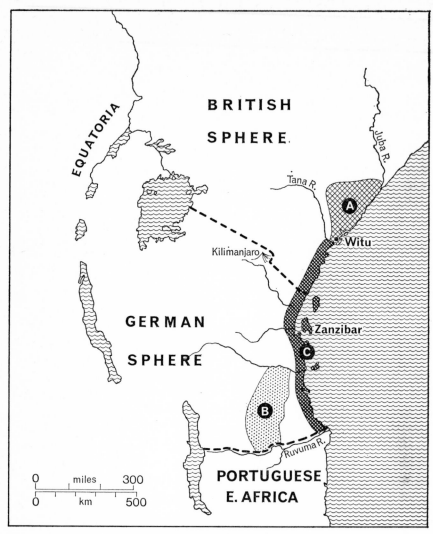

5   The partition of East Africa

Left-hand map Approximate boundaries under the Agreement of 1886:
A—Sultanate of Witu   ⎫
B—Area covered by Peters' treaties ⎬ German protectorates
C—Coastal strip, domain of Sultan of Zanzibar

Right-hand map Approximate boundaries after the Settlement of 1890:
A—Area later leased to King Leopold
B—Mackinnon's "corridor"

360

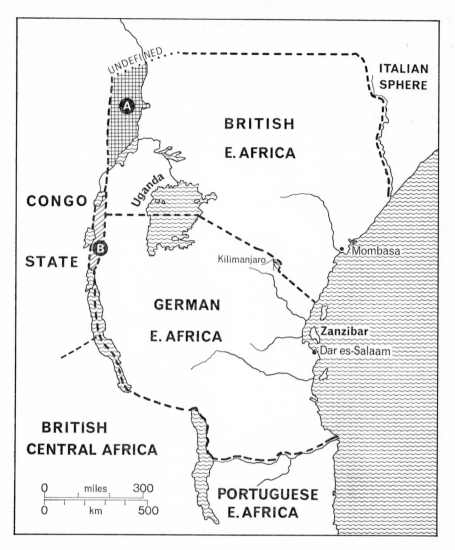

dominions. Having denied—it might almost be said at Germany's insistence—a slice of territory to its rival, the British Government was then content to do nothing whatever about its new acquisition. But as Germany's desire to annoy the British had created an opportunity for Peters to pursue the schemes to which he was privately committed, so Britain's desire to create a counter-annoyance by taking a hand in the game had given Mackinnon the chance he needed to renew his dreams of an African commercial empire. The negotiations with the dying Sultan Barghash, begun by Stanley during his stop-over in Zanzibar en route for the Congo, resulted in the Sultan's ceding to Mackinnon for a period of fifty years full administrative and commercial rights over the northern or "British" half of the coastal strip including the port of Mombasa. Meanwhile Mackinnon had pressed ahead with the formation of the commercial organisation—the British East Africa Association—through which he hoped to administer and exploit his concession. The general scheme was to tap the putative riches of the Lakes Region (an area understood to include Equatoria) via a line of posts, and eventually a railway, running between Lake Victoria and Mombasa.[18]

These plans were well advanced even before the Expedition's departure from England. It was in the name of the Association not yet formed that Stanley was briefed to conduct negotiations with the Sultan and to offer Emin the chance to continue as Governor of Equatoria. Mackinnon must have had cosiderable confidence in Stanley's power of persuasion and in Emin's willingness to co-operate since, after the Expedition had left, he gave contractual form to the agreement he supposed Emin and Stanley were going to reach. In October 1888 an agreement was concluded whereby Robert Felkin, acting on Emin's behalf, signed over to the East Africa Company the sole right to exercise military, administrative and commercial functions in Emin's province. Emin himself was to stay on as Governor during his lifetime, and an escape clause was included whereby Emin must ratify the agreement made by Felkin in his name. In signing this document Felkin believed he was carrying out Emin's wishes as expressed in letters to Felkin written during 1885, 1886 and 1887. In these, during the most anxious period of his uncertainty about the future of his Province, Emin had set out his plans for opening a route to the East Coast as a means of putting the economy of the Province on a sound commercial footing, and had asked Felkin to find support for the plan among the British business community. When the agreement became known, there were loud cries of treachery from the Germans, who saw Felkin's action as a ploy to pre-empt their own newly conceived claims on Emin's loyalties. Whether or not such an idea may have been in Mackinnon's mind, there is no doubt that Felkin for his part acted in good faith, out of a disinterested desire to promote the welfare of Emin and his Province.[19]

However, neither Emin's co-operation nor the occupation of Equatoria was indispensable to Mackinnon's plans. There was room for more than one iron in a fire the size of Kenya and Uganda combined. What was indispensable, though, was some degree of government recognition for the Association; only this could give it the quasi-sovereign status it would need to hold its own in Africa in the face of competition on an international level. Recognition, when it came, took the form of a Royal Charter granted in September 1888, by which the Association was sonorously incorporated as the Imperial British East Africa Company.[20]

The ease and speed with which Mackinnon's company obtained its charter was, on past showing, surprising. Governmental opposition to colonial adventures had so far led to what one historian has called "a series of deliberately-missed opportunities".[21] In 1878 Salisbury had sabotaged Mackinnon's negotiations with the Sultan of Zanzibar. In 1886 he had written that if Emin was to be rescued, it was up to the Germans to do it. In 1887 he had refused Mackinnon's request for special support in his new negotiations with the Sultan. Yet in 1888 Mackinnon found no difficulty in obtaining from Salisbury's government the charter which set the seal of approval on his plans. Had there been a change of heart? Strictly speaking there had not. The government still had no plans for occupying any part of East Africa in its own person, as it were. But between the departure of the Emin Pasha Relief Expedition in 1887 and its return in 1889, two events had occurred which tended to modify the neurotic apprehension with which, until then, successive administrations had viewed the prospect of embroilment in African colonial enterprises.

The first and most influential of these was the British decision to stay on in Egypt. Salisbury, following Gladstone, was both publicly and privately committed to leaving Egypt at the first possible moment. In early 1887, at the same time as Mackinnon and his associates began the campaign designed to obtain a charter for their Association, Salisbury set in motion the first steps towards a definite withdrawal from Egypt. A British envoy, Sir Henry Drummond Wolff,[22] was despatched to Constantinople to negotiate with the Sultan (still nominally the utlimate source of Egyptian authority) an agreement which would have resulted in the British leaving Egypt within five years. The negotiations went well and an agreement was actually signed, but it was never ratified. At the last moment it foundered on the opposition of France and Russia to Britain's insistence that she must retain the right to re-occupy Egypt if the need arose. This outcome convinced the government of what Baring had seen all along—the impossibility of disentanglement from Egypt in the foreseeable future.

This changed attitude to Egyptian affairs involved two corollaries. One was acceptance of the fact that sooner or later an attempt would have to be made to re-occupy the Sudan. The second was that it now became a fixed canon of British policy (though by a process of reasoning which is, it must be confessed, obscure) that Britain must control the affluents of the Nile, or at least deny them to any power capable of interfering with the flow of water on which the existence of Egypt as a country depended. This curious[23] fixation led directly to the occupation of Uganda, though as usual the method preferred was one which involved the government in no outlay of effort or money and would enable them to disclaim responsibility if things went wrong. Mackinnon and his company were a tool ready to hand; and a licence to assume responsibility for the area which the government had suddenly discovered to be so vital to British interests was exactly what Mackinnon wanted. For once the aims and aspirations of government and private enterprise coincided.

The second factor bearing on Salisbury's decision to support Mackinnon's plans was the evident possibility of a German attempt to annex Equatoria or Uganda or both.

In late 1888, while the civilised world was without news of the fate of Stanley's Expedition, Germany, in the person of Carl Peters, began to organise her own expedition for the relief of Emin. The German effort, though like the British it was presented to the public as an exercise in disinterested philanthropy, had itself been called into being as a response to the threat posed by Stanley's presence on the outer confines of the German sphere. Peters suspected (rightly) that Stanley had designs on Equatoria, though he could not be sure whether an ostensibly private undertaking concealed an intention on the part of the British Government to expand its sphere beyond the bounds of the area covered by the existing Anglo-German agreement. In any case, from Peters' point of view, the possibility of establishing a claim to Equatoria by "rescuing" Emin was no less attractive than it was to Mackinnon and his friends. It offered the chance of neatly exploiting the deficiencies of the 1886 agreement. The Germans had already managed to get a toe-hold on the Zanzibar coast north of the British strip by extending a protectorate over the small "Sultanate" of Witu.[24] Therefore, if Germany could stake a solid claim to Equatoria and/or Uganda (neither of which was covered by the agreement) the English zone would be effectively encircled and debarred from further expansion towards the headwaters of the Nile.

Unfortunately for Peters, political difficulties delayed the start of his expedition until the middle of 1889. When he finally did set off, marching westward from Witu for Lake Victoria, it was without the support of his government. By this time, of course, Equatoria had collapsed and Emin was already on his way back to the coast under Stanley's watchful eye, but Peters, knowing nothing of this, pressed on.

Meanwhile Mackinnon, ignorant of Stanley's fate and as alarmed by Peters' preparations as Peters had been by Stanley's, had had time to take counter-measures. A second Relief Expedition was mounted, which was to march inland from the Mombasa coast and find out what had happened to Stanley.[25] Command of the Expedition was given to a big-game fanatic named Swayne, a man whose enthusiasm for the chase was so great as to unfit him for any other occupation. Even his second-in-command, Frederick Jackson, himself a keen hunter, found Swayne's sporting proclivities excessive:

Swayne, the leader, neither knew nor cared about anything connected with the safari; and though very anxious to get off, had done nothing to expedite it. Big game shooting was an obsession with him, and he could think and talk of nothing else. He had, amongst other rifles, a 4-bore, and with that he would tear about the camp until he was blown, then aim at a leaf or other object, about the height of an elephant's vitals, and shout, "Am I steady, Jackson, am I steady?" The position was hopeless. . . .

Swayne was quietly dumped[26] and the Expedition left the coast under Jackson's command. Following a north-easterly route they arrived, in November 1889, at Mumia's, a village at the northern end of Lake Victoria on the borders of Uganda. (Jackson does not explain what inspired him to make for this particular point but states, confusingly, that his orders were to try to make contact with Stanley at the southern end of the Lake.) Uganda was at this time on the verge of total collapse. The feeble and vacillating policies of King Mwanga, and political strife between the three religious factions—Catholic, Muslim and Protestant—had so weakened the country's internal cohesion that it lay open to the hand of the first plausible annexationist who should happen along. But Jackson was not that man. In spite of appeals for help from the Protestant missionaries and from Mwanga himself, Jackson refused to enter Uganda on the grounds that his instructions specifically precluded such an action. Instead, he turned his back on the situation and pottered away northwards to Mount Elgon where he hoped to find elephants to shoot. Hardly had he departed than Peters, like the villain of some crude comedy, appeared at Mumia's. He could hardly believe his luck at discovering there a packet of mail which had arrived for Jackson after Jackson had left. Nothing if not unscrupulous, Peters opened and read Jackson's letters.[27] One was from Stanley, and from it Peters learnt of the collapse of Equatoria, and that Stanley and Emin were already on their way back to the coast. That left nothing for Peters to do in Equatoria; but there remained Uganda. He seized his chance with both hands, left Mumia's the next day, crossed the Nile into Uganda, and forced one of his famous treaties (treaties being to Peters what big game was to the unfortunate Swayne) on Mwanga.

At this point Jackson returned to Mumia's and found out what was going on. He appears to have been more distressed by Peters' ungentlemanly interception of his mail than by the German adventurer's having practically annexed Uganda under the noses of the British. Jackson despatched a message summoning Peters either to desist from interfering in Ugandan affairs or to face arrest, and set off for Mwanga's.[28] When he arrived it was to find that Peters had, not unnaturally, fled the scene without waiting to explain himself and was already on his way back to the coast with his precious treaty in his pocket.

Jackson left his second-in-command, Ernest Gedge, to hold the fort in Uganda and set off in turn for the coast. Both men now intended to submit the Uganda question to arbitration at a higher level—Peters hoping for ratification of his treaty, Jackson confidently expecting its annulment.

For all the good their manœuvrings did, both men might as well have stayed at home and economised on their shoe-leather. In their absence the future of Uganda had already been decided over their heads. On July 1, 1890, an Anglo-German agreement was signed which settled the fate of the disputed regions. Its principal provisions were as follows:

1. The boundary between the German and British spheres, which in 1886 had been drawn only as far as the eastern shore of Lake Victoria, was extended due west to meet the frontier of the Congo Free State at a point mid-way between the northern end of Lake Tanganyika and the southern end of Lake Albert. This

firmly excluded Germany from the headwaters of the Nile by placing Equatoria, Unyoro and Uganda squarely in the British sphere.

2. Germany renounced her claim to Witu, leaving Britain free to extend her coastal strip north to the River Juba (where it met the "sphere" claimed by Italy).

3. In return for these concessions on the part of the Germans, Britain surrendered Heligoland.[29]

Peters entered Bagamoyo to be greeted by news of the treaty. His pique is understandable at finding the fruits of his bold gamble snatched from his hands by his own government and presented to his opponents on a silver plate. On hearing the news, he shut himself up alone in a room for two hours—"to regain my composure" as he put it.[30]

Mackinnon now owned rather more than half of East Africa. On December 26, 1890, Captain Frederick Lugard at the head of an I.B.E.A.C. expedition hoisted the Company's flag in Mwanga's capital and proclaimed British "suzerainty" over his kingdom.

With Uganda, which Gordon had long ago declared to be the prize plum in the African cake, disposed of, and Mackinnon (it is to be supposed) happy, there yet remained the mess Stanley had left behind in Equatoria. Peters' appreciation of the situation in Equatoria after Emin's "retreat" is hard to quarrel with, despite its double bias (pro-German and anti-Stanley):

> The Equatorial Province is deserted. . . . Neither the ostensible nor the real purpose (of the Expedition) has been attained. Even the Mahdi himself could not have been more injurious to the civilising of the Upper Nile than Stanley has been. . . . If Stanley had stuck fast in the swamps of the Aruwimi, Emin Pasha would at this day, according to all human calculation, be still in Wadelai in a perfectly secure position. The whole territory north of Lake Victoria would be a firm bulwark, under Christian influence, which in time could have been extended step by step down the Nile against the Mahdi's influence, whereas now the Arab influence extends to the northern boundary of Uganda.[31]

If Mackinnon had plenty on his plate with his new acquisitions in Kenya and Uganda, and if the British Government was content to

leave the Mahdi-ists in Equatoria until such time as the whole of the
Sudan should be reconquered, there was yet one man who had by no
means relinquished his civilising designs on the Southern Sudan:
that was King Leopold.

Emin's departure had left Equatoria in the hands of four mutually
hostile groups. First there were the native inhabitants. They were
divided and sub-divided by linguistic, geographical and tribal
barriers; they fought among themselves; and from time to time, to
gain a temporary advantage or simply out of inability to resist,
tribes or villages would submit to, or even ally themselves with, one or
another group of northern infiltrators—Danagla slave-merchants,
Egyptian administrators or Mahdi-ist invading forces. But by and
large the natives of Equatoria maintained a policy of resistance,
active or passive according to circumstances, to foreign interference.[32]

Second in importance was the army of Omar Saleh, which, though
now much weakened by disease, desertions and continual skirmishing
with the natives and battles with Emin's troops, had pushed south as
far as to occupy Duffile. Farther south again, in the hills around Wadelai,
was Fadl el-Mulla. He had under him the majority of the Equatorial
troops, plus a locust-like and unmanageable horde of camp-followers
which severely restricted his freedom of action. Finally, in the extreme
south was Selim Bey with his followers, who, after some fighting
with the natives, had established themselves on the Lake shore in the
neighbourhood of Kavalli's.[33]

Fadl el-Mulla found it difficult to support his band in the hills,
and, seeing that the Mahdi-ists made no move to occupy the southern
stations, returned to Wadelai. At the same time he entered into a
treasonous correspondence with Omar Saleh, suggesting a merger.
Omar Saleh accepted Fadl el-Mulla's submission and sent a steamer-
load of troops down to Wadelai to arrange the formalities. But once
again the loyalty of the ordinary soldiers to the Khedive they still
supposed themselves to be serving proved stronger than the willingness of their officers to make an accommodation with the enemy.
The Mahdi-ists, instead of being welcomed with open arms, found
the station prepared to resist. A battle followed. The Mahdi-ists were
beaten off with heavy losses and Omar withdrew his whole force to
Rejaf from where he began to pester Khartoum with appeals for
reinforcements. Fadl el-Mulla's men were disgusted at their leader's
treachery. Many of them decided to throw in their lot with Selim. The
result was a mass desertion. Eight hundred soldiers and some ten

thousand of their followers left Wadelai and marched south to Kavalli's, where they arrived at about the end of May 1891.

The situation now entered a period of apparent stasis. Selim Bey hung on at Kavalli's until, in September 1891, he was visited by Lugard, who persuaded him to abandon his position and enlist with his followers under the British for service in Uganda. Fadl el-Mulla and his band continued their somewhat precarious existence of semi-brigandage. Omar Saleh and his troops frittered away their time and their strength in internal dissensions and in attempts to impose their authority on the surrounding tribes. This state of affairs might have been prolonged almost indefinitely had not a new factor appeared to unbalance the equation. It took the form of a Belgian invading force making its way into Equatoria from the Congo.

Leopold's reaction to the failure of the Emin Relief Expedition had been very different from that of Mackinnon. While Mackinnon, after the collapse of his hopes for Equatoria, had been content to shift his attention to other parts of the map, Leopold's greedy eye remained firmly fixed on the Upper Nile. Sending Stanley up the Aruwimi was neither the first nor the last of the gambits employed by the wily and enterprising monarch in pursuit of his grandiose (one might almost say, megalomaniac) dream of adding the Southern Sudan to his already enormous portfolio of African real-estate. As early as 1884 he had engaged Gordon with just this end in view. When the project was aborted after Gordon's last-minute re-engagement in the Egyptian service, Leopold had switched his line of attack: in 1886 an expedition under Van Gèle was ordered up the Welle from its junction with the Congo with a view to the possible future use of the Welle valley as an approach route to the Southern Sudan. And in 1888, while Stanley was still plodding grimly to and fro among the jungles of the Aruwimi, had come the idea for using Tippu-Tib's forces for a push northwards to Bahr-el-Ghazal. This scheme, too, had come to nothing. Any question of its revival disappeared with the ending of the uneasy truce between the Belgians and the Congo Arabs, and the smashing of Arab power in a series of short and bloody campaigns in 1892 and 1893.

Meanwhile another opening had appeared which permitted Leopold to set in motion a sustained and serious effort to take and hold the Southern Sudan. In 1889 he had begun negotiations with Mackinnon for a lease of the area between the eastern boundary of the Congo State and the west bank of the Nile. This would have given

Leopold control over the whole of the now defunct Equatorial Province west of a line drawn from Lado to Lake Albert—an area that now became known as the Lado Enclave. Mackinnon, whose Company had no plans for Equatoria, was willing. In return Leopold offered Mackinnon the lease of a corridor through Belgian territory connecting the northern end of Lake Tanganyika and the southern end of Lake Edward. Mackinnon's interest in this peculiar concession is explained by the fact that he had recently been recruited to the ranks of the so-called "Cape-to-Cairo" enthusiasts. These persons (of whom Cecil Rhodes was one) were fascinated by the notion of an all-pink road, rail and steamer route spanning the African continent from top to bottom. Their cartographical fantasies were threatened with extinction by the impending Anglo-German agreement which would, by giving Germany a common frontier with the Congo at the north end of Lake Tanganyika, nip off the proposed thin red line in the middle. Mackinnon's corridor was an expedient calculated to save the Cape-to-Cairo scheme from an untimely death. In the event it failed to do so. But the "Mackinnon Treaty", though later disowned by the British Government, gave Leopold, at least momentarily, the diplomatic cover he needed for an assault on the Southern Sudan.[34]

He chose his moment well. He had the field to himself. The agreement of 1890 had confined the Germans well to the south of Lake Albert. France was concentrating her efforts on the southern Sahara and Lake Chad and had not yet turned her attention to the Upper Nile. (When she did so, her intervention was to culminate in the Fashoda "Incident" of 1898.) England, represented for practical purposes by Mackinnon, was busy in Kenya and Uganda, while the British Government still maintained the curious attitude of indifference to Leopold's expansionist projects that it had shown at the time when the Emin Relief Expedition was being planned. But Leopold's strongest card was his willingness to man and equip an expedition to carry out his plans on the ground. This was the very thing the British Government, still harassed by memories of the Khartoum débâcle, was for its own part most unwilling to contemplate. Salisbury's whole strategy was to achieve his ends by purely diplomatic means without the risk, expense and publicity that would be involved in field operations. It was for this reason that the British Government was content to leave the exploitation of East Africa to Mackinnon's Company; for the same reason they raised no objection—at first—to Mackinnon's deal with King Leopold.[35]

370

The result was the Belgian Expedition under Van Kerckhoven, which left Leopoldville early in 1891, marched up the valley of the Welle, and in August 1892 crossed the Congo–Nile watershed into Equatoria.[36] At this point Van Kerckhoven lost his life in an accident (shot by his gunbearer), but under the leadership of the second-in-command, Lt. Milz, the column pressed on for the Nile.

Their objective was to occupy the Lado Enclave by putting garrisons into those of Emin's old stations not at present in the hands of the Mahdi-ists. This was a considerable undertaking since Milz's force would also have to hold the line of the Upper Welle in order to secure its rear. Milz therefore hoped to enlist Fadl el-Mulla and his force under the Belgian flag and use them to hold the Nile stations against the Mahdi-ists.

Fadl el-Mulla was ready to do business. His supply situation was now desperate, and he was not slow to recognize in the Belgians a heaven-sent source of weapons, ammunition and equipment. An agreement was signed. Not surprisingly, in view of Fadl el-Mulla's past record, the association failed to live up to the Belgians' expectations of it. Fadl el-Mulla had no intention of getting involved, if he could help it, in serious military operations, and was particularly lukewarm towards that aspect of the plan which involved the Equatorials' manning, as it were, the front line positions, while the Belgians lay back in their zeribas in the interior, well away from the river which would be the likely theatre of any aggressive operations undertaken by the Mahdi-ists in the northern stations. Having got what he wanted in the form of supplies, Fadl el-Mulla tacitly promoted himself from subordinate to ally—and an unco-operative ally at that. But the Belgians, short of men, soon found that they needed Fadl el-Mulla more than he needed them and the contract (which had originally been for one year) was renewed at the end of 1893 on terms even more favourable to the Equatorials.

As yet the Belgians had met difficulties in plenty but no serious opposition. But meanwhile, news of the Belgians' presence in the south had reached Khartoum. The Khalifa responded by sending strong reinforcements to Rejaf under an able, brave and energetic commander, Arabi Dafallah. After a preliminary campaign against the Bari (partly to season his troops and partly to protect his rear), Arabi marched his entire force out of Rejaf at the beginning of 1894 against Fadl el-Mulla. The Equatorial force was caught in the open near Wadelai, surprised, surrounded, and virtually wiped out. Fadl el-Mulla died with his army. Those few of his followers who escaped the slaughter—some two hundred in number—fled south to Kavalli's. There, in May 1894, they were picked up (as Selim's men had been by Lugard) by a British officer in the Uganda service, Major Thruston.[37]

With the defeat and death of Fadl el-Mulla, further happenings in Equatoria pass outside the scope of this story. There followed another five years of fighting between the Mahdi-ists, the natives, and a succession of Belgian expeditions. From being at one point only a hair's-breadth from total annihilation, the Belgians fought their way back to a position of superiority and inflicted a decisive defeat on the Mahdi-ist forces at Rejaf (February 1897). After this, Arabi Dafallah was no longer a serious threat, though he continued indomitably to harass the Belgian garrisons and maintained, in the best traditions of guerilla warfare, a tactical offensive while strategically on the defensive. But in the northern Sudan Kitchener's campaign against the Khalifa was moving inexorably to its crisis at Omdurman (September 1898) and Arabi's position was rapidly beginning to resemble that of Emin in 1885—a beleaguered outpost of an empire that had already ceased to exist.[38]

Seen in perspective, the Belgian campaigns in Equatoria and Bahr-el-Ghazal were never more than a sideshow to the larger war that was being fought out in the Northern Sudan between Kitchener's army and the forces of the Khalifa, and to the diplomatic war being carried on in the chanceries of Europe. The Belgian field forces were over-extended at all times, and even under more favourable conditions would have been quite inadequate to the task of holding and administering the vast tracts of territory to which Leopold aspired. And once France and England had entered the game in earnest, Leopold's diplomatic position, always shaky, had no chance of resisting a determined effort by his rivals to squeeze him out. It was not at Rejaf but at Omdurman that the Mahdi's power was broken. And it was not in Brussels but in Paris and London that the mastery of the Nile valley was decided.

Leopold hung on until the end to his tattered dream of an empire embracing the Congo and the Nile. With his death in 1909 the Lado Enclave reverted to Britain and was administered as part of the Sudan.

Of Leopold's dreams, however, it can at least be said that they lasted longer than Mackinnon's. The Imperial British East Africa Company, for all the magniloquence of its title, was from the start ill-managed, under-capitalised and under-planned. It did not outlive its creator. Four years after its incorporation it was bankrupt. In 1893, Mackinnon died and in the same year the government, not very willingly, assumed responsibility for Uganda. Kenya followed two years later when the muddled career of the I.B.E.A.C. was formally terminated by the surrender of the Company's charter.

NOTES AND REFERENCES

CHAPTER 10   AFTERMATH

1 Figures from Stanley's report printed in C.5906 pp. 15, 16. As Stanley's critic Fox-Bourne pointed out, the list omits all those Africans slaughtered in countless small skirmishes while resisting the Expedition's intrusion into their lands.

2 Emin's accident was generally attributed at the time to his failing sight. He was suffering from cataract and could no longer see anything clearly at a distance of more than three or four inches from his face. It should also be borne in mind that it was fifteen years since Emin had last been in a two-storey building.

3 Diary, qu. SCHWEITZER I p. 320.

4 D.A. II pp. 419–420. Cf. Emin's remarks on Stanley's cosmopolitanism, Ch. 9 above.

5 JEPHSON—E.P. pp. 475–480; PARKE pp. 506–507.

6 JEPHSON—E.P. pp. 477–478.

7 Stanley reprints a six-page selection of adulatory messages as an appendix to In Darkest Africa.

8 Tippu-Tib, summoned to present himself before the Consular Court, was furious at what he saw as another instance of Stanley's ingratitude and faithlessness. (SWANN pp. 173–174.) Stanley later withdrew his claim, and the matter was settled out of court after Tippu-Tib's return to Zanzibar with both parties agreeing to drop the dispute. (BRODE p. 236; GRAY, 1944.)

9 A feat of composition which, it must be admitted, impresses the present writer even more than the crossing of Africa.

10 JAMESON pp. 290–291.

11 PARKE p. 510.

12 The story was denied by Tippu-Tib (BRODE p. 235) and Assad Farran later retracted his accusations. Unfortunately, Assad Farran's retraction was so sweeping that it contradicted Jameson's admission. (See The Times for November 15, 1890.)

13 JEPHSON pp. 336–337.

14 JEPHSON pp. 363–364.

15 D.A. II p. 424.

16   Among the mail Stanley found waiting for him on his arrival at Msalala had been newspaper reports which indicated that rumours were already current in Europe (thanks to Assad Farran) of dark doings at Yambuya. Stanley replied with a despatch from Msalala dated August 31, 1889, in which he categorically exculpated the Rear Guard officers. This letter, besides defending Barttelot against the suggestion that he had been over-severe in his punishments, contains the assertion that: ". . . the horrible statement I have seen connected with the names of Major Barttelot and Jamieson (sic) . . . is simply inconceivable nonsense—a sensational canard." (See KELTIE pp. 160 ff.)

17   The last phrase may refer to Stanley's attempts to suppress Jameson's diary and personal papers, which he had appropriated and refused—no doubt from the worthiest motives—to restore to Jameson's family until forced to do so by the threat of legal action. The other "official reports" are presumably those of Bonny, while the mention of "affidavits" refers to the efforts of Assad Farran.

18   The idea was not, of course, Mackinnon's creation. It had originated with Gordon (hence the ill-fated Mackillop expedition) and had subsequently been advocated by Kirk and Holmwood in Zanzibar and by Emin himself.

19   This is clear from Felkin's defence of his action in his Introduction to SCHWEITZER. The letters from Emin to Felkin fully justify the interpretation Felkin put on them and would seem to be a more than adequate vindication of his action, besides being a valuable source of information regarding Emin's hopes and plans during the crucial years 1885–1887. Felkin also prints the agreement he signed on Emin's behalf, while Schweitzer (I pp. 309–311) prints letters from De Winton (as secretary of Mackinnon's company) and Felkin to Emin explaining the company's plans for Equatoria. Emin knew nothing of the Felkin agreement until his return to the Coast, by which time it was for all practical purposes a dead letter, since the chances of fruitful co-operation between Emin and Stanley (or the interests Stanley represented) had long ago receded into invisibility.

20   The Charter is printed as an appendix to MACDERMOTT, along with a number of other interesting documents relating to the history of the I.B.E.A.C.

21   J. Flint in History of East Africa Vol. I p. 361.

22   This distinguished diplomat was the son of the Rev. Joseph Wolff, the traveller and missionary, whose improbable adventures and amazing eccentricity have won him a unique position in the annals of nineteenth-century travel. (See his Mission to Bokhara, 1845, and Travels and Adventures, 1860.) In the Muslim world, calling himself the Grand Mullah of English-stan, Wolff achieved an enormous reputation both by the zeal with which he indulged his taste for learned theological disputation, and by his evident madness. He died in 1862.

23   "Curious"—because it should more logically have led to the occupation of Abyssinia, the Blue Nile being by far the more important component of the annual Egyptian flood. (On the diplomatic significance of Nile hydrology, see LANGER, pp. 102–108 and SANDERSON pp. 9–11.)

24 The establishment of the Witu Protectorate was, by almost any standards, a most dubious proceeding. The Sultan, the rascally Simba, was a declared outlaw and rebel against the Sultan of Zanzibar, whose territory he had no conceivable right to alienate. But the British negotiators of the 1886 agreement had meekly accepted the existence of this threatening beach-head on their northern flank and chosen coolly to ignore the violation of the Sultan's rights which it implied.

25 Jackson's frank comments on the slapdash way this expedition was recruited, organised, equipped and briefed, show the field organisation of the I.B.E.A. Company in a very poor light. Even the aims of the expedition appear to have been extremely ill-defined.

26 Though he missed this chance of glory, Swayne achieved a modest immortality elsewhere, and in a way he doubtless found far more congenial: an animal was named after him, *Swayne's Dik-Dik* (a small deer). A stuffed specimen is on display in the Natural History Museum.

27 A liberal scorn for certain niceties of civilised behaviour was a characteristic Peters shared with Stanley. But Peters, quite apart from the unscrupulousness of his annex-first-and-argue-later methods, earned an unsavoury reputation for his harsh treatment of the Africans, and this notoriety was possibly better-deserved in his case than it was in Stanley's. (Even Stanley's worst enemies never suggested that he *enjoyed* mistreating other human beings.) Jackson records that one of Peters' last acts before leaving Uganda was "publicly to hang his native mistress for having preferred the attentions of a native to his own". In 1892, while Commissioner for the Kilimanjaro district, Peters was indicted by a German judge for cruelty to the natives, and in 1898 was dismissed from his post for the same cause. Hitler called him a "model, if stern, colonial admini-strator". (MARSH and KINGSNORTH p. 223; *History of East Africa* Vol. I pp. 444–445, II p. 146.)

28 "Mr. Jackson is in the habit of marching very slowly," was Peters' comment when he heard that Jackson was coming into Uganda after him. He was right: Jackson did not arrive at Mwanga's until a month after his letter. (PETERS p. 432.)

29 It is odd on the face of it that Germany was prepared, under no apparent compulsion, to trade a gigantic slice of Africa for an asset so nearly invisible as a button-sized island in the North Sea. The explanation, apparently, is that Heligoland was considered indispensable to Germany's plans for naval expansion (a project particularly close to the new Kaiser's heart). The Kiel canal was at this time in the process of construction. Since one of its principal functions was to provide an easy outlet to the North Sea from Germany's Baltic bases, her strategists feared that British possession of Heligoland (covering the western outlet of the Canal) might jeopardise the whole scheme in time of war.

30 PETERS p. 557.

31 PETERS pp. 547–548.

32 And still maintain to the present day. (See Appendix III.)

33 An important factor in the calculations of both Selim and Fadl el-Mulla had been the ammunition left behind by Stanley, buried at Mazamboni's. Selim's men had dug it up after the Expedition's departure, but it had been seized from them by a raiding party from Fadl el-Mulla's group. This had left Selim in a dangerously weak position.

34 Details will be found in SANDERSON as part of a comprehensive and beauti-fully coherent account of the jockeyings between the colonial powers for control of the Upper Nile between 1882 and 1889. Some of the same ground has been covered by Collins in his *King Leopold, England and the Upper Nile, 1899–1901*, NEW HAVEN, Conn., and LONDON (Yale U.P.), 1968. For an account of the Belgian expeditions to the Bahr-el-Ghazal and Equatorial Provinces see Collins's earlier book, *The Southern Sudan*.

35 Sanderson argues that Salisbury's apparent acquiescence in Leopold's schemes sprang from a refusal to take Belgium seriously as a rival colonising power. The reality of the threat from Leopold to England's hegemony on the Upper Nile was not perceived until nearly two years after the launching of the Kerckhoven expedition. Salisbury at first accepted the Mackinnon treaty simply in order to get Mackinnon off his back during the delicate negotiations which led up to the 1890 agreement with Germany. When the news broke in England that a Belgian expedition had actually reached the Nile, there was consternation. (See SANDER-SON Ch. V, esp. pp. 90–97.)

36 The expedition consisted of 800 trained troops plus Zande auxiliaries. Among the European officers was William Hoffmann, late body servant to H. M. Stanley. Hoffmann remained in Equatoria until 1894 and after that continued in the Belgian service. Among his appointments was a term as Chef de Poste at Yambuya.

37 Emin's troops did not disappear from the notice of the world with their absorption into the Uganda garrisons. They had a last brief period of notoriety when—true to type, Stanley would have said—they mutinied against their new masters. After a year of intermittent fighting (September 1897–August 1898) they were defeated with the help of Indian troops brought up from Mombasa. It was not until the last remnants of the rebel forces had fled across Uganda's northern borders that the turbulent career of the army of Equatoria finally reached its term. (See THRUSTON, MACDONALD, LUGARD II.)

38 Even after the conquest of the Sudan and the death of the Khalifa, Arabi refused to surrender. With 3,000 followers he moved west into Dar Fur, where he sustained himself for a time in precarious independence by raiding into French Equatorial Africa. In 1902 the mutiny of his army deprived him of support, but he remained at large in Dar Fur until 1916 when he was murdered on the orders of the local Sultan. (COLLINS pp. 176–177; HILL.)

EPILOGUE

Why is it that I alone,
among all those I knew,
am still a rolling stone?

EMIN

When the Emin Relief Expedition was over and the dust had settled, the great days of Central African exploration had visibly reached their close; the era of colonial exploitation was just beginning. Of the handful of men whose journeys and whose labours had opened the heart of the continent and let in the world, few lived to make old bones and fewer still outlived their era. By the end of 1894, Burton, Speke, Grant, Baker, Gordon, Gessi, Livingstone, Mackay, Junker, Thomson and Cameron were all dead. And only one of these—Baker— had lived out his three score and ten.[1]

Among the young hopefuls who had set out with Stanley to the relief of Emin the mortality was even more dramatic. Jameson was thirty-two at his death, Barttelot only twenty-nine. And of the survivors, at least two—Jephson and Parke—never recovered from the ruinous expenditure of youth and energy that was involved in their walk across Africa. Parke died in 1893, aged thirty-six. Jephson survived until 1908, but his health was shattered. Stairs returned to Africa in 1891 at the head of a Belgian expedition to Katanga, only to die a year later on the way home. In the same year Nelson succumbed to dysentery while working in Kenya for the I.B.E.A.C. Even Stanley's magnificent physique had finally given way. The remainder of his life, though ornamented by a knighthood, assured fame, a brilliant marriage, and election to Parliament, was haunted by ill-health and the deaths of his friends. He died in 1904. It was Stanley's wish to be buried in Westminster Abbey next to Livingstone. He failed, however, to realise this last ambition in the face of opposition from the Dean— opposition which Stanley would certainly have made short work of had he been alive at the time. His remains lie in the village church- yard of Pirbright in Surrey under a massive monolith of Dartmoor granite inscribed:

HENRY MORTON STANLEY
BULA MATARI
1841–1904
AFRICA

His old enemy Tippu-Tib outlived him by one year.

The careers of Jameson, Barttelot, Jephson, Stairs and Parke began and ended with the Emin Relief Expedition. One happy exception to this rule—the case of Ward—therefore deserves to be recorded, if only to illuminate by means of contrast an otherwise gloomy picture. After Jameson had died in his arms at Bangala, Ward, who knew nothing of Stanley's return from the Lake, but had gathered from Jameson's papers the broad outlines of the disaster to the Rear Column, made his way back down the river to report these events to the Committee in London and ask for instructions. The Committee, also without news of Stanley, ordered Ward to return to Banalya, gather up the remnants of the Rear Column and bring them down to the coast. He set off once more up-river and learned *en route* of Stanley's re-union with the Rear Guard at Banalya. In the hope of being able to overtake the Expedition, Ward pressed on, but at Stanley Falls his hopes were once more dashed when Tippu-Tib informed him that Stanley and Emin had already left Equatoria and begun their march to the East Coast. Ward accordingly returned to Matadi, taking with him thirteen invalids from the Rear Guard who had been left at the Falls. It was now over a year since Barttelot had packed him off from Yambuya, and most of that time Ward had spent in fruitless and exhausting passages up and down the Congo. The energy and devotion he had shown in performing this lonely and unrewarding task are beyond praise. If his efforts achieved precisely nothing, the fault was certainly not his. The very fact that his journeys were, in the last analysis, pointless, renders even more admirable the uncomplaining loyalty he showed throughout. His feelings may be imagined, therefore, at finding on arrival at the coast, that his only reward was a slighting reference in one of Stanley's published despatches: "Ward has for the last year been rushing up and down the Congo like a shuttle in a loom." This mean ingratitude in the leader he so much admired, coming on top of Barttelot's accusations[2] and the final abandonment of the high hopes of adventure and achievement with which he had joined the Expedition, was a heavy blow. That Ward survived it unembittered bespeaks both resilience and magnanimity in his character. Nevertheless, he returned to England exhausted, and sick at heart at the miserable close to his five years' service on the Congo. In the months that followed, under Stanley's attacks on the professional conduct and private morals of the Rear Guard officers, Ward acted with a restraint which contrasted starkly with Stanley's own behaviour. When, after a long silence, Ward finally permitted himself to reply to Stanley's libels, he was no more successful than his colleagues (dead and living) had been in getting justice at the hands of their erstwhile employer. But his account of his experiences, the last to be published, won him a wide and sympathetic audience. After a spell of lecturing in England and America on his African adventures, Ward turned his energies and his talents into another field. Encouraged by a successful showing of his Congo sketches, he devoted himself seriously first to painting and then to sculpture. Between the years 1900 and 1914 he produced a series of bronze sculptures of African subjects which soon earned him notice as an artist of outstanding merit. Drawing on his memories of the Congo and on the deep sympathy he had always felt for the native African, Ward was able to inform his works with a combination of almost frightening realism and intense imaginative power. The Great War to End Civilisation put a stop to a career which might well have brought him to a position of lasting international repute. He served in France with the British Ambulance Committee and the Red Cross until the beginning of 1919. Then his health broke down and he died in the same year. After his death, his sculptures, together with the large collection of ethnographical material he had acquired during his Congo service, went to the Smithsonian Museum in Washington, where they can still be seen.

*   *   *

For Emin himself a fitting end was reserved. The outcast, the Wandering Jew as he once called himself, the man who had of his own choice spent the whole of his working life under an assumed name and an alien religion, cut off from family, home and friends, was to join the select band of African explorers who died with their boots on and their faces towards untravelled lands.

Left in the care of the German authorities at Bagamoyo after Stanley's departure, Emin made a rapid recovery from what had so nearly been a fatal accident. By the end of February 1891, though he still felt the after-effects of his fall in the shape of partial deafness, loss

381

of appetite and impaired balance, Emin already had arrangements in hand for renewing his scientific pursuits. He reopened the correspondence with his family that he had broken off at the time of his flight into Egypt fifteen years before, and redoubled that with his scientific contacts and with the numerous learned institutions which since his return had been pressing on him marks of recognition and favour. At the same time, through von Wissmann, he definitely committed himself to the German service, agreeing to lead a German expedition inland to the very regions from which Stanley had just with much ado extracted him. The terms of his original instructions, though vague in matters of detail, were explicit in intention:

> Your Excellency is to secure on behalf of Germany the territories situated south of and along the Victoria Nyanza Lake, from Kavirondo Bay (the north-east corner) and the countries between Victoria Nyanza and Tanganyika up to the Muta Nzige (Lake Edward) and Albert Nyanza, so as to frustrate England's attempts at gaining an influence in those territories. I consider that the extension of the line from . . . Kavirondo Bay to the north-west, up to the frontier of the Congo State, constitutes the Anglo-German frontier. Any extension warranted by circumstances, of the sphere of influences just described, would be regarded by me as redounding to Your Excellency's special merit.[3]

Emin's main target, therefore, was Uganda. Since the Anglo-German agreement was still some months in the future, Wissmann's opinion as to what the German-British frontier should be was as good as anybody's. The line he laid down in his letter of instructions was simply the projection of the existing Kilimanjaro line along the Nile from the north end of Lake Victoria to Lake Albert. Projected still further (to the boundary of the Congo State) it also took in a good piece of southern Equatoria. Thus Emin was about to be launched on the trail of the quarry which Stanley had just failed to bring down and which Peters, at the very moment these plans were being laid in Bagamoyo, had already, as he thought, brought to bay.

At the same time Emin was commissioned to do what he could in the way of showing the flag in the interior of the German sphere between Lake Tanganyika and the Coast. German power as yet reached no further inland than Mpwapwa, and though the rising of the Coast Arabs had, thanks to Wissmann, been crushed, nothing had yet been done to establish German authority inland, more particularly in the region of the Arab stronghold at Tabora. Wissmann therefore added to his instructions:

> When marching towards the Victoria Lake, Your Excellency will everywhere make known to the population that they are placed under German supremacy and protection. I request you to gain over and assist any well-disposed and suitable chiefs, and to break or undermine Arab influence as far as possible in all directions.

It is hard to gauge the extent of Emin's enthusiasm for, or commitment to, these imperialistic schemes. In the light of later events it is permissible to suppose that Emin consented to lead the Expedition simply because it offered a convenient means of continuing his researches and avoiding the obscure retirement he dreaded. Certainly, his sudden fervour of patriotism, being partly the product of disgust with Stanley and the English, and partly the response of his sensitive vanity to the notice that Germany was taking of him, cooled noticeably once these influences were removed by time and distance. The make-up of the caravan reflected Emin's divided interests. He took two assistants: the zoologist Franz Stuhlmann to co-operate with Emin in the scientific side of the Expedition; and Lt. Langheld in charge of the soldiery (fifty-four regulars—Sudanese, "Zulus",[4] and Zanzibaris; and fifty-odd irregular "Askaris" hired in Zanzibar). There were also three German N.C.O.s. The porters, nearly six hundred in number, were all armed, and the Expedition's equipment included a 3·5 cm Krupp quick-firing cannon.

Before leaving Bagamoyo, Emin installed his daughter Farida with her nurse in a house he had bought there. On April 26, 1890, the march began.

At Mpwapwa he met Peters hot-footing it in the opposite direction with the Uganda treaty burning a hole in his pocket. Emin greeted him with almost precisely the same words he had used to Stanley: "I do not know how I am to thank you for all you have done for me."[5] The two men discussed the political situation in the Lakes Region, especially Uganda, and debated Emin's future moves. On Peters' advice Emin decided to march first of all to Tabora. With that firmly under German control Emin would have largely neutralised Arab influence in the Lakes Region and would at the same time give himself a secure base for operations northwards into Uganda and, eventually, Equatoria.

They parted on excellent terms. While Peters pressed on to Baga-moyo and the shattering news that awaited him there, Emin accordingly made his way to Tabora and raised the German flag. He had no trouble with the Arabs, who agreed to accept German authority provided it was exercised through a Vali chosen from their own number salaried by the Germans. Emin did, however, have trouble with his own super-iors. He sent off a jubilant report announcing the annexation and asking for the instant despatch of fifty German flags ("thirty medium-sized ones and twenty large ones") only to be sharply ticked off for exceeding his instructions by going to Tabora at all.[6]

From this point on, there was a marked deterioration in Emin's relations with his employers. Despatches from the Reichskommissariat repeatedly complained of his failure to report his proceedings and of his ignoring his instructions, while Emin's reports consisted largely of complaints about inadequate equipment, instructions for the disposal of vast quantities of specimens that continued to pour back to the coast from wherever he happened to be, and demands for collecting materials and scientific literature. Both parties complained of a lack of response to their respective messages, so the root of the trouble might seem to lie in a simple failure of communication. But this was not the only cause of uncertainty and friction. After leaving Tabora Emin had turned north to the lower end of Lake Victoria and it was here, in the autumn of 1890, that he learned the terms of the Anglo-German treaty and the consequent demise of his hopes of annexing Uganda. The Treaty, by robbing the Expedition at a stroke of its main reason for being, left Emin's position awkwardly undefined, and his un-responsiveness to control made him a potential source of embarrass-ment to his superiors. Even so, the political aspect of his changed situation left Emin the Scientist serenely unruffled. Uganda might be barred to him, but there was no lack elsewhere of territories he had never visited and, hence, never collected in. His thoughts began to wander very far afield indeed.

In November 1890 Emin began building a station at Bukoba on the south-west shore of Lake Victoria, sited just south of the border separating the German and British spheres. In February the following year, when the station was well established, Emin again set off on his travels. He took Stuhlmann with him and left Langheld and half the soldiers behind to hold the fort. He gave out that his immediate aim was to tour the kingdom of Karagwe and secure the allegiance of its rulers to the German flag. But from the time of his leaving Bukoba Emin's motives and intentions are attended by a moving fog of mystery and confusion. Indeed, his subsequent movements are so puzzling as to have given rise in some observers to the conviction that Emin's reason had been adversely affected by the crack on the head he got from his fall at Bagamoyo.[7] He seems, though, to have had two plans in his mind at this time, and in his letters and reports refers now to one and now to the other, but characteristically always speaks of the one which is uppermost in his mind as if it were a settled thing. This makes his real intentions (if any) hard to establish, but is not madness.

The first plan was, after leaving Karagwe, to turn south through Ruanda (still totally unexplored) to Lake Tanganyika, and from there make his way back to the coast. Alternatively, he might turn north from Karagwe and march to Lake Albert via Lake Edward. From there he would go west into Monbuttu and make for what he called "the hinterland of the Cameroons", which he would then take possession of in the name of Germany. The first of these schemes was reasonable enough: it would give Emin a chance to show the flag in the interior of the German Protectorate without either leaving German territory or exceeding the scope of his instructions; at the same time he would be able to explore a portion of Africa in which no European had as yet set foot—a notion which had an obvious appeal for Emin as a scientist and was further justified by its political utility. The second scheme, on the other hand, was so wildly visionary that, without the clear evidence of Emin's diaries and letters to the contrary, it almost justifies the supposition that he had lost his reason. It is true that the phrase "hinterland of the Cameroons" is sufficiently vague to admit of a wide interpretation. In all probability, though, Emin had in mind the area south and west of Lake Chad, a distance of not less than fifteen hundred miles in a straight line from Lake Albert. Without lavish equipment and careful preparation—neither of which advantages Emin enjoyed—such an undertaking was of staggering difficulty, quite apart from the fact that only the most elastic imagination could suppose it to be comprehended in Emin's original instructions. ("Any extension . . . of the sphere of influences just described, would be regarded by me as redounding to Your Excellency's special merit. . . .")

Which of these plans was uppermost in Emin's mind when he left

Bukoba, it is impossible to say. Stuhlmann, Emin's only companion, does not appear to have known. Very probably Emin himself did not know but, typically, was content to wait until events should decide the question for him. The decision point would not come until Emin had passed through Karagwe and reached Lake Edward; then he must either turn south into Ruanda or north to Lake Albert. But in a sense, when Emin reached the southern end of Lake Edward in May 1891, the die had already been cast. The Lake lay outside the borders of the German Protectorate, and merely by going there Emin had automatically renounced any claim to official status for his Expedition. Henceforth he was a private individual.[8]

As if to underline the point, Emin simply ignored an order from Wissmann which reached him on April 4, ordering him to return at once to the coast.

Thus, without troubling himself to explain his intentions, Emin severed, as if by inadvertence, the links which bound him to the service of the Reichskommissariat. And having gone so far, it was logical (if that is not too strong a word) that he should choose, on leaving Karagwe, to pursue the nebulous notion of empire-building in the Cameroons and so enlarge the distance between himself and the Rubicon he had just crossed. Two things drew him northwards: the desire to visit parts of Africa he had never seen—the savannahs between the Sahara and the Great Forest; and the desire to revisit his old province and the people he had left behind there. A chance meeting with some Manyuema ivory-hunters from the north brought him news of his old soldiers: a group described as "Wa-turki" were said to have been involved in fighting to the south of Lake Albert. Emin took this as confirmation that at least some of the Equatorial troops were still in existence as an armed body. He made up his mind. He would march to Lake Albert, enroll the Equatorial troops under the Expedition's flag, and with their aid penetrate westwards to Lake Chad and take possession of that country in the name of the Kaiser and the interests of science.[9]

The caravan moved north along the flanks of Ruwenzori and down the valley of the Semliki. In July 1891, in the neighbourhood of Mazamboni's, he made contact with Selim Bey. Here Emin's attempt to put into execution his weird and visionary scheme began and ended; he was not destined ever to come within a thousand miles of the "hinterland of the Cameroons".

RESCUED!

13 RESCUED! Cartoon from Punch, December 14, 1889

BETWEEN THE QUICK AND THE DEAD.

14 (i) Justice puzzled by the conflicting demands of the living and the dead—Punch's comment on the Stanley-Barttelot controversy, November 22, 1890

14 (ii) Stanley's tomb in the village churchyard at Pirbright

At the time of Emin's arrival the position of Selim and his followers was shaky and getting worse. Their numbers were small; they had had losses from fighting and disease, and had not yet received the large reinforcement that was shortly to reach them in the form of deserters from Fadl el-Mulla's band. Relations with the natives of the plateau were uncertain. Kabba Rega's banassura were still active round the south of the Lake, and the Manyuema of the Aruwimi were encroaching steadily on the country both north and south of the Semliki valley. Most of Selim's people were now reduced to wearing roughly-dressed cow-hides in place of their cotton uniforms. Ammunition was a continual worry. There was smallpox about. Yet they clung doggedly to whatever they could preserve of the old order and to their loyalty to the flag they served under. Lugard, whose column reached Kavalli's only a few months after Emin's, wrote of what he found there, with something like admiration:

> Selim, and the few who had arrived first with him, had now been here over two years. They had brought cotton-seeds with them, and planted and gathered the produce of the fields, and in their own rough looms had woven the cloth, from which they made the coats and trousers which they wore. A coinage yet circulated among them, and the Egyptian clerks still wrote the official despatches sent by Selim to his out-stations and subordinate officers. In short, among all the outward savagery of soldiers dressed in hides, of naked women, and grass huts, there was a noticeable—almost pathetic—attempt to maintain the status they claimed as soldiers of a civilised government.[10]

Selim's band hailed Emin's arrival with joy, supposing the Expedition to be a relief party sent by the Khedive. Joy turned to dismay when the hope proved false. And when Emin announced that he had switched his allegiance from Egypt to Germany and invited Selim and his men to do the same, the response was an indignant—even contemptuous—refusal from both Selim and the majority of his people. The best Emin could do was to enlist twenty-nine men (with the inevitable complement of women and children—one hundred and fifty-three in the present case) for the march to the west.[11]

On August 20, 1891, the caravan set out. Numerically it was a strong party, four hundred and ninety-four all told,[12] but over half were women and children, and as a group it had neither cohesion nor discipline. These weaknesses might have been compensated by strong and dynamic leadership and a clearly defined goal: Emin could offer neither. Disaster overtook the Expedition piecemeal.

They struck due north from Mazamboni's towards the Nile–Congo watershed. This route took them through a spur of the Great Forest lying along the headwaters of the Ituri River. Emin, whose experience hitherto had mainly been of swamp and scrub lands, was vastly pleased by this new environment. Whatever the forest yielded of flora and fauna, everything from pygmies to pygmy shrews, was subjected by Stuhlmann and himself to the same meticulous and delighted scrutiny, measured, recorded, annotated, shot, skinned, photographed, pressed, pickled or stuffed. The rest of the caravan—soldiers, porters and camp-followers—unable to share these specialised pleasures, was left with little or nothing to write home about and all of it bad. All the dangers, difficulties and discomforts of forest travel, which had so nearly wrecked Stanley's Expedition, now combined to play havoc with Emin's unwieldy caravan. Guides deserted or led him astray. There was a perpetual shortage of food. The forest dwellers lurked about the fringes of the column, peppered its camps with arrows and speared stragglers on the march. The Sudanese decamped. The porters mutinied. The position was hopeless.

Some three weeks after it had begun, the great trek to the Cameroons straggled miserably to a stop. Emin reluctantly gave the order (permission is perhaps the more exact term) to turn south. On November 12 the disorganised remnants of the Expedition were back at Mazamboni's.

During Emin's absence Lugard had arrived at Selim's station. He found there, in addition to Selim and his original few hundred people, the horde of Wadelai men who had deserted from Fadi el-Mulla's camp after the battle with the Mahdi-ists at Wadelai. This sudden and radical increase in his ration strength was as much of a headache to Selim as his numerical weakness had been before. Among the newcomers, women, children and slaves—as always—outnumbered the fighting men by more than ten to one. It is, therefore, reasonable to suppose that the problem of feeding, housing, clothing, and protecting this locust-swarm of supernumeraries weighed heavily in Selim's decision to enroll his entire force under Lugard's flag.[13] At the beginning of October the Equatorials' station was abandoned and Lugard headed south-east for Uganda at the head of a vast caravan nearly nine thousand strong.

In this way, almost overnight, without fuss, almost casually, the evacuation of Equatoria became a fact.

Emin, returning to Mazamboni's a month later and hearing that Selim was gone, was faced with the realisation that any hopes he may still have had of marching to the Cameroons at the head of his old soldiers were gone likewise. His fortunes and his prospects were now equally at a low ebb. His expedition, his status vis-à-vis his employers, his plans, his health—all were in ruins. Where could he now turn? He could neither stay where he was, nor go on. Only one way seemed open to him—to return to the coast with his tail between his legs. But to return under such conditions, with failure behind him and disgrace and ridicule ahead, was, for a man of Emin's touchy pride, the most difficult course of all. It would require either great moral courage or else the suicidal fatalism born of complete despair. The act of disobedience Emin had committed the previous April in ignoring Wissmann's order to return was of the kind that can only be justified if it leads to some accomplishment so brilliant as to confound reproach. But Emin did not have the Nelson touch. He did not even have the Gordon touch, which makes of wrong-headedness heroism. His position was unenviable.

Worse was to come. Fortune, choosing her moment, now dealt him another shrewd stroke: smallpox broke out among his people. They began to die daily by handfuls. It seemed, indeed it was, the last straw. Yet, paradoxically, it was this that saved Emin from the agonising prospect of a return to civilisation and the ignominious termination of his career as a colonial administrator.

On the appearance of the disease Mazamboni and his people disappeared into the bush like smoke, leaving Emin and his followers alone and without resource. Unless something were done quickly to save at least a portion of his people, Emin was faced with the prospect of looking on helplessly while the epidemic reduced his Expedition to nothing. He decided to try and check the spread of the smallpox by separating the sick from those still uninfected. He therefore instructed Stuhlmann to take all the healthy people and the Expedition's baggage and remove them several days' journey to the south. Emin himself would remain behind to tend the sick and rejoin Stuhlmann when the disease had burned itself out. If, however, Emin had not overtaken him within a certain time, Stuhlmann was to make his way back to Bukoba without waiting for further orders.

Stuhlmann protested energetically against the proposed separation.

He pointed out that the "healthy" group would certainly carry the contagion with it, and that Emin, if left behind practically alone and without goods, was placing himself in a position of suicidal difficulty. Emin finally overcame Stuhlmann's loyal disobedience only by pulling rank and presenting him with a formal written order:[14]

> In view of the spread of small-pox and the decrease of available provisions in this country, I request Your Honour forthwith to take all the healthy porters and soldiers, together with the goods belonging to the expedition, and to proceed in the first instance to Tenge-Tenge (i.e. the southern Semliki valley). I myself shall remain here with the sick, their dependents, and the few guards you will leave me, until the sick recover. For use meantime you will please also leave two cases of cloth, some coloured cloth as presents for the chiefs on the route, a case of ammunition, and some powder for the muzzle-loaders.
>
> If within a month of your march no news is to hand from me, you will endeavour without delay to reach Bukoba station without awaiting my caravan.
>
> > Dr. Emin.
> > Commander of the Expedition.[15]

Thirty-eight men, and a corresponding proportion of the women and children, remained behind with Emin.[16] The remainder marched with Stuhlmann. The parting took place on December 10, 1891. It was understood between the two men that the chances of their meeting again were small (though Stuhlmann records that, on their last evening together, "tranken wir auf ein baldiges Wiedersehen ein Glas Portwein"). Stuhlmann took with him Emin's last letter to his sister. It ended with the words:

> My people are stricken with small-pox. Dr. Stuhlmann is leaving with such as are healthy, and is taking this letter. God bless you all. Half blind as I am, it would be useless to write to me at once, so please wait until you hear from me again.
>
> > Your brother,
> > Emin.

After Stuhlmann's departure Emin remained at Mazamboni's, ministering as best he could to his sick people, for almost six months.

By the end of that time Stuhlmann, following his orders, was long gone back to Bukoba and the coast, taking with him the richest harvest of scientific data that had ever been gathered by an African expedition. What those six months at Mazamboni's must have meant to Emin— oppressed by the knowledge of his failure, troubled by failing health and surrounded by the dying and the dead—can only be guessed at.[17]

When the disease had burnt itself out, he was left with a handful of followers, perhaps a score of loads (his personal baggage), and the problem of where to go next. The idea of returning to Bukoba or Bagamoyo, even had it been practical for such a small group and one so ill-furnished, was repugnant to Emin for reasons already mentioned and still valid. He therefore decided to make not for the East but for the West Coast. This plan offered several advantages: it would take him through regions he had not yet visited and in which he could still hope, by assiduous collecting and observation, to add something to the lustre of his scientific reputation before the return to civilisation put an end (as it must, in view of his failing health and sight) to his career in the field. At the same time he could compensate for the smallness of his party by attaching himself, over at least part of the route, to the only organised body in existence between Lake Albert and the Congo— the Manyuema ivory-hunters.

Since 1887, Kilonga-Longa's bands, following in Stanley's track, had pushed east to the edge of the Forest and beyond. Kilonga-Longa's lieutenant Ismaili, whose notions of hospitality had been so nearly fatal to Nelson and Parke during their stay at Ipoto, now commanded his own station near the site of Fort Bodo.

On May 28, 1892, after lengthy haggling with the Manyuema about the hire of porters, Emin and his party left Mazamboni's for Ismaili's station. From here, escorted by Ismaili in person, Emin re-traced Stanley's old route as far as Ipoto, which he reached on June 18. He then turned south-west along the track which led from the Arab stations on the Upper Aruwimi to their main strongholds on the Congo.

The sparse and jumbled notes which Emin entered in his diary during this period are the work of a man who feels his time and his strength to be running out.

30 June 1892. Ipoto. Feet very much swollen, right hand incapacitated for work, eyesight half or three parts gone; is life worth living? Kilonga came to look at pictures and Shass (*alphabetic characters*);

I asked him to come again, as I am ill. Some of my people have gone to the Arabs at Tenge-Tenge, to get some gunpowder in exchange for ivory. Muranguana sends manioc, two green pumpkins, whole rice; he is the most sensible of them all. Ismaili's wife is ill; he himself not to be seen. My people have shot various birds for me. Here in the hut I found a small snake, and a red-nosed rat with two young. For more than a week we have had nothing but sweet potatoes and watery rice—and then I am to get well!

1st August. (Leaving Ipoto.) Ready early; two loads taken up. The usual trouble about porters, ending in a razzia; women taken, put in irons, loads distributed. No one about but Ismaili. Marched at 8.48; Ismaili to follow with seven loads. . . .

3rd September. (On the march.) Four of my people decamped! At 6.10 a.m. arrived at the river Bierna. Water lower, breast high as we waded through. At 6.36 started from opposite bank. To the left we saw an enormous elephant's skull without tusks. Awful quagmire; drier only at the first hill, many winding rivulets to cross three or four times. Old clearings. First the country of the Watikalimaia up to the second clearing; then country of the Watikoakibie, chief Bunda, whose beautiful but abandoned grove we passed in an open clearing at 10.46. The people march well in spite of the mire; hunger impels them all. At 12.30 Utikvatibie camp, also named Kituka after a Manyuema tribe formerly settled here. Rice! Eight elephants on the way. A lot of diospyros fruit. . . . In clearing colonies of weaver birds: Pl. castamen fasillo? It is now half past two. A good many large huts here. Rice field. . . .[18]

These notes show that despite fatigue, confusion, disillusion, and consciousness of his failing powers, the habit of precise and meticulous observation stayed with Emin until the last. And he could still inject a note of jubilation into such an entry as:

9th May—Caught a red mouse at last!

On October 12, 1892, Emin and his party, still accompanied by Ismaili, arrived at the station called, after its chief, Kinena.[19] In his diary for that day he wrote:

Forest hilly, a good many pools. Huts immediately. At 9.15 Kinena station on the Maluma brook. Nasty dark house. . . . Halt here for some days. I hope "we" will do some collecting.

Kinena, whom Emin calls "a Nyamwesi slave of Said bin Abed" (one of the biggest names among the Arabs of the interior), was immediately subject to the orders of one Kibonge whose headquarters lay on the Congo some 100 miles away to the south-west. The halt at Kinena's was caused by the necessity of applying to Kibonge for permission to proceed. Accordingly, Ismaili and another man named Mamba were sent ahead with messages to Kibonge. In due course Mamba returned with a letter from Kibonge to Emin containing the expected *laisser passer*. Ten minutes later Ismaili returned independently bearing a second letter: this one was addressed to Kinena and contained orders to have Emin killed.

Ismaili later gave the following account of what happened next:[20]

On the verandah of the chief's house Emin Pasha was seated, surrounded by a few of his soldiers. He was writing at his table, and many birds and bugs were scattered around. These he had caught coming from the Aruwimi. The first letter, which Mamba had brought, was in front of him; and he was laughing, and seemed in cheerful spirits at the thought of leaving next morning for Kibonge. Kinena came up with a few men who were carrying guns. Kinena had in his hand the letter which I had given him. He stopped near the Pasha and began reading to himself. When he had finished he said: "Pasha, as you are leaving tomorrow for a twelve days' march, don't you think you had better send your men into the plantations, and get bananas, manioc, and peanuts for the long march which you have before you? Tell your men to get all they wish; and I hope that you won't think of paying for them, as it is my present to you, and is in return for the many little things which you have given me and my women since you have been my guest." The Pasha looked up and thanked Kinena very much. He then told one of his orderlies to have the bugler call the men, which was done.

When they arrived, Kinena said: "Tell the men to leave their arms on the side of the veranda, because if they go into the plantations carrying guns, the women working there will become frightened and run away." Thereupon Emin's men, numbering thirty or forty, placed their guns on the veranda and departed. The plantations were an hour's walk from the house. During the time it took to go to the plantations Kinena talked to Emin, expressing his regret at his

393

departure. Mamba and I were standing next to the Pasha, and at a sign from the chief we seized him by the arms as he was sitting in his chair. He turned, and asked what we meant. Kinena looked at him, and said, "Pasha, you have got to die." Emin turned, and exclaimed rather angrily: "What do you mean? Is this a joke? What do you mean by seizing me in this manner? What are you talking about my dying for? Who are you that you can give orders for a man to die?" Kinena replied: "I do not give the orders. I receive them from Kibonge, who is my chief; and when Kibonge gives an order to me, I obey it."

Three of Kinena's men came and assisted us in holding Emin, who was struggling to free himself and to get at his revolver lying on the table; but his efforts were fruitless, and we forced him back into his chair. Then Emin told Kinena that it was all a mistake, as he had just received a letter from Kibonge that morning saying that he should have safe-conduct to his village, and that the letter was on his table in front of him. Kinena replied, "Pasha, you read Arabic, don't you?"

"Yes."

"Then read this," holding the second letter close to Emin's eyes as the Pasha was nearly blind.

Emin read the letter, and saw that it was true. Drawing a long breath, he turned and said: "Well, you may kill me, but don't think that I am the only white man in this country. There are many others who will be willing to avenge my death: and let me tell you that in less than two years from now there won't be an Arab left in the entire country held by your people."

Emin showed no sign of fear, but—

... when he spoke of having care taken of his daughter, two years of age, he trembled slightly. He said: "My child is not bad; she is good. Send her to Said bin Abed at Kibonge, and ask him to look out for her."[21]

At a sign from Kinena, the Pasha was lifted out of his chair, and thrown flat on his back. One man held each leg, and I held his head, while Mamba cut his throat. . . . Emin made no effort at resistance. His head was drawn back until the skin across his throat was tight, and with one movement of the knife, Mamba cut the head half off. The blood spurted over us and the Pasha was dead.

After the murder, Emin's headless and naked body was thrown into the bush. His head, together with—

> . . . his trunks and boxes were sent to Kibonge; his cloth was distributed among Kinena's people. The soldiers who were in the plantation were made prisoners, and all of them are slaves now, and with Kibonge. . . .

The motive for Emin's murder was, and remains, a matter of some doubt. It was suggested at the time that the killing was an act of vengeance for Emin's attack, two years earlier, on an Arab slavers' village south of Lake Victoria. It is more probable, however, that Emin was simply a victim of the general deterioration in relations between Europeans and Arabs in Central Africa. The first clashes had already come—the attack on Stanley Falls, and the rising of the Coast Arabs recently suppressed by von Wissmann. The last round, which saw the elimination by the Belgians of the Arab strongholds on the Upper Congo, was, in late 1892, just getting under way. It was Emin's misfortune to have blundered myopically onto the battlefield at the very outbreak of hostilities and so to have earned the distinction of becoming the first casualty of the engagement.

Both of Kinena's superiors—Said bin Abed and Kibonge—were captured by the Belgians during their campaigns on the Congo and Aruwimi rivers in 1893. They were charged with instigating Emin's murder, court-martialled and shot. In the same year, the belongings that Emin had with him at his death, including his journals and papers, were recovered in two instalments when the Belgian forces stormed Nyangwe and Kasongo. Among these possessions was found a Koran that had been given to Emin by Gordon.[22]

The last entry in Emin's diary, under October 23, 1892, was a meteorological observation:

> *Das barometer steigt schnell.* The barometer is rising fast.

An epitaph, of a kind.

NOTES AND REFERENCES

EPILOGUE

1   For those who like figures to their facts, the average age at death of the remaining ten works out at 51·4.

2   Ward refused, to the end of his life, to defend himself against Barttelot's accusations, on the ground that Barttelot was no longer alive to speak for himself.

3   As communicated to Schweitzer by Wissmann, and qu. SCHWEITZER II p. 41.

4   Wangoni from the neighbourhood of Lake Nyasa.

5   To Stanley: "I really do not know how to express my thanks to you."

6   Wissmann's intention had been to send another agent, the trader Charles H. Stokes, to occupy Tabora. (SCHWEITZER II p. 95). Stokes was a colourful, not to say technicolour figure, who played a significant part in the opening up of East Africa. An Irishman, he had come out as part of the Uganda mission in the 70s but had then turned trader, married a chief's daughter of the Wanyamwesi, and established his headquarters at Usonga, between Tabora and Msalala. His Wanyamwesi connections were of the greatest use to him, this tribe being generally acknowledged the best porters in East Africa. In 1891 he upset the British by trying to run guns into Uganda, and in 1895 he was hanged by the Belgians for doing the same thing on the Congo. (On Stokes's death, which had the makings of an international incident, see JACKSON pp. 81–84; C.8276; *Biographie Coloniale Belge* under "Lothaire".)

7   See, for example, STIGAND, pp. 192–193.

8   In a strict sense, as Schweitzer points out (II p. 152), he was never anything but. Official confirmation of his appointment had not arrived when Emin left Bagamoyo, and when it did arrive there, never caught up with him. Emin wrote from Bukoba: 'I am still to this day in the remarkable position of leading a German expedition without knowing whether I hold an official appointment at all, and whether or not I am to draw any salary . . . This is a most comical position and my English friends would think me mad if they heard of it.'

9   STUHLMANN pp. 253–256.

10   LUGARD II p. 218.

11   It is not clear whether Emin exposed to his potential recruits the full scope of his planned trans-African ramble. According to the report based on statements made by some of Selim's people who later reached Cairo, Emin merely talked of

"exploring the country to the west and north-west". (See *The Times*, July 14, 1892.) Schweitzer offers no information on the point.

12 Emin's original column: men 177; women 96; children 39. Equatorials: men 29; women 72; children 81. (Figures from SCHWEITZER II p. 246, quoting Emin.)

13 Lugard, who was much impressed by the dogged loyalty of Selim and his men to the Khedive, makes it clear that Selim's decision was not made without considerable soul-searching. The Equatorials were only persuaded to enter the British service on the understanding (a) that the change of allegiance was provisional and would not become binding unless and until it was ratified by the Khedive personally; (b) that the British would intercede with the Khedive on behalf of Selim's men and attempt to secure a pardon for their previous disloyalty to Emin. A feeling that the British had not carried out the second stipulation, plus indignation at their rejection by the Khedive, later played an important part in stimulating the mutiny of the Equatorials in Uganda. (See LUGARD—esp. II pp. 210–215—and MACDONALD).

14 STUHLMANN pp. 603–607.

15 SCHWEITZER II p. 272. A fascimile of the original appears in STUHLMANN at p. 604.

16 Emin later sent 17 of his 38 to rejoin Stuhlmann's party. (STUHLMANN p. 606.)

17 The short remainder of Emin's life, after his parting with Stuhlmann, is very poorly documented. His correspondence had, of necessity, ceased. He continued to keep his diary and record his scientific observations. This journal and Emin's other papers from this period were recovered after his death and were available to Schweitzer when he wrote his biography of Emin. Later, all Emin's diaries passed to Stuhlmann who edited them for publication. Four volumes appeared, covering the years 1875–1889. (A fifth volume, numbered VI in the series, also appeared, containing Emin's zoological notes and ornithological correspondence.) But the fifth volume of diaries, covering the years 1890–1892 (i.e. Emin's last expedition up to his death) never appeared. After Stuhlmann's death in 1928 the original diary disappeared and was supposed lost until re-located recently in the Hamburg city archives. A photostat copy of the two notebooks in which the diary was written is now in the possession of the finder, Mr. D. H. Simpson, Librarian of the Royal Commonwealth Society and author of *A bibliography of Emin Pasha*. Unfortunately the quality of the copy is poor and the handwriting is so minute that it can only be read with a powerful magnifying glass. It is much to be hoped that in the near future some competent body will undertake to commission the editing of this important document.

18 SCHWEITZER II p. 298.

19 Station built by Kilonga-Longa's men on their way from the Congo to the Aruwimi in 1886. (See above, Ch. 4.)

20 In April 1894 Ismaili and Mamba were arrested at Kasongo by the Belgian

397

commander Dhanis after his defeat of the Arabs led by Tippu-Tib's son
Sefu. Before being hanged, Ismaili and Mamba were interrogated by an American
named Mohun, an officer in the Belgian service, to whom Ismaili made the
confession which follows.

21 The child in question was not, of course, Farida. According to Mohun:
"A copper-coloured native woman of the Equatorial Provinces, who had been his
(Emin's) companion ever since he left the East Coast, and his two-year-old
daughter, who is of yellow complexion, are now at Kibonge, and are being
cared for by the officers of the post. When the child arrives at the proper age
she will be placed in a mission school, at the expense of the Congo Free State,
where her education will be assured."

22 STUHLMANN p. 830.

APPENDIX I

DOCUMENTS

Contents:

1. Emin to the Uganda Missionaries. (In English)

Dated: October 22, 1885.

SIR—

Two and a half years are past since the last steamer left for Khartoum. During all this time we never heard a single word from our government, nor had we any intercourse whatever with the civilised world. The Bahr el Ghazal province has been overwhelmed by the Danagla mob; my poor friend Lupton, the governor, has been betrayed by his people and forced to surrender. Our province has been attacked repeatedly and we have had to undergo very severe losses in men and arms. At last the Danagla retired after having received a severe lesson at Makraka. Now the Bari and Dinka tribes have revolted and I do not know what has to happen if the revolt spreads over the land. Our ammunition runs very short; our men are few; we have barely anything to eat; from Khartoum, where probably they believe me dead, no help comes. It is therefore that I venture to address you with a request to inform immediately your Consul-General at Zanzibar of our position. He will be good enough to insist to whom it concerns that help is speedily afforded to ourselves, be it by way of Khartoum or by way of Zanzibar. If steamers should be sent up from Khartoum it should be known that our Shambe and Bor stations have been destroyed by the negroes, and that our forces are now concentrated on the river line from Lado to Wadelai. Twice I have tried to write to you by other ways; my letters never reached you. So I forward this letter in two copies; one by means of King Kabrega, who kindly sent me his men with some clothes and provisions, and the other by means of the Zanzibar merchants Abder-Rahman and Masudi, my old Uganda acquaintances. Be good enough to let me have the answer by the bearer of this letter. . . . Please inform likewise your consul that Dr. Junker and Sgr. Casati, the explorers, are in our country and well. If you can spare some old newspaper you will greatly oblige me by sending it. From April 1883 we have not heard so much as a word about what has happened in the Sudan, nor in Egypt and Europe. Should you be able to forward some letters of ours—official and private—to Zanzibar, be kind enough to tell me. I shall send them at once.

Accept, Sir. . . . &c.

(Emin wrote four copies of this letter, two in English and two in French. Two separate packets, each containing one copy of the English version and one of the French, were despatched to Uganda by different routes.) See Uganda Journal XXVII–i, 1963.

2. The Mahdi to Keremallah reporting the fall of Khartoum and the death of Gordon. (Translation)

Dated: January 29, 1885.

(Keremallah sent a copy of this letter to Emin on April 28, 1885. Emin passed it on to Mackay, Mackay to Holmwood in Zanzibar, and Holmwood to Lord Iddesleigh, who received it on November 22, 1886.)

From the miserable Mahomed Ahmed, who is called El Mahdi, to his miserable Wali, Keremalla-el-Sheikh.

After praises to Almighty God—

From the poor slave of God, Mahomed El Mahdi-bin-Abdullah, to his friend and his Governor, Keremalla-bin-Sheikh Mahomed, God grant him, &c. I present to you excellent salaams, &c. Then I inform you, O my dear friend, that according to the fulfilled promise of God, the city of Khartoum was entered by the help of God on the 26th January, 1885, at the instant of daybreak, through the helpers of our religion, who were ready, and jumped over the ditch acting upon the command of the Lord of the whole world; it was a quarter of an hour or less that they came upon the enemies of God, their cutting off even from the beginning to the end of them, and the surrounding of them, notwithstanding they were strong in their arms of strength. From the commencement they fled away from before the troops of God, and though thinking to obtain safety by entering enclosures and shutting the doors, they were met face to face, and hewn with swords or stabbed with spears until their cries were terrible, and they were cut to pieces at once there upon the ground, and then the troops of God fell upon the rest of the people who had shut the doors fearing the same fate, who were taken up and killed properly, and there were none left remaining of them but little children and free slaves.

But as to the enemy of God, Gordon, though we had warned him and talked kindly to him that he might return to God, yet he never did so, because his miserable state had been fore-ordained, and also the access of his foolishness, before his fate was ended, and he was sorry for the sins he had sown in this world; and he was removed by God to the place of His wrath, which is a bad place to remain in.

The end of this guilty people is that they were cut off, which, thanks to God befalls those who are to receive fire as their reward, whilst light is reserved for those who shall receive Heaven as their dwelling-place.

Then he began to bless himself and his people in prayer. There were ten persons only of our people who were killed in this holy strife for the conquest of Khartoum, and the rest of our people neither received wound nor hurt.

All has happened by the Providence of God, &c. And we bow our heads in thanks to God for the help we have received from Him. May you also do so. Bow the head to God, and thank his holy name.

(This version of the Mahdi's letter is taken from C.5601, No. 7. The version printed by Wauters (pp. 90–91) exhibits a number of variations, most of which can be accounted for by differences of translation.)

3. Nubar Pasha to Emin. (Translation)

Dated: Cairo, May 27, 1885.
Received: February 26, 1886.

To EMIN PASHA, Commandant of Gondokoro—

The seditious movement in the Soudan compels the Government of His Highness to abandon this territory. Consequently we cannot send you any assistance. On the other hand, we do not know the exact circumstances in which you and your garrisons at present may be. Nor can we give you instructions as to the course to be adopted, and if we contemplated asking you to furnish us with a report on the state of affairs, with a view to making it the basis of our instructions, it would take far too long, and the loss of time might be prejudicial to you.

The object of this letter, which you will receive via Zanzibar by the intermediary of Her Britannic Majesty's Consul-General at Zanzibar, Sir John Kirk, is to leave you unlimited freedom of action. If you consider it safer for yourself and your garrison to withdraw and return to Egypt, Sir John Kirk, as well as the Sultan of Zanzibar, would write to the chiefs of the various negro tribes on the road, and use every care to facilitate your retreat.

You are hereby empowered to raise funds by drawing bills on Sir John Kirk. I repeat that you have *carte blanche* to do the best for yourself and the garrisons. We may inform you that the only road you can take, if you decide to leave Gondokoro, is that of Zanzibar. As soon as your decision is arrived at, please let me know.

The President of Council,

NUBAR PASHA.

P.S. Sir John Kirk will also write to apprise you of the ways and means he could endeavour to employ in order to facilitate the withdrawal of your garrisons on all sides.

15 (i) EMIN, in the uniform
of the German
Colonial Service

A LITTLE PARTY IN EAST AFRICA ONLY GOING TO COLLECT A FEW
BUTTERFLIES AND FLOWERS FOR THE DEAR KAISER, THAT IS ALL!!

"We came very near to having Kilima-Njaro attached to the British Empire, only the
German Emperor said he would very much like it, because he was so fond of the *flora* and
fauna of the place . . . Would the English have expected to get any territory on account
of their great interest in the *flora* and *fauna* here."—*Stanley speaking at Chamber of
Commerce, May 21.*

15 (ii) Cartoon from
Punch (May 31, 1890)
commenting on Emin's
expedition for the Germans

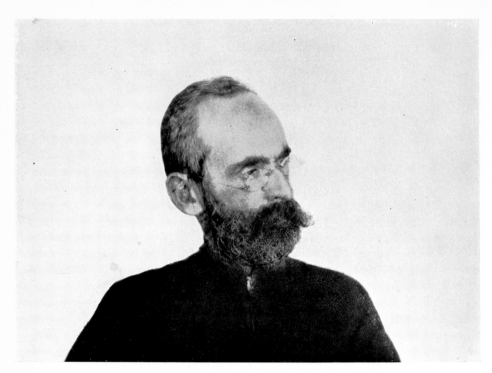

16 (i) EMIN. Photograph taken at Bukoba on
December 9, 1890

16 (ii) EMIN on the march west of Lake Albert

4. Emin to R. W. Felkin.

(The extracts which follow have been chosen to illustrate the development of Emin's thinking, during the years 1885–1887, about his own future and that of his Province. They are taken from the letters which Felkin printed in his introduction to Schweitzer's Emin Pasha in order to justify his action in signing, in Emin's name, an agreement with the I.B.E.A.C.)

(i) From letter dated December 31, 1885.

Naturally I have been compelled by the events which have happened to give up our most distant stations and to concentrate my few soldiers to the river banks, still in the hope that our Government will come to help us. In this, however, I have made a mistake, it appears, for since the month of April, 1882, I have received no kind of news from the north. The people in Khartoum have not acted well towards us. Before they evacuated Fashoda, they ought to have remembered that Government officials were living here who had performed their duty, and had certainly not deserved to be left to their fate without more ado. Even if it were the intention of the Government to deliver us over to our fate, the least they could have done would have been to release us from our duties. We should then have known that we were considered to have become valueless. . . .

As to my future plans, I intend to hold this country as long as ever it is possible. I hope, when our letters arrive in Egypt in seven or eight months, to receive an answer either via Khartoum or by Zanzibar. If the Egyptian Government still exists in the Soudan, we naturally expect them to send us help. If, however, the Soudan has been evacuated, we shall all go towards the south. I will then send the whole of the Egyptian and Khartoum officials via Uganda or Karagwe to Zanzibar, but shall remain myself, and my negroes, either at Kabrega's or in Uganda until the Government has informed me as to their wishes, and until I know that the people committed to my care are in safety. . . .

(ii) From letter dated May 5, 1886.

During his (Junker's) stay with Kabrega, messengers have in the most friendly way been provided him to go to Uganda, and they have now returned with the post containing a dispatch from Egyptian Government to me, accompanied by a very friendly letter from Sir John Kirk. . . . At last, therefore, I have received trustworthy intelligence of the events which have happened in the Soudan, of Gordon's death, of the taking of Khartoum, and of the abandonment of the Soudan, and many other startling details.

The Government has had the goodness to invest me with full powers in all my actions, and also, in case we made up our minds to march to Zanzibar, a credit has been opened for me with Sir John Kirk. So, heartily thankful as I am for this friendliness received after three years of seclusion, still it does appear to me that, to a certain extent at least, the people in Egypt have false ideas as to our position, and especially about the possibility of a march from here to Uganda and to Zanzibar. That it is easy to march into Uganda, but very difficult to get out again, you know by your own experience. Add to that the difficulty that we possess a considerable number of arms, which would be a terrible temptation to the ruler of Uganda—whatever his name may be—and you will readily understand that I shall think twice before I lead my people into such a mouse-trap. . . .

The Soudanese will not go to Egypt; and if I tried to compel them to do so, they would shoulder arms and decamp, if they did not do worse. I have, therefore, till now had to temporise with them in order to prevent an outbreak of their growing discontent, and I shall indeed be glad when I succeed in getting rid of the Egyptians, and sending them through Uganda to their homes, or at least sending them away from here. Whether, however, I shall succeed in this is up to the present time doubtful, although I have thrown into the scale the whole weight of my personal influence with the Soudanese, and have promised to remain with them until we see a clear way open to us, and have thus kept the peace for the present. . . .

That I personally am in no hurry to return to Egypt, you will, no doubt, easily understand; the work to which I have devoted my efforts and my hopes during the last ten years, for the sake of which I have suffered gladly difficulties and hardships, is now broken down, and so all that I have accomplished, and all my struggles, have been in vain. The knowledge of a wasted life, of a useless work, hangs like a veil over the future, and robs me of all joy in life, and of all courage for further efforts. Shall I, then, go to Egypt and be laughed at, or, at the best, after a few cool words of thanks, see myself dismissed? The little that I have been able to save was lost at the fall of Khartoum. Shall I, then, go to Egypt to beg? It is quite clear to me that there would be no calling or position for me in Egypt after the loss of the Soudan, and I should therefore be more of a burden than of use to the great lords there. I must, therefore, be thankful to the soldiers that they will not let me go. . . .

(iii) *From letter dated July 7, 1886.*

. . . I have written . . . to Sir John Kirk and to the Government in Cairo, telling them of the state of affairs, and also of my determination to hold on here; besides this, I have certainly still the hope that, as Egypt is incapable of supporting us, England may perhaps one of these days come to the determination to occupy these countries, and in this way remain true to her humanitarian and civilising mission To-day, when the European Powers are striving with one another to gain possession of countries in Africa, is it possible that no one in England has ever thought of how easy and free of cost it would be to occupy our districts . . . ?

(iv) *From letter dated July 22, 1886.*

According to my opinion, the time is now come for England to secure her part in North East Africa before it is too late, and you will probably say that I am correct when I believe that a State—this province—which should, I think, include Uganda and Unyoro, if under British control, would be indeed a great blessing to Central

Africa, and it would form a central point from which the annexation and exploitation of a healthy, fruitful, and compact district could be easily carried out. True, I do not exactly know now the condition of politics in your country, and whether they are at the present time likely to favour my plans or not. I should, however, imagine that as this plan has in its forefront a philanthropic object, one of the very utmost importance—an attack on the slave trade and on the slave dealers—England would not dare to be untrue to the humanitarian position she has hitherto occupied, whether Liberals or Conservatives are at the helm. . . . In the meantime, however, come who will, if only some one will come. Till then I shall do everything possible to hold out with my people until we know whether we can receive support from England or not. . . .

(v) *From letter dated October 22, 1886. (?)* *

The reoccupation of the districts which I have in the meantime given up, can take place with very little difficulty, and a few caravans with arms and ammunition via Mombasa . . . either direct here or to Kabrega's, will be quite sufficient. People can easily be found. Of course, the old Egyptian system of plunder must be put an end to, and the natural capabilities of the country be developed. All this can certainly be easily done, but who will help us? Will your countrymen really wait until it is too late? The cardinal question is now, according to my opinion, not the holding of the Soudan and the sacrificing in a needless manner of men and money for deserts and sands, but the occupation of our districts. The Soudan, that is to say, Khartoum, etc., must fall to the share of whoever takes these countries in hand. . . .

. . . it is perfectly certain that England, who has declared as her own the district between Mombasa, Kavirondo and this province, does not intend this country to lie fallow, but much more to develop it. Sooner or later, therefore, they must begin to found stations in order to render it easy for commercial men to penetrate into the interior, and also to regulate the transport. For this purpose the presence of camels in the Lango and Masai districts will be of the greatest assistance. The opening up of this route can only be a question of time; and if I live to see them commencing at the coast, and they come to an agreement with me about it, it will be an easy thing for me to concentrate a few troops, and by the erection of a few stations to help those coming from the coast. . . . It is pretty clear to me that on account of the present political aspect, I dare hardly expect from England official help, and I must to my shame confess that I would rather be without it. The noble manner in which private persons equipped Stanley's expedition, the manifestation of sympathy and recog-

---

*Internal evidence suggests the date given by Felkin must be wrong. In this letter Emin speaks of Stanley's Expedition as a settled thing, and refers to receiving newspapers dated up to November 1886. This can hardly have been written earlier than the beginning of 1887—say February or March. And since the next letter printed by Felkin (dated April 17, 1887) speaks of a relief expedition in the conditional—"If Stanley or Thomson really comes here . . ."—it would seem more than possible that the dates of the two letters have been accidentally transposed, either by Felkin or by his printer.

nition which it contains, and the possibility of being able to arrange our affairs at length in a satisfactory manner, satisfy me to the full. . . .

Let us suppose then that Egypt intends to gradually evacuate this province, and that on the other hand England, on account of her political situation, is prevented from undertaking its annexation, then comes the eventuality which you have foreseen. I should be independent like the Rajah of Sarawak, and that it would be possible for me to govern my country in the same way as Rajah Brooke does, you will, I hope, agree. After these suppositions, two methods are again open to me—the one is for me to seek for the protection of England, which I hardly think they would refuse, as doubtless public opinion would be on my side; the other method would be for me to establish myself in a perfectly independent position; this would also not be difficult, but might possibly cause me difficulties in the future. A definite arrangement with a syndicate of English commercial men would in neither case be difficult. . . .

. . . apart from ivory, we have many other articles of trade in the country which with anything like proper trade could be developed to great advantage, and which I have previously been only able to partially attend to, because the goods which were sent me by the steamers from Khartoum were never sufficient for the requirements of my own people, and it was out of the question, therefore, to use them for purposes of trade. . . . The eastern districts of our province yield ivory, ostrich feathers, oil, vegetable fat, etc.; the western districts yield ivory, indiarubber, palm-oil, skins, etc.—certainly sufficient. . . .

(vi) *From letter dated April* 17, 1887.(?)

I should like . . . to remark here that if a relief expedition comes to us, I shall on no account desert my people. We have passed through sorrowful and hard days with one another, and I should indeed consider it shameful to desert my post just now. My people are, notwithstanding many wants, brave and good, with the exception of the Egyptians. We have known one another now for many years, and I do not think that it would be easy for one following me to gain their perfect trust. There is no question about it; I shall remain here. England should try to establish affairs upon a firm basis in Uganda. Obtain for us a free and safe route to the coast. Evacuate our country? Certainly not. . . .

(vii) *From letter dated August* 15, 1887.

Already in my last letter to you I indicated that I intended to remain here; and even if Mr. Stanley brings me ammunition, I shall only use it for the consolidation of our position and for defence in case we are attacked. In no case shall I think of quitting my post. I am strengthened in this decision, in the first place by the wish only to leave this province when the territories which have been given up are reoccupied, and when a safe route has been opened up by which the necessities of my people may be supplied; and again, by the acknowledgements which I have received, which have made it my duty to work and labour as long as ever it is possible. . . .

5. Contract of engagement for the Emin Pasha Relief Expedition.

1. I, Edmund Musgrave Barttelot, Major, 7th R.F., agree to accompany the Emin Pasha Relief Expedition, and to place myself under the command of Mr. H. M. Stanley, the leader of the Expedition, and to accept any post or position in that Expedition to which he may appoint me.

2. I further agree to serve him loyally and devotedly, to obey all his orders, and to follow him by whatsoever route he may choose, and to use my utmost endeavours to bring the Expedition to a successful issue.

3. Should I leave the Expedition without his orders, I agree to forfeit all claim to pay due to me, to return passage-money, and to become liable to a refund of all the moneys advanced to me for passage to Zanzibar and outfit.

4. Mr. H. M. Stanley also agrees to give £40 (forty pounds) as an allowance for outfit, and to pay my passage to Zanzibar, and my return passage to England, provided I continue during the whole period of the Expedition.

5. I undertake not to publish anything connected with the Expedition, or to send any account to the newspapers for six months after the issue of the official publication of the Expedition by the leader or his representative.

6. In addition to the outfit, Mr. Stanley will supply the following: tent, one Winchester rifle, one revolver, ammunition for the same, canteen, a due share of European provisions taken for the party, besides such provisions as the country can supply.

EDMUND M. BARTTELOT.
Major, 7th. R.F.

(*The other officers signed similar contracts. Those of Jephson and (presumably) Jameson included the stipulation that they would forfeit their contributions of £1,000 if they left the Expedition. Ward's contract is printed in* WARD *pp. 12–13, Jephson's in* JEPHSON *p. 426*).

6. The Khedive to Emin. (Translation)

Dated: February 1, 1887.
Delivered to Emin by Stanley, April 28, 1888.

We have already thanked you and your officers for the plucky and successful defence of the Egyptian Equatorial provinces entrusted to your charge, and for the firmness you have shown with your fellow-officers under your command.

And we therefore have rewarded you in raising your rank to that of Lewa Pasha (Brigadier General). We have also approved the ranks you thought necessary to give to the officers under your charge. As I have already written to you on the 29 November, 1886, No. 31, and it must have reached you with other documents sent by His Excellency Nubar Pasha, President of the Council of Ministers.

And, since it is our sincerest desire to relieve you with your officers and soldiers from the difficult position you are in, our Government have made up their mind in the manner by which you may be relieved with officers and soldiers from your troubles.

And as a mission for the relief has been formed under the command of Mr. Stanley, the famous and experienced African explorer, whose reputation is well known throughout the world; and as he intends to set out on his expedition with all the necessary provisions for you so that he may bring you here with officers and men to Cairo, by the route which Mr. Stanley may think proper to take, consequently we have issued this High Order to you, and it is sent to you by the hand of Mr. Stanley to let you know what has been done, and as soon as it will reach you, I charge you to convey my best wishes to the officers and men—and you are at full liberty with regard to your leaving for Cairo or your stay there with officers and men.

Our Government has given a decision for paying your salaries with that of the officers and men.

Those who wish to stay there from the officers and men they may do it on their own responsibility, and they may not expect any assistance from the Government.

Try to understand the contents well, and make it well known to all the officers and men, that they may be aware of what they are going to do.

MEHMET TEWFIK.

(*The translation above is that given by Stanley in* D.A. 1 *pp* 56–57. *Jephson's* Emin Pasha *prints an alternative translation at p.* 45.)

7. Nubar Pasha to Emin. (Translation)

Dated: Cairo, February 2, 1887.
Delivered to Emin by Stanley, April 28, 1888.

MY DEAR EMIN PASHA,
I had sent you, by the kind favour of her Britannic Majesty's Consulate at Zanzibar, a letter addressed to you by his Highness complimenting you on your conduct, and congratulating you, your officers, and your soldiers on having overcome the difficulties with which you had to cope.

His Excellency made you aware in that letter that he had promoted you to the rank of General, and would confirm all promotions and rewards given by you to your officers and others. I informed you myself of the preparation of an expedition for your relief. The expedition is now formed; it is commanded by Mr. Stanley, who will himself hand you my letter with that which his Highness is writing to you, and another which I am writing to you in Arabic.

The expedition commanded by Mr. Stanley has been formed and organised in order to go to you with the provisions and stores, of which you must certainly be in want. Its object is to bring you, your officers, and soldiers back to Egypt by the way which Mr. Stanley shall think most suitable. I have nothing to add to what I have just said of the objects of the expedition. Only his Highness leaves you, your officers, your soldiers and others entirely free to stay where you are, or to make use of the help he sends for your return.

But, of course, and this must be made clear to your officers, soldiers, or others, if some do not wish to return they are free to remain, but at their own risk and by their own desire, and that they cannot expect any other help from the Government. That is what I wish you to make clear to those who may wish to remain.

I have only to add that you, your officers, your soldiers and other officials will have your accounts settled and be paid on your arrival in Egypt what is due to you on account of salaries and other allowances, as all your promotions have already been confirmed by his Highness.

I hope, my dear Pasha, that Mr. Stanley will find you all safe and sound, and enjoying good health. That is what we all wish with all our hearts and it is with these wishes that I beg you to accept these expressions of my devotion and my sincere compliments on your fine conduct.

N. NUBAR.

(The original of this letter is in French.)

8. Stanley to Emin.

Dated: Zanzibar, February 23, 1887.
Undelivered.

DEAR SIR,

I have the honour to inform you that the Government of His Highness the Khedive of Egypt, upon the receipt of your urgent letters soliciting aid and instructions, have seen fit to depute me to equip an Expedition to proceed to Wadelai to convey such aid as they think you require, and to assist you in other ways agreeably with the written instructions which have been delivered to me for you.

Having been pretty accurately informed of the nature of your necessities from the perusal of your letters to the Egyptian Government, the Expedition has been equipped in such a manner as may be supposed to meet all your wants. As you will gather from the letters of His Highness and the Prime Minister of Egypt to you, all that could possibly be done to satisfy your needs has been done most heartily. From the translation of the letters delivered to me, I perceive that they will give you immense satisfaction. Over sixty soldiers from Wady Halfa have been detailed to accompany me in order that they may be able to encourage the soldiers under your command, and confirm the letters. We also march under the Egyptian standard.

The Expedition includes 600 Zanzibari natives, and probably as many Arab followers from Central Africa.

We sail tomorrow from Zanzibar to the Congo, and by the 18th June next we hope to be at the head of navigation on the Upper Congo. From the point where we debark to the southern end of Lake Albert is a distance of 320 miles in a straight line, say 500 miles by road, which will probably occupy us fifty days to march to the south-western or southern end, in the neighbourhood of Kavalli.

If your steamers are in that neighbourhood, you will be able to leave word perhaps at Kavalli, or in its neighbourhood, informing me of your whereabouts.

The reasons which have obliged me to adopt this route for the conveyance of your stores are various, but principally political. I am also impressed with the greater security of that route and the greater certainty of success attending the venture with less trouble to the Expedition and less annoyance to the natives. Mwanga is a formidable opponent to the south and south-east. The Wakedi and other warlike natives to the eastward of Fatiko oppose a serious obstacle, the natives of Kishakka and Ruanda have never permitted strangers to enter their country. En route I do not anticipate much trouble, because there are no powerful chiefs in the Congo basin capable of interrupting our march.

Besides abundance of ammunition for your needs, official letters from the Egyptian Government, a heavy mail from your numerous friends and admirers, I bring with me personal equipments for yourself and your officers suitable to the rank of each.

Trusting that I shall have the satisfaction of finding you well and safe, and that nothing will induce you rashly to venture your life and liberty in the neighbourhood of Uganda, without the ample means of causing yourself and your men to be respected which I am bringing to you,

                    I beg you believe me,
                        Yours very faithfully,
                            HENRY M. STANLEY.

9. Tippu-Tib's contract with the E.P.R.E.

The following agreement has been entered into between Henry Morton Stanley and Hamed bin Mohammed el Marjebi Tippoo Tib:

I. Henry Morton Stanley agrees to accept the services of a number of able-bodied men in Hamed bin Mohammed's employ who shall accompany him to the Albert Nyanza in the capacity of armed porters, that is, who shall be effective in the use of a gun for defence and shall be capable of carrying a load not exceeding sixty-five pounds in weight from the Congo River to the Lake and back at the following rates and following conditions.

II. Each man shall be armed with a gun at Hamed's expense and further be provided with one hundred bullets.

III. Each man shall be at the disposition of Mr Stanley for carrying any load not exceeding sixty-five pounds weight or for the defence of the caravan as circumstances may require.

IV. His service begins on the date of leaving the Congo River with the expedition for the Albert Nyanza and terminates on the return of any portion of the expedition to the Congo.

V. The time occupied by the journey from the Congo to the Albert Nyanza and back to the Congo shall not exceed six months, or if longer no increase of pay shall be due.

VI. For the service each man shall receive Thirty dollars together with food during the time of his employment.

VII. All of these men, if loaded with ivory at the Albert Nyanza, shall deposit the said ivory at the Congo and within the district of Stanley Falls as the officer in charge shall direct, and his receipt for the safe arrival of the same on the Congo shall be a sufficient voucher for the discharge of their part of this agreement.

VIII. If circumstances shall warrant a re-engagement of these men or any number of them for a repetition of this duty, then the above articles shall stand for a second contract upon the same terms and conditions.

IX. Powder and caps shall be supplied by Mr Stanley.

X. For every round journey thus made Sheikh Hamed shall be entitled to a bonus of one thousand dollars.

> (signed)   Henry M. Stanley
> Hamed bin Mohammed el Marjebi (in *Arabic*)
>
> (witnessed)   Frederick Holmwood
> Khoja Kanji Raipar (in *Gujarati*)

10. *Stanley's letter of instructions to Barttelot.*

Dated: Yambuya, June 24, 1887.

SIR,

As the senior officer of those accompanying me on the Emin Pasha Relief Expedition, the command of this important post naturally devolves on you. It is also for the interest of this Expedition that you accept this command, from the fact that your Soudanese company, being only soldiers and more capable of garrison duty than the Zanzibaris, will be better utilised here than on the road.

The steamer *Stanley* left Yambuya on the 22nd of this month for Stanley Pool. If she meets with no mischance she ought to be at Leopoldville on the 2nd July. In two days more she will be loaded with about 500 loads of our goods, which were left in charge of Mr. J. R. Troup. This gentleman will embark, and on 4th July I assume that the *Stanley* will commence the ascent of the river, and arrive at Bolobo the 9th July. Fuel being ready, the 125 men in charge of Messrs. Ward and Bonny, now at Bolobo, will embark, and the steamer will continue her journey. She will be at Bangala 19th July, and arrive 31st July. Of course the lowness of the river in that month may delay her a few days; but having great confidence in her captain, you may certainly expect her before the 10th of August.

Though the camp is favourably situated and naturally strong, a brave enemy would find it no difficult task to capture if the commander is lax in discipline, vigour, or energy. Therefore I feel sure that I have made a wise choice in selecting you to guard our interests here during our absence. The interests now entrusted to you are of vital importance to this Expedition. The men you will eventually have under your command consist of more than an entire third of the whole Expedition. The goods that will be brought up are the currency needed for transit through the regions beyond the Lakes. There will be a vast store of ammunition and provisions, which are of equal importance to us. The loss of these goods and men then would be certain ruin to us, and the advance force would in its turn need to solicit relief. Therefore, weighing all these matters well, I hope you will spare no pains to maintain order and discipline in your camp, and keep them in such a condition that, however brave an enemy may be, he can make no impression on them. For this latter purpose I would recommend you to make an artificial ditch of six feet wide, three feet deep, leading from the natural ditch, where the spring is, round the stockade. A platform like that on the southern side of the camp, constructed near the eastern as well as the western gate, would be of advantage to the strength of the camp. For, remember, it is not the natives alone you have to fear, or who may wish to assail you, but the Arabs and their followers may, through some cause or other, quarrel with you and assail your camp.

Our course from here will be true east, or, by magnetic compass, east by south, as near as possible. Certain marches that we may take may not exactly lead in the direction aimed at; nevertheless, it is the south-west corner of Lake Albert, near or at Kavalli, that is our destination. When we arrive there, we will form a strong camp in the neighbourhood, launch our boat, and steer for Kibero, in Unyoro, to hear from Signor Casati, if there, of the condition of Emin Pasha. If the latter is alive and in the neighbourhood of the lake, we shall communicate with him, and our after conduct must be guided by what we learn of the intentions of Emin Pasha. We may assume that we shall not be longer than a fortnight with him, before deciding on our return to this camp, along the same route traversed by us when going east.

We will endeavour, by blazing trees and cutting saplings along our road, to leave sufficient traces of the route taken by us. We shall always take by preference tracks leading eastward. At all crossways where paths intersect, we shall hoe up and make a hole a few inches deep across all paths not used by us, besides blazing trees when possible. It may happen, should Tippu-Tib have sent the full number of adults promised by him to me—viz., 600 men (able to carry loads)—and the *Stanley* has arrived in safety with the 125 men left by me at Bolobo, that you will feel yourself sufficiently competent to march the column, with all the goods brought by the *Stanley*, and those left by me at Yambuya, along the road pursued by me. In that event, which would be desirable, you will follow closely our route, and before many days we should most assuredly meet. No doubt you would find our bomas intact and standing, and you should endeavour to make your marches so that you could utilize these as you marched. Better guides than these bomas of our routes could not be made. If you do not meet them in the course of two days' march, you may rest assured that you are not in our route.

It may happen also that, though Tippu-Tib has sent some men, he has not sent enough to carry the goods with your own force. In that case you will, of course, use your discretion as to what goods you can dispense with to enable you to march, For this purpose you should study your list attentively, viz.:

1. Ammunition, especially fixed, is important.
2. Beads, brass wire, and cowries rank next.
3. Private baggage.
4. Powder caps.
5. European provisions.
6. Brass rods as used in the Congo.
7. Provisions (rice, beans, peas, Matama, biscuit).

Therefore you must consider after those, sacking, tools, such as shovels (never discard an axe or a billhook), how many sacks of provisions you can distribute among your men to enable you to march, whether half the brass rods in your boxes could not go also, and there stop. If you still cannot march, then it would be better to make marches of six miles twice over (if you prefer marching to staying for our arrival) than throw too many things away.

With the *Stanley*'s final departure from Yambuya, you should not fail to send a report to Mr. Wm. Mackinnon, of Gray, Dawes, and Co., 13 Austin Friars, London, of what has happened at your camp in my absence, of when I started away eastward, whether you have heard of or from me at all, when you expect to hear, and what you purpose doing. You should also send him a true copy of this Order, that the Relief Committee may judge for themselves whether you have acted or propose to act judiciously. Your present garrison shall consist of eighty rifles and from forty to fifty supernumaries (the *Stanley* is to bring you within a few weeks fifty more rifles and seventy-five supernumaries under Messrs. Troup, Ward, and Bonny).

I associate Mr. J. S. Jameson with you at present. Messrs. Troup, Ward, and Bonny will submit to your authority in the ordinary duties of the defence and the conduct of the camp or of the march. There is only one chief, which is yourself; but should any vital steps be proposed to be taken, I beg of you to take the voice of Mr. Jameson, and when Messrs. Troup and Ward are here, pray admit them to your confidence, and let them speak freely their opinions.

I think I have written very clearly upon everything that strikes me as necessary. Your treatment of the natives, I suggest, should depend entirely on their conduct to you. If they do not molest you, suffer them to return to the neighbouring villages in peace, and if you can in any manner, by moderation, small gifts occasionally of brass rods, &c., hasten an amicable intercourse, I should recommend your doing so. Lose no opportunity of obtaining information respecting the natives, the position of the various villages in your neighbourhood, &c.

I have the honour to be,
Your obedient servant,
HENRY M. STANLEY.

P.S. In the bottom of your ditch put splinters. Keep four or five weak men doing this light job; cut fuel ten days for *Stanley*.

Give one brass rod per week to each man to buy fish, &c.; in five months these amount to 2580. Give also six cowries per man per week; in five months these will number 15,480.

Let Mr. Jameson attend to the sick daily.
H.M.S.

(*The above, certified a true copy by Barttelot, was forwarded to Mackinnon according to instructions, and appeared, together with Barttelot's report, in* The Times, *November 28, 1887.*)

11. Reports from Ipoto.

(i) *Jephson to Stanley.*
Report on the relief of Nelson.
Dated: Ipoto, November 4, 1887.

DEAR SIR,

I left at midday on October 26th, and arrived at the river and crossed over with 30 Manyuema and 40 Zanzibaris under my charge the same afternoon and camped on landing. The next morning we started off early and reached the camp where we had crossed the river when we were wandering about in a starving condition in search of the Arabs ... the signs and arrow heads we had marked on the trees to show the chiefs we had crossed were still fresh. I reached another of our camps that night. The next day we did nearly three of our former marches. The camp where Feruzi Ali had got his death wound, and where we had spent three such miserable days of hunger and anxiety, looked very dismal as we passed through it. During the day we passed the skeletons of three of our men who had fallen down and died from sheer starvation, they were grim reminders of the misery through which we had so lately gone.

On the morning of the 29th I started off as soon as it was daylight, determining to reach Nelson that day and decide the question as to his being yet alive. Accompanied by one man only, I soon found myself far ahead of my followers. As I neared Nelson's camp a feverish anxiety to know his fate possessed me, and I pushed on through streams and creeks, by banks and bogs, over which our starving people had slowly toiled with the boat sections. All were passed by quickly today, and again the skeletons in the road testified to the trials through which we had passed. As I came down the hill into Nelson's camp, not a sound was heard but the groans of two dying men in a hut close by, the whole place had a deserted and woe-begone look. I came quietly round the tent and found Nelson sitting there; we clasped hands, and then, poor fellow! he turned away and sobbed, and muttered something about being very weak.

Nelson was greatly changed in appearance, being worn and haggard looking, with deep lines about his eyes and mouth. He told me his anxiety had been intense, as day after day passed and no relief came; he had at last made up his mind that something had happened to us, and that we had been compelled to abandon him. He had lived chiefly upon fruits and fungus which his two boys had brought in from day to day. Of the fifty-two men you left with him, only five remained, of whom two were in a dying state. All the rest had either deserted him or were dead.

He has himself given you an account of his losses from death and desertion. I gave him the food you sent him, which I had carefully watched on the way, and he had one of the chickens and some porridge cooked at once, it was the first nourishing food he had tasted for many days. After I had been there a couple of hours my people came in and all crowded round the tent to offer him their congratulations.

You remember Nelson's feet had been very bad for some days before we left him, he had hardly left the tent the whole time he had been there. At one time he had had ten ulcers on one foot, but he had now recovered from them in a great measure and said he thought he would be able to march slowly. On the 30th we began the return march. I gave out most of the loads to the Manyuema and Zanzibaris, but was obliged to leave thirteen boxes of ammunition and seven other loads, these I buried, and Parke will be able to fetch them later on.

Nelson did the marches better than I expected, though he was much knocked up at the end of each day. On the return march we crossed the river lower down and made our way up the right bank and struck your old road a day's march from the Arab camp. Here again we passed more skeletons, at one place there were three within 200 yards of each other.

On the fifth day, that is November 3rd, we reached the Arab camp, and Nelson's relief was accomplished. He has already picked up wonderfully in spite of the marching, but he cannot get sleep at night and is still in a nervous and highly strung state; the rest in the Arab camp will, I trust, set him up again. It is certain that in his state of health he could not have followed us in our wanderings in search of food, he must have fallen by the way.

I am, etc.,

A. J. MOUNTENEY JEPHSON.

(ii) *Nelson to Stanley.*
    Dated: Ipoto, November 6, 1887.

DEAR SIR,

Mr. Jephson arrived at my camp on the 29th October with the men for the loads and with the food you sent for me. Many thanks for the food, it was badly needed. He will tell you what state he found me in and of the few men still alive.

You left me on the 6th October last; on the morning of the 9th I got up a canoe* and sent Umari and thirteen of the best men I could find (they were all very bad) over the river to look for food. On the 8th Assani (No. 1 Company) came to me and said that he had returned from the column sick. Same day Uledi's brother came into camp, told me he had lost the road while looking for bananas, near the camp where we met the Manyuema. On the 10th I found that Juma, one of Stairs' chiefs, had cleared in the night with ten men, and stolen a canoe and gone down river. On the 14th one man died. Umari returned with very few bananas, about enough for two days; however, they were very welcome, as I had nothing but herbs and fungi to eat up to this time. On the 15th another man died, and I found that Saadi (No. 1) with some other men had come into the camp in the night and stolen the canoe (Umari had re-crossd the river in) and gone down river. On the 17th Umari went away with twenty-one men to look for food; 19th, man died; 22nd, two men died; 23rd, man died; 29th, two men died; Jephson arrived; 30th, one man died; we left camp on way here. Umari had not returned; he, however, if alive, will come on here, I feel sure, but how many men with him I cannot tell, perhaps five or six

---

The canoes had been filled with stones and sunk in a spot where they could be retrieved on the return march to Yambuya.

may reach here with him. With the exception of the few bananas I got from Umari I lived entirely on herbs, fungi, and a few mabengu. I had ten ulcers on my left leg and foot and so was unable to look for food myself and was kept alive entirely by my two boys and little Baruk, one of my company, and Abdalla, a man Stairs left with me. I was very weak when Jephson arrived. Now, however, I feel a little better. We arrived at the village on the 3rd November, the chief Ismail brought me the day I came a very small quantity of coarse meal and two small dried fish, about enough for one meal.

Yesterday, no food having come for two days, we sent for it, and after a good deal of trouble Ismail sent us a little meal. At present I am living on my clothes; we hardly get anything from the Chief. Today Dr. Parke and I went to the Chief, with Hamis Pari as interpreter, and talked to him about food. He told us that *no arrangement had been made by you* for my food, and that he was feeding the Doctor and me entirely from his own generosity, and he refused to feed our boys, three in number (fewer we cannot possibly do with), as you never told him to do so.

I have the honour to be, etc.,
R. H. NELSON.

(iii) *Parke to Stanley.*
  Dated: Ipoto, November 6, 1887.

MY DEAR MR STANLEY,
Captain Nelson and Mr Jephson arrived here on the 3rd inst. a few of the Zanzibaris and Manyuema men getting in with their loads the previous day. Of all those men left at Nelson's camp, only five have arrived here, the remaining live ones were away on a foraging tour with Umari when the relief party arrived. It is very likely that some of them may find their way here; if so, I shall get Ismaili to allow them to work for their food. Nelson staggered into camp greatly changed in appearance, a complete wreck after the march, his features shrunken and pinched, and a frame reduced to half its former size. I have done the best I could for him medically, but good nourishing food is what he requires to restore him to his health: and I regret to say that my experience here and the conversation which we had today with Ismaili goes to show that we shall have to exist on scanty fare. Since you left, I have had some flour and corn from the chiefs, but this was generally after sending for it several times. By a lucky accident I got a goat, most of which I distributed amongst the sick men here, for I am informed by Ismaili, through H. Pari, that only those who work in the field get food, and there are some here who certainly cannot do so; therefore they are trusting to the generosity of the other men, who get five heads of corn each day they work. Both Nelson and myself have much trouble in getting food from Ismaili for ourselves, and he has refused to feed our boys, who are absolutely necessary to draw water, cook, &c., &c., although I have reduced mine to one.

Nelson and myself went and saw him today (Hamis Pari, interpreter), and Ismaili stated that you had told the chiefs that a big Mzungu was to come (Nelson), and he would make his own arrangements about food, and that I was living here on his (Ismaili's) generosity, as no arrangements had been made for me. I reminded him of the conversation you had with him in your tent the evening you called me down and gave me your gold watch, and I said that you had told me that you had made a written arrangement with the chiefs that both Nelson and myself should be provisioned. We both told him that we did not want goats and fowls, but simply what he can give us. Not having seen any agreement, I could not argue further, but asked to see the document, so that we might convince him; this he said he could not do, as Hamis, the Chief, had it, and he was away, and would not return for two months. He however sent us up some corn shortly afterwards. This is a very unhappy state of affairs for us who shall have to remain here for so long a time. Nelson has sold much of his clothes, and out of my scanty supply (my bag having been lost on the march), I have been obliged to make a further sale so as to provide ourselves with sufficient food.

We shall get along here as best we can, and sacrifice much to keep on friendly terms with the Arabs, as it is of such essential importance. I sincerely hope you will have every success in attaining the object of the Expedition, and that we shall all have an opportunity of meeting soon and congratulating Emin Pasha on his relief.

With best wishes, &c.,
T. H. PARKE.
A.M.D.

(*The three letters above were delivered to Stanley by Jephson when he rejoined the main column on November* 16, 1887.)

12. *Parke's report on his stay at Ipoto.*

Dated: Fort Bodo, February 8, 1888.

SIR,

I have the honour to forward this report for your information. In compliance with your orders dated 24th October, 1887, I remained at the Manyuema Camp to take charge of invalids and impedimenta left there on your departure, 28th Ocober, up to the time the relief party arrived, 25th January, 1888. Of those invalids whom you left at camp, seven were sufficiently recovered to send on with Captain Jephson, 7th November; those remaining were increased in number by the arrival of Captain Nelson, his two boys, and two men, 3rd November; also headman Umari and nine men, who were found in a starving condition in the bush by Kilonga-Longa, and brought to camp by him 9th January; this made a total of one sick officer and thirty-nine invalids remaining in camp; of this number Captain Nelson and sixteen men left with the relief party. Twelve men were away on a journey looking for food, therefore remain at Manyuema Camp, and eleven deaths occurred; this extremely high mortality will no doubt astonish you, especially as it was entirely due to starvation, except in two instances only. From the time you left the Manyuema until our departure, 26th January, the chiefs gave little or no food to either officers or men; those men who were sufficiently strong to do a good day's work, sometimes got as many as ten heads of corn (Indian) per man, but as the working men were not constantly employed, their average ration of corn was about three per day; those invalids unable to work, of whom there were many, received no food from the chiefs, and were therefore obliged to exist on herbs. Remembering the wretched and debilitated condition of all these men, both from privation and disease, you will readily understand that the heartless treatment of the Manyuema chiefs was sufficient to cause even a much greater mortality.

The men were badly housed, and their scanty clothing consisted of about half a yard of native bark-cloth, as they sold their own clothes for food; they experienced not only the horrors of starvation, but were cruelly and brutally treated by the Manyuema, who drove them to commit theft by withholding food, and then scored their backs with rods, and in one case speared a man to death (Asmani bin Hassan) for stealing.

Captain Nelson arrived in a very weak condition, requiring good food and careful treatment. He visited the chiefs, and made them handsome presents of articles costing about £75, with a view to win their sympathy; however, they continued to give little or no food to officers or men: they said that no arrangement had been made for provisioning Captain Nelson, and any food they sent to me was entirely of their own generosity, as no arrangement had been made by you. I asked them to let me see the written agreement between you and them, which they did; also another document written in Arabic characters, which I could not read. In their agreement with you I saw that they had promised to provision the officers and men whom you would leave. I appealed to them, and remonstrated with them, nevertheless they supplied less and less food, until finally they refused to give any on the plea that they had none. The height of this generosity would be reached when they would send two or three cups of Indian meal to feed Captain Nelson, myself and the boys, until the next donation would turn up in six or seven days afterwards. During the last seven weeks we did not receive any food whatever from the chief. Owing to their refusal to give us food, we were obliged first to sell our own clothes, and eight rifles belonging to the Expedition to provide ourselves and boys with food. I repeatedly reminded Ismaili (the Chief) of the conversation he had with you in your tent the night before you left the camp, when he promised to look after and care for the officers and men whom you left in camp. Although the chiefs had no food to supply according to their agreement, yet they had always plenty to sell, their object being to compel us to sell the arms and ammunition for food. I send you a complete list of effects left in my charge by Captain Jephson, 7th November, all of which were correct when the relief party arrived, with the following exceptions, viz.:—two boxes Remington ammunition, and one rifle, which were stolen by a Zanzibari (Saraboko), and, I believe, sold to the Manyuema chiefs.

Several attempts were made to steal the arms, boxes, &c.; on the night of November 7th, the hut in which the baggage was stored was set on fire with a view to taking everything with a rush in the confusion caused by the fire: however, their dream was frustrated, as Captain Nelson, who was ever awake saw the blaze, and gave the alarm just in time for ourselves and our boys to put out the fire before it got to the baggage. I then had the tents pitched according to your directions, not being able to do so earlier, as I had no assistance. All the rifles, ammunition, boxes, &c., were packed in the tents, one of which was occupied by Captain Nelson, and the other by myself. Every effort was made to prevent things being stolen; nevertheless, even Captain Nelson's blankets were taken by a thief who got under the tent from behind. On another occasion I heard a noise at my tent-door, and, jumping out of bed quickly, I found a box of ammunition ten yards off, which had just been taken out of my tent. The thief escaped in the dark.

On the night of January 9th, I heard a noise outside my tent, and, suspecting a thief, I crept out noiselessly to the back, where I caught Camaroni, a Zanzibari, in the act of stealing a rifle through a hole which he had cut in the tent. For this offence I flogged him severely. Many cases of stealing corn by the Zanzibaris were brought up by the chiefs, and in every case where there was proof the Zanzibaris were punished. Life at the Manyuema Camp was almost intolerable. The people, their manners and surroundings, were of the lowest order, and, owing to the mounds of fecal matter and decomposing vegetation which were allowed to collect on the paths and close to their dwellings, the place was a hotbed of disease. Captain Nelson was confined to his bed from sickness for over two months, and I got blood-poisoning followed by erysipelas,which kept me in bed for five weeks. During our illness the chiefs paid us frequent visits, but always with a view to covet something which they saw in our tents. Their avarice was unbounded, and they made agreements one day only to be broken the next. After the arrival of Kilonga-Longa and his force of about 400, including women, children and slaves, food became really scarce, therefore the Manyuema were obliged to send out large caravans to bring in food. Twelve Zanzibaris who are absent accompanied these caravans in search of food, and had not returned when I left the camp with the relief party. Starvation was so great just before we left that the native slaves seized one of their comrades, who had gone some distance from the camp to draw water, cut him in pieces and ate him.

In conclusion, I may mention that Captain Nelson and myself did everything we could to preserve a good feeling with the Manyuema chiefs and people, and we parted on friendly terms.

Yours obediently,
T. H. PARKE.
Surgeon, A.M.D.

(Parke's report as printed by Stanley—D.A. I pp. 338–340—shows minor variations from the version copied into his diary by Jephson—JEPHSON pp. 434–436. In the version reproduced here, one or two small omissions from Stanley's version have been supplied from Jephson's.)

13. Three letters to Barttelot.

(i) *Stanley to Barttelot.*
    Dated: (Ugarrowa's) September 18, 1887.
    Undelivered.

MY DEAR MAJOR,
You will, I am certain, be as glad to get news—definite and clear—of our movements, as I am to feel that I have at last an opportunity of presenting them to you. As they will be of immense comfort to you and your assistants and followers, I shall confine myself to giving you the needful details. We have travelled 340 English miles to make only 192 geographical miles of our easterly course. This has been performed in eighty-three days, which gives us a rate of four and one-tenth miles per day. We have yet to make 130 geographical miles, or a winding course, perhaps, of 230 miles, which, at the same rate of march as hitherto, we may make in fifty-five days. We started from Yambuya 389 souls, of whom fifty-six are so sick that we are obliged to leave them behind us at this Arab camp of Ugarrowa. We are fifty-six men short of the number with which we left Yambuya. Of these, thirty men have died—four from poisoned arrows, six left in the bush or speared by the natives—twenty-six have deserted en route, thinking that they would be able to follow a caravan of Manyuema, which we met following the river downwards. But this caravan, instead of going on, returned to this place, and our deserters, misled by this, will probably follow our track downwards until they meet you, or are extermin-ated by the natives. Be not deluded by any statements they may make. Were I to send men to you, I, of course, would send you a note; but in no instance a verbal message, or any message at all by the scum of the camp. Should you meet them, you will have to secure them thoroughly.

The first day we left you we made a good march, which terminated in a fight, the foolish natives firing their own village as they fled. Since that day we have had, probably, thirty fights. The first view of us the natives had inspired them to show fight. As far as Panga Falls we did not lose a man or meet with any serious obstacles to navigation. Panga is a big cataract, with a decided fall. We cut a road round it on the south bank, and dragged our canoes and went on again.

We had intended to follow a native path which would take us toward our destina-tion, with the usual windings of the road. For ten days we searched for a road, and then took an elephant track, which led us into an interminable forest, totally uninhabited. Fearing to lose ourselves altogether, we cut a road to the river, and have followed the river ever since. From the point where we struck the river to Mugwye's country—four days' journey below Panga—we fared very well. Food was abundant; we made long marches, and no halts whatever. Beyond Mugwye's up to Engweddeh was a wilderness, eleven days' march, villages being inland, and mostly foodless. From this day our strength declined rapidly. People were lost in the bush as they searched for food, or were slain by the natives. Ulcers, dysentery, and grievous sickness, ending in fatal debility, attacked the people. Hence our enormous loss since leaving Panga—thirty dead and twenty-six deserters. Besides which, we are obliged to leave fifty-six behind, so used up that, without a long rest they would also die.

Of the Somalis, one is dead (Achmet); the other five are at this camp until our return from the Lake. Of the Soudanese, one is dead; we leave three behind today. All the whites are in perfect condition—thinnish, but with plenty of go.

Among our fights we have had over fifty wounded, but they all recovered except four. Stairs was severely wounded with an arrow, which penetrated an inch and a half within a little below the heart, in the left breast. He is all right now.

We have had one man shot dead by some person unknown in the camp; another was shot in the foot, resulting in an amputation. This latter case, now in a fair state of health, we leave behind today. The number of hours we have marched ought to have taken us back to you by this time, but we had to hew daily our path through forest and jungle to keep along the river, because the river banks were populated. The forest inland contains no settlements that we know or have heard of. By means of canoes we were able to help the caravan, carry the sick, and several loads. The boat helped us immensely. Were I to do the work over again, I should collect canoes as large as possible, man them with sufficient paddlers, and load up with goods and sick. On the river between Yambuya and Mugwye's country the canoes are numerous, and tolerably large. The misfortune is that the Zanzibaris are exceedingly poor boatmen. In my force there are only about fifty who can paddle or pull an oar; but even these have saved our caravan immense labour, and many lives which otherwise would have been sacrificed.

Our plan has been to paddle from one rapid to another. On reaching strong water, or shoals, we have unloaded our canoes and poled or dragged them up with long rattan or other creepers through the rapids, then loaded up again and pursued our way until we met another obstacle. The want of sufficient and proper food regularly pulls people down very fast, and they have not that strength to carry the loads which has distinguished them while with me in other parts of Africa. Therefore, any means to lighten the labour of the caravan is commendable.

If Tippu-Tib's people have not yet joined you, I do not expect you will be very far from Yambuya. You can make two journeys by river for one that you can do on land. Slow as we have been coming up, and cutting our way through, I shall come down river like lightning. The river will be a friend indeed, for the current alone will take us twenty miles a day, and I will pick up as many canoes as possible to help us on our second journey up river. Follow the river closely, and do not lose sight of our track. When the caravan which takes this passes you, look out for your men, or they will run in a body, taking valuable goods with them.

Give my best salaams and kind remembrances from us all to your fellows. Bid them cheer up; so many miles a day will take you here in so many days. It depends on your own going, and your power, how many or how few you will be.

I need not say that I wish you the best of health and luck and good fortune, because you are a part of myself; therefore good-bye.

> Yours very truly,
> HENRY M. STANLEY.

(ii) *Stanley to Barttelot.* (Extract)
    Dated: Fort Bodo, February 14, 1888.
    Undelivered.

(Stanley's second letter to Barttelot, a long one, shows Stanley preoccupied with the question of what might happen to Barttelot's column if, having left Yambuya, it penetrated as far as the country devastated by the Manyuema. Therefore, apart from a brief account of his past proceedings and future plans, Stanley concentrates on an enumeration of places at which Barttelot's column could establish itself away from the Manyuema influence and its twin corollaries: starvation and desertion. The last part of the letter is of particular interest since in it Stanley specifically orders Barttelot to take precisely that action which subsequently became the principal charge in the catalogue of Stanley's accusations against his second-in-command—namely, to stay where he was and await Stanley's return.)

Assuming that Tippu-Tib's people are with you . . . and the *Stanley* steamer arrived within reasonable time, you have arrived at some place about twenty-two or twenty-four of our former journeys from Yambuya, below Mugwye's, as I take it. Hence, before you get near the Arab influence, where your column will surely break up if you are alone, I order you to go to the nearest place (Mugwye's, Aveysheba, or Nepoko confluence) that is to you, and there to build a strong camp and wait us; but whatever you decide upon, let me know. If you come near Ugarrowa's you will lose men, rifles, powder—everything of value; your own boys will betray you, because they will sell food so dearly that your people, from stress of hunger, will steal everything.

At either of the three places above you will get safety and food until we relieve you. So long as you are stationary, there is no fear of desertion; but the daily task. added to constant insufficiency of food, will sap the fidelity of your best men. (These directions are only in case of your being alone, without Arab aid. If Tippu-Tib's people are with you, I presume you are coming along slowly.)

With everybody's best wishes to you, I send my earnest prayer that you are, despite all unwholesome and evil conjectures, where you ought to be, and that this letter will reach you in time to save you from that forest misery, and from the fangs of the ruthless Manyuema blackguards. To every one of your officers also these good wishes are given, from,

Yours most sincerely,
HENRY M. STANLEY.

(iii) *Parke to Barttelot.*
    Dated: Fort Bodo, February 15, 1888.
    Undelivered.

MY DEAR OLD BARTTELOT,
I hope you are 'going strong', and Jameson 'pulling double'. None of us here have any idea where you are. Some of us officers and men say you are on the way up river, others say you are still at Yambuya, unable to move with a large number of

loads, and amongst the men there is an idea that your Zanzibaris may have gone over to Tippu-Tib. Stanley reached the Lake 14th December, 1887, but could not communicate with Emin Pasha, as he had not got his boat. He then came back from the Lake into the bush, and made this fort to store his baggage, while he again goes on to the Lake with Jephson and boat. Stairs goes to Ugarrowa's tomorrow with twenty men, who are to go on to you and who bring this letter. Stairs returns here with about forty or fifty men who were left at Ugarrowa's, and then goes on after Stanley, as the place is only 80 or 100 miles from the Lake. I am to stay at this fort with forty or fifty men. Nelson, who has been ailing for months, therefore also remains here. We had an awful time coming here. I often said I was starved at school, but it was stuffing compared with what we have gone through. I am glad to say all the white men are very fit, but the mortality amongst the men was enormous, something like 50 per cent. Up to Ugarrowa's there is plenty of food, but little or none along the river this side of Ugarrowa's. Stanley, I know, is writing you all about the starvation and the road. Today, Stanley fell in all the men, and asked them all if they wanted to go to the Lake or back for you. Most of the men at first wanted to go back, but afterwards the majority were for the Lake; both Stairs, Jephson, and myself were for the Lake, so as to decide if Emin Pasha was alive or not, so as not to bring your column up all this way and then go back to Muta Nzige. All the men are as fat as butter, some of them, however, who stayed with me at an Arab camp for three months, where I was left to look after Nelson, and sick men, and boxes, etc., are reduced to skin and bone. Out of thirty-eight, eleven died of starvation. Stairs was the only officer wounded, but many of the men died from their wounds.

We are all in a bad way for boots; none of us have a good pair. I have made two pairs, but they did not last long, and all my clothes have been stolen by Rehani, a Zanzibari. Stanley has had me working hard all day, and I have only time to write these few lines as the sun is going down. Our party have lost and sold a great quantity of ammunition.

Give my best wishes to old Jameson, also the other fellows whom I know; and hoping to see you up here before long.

Believe me, yours very sincerely,
T.H.P.

(*The three letters above were returned to Stanley by Ugarrowa on August 11, 1888.*)

14. *Stanley to Emin.*

Dated: Kavalli's, April 18, 1888.
Received: April 27, 1888.

DEAR SIR—

Your letter was put into my hands by Chief Mbiassi, of Kavalli (on the plateau), the day before yesterday, and it gave us all great pleasure.

I sent a long letter to you from Zanzibar by carriers to Uganda, informing you of my mission and of my purpose. Lest you may not have received it, I will recapitulate in brief its principal contents. It informed you first that, in compliance with instructions from the Relief Committee of London, I was leading an Expedition for your relief. Half of the fund necessary was subscribed by the Egyptian Government, the other half by a few English friends of yours.

It also informed you that the instructions of the Egyptian Government were to guide you out of Africa, if you were willing to leave Africa; if not, then I was to leave such ammunition as we had brought with us for you, and you and your people were then to consider yourselves as out of the service of Egypt, and your pay was to cease upon such notification being given by you. If you were willing to leave Africa, then the pay of yourself, officers and men, was to continue until you had landed in Egypt.

It further informed you that you yourself was promoted from Bey to Pasha.

It also informed you that I proposed, on account of the hostility of Uganda, and political reasons, to approach you by way of the Congo, and make Kavalli my objective point.

I presume you have not received that letter, from the total ignorance of the natives at Kavalli about you, as they only knew of Mason's visit, which took place ten years ago.

We first arrived here after some desperate fighting on the 14th December last. We stayed two days on the shore of the Lake near Kavalli, inquiring of every native that we could approach if they knew of you, and were always answered in the negative. As we had left our boat a month's march behind, we could get no canoe by fair purchase or force, we resolved to return, obtain our boat, and carry it to the Nyanza. This we have done, and in the meantime we constructed a little fort fifteen days' march from here, and stored such goods as we could not carry, and marched here with our boat for a second trial to relieve you. This time the most violent natives have received us with open arms, and escorted us by hundreds on the way. The country is now open for a peaceful march from Nyamsassi to our fort.

Now I await your decision at Nyamsassi. As it is difficult to supply rations to our people on the Nyanza plain, I hope we shall not have to wait long for it. On the plateau above there is abundance of food and cattle, but on the lower plain, border-ing the Nyanza, the people are mainly fishermen.

If this letter reaches you before you leave your place, I should advise you to bring in your steamer and boats, rations sufficient to subsist us while we await your removal, say about 12,000 or 15,000 lbs. of grain, millet, or Indian corn, &c., which, if your steamer is of any capacity, you can easily bring.

427

If you are already resolved on leaving Africa, I would suggest that you should bring with you all your cattle, and every native willing to follow you. Nubar Pasha hoped you would bring all your Makkaraka, and not leave one behind if you could help it, as he would retain them all in the service.

The letters from the Ministry of War, and from Nubar Pasha, which I bring, will inform you fully of the intention of the Egyptian Government, and perhaps you had better wait to see them before taking any action. I simply let you know briefly about the intentions of the Government, that you may turn the matter over in your mind, and be enabled to come to a decision.

I hear you have abundance of cattle with you; three or four milk cows would be very grateful to us if you could bring them in your steamer and boats.

I have a number of letters, some books and maps for you, and a packet for Captain Casati. I fear to send them by my boat, lest you should start from your place upon some native rumour of our having arrived here, and you should miss her. Besides, I am not quite sure that the boat will reach you; I therefore keep them until I am assured they can be placed in your hands safely.

We shall have to forage far and near for food while we await your attendance at Nyamsassi, but you may depend upon it we shall endeavour to stay here until we see you.

All with me join in sending you our best wishes, and are thankful that you are safe and well.

Believe me, dear Pasha,

Your most obedient servant,

HENRY M. STANLEY.

Commanding Relief Expedition.

15. Stairs's report on his journey to Ugarrowas.'

Dated: Fort Bodo, June 6, 1888.

SIR—

I have the honour to report that in accordance with your orders of the 15th February, 1888, I left this place on the 16th of that month with an escort of twenty couriers and other details, to proceed to Ugarrowa's station on the Ituri, forward the couriers on their journey to Major Barttelot's column, relieve the invalids left in charge of Ugarrowa, and bring them on to this station. . . .

. . . Reaching Kilonga Longa's on the 22nd, we arranged for a party to take us by a road south of Ituri, and on the 24th left. On the 1st of March crossed the Lenda, courses now N.W. and N.N.W. On the 9th reached Farishi, the upper station of Ugarrowa. On the 14th we reached Ugarrowa's, on the Ituri, early in the morning. For many days we had been having rains, and owing to these I suffered very much from fevers, and on getting to Ugarrowa's had to remain in bed for two days.

At U.'s some eight or ten (of the invalids) were away foraging, and to get these required three and a half days.

Fifty-six (56) men were left with Ugarrowa, viz., five Somalis, five Nubians, and forty-six Zanzibaris, on the 18th of September, 1887. Of this total twenty-six had died, including all the Somalis except Dualla. There were still two men out when I left. Baraka W. Moussa I detailed as a courier in place of another (who had been left at Ipoto with a bad ulcer), and Juma B. Zaid remained with Ugarrowa.

The majority of the men were in a weak state when I arrived, and on leaving I refused to take seven of these. Ugarrowa, however, point blank refused to keep them, so thus I was obliged to bring on men with the certainty of their dying on the march.

Early on the 16th, Abdullah and his couriers were despatched down river. On the 17th took our forty-four rifles from Ugarrowa, and out of these made him a present of two and forty-two rounds Remington ammunition.

On the 18th closed with U. for $870, being $30 for twenty-nine men; also handed him his bills of exchange and your letter.

On same day left for Ibwiri (Fort Bodo) with following.

From the 19th to 23rd, when I reached Farishi, the rain was constant, making the track heavy and the creeks difficult in crossing. From here on to Ipoto I had bad fevers day after day, and having no one to carry me, had to make marches of five to seven miles per day. The constant wettings and bad roads had made all the men very low-spirited, some doubting even that there was help ahead. Reached Ipoto April 11th, left 13th; and after more trouble from fever reached here on 26th April. All glad to see the Fort. Dualla, the Somali, I was obliged to leave at Ipoto. Tam, a former donkey-boy, deserted on the road. Of the draft of invalids (twenty-six) ten had died. Kibwana also died from chest disease in camp near Mambungu. Out of fifty-six invalids brought fourteen alive to the Fort.

On reaching Fort Bodo I found you had been so long gone that I could not follow up with safety with the few rifles I could command, and so remained at this station and reported myself to Captain Nelson, who was left in charge of the Fort by you.

Floods, rains, fevers, and other illnesses had been the cause of our long delay, and those of us who were in fit condition at all, felt bitterly the disappointment at not being able to reach you.

I have the honour to be, &c.,
W. G. STAIRS.
Lieut. R.E.

16. Barttelot to Sir Redvers Buller.

Dated: Yambuya, June 1, 1888.

DEAR SIR REDVERS BULLER—
I thought perhaps you might like to have a short account of our Expedition, which, as far as the rear-guard is concerned, and we can judge, has turned out a fiasco and a delusion. . . .

(After dealing with the trip to Yambuya and the early part of the Rear Guard's stay there, the letter goes on—)

I had no means of moving, for my men were dying fast from want of proper food and medicine; they have nothing but makago or manioc. Our number of loads trebled the men who were fit to carry. Deserters had come in and stated that Stanley had had great trouble on the road; so I expected he would be late, but not so late as this.

In the meantime, on November 15, Tippu had gone to Kasongo, and was expected back on February 1, 1888. But on February 1 we heard that men were scarce, and that Tippu would not return for several months.

About fifty men had been sent, ostensibly for us, to Salem Mohammed, but we were not to use them till Tippu came.

From October, 1887, to March, 1888, about 800 Arabs were sent up eastward on Stanley's track, and we are completely surrounded by their camps. The paucity of men, and Tippu's protracted absence, determined me to hunt him, and on February 14, 1888, Jameson and I started for the Falls for that purpose. We got to the Falls February 20, and we were told Tippu would come in ten days; however, he did not. Then, that a big caravan entirely for us would arrive with Tippu on the new moon, March 12. A caravan of 300 came on the 14th, but only fifty small-poxed men for us. Sick and disheartened at this, I sent Jameson to Kasongo, March 18, with full instructions to offer Tippu money for 1,000 men—600 carriers and 400 fighting men. And I hastened back to camp, got there on March 24, and sent Ward down river to Banana Point with a telegram to Mackinnon. Salem Mohammed, meanwhile, had got troublesome, and had undoubted designs on our camp and the stores, but I frustrated him.

The natives I have found quite peaceful, and willing to trade, till they were stopped by the Arabs. The Arabs are the danger here, not the natives.

On May 8 the Belgian steamer A.I.A., with two officers on board, arrived here, bringing back Ward's escort. They stayed three days, and then went round to the Falls.

Three days later I went to the Falls overland, and caught them up—we both arriving together on May 18.

No news of Jameson, Tippu, or Stanley, beyond a vague report that the latter was dead, which is not true. I came to the Falls to watch the Belgians and the head Arab, Nzige, and because I heard from up river of a large caravan coming to the Falls; also I reckoned that Jameson should return about the 14th.

On May 22, unexpectedly, Jameson and Tippu came back with 400 men, all for us. And Tippu told Jameson that 800 men would be forthcoming, which Jameson told me. But on the 23rd, when I had my palaver with Tippu, he said he could only let us have 400 men, and these were only to come on condition they only carried 40 lb., our original weight being 60 lb. He said he knew nothing about the 800 men, and that as he had much fighting to do he could give us no more. He would enter into no written agreement with me.

The truth came out in a few days. It has been apparent to me for the last eight months that Tippu had designs on Bangala: it is a country rich in ivory and slaves. The Belgians became aware of it on its being pointed out to them, and to avert it asked Tippu to send a strong force to the Mobangi River, before anyone else took it. It abounds in ivory, slaves, and food, lying north of the Free State territory, and entering the Congo west of Bangala, on the north bank, at Equator Station.

Tippu's ambition aroused, his promises of help to us were immediately placed on one side. Seeing how matters stood, I said nothing, but took the 400 men and came on here with all speed.

Tippu should be here tomorrow, and then I will tackle him, and, I hope, get another 200 out of him. I am very busy now rearranging stores, etc.

Tippu, of course, could have let us have the men long ago if he had wished, and if it had not been for Holmwood, the Consul at Zanzibar, we should not have got them now.

All the Arabs are dead against Tippu helping us—Tippu and all hating Stanley for his mean treatment of them when he crossed Africa.

I hope to start not later than June 12, to look for Stanley and find out about Emin Pasha. During my long stay here, I have never been idle; the village chiefs, etc., for miles around I know, and I know more of the Arab movements than they dream of.

The camp is a healthy one, our men dying chiefly from debility caused by the food; out of 240 I have lost eighty-seven since June 28, 1887.

The English officers are all well but Troup, and he is in a dying state, and is going home as soon as the steamer *Stanley* arrives, which she should do in a few days.

The officers are Jameson; Troup, son of the late General Troup; Bonny, an ex-sergeant of A.M.D., and who got the D.S. order at Sekouni's stronghold; and Ward, nephew of the naturalist.

Jameson, Bonny, and self will be the three to go up. Ward goes to Bangala with the stores I cannot carry.

A better officer than Jameson I could not have; and Bonny, though rough and slow, is steady, honest, and sure.

I hope to be in England this time next year; but time in Africa is uncertain.

The country for miles is a dense jungle, only clearings on the waterway; food scarce, the roads execrable. I would far sooner be in the desert again; I am looking forward with the keenest pleasure to this trip, though I am afraid it may not be productive of anything, for Stanley is such a funny fellow, that very likely he may be in England now. At the same time he may be in a scrape, out of which I may perchance rescue him, though, if ever I do get to him, I shall catch it.

I trust you are well, and that all fighting may be postponed until I arrive home. I will put in below if I get more men, and the day I start. With kind regards,

Believe me, yours sincerely,

EDMUND M. BARTTELOT.

We leave this to-morrow, June 11, 1888. So good-bye, sir.

17. Two letters written by Stanley from Banalya.

(i) *Stanley to Tippu-Tib.*
  Dated: August 17, 1888.

To Sheikh Hamad bin Mohammed, from his
good friend, H. M. Stanley.

Many salaams to you.
I hope you are in good health as I am, and that you have remained in good health
since I parted with you on the Congo. I have many things to say to you, but I hope I
shall see you face to face before many days. I reached this place this morning with
130 Wangwana, three soldiers, and sixty-six natives from Emin Pasha. This is now
the eighty-second day since I left Emin Pasha on the Nyanza, and we have only lost
three men on the way—two have been drowned and one ran away.
  I found the white man whom I was looking for, Emin Pasha, quite well, and the
other white man, Casati, quite well also. Emin Pasha has ivory in abundance,
cattle by thousands, sheep, goats, fowls, and food of every kind. We found him to be
a very good and kind man. He gave a number of things to all our white and black
men. His liberality could not be exceeded. His soldiers blessed our black men for
coming so far to show them the way, and many of them were ready to follow me at
once out of the country, but I asked them to stay quiet yet a few months that I
might come back and fetch the other men and goods that I have left in Yambuya. And
they prayed God to give me strength that I might finish my work. May their prayer
be heard! And now, my friend, what are you going to do? We have gone the road
twice over. We know where it is bad and where it is good. We know where there is
plenty of food and where there is none—where all the camps are, and where we shall
sleep and rest. I am waiting to hear your words. If you go with me it is well. If you do
not go with me it is well also. I leave it to you. I stay here ten days, and then I
go on slowly. I move from here to a big island two hours' march from here, and
above this. There are plenty of houses and plenty of food for the men. Whatever you
have to say to me my ears will be open with a good heart as it has always been
towards you. Therefore, come quickly, for on the eleventh morn from this I will
move on. All my white men are well, but I left them all behind except my servant
William, who is with me.
  Salaams, &c., to all (*enumerating several Arabs' names*).

                                                    HENRY M. STANLEY,

(*The above was passed on to the Committee by Ward, who does not state (cf.* WARD *p. 138)*
whether the original letter was in English, Arabic or Swahili. The first is unlikely).

(ii) *Stanley to Jameson.*
  Dated: "On march above Bonalya", August 30, 1888.
  Undelivered—Jameson being dead since August 17.

DEAR SIR,
I know that Bonny has written to you about my arrival, so I may be brief. Arriving

at Bonalya 17th inst. I have been busy ever since reorganising the Expedition, which I found to be in a terrible state. Today the second march from Bonalya has begun and we shall continue on. Bonny showed me your letter of the 12th inst., wherein you stated it to be your purpose to go to Bangala. I cannot make out why the Major, you, Troup, and Ward have been so *demented*—demented is the word! You understand English—an English letter of instructions was given you. You said it was intelligible, yet for some reason or another you have not followed one paragraph. You paid a thousand pounds to go on this Expedition, you have voluntarily thrown your money away by leaving the Expedition. Ward is not a whit better; he has acted all through, as I hear, more like an idiot than a sane being. You have left me naked—I have no clothes, no medicine; I will say nothing of my soap and candles, a photograph apparatus and chemicals, two silver watches, a cap, and a score of other trifles. You believed I was dead, yet you brought along my boots, and two hats, and a flannel jacket. You believed the Expedition had gone to Ujiji, yet you took Stairs' and the other officers' goods along. Is this not rather inconsistent?

I shall proceed along the south bank of the river for nearly two months and then cross the river to the north bank, then straight to the Nyanza. If you can bring my kit with you you are welcome to go on with us if you can catch us up. Forty guns will take you along safely to the point where we cross the river. Emin Pasha is quite well. All our officers are well; we have lost 50 per cent. of men. I have come from the Nyanza in eighty-two days and from our fort in sixty-one days.

Our track will be quite clear as a highway, two marches from Bonalya or, as you call it, Unaria. It will be white all the way to the crossing. If you can find where we landed on the north bank—it will be one march above Nepoko confluence with the Aruwimi—you will be able to follow us with forty guns; with less it would be dangerous. The plains are twenty-five marches from the crossing place. Splendid young country—game of all kinds. I have left all the officers at Fort Bodo except Jephson, who is with Emin Pasha. Though, as reported to me, you, and all of you, seemed to have acted like madmen, your version may modify my opinion. Therefore I write this brief note to you in the midst of bustle and hurry.

Yours truly,
HENRY M. STANLEY.

18. *Stairs's report on his tenure of command at Fort Bodo.*

Dated: Fort Bodo, December 21, 1888.

SIR,

I have the honour to report that, in accordance with your letter of instructions dated Fort Bodo, June 13th, 1888, I took over the charge of Fort Bodo and its garrison.

The strength of the garrison was then as follows: Officers, 3; Zanzibaris, 51; Soudanese, 5; Madis, 5; total, 64.

Soon after your departure from (sic—? for) Yambuya, the natives in the immediate vicinity became excessively bold and aggressive; gangs of them would come into the plantations nearly every day searching for plantains, and at last a party of them came into the gardens east of the Fort at night-time and made off with a quantity of tobacco and beans. On the night of the 21st August they again attempted to steal more tobacco; this time, however, the sentries were on the alert. The lesson they received had the effect of making the natives less bold, but still our bananas were being taken at a great rate. I now found it necessary to send out three parties of patrols per week; these had as much as they could do to keep out the natives and elephants. If fires were not made every few days the elephants came into the bananas, and would destroy in a single night some acres of plantation.

By November 1st we had got the natives well in hand, and at this time I do not believe a single native camp exists within eight miles of the Fort. Those natives to the S.S.E. of the Fort gave us the most trouble, and were the last to move away from our plantations.

At the end of July we all expected the arrival of Mr. Mounteney Jephson from the Albert Nyanza to relieve the garrison, and convey our goods on to the Lake shore. Day after day, however, passed away, and no sign of him or news from him reaching us made many of the men more and more restless as each day passed. Though most of the men wished to remain at the Fort till relief turned up, either in the shape of Mr. Jephson or yourself, still some eight or ten discontented ones, desirous of reaching the Lake and partaking of the plenty there, were quite ready at any time to desert the loads, the white men, and sick.

Seeing how things stood I treated the men at all times with the greatest leniency, and did whatever I could to make their life at the Fort as easy for them as was possible.

Shortly after the time of Mr. Jephson's expected arrival, some of the men came to me and asked for a "shauri"; this I granted. At this shauri the following propositions were made by one of the men (Ali Juma), and assented to by almost every one of the Zanzibaris present: (1) To leave the Fort, march on to the Lake by way of Mazamboni's country, making double trips, and so get on all the loads to the Lake and have plenty of food. (2) Or, to send say fifteen couriers with a letter to the edge of the plain, there to learn if the Bandusuma were still our friends or no; if unfriendly, then to return to the Fort; if friendly, then the couriers would take on the letter to Mr. Jephson, and relief would come.

To the first proposal I replied: (1) Mr. Stanley told me not to move across the plain, whatever else I did, without outside aid. (2) Did not Mr. Stanley tell Emin

Pasha it was not safe to cross the plains, even should the natives be friendly, without sixty guns? (3) We had only thirty strong men, the rest were sick; we should lose our loads and sick men.

We all lived on the best of terms after I had told them we could not desert the Fort. We went on hoeing up the ground and planting corn and other crops, as if we expected a prolonged occupation. On the 1st September a severe hurricane accompanied by hail passed over the Fort, destroying fully 60 per cent. of the standing corn, and wrecking the banana plantations to such an extent that at least a month passed before the trees commenced to send up young shoots. Had it not been for this we should have had great quantities of corn; but as it was I was only able to give each man ten corns per week. The weakly ones, recommended by Dr. Parke, got one cup of shelled corn each per day. At one time we had over thirty men suffering from ulcers, but, through the exertion of Dr. Parke, all their ulcers on your arrival had healed up with the exception of some four.

Eight deaths occurred from the time of your departure up to the 20th December, two were killed by arrows, and two were captured by natives.

In all matters where deliberation was necessary the other officers and myself took part. We were unanimous in our determination to await your arrival, knowing that you were using every endeavour to bring relief to us as speedily as possible.

On the 20th December I handed over the charge of the Fort to you, and on the 21st the goods entrusted to my care.

I have the honour to be, Sir,

Your obedient servant,

W. G. STAIRS.

Lieut. R.E.

19. *The reported capture of Stanley and Emin.*

(i) *Osman Digna to General Grenfell.* (Translation)

In the name of the Great God, &c. This is from Osman Digna to the Christian who is Governor of Suakin. Let me inform you that some time ago Rundle* sent me a letter asking me of the man who was governor in the Equator Province. On the arrival of the said letter I sent it at once to the Khalifa. The Khalifa has sent me the answer, and has informed me that the said Governor of the Equator has fallen into our hands, and is now one of the followers of the Mahdi. The details of his fall are as follows: The Khalifa sent steamers to the Equator commanded by one of our chiefs named Omar Saleh; they reached Lado, and on their arrival there they found that the troops of the said Governor, which were composed of military men and officers, had captured the Governor, with a traveller who was with him; they put them in chains and delivered them into the hands of our Chief. Now all the province is in our hands, and all the inhabitants have submitted to the Mahdi. We have taken all the arms and ammunition which was there, and also brought all the officers and the Chief Clerk to the Khalifa, who received them kindly, and now they are staying with him. They have also handed all the banners they had to him; therefore, as Rundle wishes to know what has become of that Governor, you tell him of this message. I inclose a copy of the letter which Tewfik had sent to said Governor. I also send you a dozen of the ammunition which was brought from the Equator.** I praise God for the victory of the believers and the defeat of the infidels.

(Sealed)

(ii) *Omar Saleh to the Khalifa.* (Translation.)
Dated: October 15, 1888.

In the name of the Great God, &c. This is from the least among God's servants to his Master and Chief Khalifa, &c. We proceeded with the steamers and army, and reached the town Lado where Emin, Mudir (*Governor*) of Equator, is staying. We reached this place 10th October, 1888. We must thank officers and men who made this conquest easy to us before our arrival. They caught Emin and a traveller staying with him, and put both in chains.

The officers and men refused to go to Egypt with the Turks. Tewfik sent Emin one of the travellers, whose name is Mr. Stanley. This Mr. Stanley brought with him a letter from Tewfik to Emin dated February 1, 1887, telling Emin to come with Mr. Stanley, and gave the rest of the force the option to go to Cairo or remain. The force refused the Turkish orders, and gladly received us. I found a great deal of (ostrich) feathers and ivory. I am sending with this on board the "Bordein" the officers and

---

* Sir Leslie Rundle (*called "Sir Leisurely Trundle" for the speed of his movements*), *Commanding the garrison at Suakin.*
** *Snider ammunition dated* 1869.

Chief Clerk. I am also sending the letter which came to Emin from Tewfik with the banners we took from the Turks. I heard that there is another traveller who came to Emin, but I heard that he returned. I am looking out for him. If he comes back again I am sure to catch him. All the chiefs of the province with the (? *native*) inhabitants were delighted to receive us. I have taken all the arms and ammunition. Please return the officers and Chief Clerk, when you have seen them and given the necessary instructions, because they will be of great use to me.

(*Baring, in Cairo, communicated the two despatches above to London, where they arrived on December 15, 1888. They were widely circulated in the European press and printed in England as a Command Paper, No. C.5602.*)

20. *Two reports on the battle for Duffile, November 1888.*

(i) *Omar Saleh to the Khalifa.* (Translation)

After three days of hard siege (*the garrison*) sallied forth in a square; but the Ansar attacked them sharply and they fled back to their fortifications. On the fourth day we agreed to rush their station by night. Nine colours proceeded to carry out the plan ... Some besieged the fortress on the south and some on the west. At dawn, after prayers, they attacked the station in one body, and some who were near the river ıound an entrance and got in with difficulty; but the rest could not discover any passage to enter, because the station was well fortified and strengthened from the inside by wood and earth and having very strong doors, with trenches outside. The infidels, being well screened inside their fortress began to fire on our brethren who were crowded at the door, striking it with axes and swords, but it was too strong and well covered with iron, while all the time our enemies were shooting at them. God did not wish the fall of the Post, and our brethren did not like to retreat and so the bearers of eight colours fell dead with those fighting under them. Our brave brethren could have been heard one saying to the other, "Forward to the infidels, I am dying." The other would answer him, "I am dying also." The wounded would also say to their stout companions, "Forward." When they despaired from getting in and being ashamed to have God see them retreating, you could have seen the one clasp his hands as in a state of praying and bow his head to the ground, being ashamed of heaven and remain so up to his death, until nearly all were killed and the colours with the gallant commanders fell on the ground lifeless. But God saved the ninth colour of Adam qad ar-Rab. Those who entered the station, although few, crushed many of God's enemies and killed the Captain and those with him. The bugle was sounded and the enemies surrounded our friends and the majority were killed but some were captured.

(ii) *Selim Aga to Emin.* (Translation)

My Master—
On November 18th the soldiers arrived here from Muggi and Labore stations, and with them 120 soldiers belonging to the 1st Battalion, who had escaped from Rejaf. I ordered Bachit Aga Mahmoud to take a small party of soldiers to Labore to find where the Donagla (*Mahdi-ists*) were encamped. At 11 a.m. some of the soldiers returned, and told us they had encountered some of them near Khor Itteen, and towards evening the rest returned and brought a letter from the chief of the Donagla, Omar Saleh, commanding us to surrender. The letter told us of the deaths of Hamad Aga, the Major, Abdullah Vaab Effendi, Ali Aga Djabor, Salem Effendi, and Hassan Effendi Lutvi, and threatened to destroy us if we did not obey. To this demand we made no answer, but burned the letter.

On November 25th the Donagla surrounded the station and shouted out on all sides, "We are the Mahdi's people." At 4 p.m. they sent us another letter, repeating their commands to surrender, but the soldiers threw the letter out of the station back at them. . . . On the 26th they approached, and firing went on between us from 9 a.m. to 3 p.m., when a body of soldiers sallied out and drove away the attacking party, and killed twelve of them, besides wounding many; among our soldiers there were no losses. On the 27th the Donagla again approached, and a good deal of firing went on from both sides. On the 28th a night attack was made, and we had to beat the soldiers up to their posts at 4 a.m., and firing went on until dawn. On this day were wounded Achmet Aga el Assinti, Bachit Aga Ali, and Suliman Aga Soudan; some were shot, and others were wounded by sword thrusts in their hands and feet. Some few soldiers and non-commissioned officers were also wounded in the same way. In the midst of the affray some of the Donagla actually entered the station and killed Mahomet Effendi el N'djar, the captain of the "Nyanza" steamer, and Ali Achmet, the engineer, Mooragan Derar, the pilot, Khamis Salim, the chief fireman, and Farajala Moru, second fireman, all belonging to the "Khedive" steamer. After these accidents we mustered up all our energy to try to kill the Donagla who had entered the station. Towards 8 o'clock, a.m., the battle was won by our soldiers, and the enemy dispersed. They left behind them 210 killed, besides those we were unable to count, and such wounded people as reached their camp. We captured eleven flags, and among them that of the Emir, some Remington rifles, percussion guns, and a lot of swords and spears; we also took one prisoner.

After the soldiers had celebrated this victory with a little ceremony, they returned to their quarters. . . .

(Selim goes on to describe the means by which the garrison ascertained the withdrawal of the enemy to Rejaf, and concludes—)

They had with them 150 wounded, and many died on the road. They burnt the stations of Khor Ayu and Labore and every station they passed through. And this is what I have to report to your Excellency about the Government soldiers.

P.S. Some of the chief men and the Kadi of the Donagla were killed in this fight.
                    SELIM AGA MATARA.
                    Bimbashi.

(A facsimile of Selim's original letter is printed in CASATI II pp. 202–203.)

APPENDIX II

CONRAD, KURTZ, KLEIN, AND BARTTELOT

In May 1890 Joseph Conrad was engaged as a steamer captain for the Upper Congo. His employers were the "Société Anonyme Belge pour l'Industrie et le Commerce du Haut Congo", the successor company to the Sanford Exploring Expedition. He was to command the *Florida*, one of the vessels in which Stanley had ferried his expedition to Yambuya three years earlier, and which had been absorbed by the "S.A.B." along with the other assets of the Sanford company. On June 12, 1890, Conrad disembarked at Boma from the steamer *Ville de Maceio*. The next day he reached Matadi,* ready to begin the overland journey to Stanley Pool. He made the crossing in nineteen days' marching. Reaching Kinshasa at the beginning of August, Conrad found the *Florida* undergoing repairs (it had been holed on a snag and sunk a couple of weeks earlier). But a new steamer, the *Roi des Belges*, was just leaving on the up-river run to Stanley Falls and Conrad embarked under her captain, a Dane named Koch, in order to gain some first-hand experience of river-navigation on the Congo.

They reached Stanley Falls on September 1, twenty-eight days after leaving the Pool. Since their reoccupation of the Falls in 1888, the Belgians had built up a large station whose principal function was to serve as a collecting-point for ivory from the Stanley Falls and Aruwimi districts. The Falls was still, however, an Arab strong-hold, and between the Belgian and Arab stations was maintained—for the moment— an outward show of peaceful intercourse.

The "S.A.B." had an agent at the Falls, a Frenchman named Georges Klein, twenty-seven years old, who had been less than two years on the Congo and now was being invalided home. He was taken on board the *Roi des Belges* together with a load of ivory, and on or about September 6, the steamer began the return journey. Meanwhile Captain Koch, too, had fallen ill, leaving Conrad in temporary command. During the voyage down river Klein died (September 21) and was buried at Bolobo.

By the time the *Roi des Belges* returned to Stanley Pool, Conrad had already had

---

* It was here that he met Casement, of whom he noted in his diary: "Thinks, speaks well, most intelligent, and very sympathetic." Years later, Conrad was to recall Casement with the same admiration: "There is a touch of the conquistador in him; for I've seen him start off into an unspeakable wilderness swinging a crook handled stick for all weapons, with two bull-dogs, Paddy (white) and Biddy (brindle) at his heels, and a Loanda boy carrying a bundle for all company. A few months afterwards it so happened that I saw him come out again, a little leaner, a little browner, with his stick, dogs and Loanda boy, and quietly serene as though he had been for a stroll in the park." (Conrad to Cunninghame Graham, 26–12–1903. Qu. Jean-Aubry, p. 52.)

enough of the Congo and was beginning to regard his presence there as a mistake. The country depressed him. The climate sapped his health. The Belgians disgusted him. And the aims, methods and motives of their commercial, colonising and civilising enterprises filled him with a contempt to which, in later years, he gave full expression in the beautifully-controlled irony of his two Congo stories, *Heart of Darkness* and *An Outpost of Progress*. A quarrel with his superiors now resulted in his being denied command of the *Florida* (which was about to take part, under Camille Delcommune, in the Katanga Expedition). This, together with an alarming deterioriation in his health, decided Conrad to throw up everything and return to civilisation without waiting for the expiry of his three-year contract. In January 1891 he was back in Europe.

Conrad was permanently to bear the marks of his Congo experience—not only in the attacks of fever and gout which tormented him intermittently until the end of his life, but also in its effects on his intellectual outlook. His brief contact with Darkest Africa had so profound an impact on him that in later life he looked back on the experience as a watershed; once he declared to his friend Edward Garnett, "Before the Congo I was only a simple animal."

In the record of Conrad's Congo venture there are numerous coincidental details which reflect, echo or underline the events of the Emin Pasha Relief Expedition. Some of these have already been touched on—his meeting with Casement, his posting to the *Florida*, his meeting with the skeleton on the road to Stanley Pool. But there is one parallel in particular which is of interest both to students of Conrad and to students of Stanley's ill-fated outing: the possibility that the model for Kurtz, the central character in Conrad's *Heart of Darkness*, was none other than Major Edmund M. Barttelot of the Seventh Royal Fusiliers.

Briefly, the thinking behind this theory is as follows.

Even a cursory comparison of the facts of Conrad's life with his novels and stories reveals that, to an extent much less common than might be supposed in writers of fiction, the events and people in his books are drawn from life. This correspondence is particularly striking in *Heart of Darkness*. It is also particularly easy to trace since the real events are well documented in Belgian records, in the published reminiscences of old Congo hands such as Ward, Troup and Werner, and in Conrad's own letters, papers and memoirs. Among the records left by Conrad himself is a diary—the only one Conrad ever kept. It is in two parts: the first covers the journey from Matadi to Kinchasa; the second contains technical information on river navigation between Stanley Pool and the Falls. Thus a point by point comparison is possible between Conrad's own Congo journey and that in *Heart of Darkness*.

In the book, the narrator, Marlowe, is engaged as a steamer captain for the Congo, travels to Matadi by steamer, and from there travels overland to Stanley Pool. There, he finds his boat wrecked, repairs her, and takes her up river to the limit of navigation (the place is not named but is referred to simply as the Inner Station) to relieve the Company's agent there, a man named Kurtz. The agent and a load of ivory are duly embarked, but on the journey down river Kurtz dies, and is buried ignominiously "in a muddy hole". Marlowe himself then falls ill and returns to Europe.

In outline, not to mention in hundreds of details, the story is plainly autobiographical. Conrad himself described *Heart of Darkness* as "experience pushed a little

443

(and only very little) beyond the actual facts of the case". This simple story of a river journey is, however, merely the skeleton on which Conrad hangs the real meat: the central interest of *Heart of Darkness*, and the feature of it which most concerns us here, lies in the character of the dying agent, Kurtz. As described by Marlowe, Kurtz is a man in whom the sickness of the body is merely an added symptom of intellectual, spiritual and moral disorder. He has, in fact, gone bush to a quite startling degree; by participation in "unspeakable rites" he has gained some kind of psychological hold over the native inhabitants and the same time gained access to the diabolical power which, though enabling him to gratify all manner of weird, dark and primitive lusts, ends by destroying him. The steps which led to Kurtz's moral collapse are not set out; the precise nature of his misdeeds is not detailed to us. We see him already broken and dying and must rely on the deductions of Marlowe—expressed in elliptical generalisations—for information about Kurtz's road to ruin. But the point Conrad was making is quite clear: Africa was for him the home of a malign and horrible primeval power (symbolised by the "darkness" of the title). It is this power, not the jungle, the climate or the cannibal inhabitants, which is the real enemy of civilised man in Africa. It is this power which has found out the weaknesses in Kurtz's moral make-up, smashed through the protective veneer of civilisation, and, having beaten down these too-fragile defences, claimed its victim body and soul.*

All the characters in *Heart of Darkness* have easily identifiable counterparts in real-life people Conrad met during his Congo service. As for Kurtz himself, the parallel with Klein, the agent at Stanley Falls, is clear, at least for the place and manner of his death and for Conrad-Marlowe's involvement in it. If there were any doubt about the validity of identifying Kurtz with Klein, it would be dispelled by the further fact that, in the manuscript of *Heart of Darkness*, Conrad actually used the name Klein for the fictitious agent but afterwards crossed it out and substituted the name Kurtz. But beyond the facts of his birth and death and the date of his engagement for the Congo, almost nothing is known of Georges Klein, and nothing whatever to suggest that he was in any way different from the hundreds of young men who met an early but otherwise undistinguished death after a short but otherwise banal career in the Belgian service. This paucity of information has led modern researchers into the antecedents of Conrad's fiction to look elsewhere for the prototype of Kurtz's spectacular moral collapse.

A solution to the dilemma has recently (1967) been proposed by Miss Jerry Allen

---

* There is also a Faustian angle to Kurtz's tragedy in that intellectual pride and the lust of forbidden knowledge play an important part in his downfall. He is represented as a man whose intelligence and attainments were as far beyond the ordinary as was "the colossal scale of his vile desires". Here Conrad is implying a distinction between Kurtz and the other characters in the story (Marlowe excepted)—the latter being men in whom an almost total lack of intelligence and sensibility is parallelled by mean, squalid and petty vices: materialism, greed, selfishness and vanity. It is almost as though Conrad saw them as immune to real evil through the sheer brutishness of their natures. Thus it is Marlowe, the only character immune to corruption, who alone can penetrate the nature of Kurtz's degradation.

444

in her book *The Sea Years of Joseph Conrad*: that Kurtz's madness and misdeeds are the fictional embodiment of the madness and misdeeds of Major Barttelot.

There is nothing inherently improbable in this idea. It is reasonable to assume that Conrad, on the Congo in 1890, the year that the Rear Column controversy was raging in Europe, was familiar with the wildly distorted rumours that had been circulated about the behaviour of Barttelot and Jameson. And, superficially at least, these stories of cannibalism, madness, orgies, sadistic punishments, murderous rages, and heaven knows what besides, offer points of resemblance to the eccentricities of Agent Kurtz. Miss Allen's hypothesis is sufficiently plausible to have gained it acceptance among other writers on Conrad. She herself plainly looks on the identity of Kurtz and Barttelot not as a hypothesis but as a fact, and her readers may be forgiven for doing the same. There are, however, a number of objections to Miss Allen's theory which it can do no harm to state before the Kurtz–Barttelot hypothesis is set in concrete and passes into the folklore of literary criticism.

1. In the first place, the theory is otiose; there is no need to find a real-life model for Kurtz's madness. Conrad's method as a writer was, in general, to select the physical facts of people, places and incidents from his own experience; but the psychological drama of his stories, the inner life of his characters, is nearly always his own creation. Thus it is sufficient to find, in Klein, a model for the biographical facts of Kurtz's career; his character can be left to Conrad's imagination.

2. Secondly, while Miss Allen states as a fact what is, at best, a plausible coincidence, she offers no *documentary* evidence for what she asserts. Nowhere in Conrad's letters or biographical reminiscences is there a line or a word to show that Conrad had ever heard of Barttelot. (I do Miss Allen the credit of supposing that, had such evidence existed, she would have found it.)

3. Thirdly, there are as many points of resemblance between Kurtz and Jameson as there are between Kurtz and Barttelot. But Miss Allen ignores Jameson's existence apart from a single reference to the cannibalism story, in which (a) she appears to state that it was Barttelot, not Jameson, who instigated the orgy, and (b) she spells Jameson's name wrong ("Jamieson").

4. It is central to Conrad's portrayal of Kurtz that Kurtz was a man of great intellect, profound culture, wide attainments, and lofty principles. Barttelot was none of these. He was a half-educated, barely-articulate, upper-class, fox-hunting subaltern, whose interests, attitudes, ambitions and attainments adhered rigidly to the norms laid down by the *Boy's Own Paper*. Indeed, he was a specimen so typical of his class and his era as to seem almost a caricature. Miss Allen can find nothing of Faust in Major Barttelot.

5. Finally, it should be pointed out that Miss Allen has got her facts woefully wrong as regards the events of the Emin Pasha Relief Expedition. Hence her grasp of the background to the Stanley-Barttelot controversy is inadequate to her purpose. For this she is not entirely to blame since her main source of information appears to be the *New York Times* for the year 1890, and that paper's main informant was Henry M. Stanley. Thus, quite apart from the truth or otherwise of the stories about Barttelot (which Miss Allen unhesitatingly accepts in their most lurid form) there are over a dozen plain mistakes in the few lines she devotes to the events of the Expedition. (For example, the statement that Barttelot was killed at Yambuya, that

Stanley and Emin met at Wadelai, that the Mahdi-ist insurrection occurred in 1885, and so on).

These points have not been raised with the intention of refuting Miss Allen's hypothesis, but merely to indicate that her case has not been proved. It cannot, on the other hand, be disproved. Therefore, should anyone—with the above reservations in mind—choose to believe that Barttelot, through Conrad, has found his place among the immortals of English fiction, there is no reason why he should not do so.

*   *   *

The most thorough examination to date of the correspondences between Conrad's Congo journey and the events of *Heart of Darkness* is contained in Professor Norman Sherry's book *Conrad's Western World* (1971). Curiously, Professor Sherry neither accepts nor rejects Miss Allen's theory that Barttelot was the model for Kurtz. He ignores it altogether, while putting forward his own theory—that the original ("at least in part") for Kurtz was a Belgian agent by the name of Hodister. Professor Sherry's case is rather better-documented than Miss Allen's, and he has unearthed some striking pieces of circumstantial evidence in support of his thesis, the merits of which, however, do not concern us here. But by a curious concidence there exists a connection between Hodister and Emin Pasha, since it is possible that Hodister was indirectly responsible for Emin's death.

Hodister was a crack agent of the "S.A.B." and former employee of the Sanford Expedition. He was a conspicuously successful ivory collector, had explored and opened up new territory on the Upper Congo, and had been made Chef de District at Bangala in 1889. In 1890, during Conrad's stay on the Congo, he had been busy exploring the commercial possibilities of the Lomami and Lualaba Rivers. At the beginning of 1892, as Director of the newly-formed "Syndicat Commercial du Katanga", he led an expedition back into those regions with the intention of founding trading stations there. The venture ended badly; Hodister and his followers were massacred in detail by the Nyangwe Arabs. It was supposed at the time that the massacre was committed in retaliation for Van Kerckhoven's depredations (while leading his Expedition to Equatoria) against the slaving stations established in the Welle Valley. This may well have been the case. It is as reasonable, however, to suppose that the Nyangwe Arabs simply resented Hodister's blatant attempt to extend Belgian commercial interests into the very heart of the territory which the Zanzibar traders had always—and with good reason—considered indisputably their own.

The Hodister massacre occurred some five months before Emin's arrival at Kinena's, the place where he met his death. In all probability, Emin knew nothing of it. But Kibonge, of course, did, and, according to the testimony of Ismaili, it was jealousy of Muni Mohara (the Nyangwe chieftain) and desire to emulate his bloody exploit, that inspired Kibonge to order Emin's death. Ismaili further stated that Emin's head, sent in the first instance to Kibonge as proof that his orders had been carried out, was then forwarded by him to Muni Mohara at Nyangwe.

References

ALLEN, JERRY. *The Sea Years of Joseph Conrad.* Methuen, London, 1967.

SHERRY, NORMAN. *Conrad's Western World.* C.U.P., Cambridge, 1971.

BAINES, JOCELYN. *Joseph Conrad, a critical biography.* Weidenfeld & Nicolson, London, 1960.

JEAN-AUBRY, G. *Joseph Conrad in the Congo.* Bookman's Journal, London, 1926.

CONRAD, JOSEPH. *Heart of Darkness.* 1902. (1st book publication.)

CONRAD, JOSEPH. *An Outpost of Progress.* 1898. (1st book publication.)

CONRAD, JOSEPH. *Geography and some explorers.* (In *Last Essays*, 1926.)

CONRAD, JOSEPH. *A Personal Record.* 1926.

MOHUN, R. DORSEY. "The Death of Emin Pasha." Century *Magazine*, February 1895, pp. 591–598.

Biographie Coloniale Belge. Entries for "Korzeniowski" and "Hodister'.'

APPENDIX III

THE PRESENT WAR IN THE SOUTHERN SUDAN

The struggle of the South Sudanese peoples against oppression and exploitation by invaders from the North has now been going on for something like 130 years. Since the arrival of the first Khartoum traders in or around the year 1840, the tribes of Equatoria and Bahr-el-Ghazal have seen, and suffered under, a continuous succession of alien intruders: Danagla slave-hunters, Egyptian governors (Baker, Gordon, Emin), Mahdi-ist jihadiya, Manyuema ivory-hunters, Belgian colonial troops and British administrators. All these people—whatever their motives—have made their contribution, greater or larger, towards destroying the complex and delicately-balanced social and economic way of life of the native inhabitants. And yet, though domination by outsiders—whether benevolent or purely predatory—has lasted more than a century and a quarter, the tribes have consistently attempted (and still are attempting) to maintain their integrity and independence. This has entailed a great deal of fighting, such as that which has formed part of the background to the events of this book.

Under the Anglo-Egyptian Condominium, established in 1899 after the chaotic interlude which followed Emin's withdrawal, the Southern Sudan saw a long period of comparative peace. During this time, as a matter of policy, the South was as far as possible kept isolated from the influence of the Arabised North. This policy —principally intended to facilitate the extirpation of slave-raiding—was well-meant, but it had the effect of further accentuating the differences between the two populations. And this process was taken a long step further by the Christianisation of a large section of the southern population during the same period. When the Condominium ended in 1955, and the British handed over to an independent Sudanese Republic, the aversion of the southerners to domination by "Arabs" from the north remained as powerful as it had always been. Even before the British withdrawal, demands for southern autonomy began to be heard. These were ignored by the British in their arrangements for the hand-over, while their successors, the Khartoum Government, promptly instituted a heavy-handed programme of forced Arabisation accompanied by blatant economic exploitation and a resolute denial of southern political aspirations.

In 1955, before the hand-over was even completed, it was clear to the southerners that they were to be denied control of their own affairs, let alone a voice in the affairs of the Sudan as a whole. Disillusion rapidly gave place to violence. In July there were riots following the dismissal of 300 African workers from Nazara cotton factory and their replacement by "Arabs". Police fired on the crowds, killing 25 and wounding many more. The disturbances spread. Hundreds of Northerners were massacred in the course of spontaneous uprisings. The garrison of Torit (near the Uganda border) mutinied and murdered its officers. A State of Emergency was declared. It remains in force to this day.

Since 1963 the main burden of southern resistance has been borne by a guerrilla organisation calling itself Anyanya (the local name for a species of scorpion). Anyanya activities have followed the classic pattern—harassing road and rail communications, attacks on isolated outposts, confinement of government forces to the towns and main roads, provision of an alternative government (including schools and medical services) in guerrilla-held areas of the countryside. The Government's response has taken equally familiar forms: concentration camps, mass arrests, torture, destruction of villages, crops and cattle by ground forces and by bombing (with Egyptian MIGs), massacres of rebel sympathisers, and so on. The net result to date is an estimated quarter of a million refugees living in camps in neighbouring countries,* and twice that number either killed in the fighting or dead of malnutrition, disease and exposure as a direct result of the fighting.**

All this has gone on almost totally ignored by the outside world. The events which have left half a million people dead and a quarter of a million homeless have earned less coverage in the British press than a Miss World Competition, a Liberal Party conference, or a pile-up on the M.1.

At the time of writing (March 1972) there is hope that a term to the long agony of the Southern Sudan may actually be in sight. On February 28 this year a cease-fire agreement between the Sudanese Government and the Southern insurgents was signed at Addis Ababa. The proposed settlement envisages the withdrawal of southern demands for outright secession in return for: large, but limited regional autonomy; incorporation of Anyanya personnel into the national armed forces; southern representation in the central government; and abandonment of the policy of forcible Arabisation. Whether or not this agreement will be found workable in practice, remains to be seen. If it is, then we shall be witnessing not only the end of 17 years of bloody misery for the South, but perhaps even the final realisation of the 130 years' struggle of its peoples for the right to manage their own affairs.

---

* B. H. MacDermot, Chairman, South Sudan Association, in *Grass Curtain* (Vol. 1 no. 4, April 1971, p. 39). There are 176,000 registered refugees in camps administered by the U.N. High Commission for Refugees. The figure of 250,000 contains an allowance for unregistered refugees.

** Statement by the Anti-Slavery Society to the U.N. Commission on Human Rights, Geneva, March 1971. These figures are put forward simply as "estimates". No objective and authoritative assessment exists of the loss of life resulting from the war. Epidemic diseases have undoubtedly contributed to the total, though again no reliable figures exist. Reports reaching the W.H.O. of 1,345 deaths from cholera in the Southern Sudan were flatly denied by the Khartoum Government. (*Guardian*, June 22, 1971.)

APPENDIX IV

SLEEPING SICKNESS IN UGANDA

Sleeping sickness in humans is caused by one of two closely-related organisms, *Trypanosoma gambiense* or *Trypanosoma rhodesiense*, the first of which is found in a broad belt stretching from the Gulf of Guinea east to the Lakes Region and south to Angola, and the second of which is restricted to the highlands of central East Africa. These two pathogens are indistinguishable—except in their effects—from the third member of the gang, *Trypanosoma brucei*, which causes the fatal "nagana" disease in cattle and horses but does not affect humans.

The trypanosomes are carried to the victim by the tsetse fly (*Glossina palpalis*, *Glossina morsitans*), which takes them up in a blood meal from the host. In the alimentary tract of the fly they multiply and develop before passing to the salivary glands. They are then passed to the victim along with the saliva which the fly injects while feeding to prevent coagulation.

Trypanosoma gambiense—and the sickness resulting from it—was originally confined in its habitat to the west coast of Africa, and as far as anyone knew this was the case until the end of the nineteenth century. No one was prepared, therefore, for the devastating outbreak of sleeping sickness which raged through the Uganda Lakes Region at the turn of the century. Since the area had previously been unaffected, the population had no immunity. As a result, the outbreak achieved a terrifying virulence. In the Lake Albert–Lake Victoria district between 1901 and 1906, two hundred thousand people died. This figure represents something like two-thirds of the population of the directly-affected areas (lake- and river-margins).

The epidemic was all the more alarming in that, at the time, the mechanisms of the disease were understood dimly, if at all. The life-cycle of the trypanosome is a complex affair whose elucidation was to take many years of patient research (and is a story worth a book in itself). But later, once the causative agent had been isolated and its relations with host, vector and victim scientifically established, it became natural to ask how it had come about that a disease endemic to the West African coast had made its appearance so suddenly and so devastatingly in an area nearly two thousand miles away.

It is now generally accepted—though of course it can never be proved—that *Trypanosoma gambiense* arrived in Uganda in the bloodstream of a member or members of the Emin Pasha Relief Expedition.

References

INGRAMS, HAROLD: *Uganda.* H.M.S.O. 1960 p. 165.
FIENNES, RICHARD: *Man, nature and disease.* Weidenfeld & Nicolson, 1964 pp. 57 ff.
Encyclopaedia Britannica—articles under "Sleeping sickness" and "Tsetse fly".

APPENDIX V

EMIN'S COLLECTIONS

The facts of Emin's life leave us in no doubt of the capital importance he attached to his scientific work, especially as a collector and naturalist. It would be of something more than academic interest to know whether the scientific world of the day attached as much importance to Emin as he did to it (so to speak). It certainly seems to be the case that the staffs of the various museums and institutes who undertook the description and classification of the specimens received from Emin were prepared to take him very seriously indeed. But an assessment of Emin's true place in the constellation of nineteenth-century naturalists is beyond the competence of the present writer.

For the benefit of whoever might wish to investigate the question, I append the following results of enquiries I made at the British Museum (Natural History) regarding the fate of the collections despatched by Emin from Equatoria and elsewhere. For this information I am indebted to the kindness of Dr. D. W. Snow of the Museum's Ornithology Section, and Mr. John Edwards Hill of the Mammal Section, whose communications I reproduce with their permission.

Regarding Emin's bird collections, Dr. Snow writes:

> . . . some of these came to the Britsh Museum, where they were described by Shelley in Proc. Zool. Soc. London, 1888, pp. 17–50. They were referred to by Bowdler Sharpe, in his history of the Museum's bird collections, as some of the most valuable ever received. A further collection was sent by Emin Pasha to the Museum shortly before his death; but it was entrusted to somebody who proved not to be trustworthy, and it found its way eventually to Germany, where it was described by G. Hartlaub in 1882 (Abh. Naturwiss. Vereins Bremen, pp. 183–232).

Concerning the mammal specimens, I received the following information from Mr. J. E. Hill:

> Emin Pasha was an enthusiastic collector of mammals, his specimens being the first of this group to be obtained from the eastern Congo forest region. Three separate collections are recorded in the archive here. They are:
>
> B.M. 82.2.3.1–3   Bats from the Upper Nile.
> B.M. 87.12.1.1–106 A large collection of Equatorial mammals.
> B.M. 90.6.8.1–35   A further collection of Equatorial mammals.

Two accounts are devoted solely to mammals collected by Emin Pasha. These are:

Thomas, O. On a collection of mammals obtained by Emin Pasha in Equatorial Africa, and presented by him to the Natural History Museum. (*Proc. Zool. Soc. Lond.* 1888: 3–17, 2 plates.)

Thomas, O. On a collection of mammals obtained by Dr. Emin Pasha in Central and Eastern Africa. (*Proc. Zool. Soc. Lond.* 1890: 443–450, 1 plate.)

Numerous mammals were discovered by and named after Emin Pasha. These are:

Crocidura pasha Dollman, 1916, a shrew.
Nyctinomus emini De Winton, 1901, a bat.
Calogale emini Matschie, 1914, a mongoose, of uncertain status.
Sciurus rufobrachiatus pasha Schwann, 1904, a squirrel.
Sciurus emini Stuhlmann, 1894, a striped squirrel.
Gerbillus emini Thomas, 1892, a gerbil.
Leggada pasha Thomas, 1910, a pygmy mouse.
Cricetomys emini Wroughton, 1910, a giant rat.
Heliophobius emini Noack, 1893, a mole rat.
Dendrohyrax emini Thomas, 1887, a tree hyrax.
Cephalophus emini Matschie, 1914, a duiker.

I have listed these names exactly as they were described. Some are now in synonymy, i.e. the animals to which they refer have been found identical with others already described; some have been transferred to genera other than those in which they were described, i.e. *Gerbillus emini* is now *Taterillus emini* (Thomas, 1892), and some have been reduced to subspecific rank. *Dendrohyrax emini*, for example, is now *Dendrohyrax dorsalis emini* Thomas, 1887 and still in use.

The original specimens of species described by Thomas, De Winton and Dollman are in the collections here, as is that described by Schwann. Those described by Matschie, Noack and perhaps Stuhlmann are probably in the Zoologischer Museum, Berlin. The point can only be established by reference to the original descriptions, which can be done in the Library here.

I would suggest that if you wish to pursue this enquiry further you should arrange to visit the Mammal Section, where the extensive literature relating to Emin Pasha is available and some of his specimens can be examined. There is no certainty that all his specimens are here, however, since it seems that some at least went to Berlin.

The *Proceedings of the Zoological Society of London* proved on inspection to contain, in addition to the birds and mammals described by Shelley and Thomas, accounts of collections received from Emin at the same time (December 1888) of butterflies, beetles and shells. A hint of the esteem in which Emin was held as a collector may be found in Thomas's description of Emin's mammals, referring to *Dendrohyrax emini*: "I have very great pleasure in connecting with this interesting animal the name of its discoverer, to whom science is indebted for so large a contribution to our knowledge of the fauna of Central Africa" (p. 16).

The *Proceedings* for 1890 contains an account of the specimens collected by Emin while on the march to the Coast and from the district round Bagamoyo (received June 3, 1890). The same publication revealed an unexpected, and indeed rather surprising item—a collection of beetles and butterflies made at Yambuya by Mr. William Bonny, late of the Army Medical Department. This contribution earned Bonny the accolade of his name attached to a brace of bugs; *Procilia bonnyi, Craspedophorus bonnyi.*

The collections (birds and butterflies) made by Jameson at Yambuya are described in an appendix to his *Story of the Rear Column.*

Emin's own notes and correspondence on Natural History subjects are collected in the final volume of his published diaries (*Zoologische Aufzeichnungen Emins und seine Briefe an Dr G. Hartlaub, 1921*).

BIBLIOGRAPHY

In the list below, primary sources are marked *; secondary sources are marked † for modern works, and ‡ for works by writers contemporary with the events they describe.

†AIMOT, J. M. *Stanley, le dernier Conquistador*. Editions Sfelt, Paris, 1951.

†ANSTEY, R. T. *Britain and the Congo in the Nineteenth Century*. O.U.P., London, 1962.

*BAKER, SIR SAMUEL W. *Albert Ny'anza*. Macmillan, London, 1866.

*BAKER, SIR SAMUEL W. *Ismailia*. 2 vols. Macmillan, London, 1874.

*BARTTELOT, WALTER G. *The life of Edmund Musgrave Barttelot . . . from his letters and diary*. Richard Bentley, London, 1890.

*BIRKBECK HILL, G. *Colonel Gordon in Central Africa*. De La Rue, London, 1881.

*BRODE, HEINRICH. *Tippoo Tib*. Tr. H. Havelock. Edward Arnold, London, 1907.

*CASATI, GAETANO. *Ten years in Equatoria and the return with Emin Pasha*. Tr. Mrs. J. R. Clay and I. W. Savage Landor. 2 vols. Warne, London, 1891.

†COLLINS, ROBERT O. *The Southern Sudan, 1893–1898—a struggle for control*. Yale U.P., New Haven, Conn., 1962.

†COUPLAND, SIR REGINALD. *The Exploitation of East Africa, 1856–1890—the slave trade and the scramble*. London, 1939. (New ed., Faber, 1967.)

†COUPLAND, SIR REGINALD. *Livingstone's Last Journey*. Collins, London, 1947.

‡DRUMMOND, HENRY. *Tropical Africa*. Hodder & Stoughton, London, 1888.

‡FELKIN, ROBERT W. "The position of Emin Bey." *Scottish Geographical Magazine*, vol. II, pp. 705–719, 1886.

‡FOX-BOURNE, H. R. *The other side of the Emin Pasha Relief Expedition*. Chatto & Windus, London, 1891.

*GESSI, ROMOLO. *Seven Years in the Sudan*. Tr. Wolffsohn and Woodward. Sampson Low, London, 1892.

†GRAY, SIR JOHN. "Stanley versus Tippoo Tib." *Tanganyika Notes and Records*, XVIII, p. 11, 1944.

*GRAY, SIR JOHN. "The diaries of Emin Pasha: extracts i–xii." *Ugand Jaournal*, XXV–XXXI, 1961–1967.

†GRAY, RICHARD. *History of the Southern Sudan, 1839–1889*. O.U.P., London, 1961.

*HASSAN, VITA. *Die Wahrheit über Emin Pascha*. Berlin, 1893. (Also published in French as *La vérité sur Emin Pacha*.)

†HILL, RICHARD. *A biographical dictionary of the Sudan*. Frank Cass, London, revised ed. 1967.

*HOFFMAN, WILLIAM. *With Stanley in Africa*. Cassell, London, 1938.

†INGRAMS, HAROLD. *Uganda*. H.M.S.O., London, 1960.

*JACKSON, SIR FREDERICK. *Early days in East Africa*. Edward Arnold, London, 1930.

*JAMESON, JAMES S. *The Story of the Rear Column of the Emin Pasha Relief Expedition*. Ed. Mrs. J. S. Jameson. Pater, London, 1890.

*JEPHSON, A. J. MOUNTENEY. Emin Pasha and the rebellion at the Equator. Sampson Low, London, 1890.

*JEPHSON, A. J. MOUNTENEY. Diary of the Emin Pasha Relief Expedition. Ed. Dorothy Middleton. C.U.P., Cambridge, 1969. (For the Hakluyt Society, Extra Series, No. XL.)

*JUNKER, WILHELM. Travels in Africa—1882–1886. Tr. A. H. Keane. Chapman & Hall, London, 1892.

*KELTIE, J. SCOTT. The true story of Emin's rescue as told in Stanley's letters. Harper, New York, 1870.

†KIEWIET, M. J. de. "History of the I.B.E.A.C., 1876–1895." Unpublished Ph.D. thesis. Senate House Library, London, 1955.

†LANGER, W. L. Diplomacy of Imperialism. Knopf, New York, 2nd. ed., 1951.

†LUDWIG, EMIL. The Nile, life story of a river. Allen & Unwin, London, 1936.

*LUGARD, FREDERICK DEALTRY. The rise of our East African Empire. 2 vols. Blackwood, London and Edinburgh, 1893.

‡MACDERMOTT, P. L. British East Africa or I.B.E.A. Chapman & Hall, London, 1895. Repr. 1970.

*MACDONALD, MAJOR J. R. Soldiering and surveying in British East Africa. Edward Arnold, London, 1897.

‡MACKAY, J. W. H., The story of the life of Mackay of Uganda. Hodder & Stoughton, London, 1890.

†MANNING, OLIVIA. The Remarkable Expedition. Heinemann, London, 1947.

†MARSH, Z. A. and KINGSNORTH, G. An introduction to the history of East Africa. C.U.P., Cambridge, 1957.

†MEISSNER, HANS-OTTO. An der Quellen des Nils. Cotta, Stuttgart, 1969.

*MOHUN, R. DORSEY. "The death of Emin Pasha." Century Magazine, pp. 591–598, Feb. 1895.

*MOOREHEAD, ALAN. The White Nile. Hamish Hamilton, London, 1960.

†OLIVER, R. and MATHEW, G. (eds.). History of East Africa. Vol. I. O.U.P., London, 1963.

*PARKE, THOMAS HEAZLE. My personal experiences in Equatorial Africa as medical officer of the Emin Pasha Relief Expedition. Sampson Low, London, 1891.

†PERHAM, M. Lugard, the years of adventure. Collins, London, 1956.

*PETERS, CARL. New Light on Darkest Africa. Tr. H. W. Dulcken. Ward Lock, London, 1891.

†RICHARDSON, LEWIS F. Statistics of deadly quarrels. Stevens, London, 1960.

†SANDERSON, G. N., England, Europe and the Upper Nile. Edinburgh University Press, 1965.

*SCHWEINFURTH, Georg, and others (eds.). Emin Pasha in Central Africa. Tr. Mrs. R. W. Felkin. Int. by R. W. Felkin. George Philip, London, 1888.

‡SCHWEITZER, GEORG. Emin Pasha, his life and work. 2 vols. Int. by R. W. Felkin. Constable, London, 1898.

*SCHYNSE, AUGUSTE. A travers l'Afrique avec Stanley et Emin Pacha. Paris, 1890.

*SCOTT, ADMIRAL SIR PERCY. Fifty years in the Royal Navy. Murray, London, 1919.

†SIMPSON, D. H. "A bibliography of Emin Pasha." Uganda Journal, XXIV/2, 1960.

†SLADE, RUTH. King Leopold's Congo. O.U.P., London, 1962.

*SLATIN, RUDOLF C. Fire and sword in the Sudan. Tr. Sir F. R. Wingate. Edward Arnold, London, 1896.

†SMITH, A., HARLOW, V. and CHILVER, E. M. (eds.). History of East Africa. Vol. II. O.U.P. London, 1965.

*SPEKE, JOHN HANNING. *Journal of the discovery of the source of the Nile.* Blackwood, London and Edinburgh, 1863.

*STANLEY, LADY D. (ed.). *The Autobiography of Henry M. Stanley.* Sampson Low, London, 1909.

*STANLEY, H. M. *How I found Livingstone.* Sampson Low, London, 1872.

*STANLEY, H. M. *In Darkest Africa, or, the quest, rescue and retreat of Emin, Governor of Equatoria.* 2 vols. Sampson Low, London, 1890.

*STANLEY, RICHARD and NEAME, ALAN (eds.): *The exploration diaries of H. M. Stanley.* William Kimber, London, 1962.

‡STIGAND, C. H. *Equatoria, the Lado Enclave.* Constable, London, 1923.

*STUHLMANN, FRANZ. *Mit Emin Pascha ins Herz von Afrika.* Reimer, Berlin, 1894.

*STUHLMANN, FRANZ. (ed.). *Die Tagebücher von Dr. Emin Pascha.* 5 vols: I (1916); II (1919); III (1922); IV (1927); V (not publ.); VI (1921). Westermann; Hamburg, Brunswick and Berlin.

*SWANN, ALFRED J. *Fighting the slave-hunters in Central Africa.* Seeley, London, 1910.

†SYMONS, A. J. A. *Emyn.* Fleuron Press, London, 1928.

†THEOBALD, A. B. *The Mahdiya, a history of the Anglo-Egyptian Sudan, 1881–1899.* Longmans, London, 1951.

*THRUSTON, A. B. *African Incidents.* Murray, London, 1900.

†TOUSSAINT, A. *A history of the Indian Ocean.* Routledge & Kegan Paul, London, 1966.

*TROUP, JOHN ROSE. *With Stanley's Rear Column.* Chapman & Hall, London, 1890.

†VATIKIOTIS, P. J. *The modern history of Egypt.* Weidenfeld & Nicolson, London, 1969.

*WARD, HERBERT. *My life with Stanley's Rear Guard.* Chatto & Windus, London, 1891.

†WARD, SARITA. *A valiant gentleman, being the biography of Herbert Ward, artist and man of action.* Chapman & Hall, London, 1927.

‡WAUTERS, A. J. *Stanley's Emin Pasha Expedition.* Nimmo, London, 1890.

*WERNER, J. R. *A visit to Stanley's Rear Guard. . . .* Blackwood, London and Edinburgh, 1891.

†WHITE, JAMES P. "The Sanford Exploring Expedition." *Journal of African History,* VIII/2, pp. 291–302. 1967.

*WHITELEY, W. H. (tr.) "Maisha ya Hamed bin Muhammed el Murjebi yaani Tippu Tip." (Tippu-Tib's autobiography: Swahili text with English translation.) Supplement to the *East African Swahili Committee Journals,* 28/ii (1958) and 29/i (1959). Int. by Alison Smith.

*WILSON, C. T. and FELKIN, R. W. *Uganda and the Egyptian Soudan.* London, 1882.

*ZUCCHINETTI, PAOLO VIRGINIO. *Souvenirs de mon séjour chez Emin Pasha el Soudani.* Imprimerie de l'auteur, Cairo, 1890.

‡*Stanley and Africa.* (Anonymous popular account of the exploits of Speke, Baker, Livingstone and Stanley.) Walter Scott, London, (?)1890.

Dictionary of National Biography.
Biographie Coloniale Belge.
The Times for the following dates:
Nov. 24, 1886; Dec. 15, 1886; Jan. 13, 1887; June 6, 1887; June 17, 1887; Nov. 28, 1887; Aug. 22, 1888; Nov. 8, 1890; Nov. 15, 1890; Nov. 17, 1890; Nov. 18, 1890; Nov. 19, 1890; Nov. 22, 1890; Nov. 24, 1890; Nov. 25, 1890;

Dec. 4, 1890; Dec. 9, 1890; Dec. 10, 1890; Dec. 13, 1890; Dec. 20, 1890; July 14, 1892.

Parliamentary papers:

C.5601 (1887)   *Correspondence respecting the expedition for the relief of Emin Pasha.*

C.5602 (1888)   *Paper respecting the reported capture of Emin Pasha and Mr. Stanley.*

C.5906 (1890)   *Correspondence respecting Mr. Stanley's expedition to relieve Emin Pasha.*

C.8276 (1896)   *Papers relating to the execution of Mr. Stokes in the Congo State.*

Cd. 9146 (1918)   *Report on the natives of S.W. Africa and their treatment by Germany.*

INDEX